Contract  and

Third Edition

Hector L MacQueen LL.B, Ph.D, F.B.A., F.R.S.E.
Scottish Law Commissioner and Professor of Private
Law, University of Edinburgh

Joe Thomson LL.B, F.R.S.E.
Formerly Regius Professor of Law, University
of Glasgow and Commissioner, Scottish Law
Commission

Bloomsbury Professional

Bloomsbury Professional Limited, Maxwelton House, 41–43 Boltro Road, Haywards Heath, West Sussex, RH16 1BJ

© Bloomsbury Professional Limited 2012

Bloomsbury Professional, an imprint of Bloomsbury Publishing Plc

A CIP Catalogue record for this book is available from the British Library.

ISBN: 978 1 84766 163 0

Typeset by Phoenix Photosetting, Chatham, Kent
Printed in the United Kingdom by
Hobbs the Printers Ltd, Totton, Hampshire

Dedication

To our students, past, present and to come

Preface to the Third Edition

As this book approaches its teenage years its aims remain nonetheless constant. We have again endeavoured to take account of the major developments in the Scots law of contract since the previous edition in 2007 while also keeping pace with European and other comparative work on our subject. We are grateful for research assistance from Megan Dewart, first-class LLB (Hons) from Edinburgh, BCL with distinction from Oxford, and a DipLP from Edinburgh again. We have also benefited hugely from the work and comments of various friends sharing our interest in contract law. These include once more Martin Hogg and Laura Macgregor as well as Gillian Black and David Cabrelli (all of the Edinburgh Law School), plus colleagues in other law schools around the world and in the Scottish Law Commission. Amongst those less interested in contract law as such, we are again especially grateful wish to our respective spouses for their support, much needed by authors in search of time and space in which to think and write. We have tried to state the law as at 1 June 2012.

Hector MacQueen and Joe Thomson
Edinburgh and Campbeltown
6 June 2012

Preface to the Second Edition

The aims of the second edition of this book remain the same as those of the first. We have endeavoured to take account of the major developments in the Scots law of contract in the last seven years (which cannot be described as lean in terms of the case law!). We are grateful for research assistance from Jamie MacQueen, a law student at Glasgow University, who brought to bear the perspectives of a consumer of the first edition. As with the first edition thanks must be given to friends and colleagues with whom we discussed various aspects of this subject. These include the Honourable Lord Eassie, Martin Hogg, Laura Macgregor and Professor Bill McBryde. Again we wish to thank our spouses for their much appreciated encouragement arising perhaps from their anticipated share of our royalties. We have tried to state the law as at 1 July 2007.

Hector MacQueen and Joe Thomson
Edinburgh
9 July 2007

Preface to the First Edition

This book was conceived in wine at a party in 1993 to celebrate the publication of volume 18 of the Stair Memorial Encyclopaedia. Subsequently, the early stages of the book's gestation proceeded most promisingly in the convivial atmosphere of the Glasgow Art Club. We then became entangled amidst the tares and thistles of university administration, prolonging the book's embryonic life beyond even that of an elephantine pregnancy. We have therefore been most fortunate that Butterworths did not exercise against us the remedies described in chapters 5 and 6 but rather have allowed us eventually to bring our work to fruition.

While this book took seven years to write, between us we have taught contract law for 50 years. We have therefore had chiefly in mind the difficulties faced by our students as they come to grips with the complexities of the Scots law of contract. The text emphasises principle over precedent (as much as possible) and we have endeavoured to provide the clearest explanations that the limitations of space allow. We thought it important to show that contract is not just about disputes in court but also about drafting clauses to avoid disputes arising in the first place. More than is perhaps usual, the text emphasises the creation and analysis of contract terms which deal with practical problems. That said, we have treated remedies at length since this is a subject of increasing academic, as well as practical, importance. We trust that the book will therefore be of use to the practitioner.

We have also tried to remember the needs of lawyers from other legal systems who, for various reasons, may need a bird's eye view of the essential features of Scots contract law. Our account has been placed in a comparative context and draws on the principles of contract law published by Unidroit and the Commission for European Contract Law. Sometimes such comparisons point out the need to modernise Scots law, and we have given consideration to the reform proposals of the Scottish Law Commission where relevant.

We would like to thank the many colleagues who have – so helpfully – inquired on the progress of our work over the last seven years! We are even more grateful to Annie and Frances, who stoically bore the demands on the time which we might otherwise have spent with them, especially in the final stages of composition as 1999 became 2000.

We have attempted to state the law as we saw it at 1 January 2000, although in one or two places we have been able to take account of developments since then.

Hector MacQueen and Joe Thomson
Edinburgh
22 March 2000

Contents

Table of Statutes

Table of Orders and Regulations

Table of Other Enactments

Table of Cases

PARA

O

P

Abbreviations

Burrows	A Burrows, Remedies for Torts and Breach of Contract (2nd edn, 2004)
CESL	Proposal for a Common European Sales Law, Brussels, 11 October 2011, COM (2011) 635 final
CISG	Convention on the International Sale of Goods 1980 (Vienna Convention)
DCFR	C von Bar and E M Clive (eds), Principles, Definitions and Model Rules of European Private Law: Draft Common Frame of Reference, 6 volumes (2009)
EdinLR	Edinburgh Law Review
Gloag	W M Gloag, The Law of Contract in Scotland, 2nd edn (1929)
Hogg	M A Hogg, Obligations, 2nd edn (2006)
JR	Juridical Review
LQR	Law Quarterly Review
McBryde	W W McBryde, The Law of Contract in Scotland, 3rd edn (2007)
McKendrick	Contract Law, 9th edn (2011)
MLR	Modern Law Review
PECL	Principles of European Contract Law, Parts I and II (1999); Part III (2002)
PICC	Unidroit, Principles of International Commercial Contracts, 3rd edn (2010)
Stair Memorial Encyclopaedia	The Laws of Scotland: Stair Memorial Encyclopaedia (26 volumes and Reissue)
Thomson	J M Thomson, Delictual Liability, 4th edn (2009)
Treitel	G H Treitel, Remedies for Breach of Contract: a comparative survey (1988)
Zweigert and Kötz	K Zweigert and H Kötz, Introduction to Comparative Law, trans T Weir, 3rd edn (1998)

1. Introduction

1.1 This book deals with the Scots law of contract. The subject is a central one in the study and practice of law in most legal systems but the Scottish example has an added interest. The law of Scotland, at least in its private dimension, is a leading instance of what comparative lawyers call a 'mixed' legal system: that is to say, a system in which are combined major features from two legal traditions generally thought to represent opposed ways of looking at law: namely, the Civilian system based ultimately on the law of ancient Rome, which dominates in Continental Europe, and the Common Law system first developed in England and then carried around the world by the expansion of the British Empire in the eighteenth and nineteenth centuries. Scots law has drawn on both traditions throughout its history, and the law of contract is no exception to this pattern[1].

1 On mixed legal systems in general, see Palmer (ed), *Mixed Jurisdictions Worldwide: The Third Legal Family* (2001).

1.2 The interest of this mixed tradition in Scotland has now taken on a practical slant. Later in this chapter, we will see how contract law plays an important role in a market economy. The European Union has moved far towards the realisation of a single market amongst its member states, while a global economy is also developing with the process being accelerated by the growth of electronic commerce untrammelled by national frontiers. As a result, there is a growing need for harmonisation and convergence of the contract laws of Europe and the world so that wherever problems occur lawyers and courts can give the same or similar results. The process requires reconciliation of the conflicting legal traditions and the contract law of Scotland and other mixed legal systems, such as those of South Africa, Israel, Louisiana and Quebec, may provide models of how this can be achieved[1].

1 See further Smits *The Making of European Private Law: Towards a Ius Commune Europaeum as a Mixed Legal System* (2002); Du Plessis 'Comparative law and the study of mixed legal systems' in Zimmermann (ed) *Oxford Handbook of Comparative Law* (2006).

1.3 In consequence, while this book is primarily an account of Scots contract law, it also makes a modest effort to set that law in a wider comparative context. Not only may this enable students to be aware of other solutions to the problems with which contract law has to cope but readers from other jurisdictions may also come to understand the Scottish approach more easily. Some of the answers to problems not yet directly addressed in the Scottish courts may even be suggested.

CONTRACT, OBLIGATIONS AND PRIVATE LAW

1.4 Contract law is included in the definition of Scottish private law in the Scotland Act 1998 (SA 1998) which set up the Scottish Parliament and included private law within its legislative competence[1]. The distinction between *public law* (the law relating to the state in all its manifestations and to its relationship with its citizens and other persons within its borders) and *private law* (the law concerning all other relationships) is ancient, but prior to the SA 1998 had had little other than some descriptive and pedagogic utility in Scotland[2]. However, the Act's definition does provide a convenient starting point in trying to outline the scope of contract law.

1 SA 1998, s 126(4).
2 See, for example, the rejection of a public/private dichotomy as a basis for judicial review in *West v Secretary of State for Scotland* 1992 SC 385. Note also *Davidson v Scottish Ministers* 2006 SC (HL) 41 per Lord Rodger of Earlsferry at para 77.

1.5 Under the SA 1998, private law includes, amongst other things, the law of property and the law of obligations. The basic distinction between the law of obligations and the law of property is usually expressed in terms of the kinds of right or relationships with which each deals[1]. *Property law* is about the relationship between persons and things, or the right which a person may have in a thing[2]. Things can be either tangible, or corporeal (eg land and goods), or intangible, or incorporeal (a category to which we will return in a moment). The rights generally take the form of a right to use the thing and to prevent anyone else using it. The typical (but not the only) property right is ownership of the thing. Property rights, or, as they are more usually known, *real rights*, are potentially enforceable against anyone and everyone; although in reality they will normally only have to be enforced against actual intruders.

1 On property law in general see Thomson *Scots Private Law* (2006), chs 2–4; Reid *The Law of Property in Scotland* (1996); Gretton and Steven *Property, Trusts and Succession* (2009).
2 Expressed in Latin as *jus in re* or *jus in rem*.

1.6   In contrast, rights under the *law of obligations* are enforceable only against particular persons, or a determinate group of persons, and have nothing to do with things. Such a right is known as a *personal right*[1]. Obligations are links or ties between persons under which each may have rights and duties (or be bound) to do, or to abstain from doing something[2]. Central to the idea of obligation, therefore, is the necessity of making some performance.

1 Expressed in Latin as *jus in personam*. See further Thomson *Scots Private Law* chs 5–9; Hogg *Obligations* (2nd ed, 2006).
2 The etymology of the word 'obligation', from the Latin '*ligatio*', meaning 'a binding', manifests the central nature of the concept of a bond, link or tie. Compare other English words such as 'ligature' and 'ligament'.

1.7   A person with a right, or to whom the obligation is owed, is known as the *obligee* or the *creditor*. A person with a duty, or who must perform under the obligation, is the *obligor*, *obligant* or *debtor*. The personal right belongs to the obligee or creditor who therefore has as such a real right, good against the world, to the personal right, or, as it has been expressed, a right in a right[1]. This is one of the prime examples of the category of incorporeal property mentioned a couple of paragraphs ago.

1 See *Reid*, para 16. For further analysis of some of the conceptual and logical difficulties thus arising, see also the same author's 'Obligations and property: exploring the border' [1997] *Acta Juridica* 225, and Gretton 'Ownership and its objects' (2007) 71 *Rabelszeitschrift* 802.

1.8   The first task of the law of obligations is to say when legally enforceable personal rights and duties occur. Contract is listed as part of the law of obligations in the SA 1998 along with 'unilateral promise, delict, unjustified enrichment and *negotiorum gestio*'. These subheadings make up a list of some of the technical terms used in Scots law to describe the circumstances giving rise to obligations. Very similar lists can be found in other legal systems since by and large the categories which they describe go back ultimately to Roman law, the root of much of private law in western Europe. The subheadings can be defined and elaborated as follows:

Contract

1.9 Contract can be defined as an agreement between two or more parties having the capacity to make it, in the form demanded by law, to perform, on one side or both, acts which are not trifling, indeterminate, impossible or illegal. If necessary, the courts can be used to compel the parties to make the agreed performances or to provide a legally recognised substitute therefor, such as damages. Most aspects of this definition will be amplified elsewhere in this book but a number of specific points may be made briefly here.

1.10 First, a contract requires only agreement and, some specific instances apart, need not be in writing of any kind despite a common belief to the contrary amongst non-lawyers. The agreement may be manifested by writing, the spoken word, other conduct, or some combination of these. Where an agreement is spelled out from parties' conduct rather than their written or spoken words, it is sometimes said to be an *implied contract*.

1.11 Second, to be a contract the agreement must be one under which action, or performance, is to take place (or inaction where apart from the agreement there would be a right to act[1]) rather than, for example, an agreement that the weather is good today or that all politicians are corrupt. Thus contracts include:

- *sales*, under which the seller transfers ownership of goods or land in return for payment of a price by the buyer;
- *leases or hires*, under which the lessor or owner transfers to the lessee or hirer possession of goods or land for a period of time in return for a payment or payments usually known as the rent or rental or hire charge;
- *loans*, under which the lender transfers property (usually money) to the borrower, to be returned or repaid over or after a certain period of time;
- *employment*, under which the employer hires and controls the services of the employee as an integral part of the employer's business in return for the payment of a wage or salary;
- *other services* where it is the provider, not the recipient, that is usually acting as a business (such as a solicitor, accountant or street shoe-polisher), but for which the recipient none the less makes payment; and
- *supply of services together with a tangible end-product*, as in building and civil engineering contracts, or the installation

of a central heating system, double glazing or a new kitchen in your home; again, the recipient pays for what is received.

1 An example of this discussed in greater detail elsewhere in this book is a restrictive covenant: see below, paras 7.30–7.47.

1.12 The categories of contracts just listed are in many cases very old, going back ultimately to Roman law. In the second half of the twentieth century, another categorisation emerged, distinguishing between commercial, consumer and other contracts. A *consumer* is a person, usually but not always a private individual, acquiring property or services under a contract with another person, usually but not always a company, who is transacting in the course of a business. The consumer is so called because he or she is the end-user of the subject matter of the contract. Reacting to the view that in dealing with businesses individuals usually lack the knowledge and economic power to obtain contractual terms in their favour, and that this weakness is often exploited by businesses to make unequal and unfair contracts, a great deal of legislation has been passed to give consumers special rights in contract law[1]. We shall return later to the significance for the theory of contract as agreement of this power to override in the interests of the consumer what parties actually agree; it suffices for present purposes to note that the concept of a *consumer contract* enables us to distinguish (1) the *commercial contract*, in which both or all parties are dealing in the course of business; and (2) the *private contract*, in which neither party is dealing in the course of business (for example, the sale of a house). In these contracts, since the parties should be more equal, there is generally thought to be less need to offer special protection to the interests of one or other party.

1 See Ervine *Consumer Law in Scotland* (4th edn, 2008).

1.13 It is not clear whether the categories of commercial, consumer and private are exhaustive: for instance, where does the contract of employment fit in? But this is another example of where much legislation has been passed to protect the interests of one party – the employee – who has generally been perceived as not bargaining on equal terms with the employer. The employee is, however, not really a consumer – if anything, it is the employer who is consuming the services of the employee – and it is only by stretching a point that the employee can be seen as acting either in the course of his business or in a purely private capacity[1].

1 See Brodie, *The Contract of Employment* (2008).

1.14 Finally, returning to our initial definition, a contract requires two or more parties, but the obligation of performance under it may exist for only one of them (in which case the contract is *unilateral*) or for both (a *bilateral* or *mutual* contract). The typical contract involves obligations for both parties. In other words, a contract usually results in an exchange of performances by the parties, normally, as we have seen above, the payment of money on one side and the supply of things such as goods or land, or the provision of services, on the other. By contrast, in a unilateral contract only one party is obliged to perform, while the other is free, making it possible to characterise the arrangement as one of 'something for nothing'. As we will see in another chapter[1], in fact this is not always, or even very often, the case; but the *gratuitous* nature of the obligation in a unilateral contract goes some way to explaining the reluctance of some legal systems to recognise its enforceability other than in exceptional circumstances[2].

1 See below, para 2.54 ff.
2 Eg in England, thanks to the doctrine of consideration (unknown in Scots law). See further on 'unilateral' and 'gratuitous' *Hogg*, paras 1.16–1.17, 2.04, 2.06–2.11.

Unilateral promise

1.15 The same comment could be made about the second subheading in the Scots law of obligations, namely unilateral promise. This is an undertaking by one party only to perform, not requiring the agreement of the beneficiary to be enforceable. The difference between a unilateral contract, requiring agreement of both parties, and a unilateral promise may be very fine, but can be significant in law. The main issue is to determine when a statement can be seen as a binding promise, as opposed to, say, a non-binding declaration of future intention. Take, for example, a statement by an elderly bachelor to his housekeeper that 'I would like to make provision for you in my will so that you do not need to work again after my death'. Is this a binding promise to make the provision mentioned, or is it simply an expression of the goodwill and gratitude the old man feels to his carer? We would need to know more about the context to provide the answer. Does the old man have the resources enabling the declaration to be made good? Are there other commitments for his estate already? Has he made a will or not? Did he ask the housekeeper to obtain the services of a solicitor to draw up a will after this conversation? How relevant is it that wills can always be changed up to the moment of the testator's death? Only with knowledge of all these and perhaps other facts will we be able to tell whether or not the statement was made with the intention to be committed legally and to give the housekeeper an enforceable personal right[1].

1 For a real-life example of the difficulty, see *Cawdor v Cawdor* 2007 SC 285.

Delict[1]

1.16   The word 'delict' comes from the Latin '*delictum*', meaning 'wrong'[2]. Delict can be defined as the obligation to refrain from wrongful acts harming the persons, property or other interests of other members of society, and, if nevertheless a wrong is committed and harm is inflicted, the obligation of the wrongdoer to make compensation to the injured party by way of damages (often known in Scotland as the obligation of reparation). In most cases coming before the courts, the harm will have occurred, and the questions will be whether or not it was caused by wrongful conduct and what reparation should be made. This may make it rather artificial to talk in addition of the obligation to refrain from wrongful conduct as part of the law of delict, since it is unusual for the obligee to demand not to be harmed, in advance of it actually occurring. But there are cases where a party goes to court to seek an order (generally an interdict) preventing another acting in a way which she anticipates will cause her harm, although usually the threat of harm must be real or, indeed, being realised before the court will act[3].

1 See generally Thomson *Delictual Liability* (4th edn, 2009); Thomson *Scots Private Law*, chs 7–8; 15 *Stair Memorial Encyclopaedia* paras 144–610.
2 Similarly the Common Law term for delict – tort – comes from a French word meaning 'wrong'.
3 Eg nuisance or breach of confidence: see Thomson *Delictual Liability*, pp 33–39, 200–205.

1.17   At the heart of the law of delict is the definition of wrongful conduct. Harm may occur to someone as a result of another's conduct without giving rise to liability in law. For example, I may set up a hairdressing business next door to your barber's shop with the result that you lose customers and profit to me; but since business competition as such is lawful, you have no claim against me despite the losses flowing to you from my activity[1]. The kind of conduct denoted as wrongful is in the end a matter of policy for the law and over time that policy develops and changes along with the perceived needs of society.

1 Note, however, that competition is regulated under eg the Competition Act 1998, the Enterprise Act 2002 and the Treaty on the Functioning of the European Union (TFEU), arts 101 and 102. In some legal systems there is a delict of unfair competition, to which the nearest cognate in Scots (and English) law is the action of passing off (for which see Thomson *Delictual Liability* pp 28–33).

1.18 Wrongful conduct may be intentional on the part of the wrongdoer but in practice the most important type of wrongful conduct is negligence. This occurs when a party acts carelessly (ie not intentionally) and so causes damage to another which would not have happened had the party taken care. Typical examples would include the momentarily inattentive car driver who runs over and injures or kills a pedestrian, and the employer who fails to provide safe conditions for his employees to work in, again resulting in injury or death. In yet other instances the law may have no regard to the intention or the fault of the wrongdoer but simply find him liable on the basis of the causal connection between the harm and his conduct. This is known as *strict liability*; the leading example is a producer's liability under the Consumer Protection Act 1987 for unsafe products causing personal injury or property damage[1].

1 Thomson *Delictual Liability* pp 174–183.

1.19 The typical harm, damage or injury for which compensation may be sought under the law of delict is to a person's physical integrity, but other types of damage may be recognised. Thus property damage, economic or financial damage, and damage to a person's reputation may all give rise to claims in certain circumstances. As with wrongful conduct, the kinds of harm (or interests) to which the law gives protection change over time in accordance with the perceptions of what legal policy requires.

Unjustified enrichment[1]

1.20 The basis of the law of unjustified enrichment was stated in the second century AD by the Roman jurist Pomponius: 'For this by nature is equitable, that no-one be made richer through the loss of another'[2]. The basic idea is, then, that a party who has been enriched at another's expense must restore the enrichment to that other. This reads a little curiously to the modern eye accustomed to the legitimacy of the pursuit of wealth even when that involves loss to another. Thus in the example of the competing hairdressers given in the discussion of delict above, just as you could not seek compensation in delict for the losses caused by my competing with you, so you could not claim my profits under the law of unjustified enrichment. But there are limits to this freedom from liability. For example, we are not allowed to increase our wealth by stealing from other people. Again, if I pay you £100 by mistake (for example, if I owe you only £10, or if I think I owe you when in fact I owe the debt to your friend), then there is no good reason for you to retain either the excess or the undue payment. A final, rather different, example is the rings which a couple engaged to marry may exchange as a symbol of their engagement: if the wedding is called off, then the purpose of the exchange has failed, and the rings should be returned.

1 See generally Evans-Jones *Unjustified Enrichment* vol 1 (2003); MacQueen *Unjustified Enrichment Law Basics* (2nd edn 2009); *Hogg* ch 4; Thomson *Scots Private Law*, ch 9; *Gloag & Henderson* ch 25.
2 *Digest* 12.6.14; 50.17.206.

1.21 The law of unjustified enrichment is primarily about transactions which benefit one party as a result of another's expenditure or loss and that have occurred despite the absence of a legal reason for their occurrence, such as a valid contract or gift, or where the reason for the transaction has ceased to exist. Everything in this area turns around the content which the law gives to the adjective 'unjustified'. Just as with 'wrongfulness' in the law of delict, so the enrichments which the law regards as unjustified, and therefore as reversible, are determined ultimately as a matter of legal policy. The main situations are (1) *transfers* of value where something has gone wrong, such as paying too much, paying the wrong person[1], or where the performance or payment was made for a purpose which then fails to materialise (eg A contributes to the cost of building an extension to B's house because they live together there and plan to get married; but their relationship breaks down, B ejects A from the house and no marriage takes place[2]); (2) *impositions* of value, as where C improves D's property without D's permission in the erroneous belief that it is his own, and D is now enjoying the benefit of the work[3]; and (3) *takings* of value, where E is benefited by using or interfering with F's property or rights without F's permission. An example is where E is the good faith jeweller-buyer of a ring which he then resells for a profit to an innocent third party who cannot now be traced; it turns out however that the ring had originally been stolen from F. E is liable to F for the profit on the sale[4]. There are three main remedies for unjustified enrichment, the definitions of which can be related to the different situations in which enrichment occurs. First there is *repetition*, which is the remedy for the repayment of money paid when not due, or for a purpose which has failed to materialise. Second is *restitution*, the remedy for the return of property other than money, which is otherwise similar to repetition. Finally, there is *recompense*, a broad remedy dealing with all other kinds of unjustified enrichment such as arise from impositions and takings.

1 *Bank of New York v North British Steel Group* 1992 SLT 613.
2 *Shilliday v Smith* 1998 SC 725.
3 *Newton v Newton* 1925 SC 715.
4 *Jarvis v Manson* 1954 SLT (Sh Ct) 93. F is of course entitled to the return of the ring if he can trace the third party buyer.

1.22   Following a number of leading cases in the 1990s[1], Scots law has now moved to a position where in principle an enrichment is unjustified and should be reversed if its retention is supported by no legal ground. Examples of 'legal grounds' or justifications for enrichments include receipt under a gift or a valid contract, as well as gain through lawful competition. For present purposes, the most important point is that transfers, impositions and takings made under a valid and subsisting contract are justified enrichments[2]. The categories of transfer, imposition and taking all come under the generalization about lack of legal ground but do not exhaust the ways in which the courts may reverse unjustified enrichment. As with delict, the law of unjustified enrichment is couched in sufficiently broad terms to ensure that its precise limits can never be definitively stated, and the law is very much in a state of development at present.

1 See *Morgan Guaranty Trust Co of New York v Lothian Regional Council* 1995 SC 151; *Shilliday v Smith* 1998 SC 725; and *Dollar Land (Cumbernauld) Ltd v CIN Properties Ltd* 1998 SC (HL) 90.
2 See especially the *Dollar Land* case; note also *Compagnie Commerciale Andre SA v Artibell Shipping Co Ltd (No 2)* 2001 SC 653; *Wiltshier Construction (Scotland) Ltd v Drumchapel Housing Cooperative Ltd* 2003 SLT 443; *Castle Inns (Stirling) Ltd v Clark Contracts Ltd* 2006 SCLR 663.

Negotiorum gestio (benevolent intervention)[1]

1.23   As is apparent from its Latin name meaning 'administration or management of affairs', this part of the law of obligations also originated in Roman law. By comparison with the previous categories, however, *negotiorum gestio* is of rather narrow scope. The situation envisaged is one where you step in to manage my affairs when I am unable (through absence, ignorance or incapacity) to deal with them myself. As a result of my inability, your actions cannot be based upon a contract between us, nor have I otherwise authorised your intervention. None the less, I am liable for the expenses and outlays which you incur in your management. Note that this is essentially a claim for your loss rather than for any enrichment which I might have as a result of your intervention in my affairs. You must intend your management to be of benefit to me, and for this reason nowadays this area of law is sometimes termed 'benevolent intervention'. That in acting you also intended some benefit to yourself does not matter; only if you were acting entirely in your own interests, ie with no element of benevolence, is the claim of *negotiorum gestio* generally excluded. It may be that you intended to donate your services to me in which case again there is no *negotiorum gestio*; it would seem from this that your actions must be undertaken with a view to recovering your costs from me, although, given that there is a presumption against donation in Scots law, it would probably be for me to prove that you intended a gift as otherwise it would be assumed that you had not intended to act gratuitously[2]. Finally, your intervention must be of at least initial utility to me.

1 See generally *MacQueen*, § 9; *Hogg*, paras 5.03–5.12; *Gloag & Henderson* ch 25.24–25.28 15 *Stair Memorial Encyclopaedia* paras 87–143.
2 On gifts see *MacQueen and Hogg*, 'Donation in Scots law', 2012 JR 1.

1.24 The classic illustration of *negotiorum gestio* is where you find my house burning down while I am away on holiday. Your attempt to put out the fire is unauthorised but is probably a justified effort to protect my interests. You may also have been motivated by a desire to stop the fire spreading to your house next door but that does not stop the situation being one of *negotiorum gestio*. Nor does the failure of your intervention; even if my house is completely destroyed, you will still be entitled to claim your fire-fighting expenses. On the other hand, if you negligently used inappropriate means of tackling the fire and made the situation worse, I might have a delictual action against you to compensate me for the loss you have caused me. There is also a link with unjustified enrichment in that if you make a profit from your intervention, you must account to me for it.

1.25 Not every legal system recognises the obligation of *negotiorum gestio*. The obvious problem is the encouragement which it may give to those who meddle without authority in other people's business. It is a perfectly tenable view that in general such interference should not impose legally enforceable obligations upon the recipient. On the other hand, it would be a wretched kind of society in which people helped each other only when specifically asked or authorised to do so, particularly when the person in difficulty was unable to help him- or herself for some reason. The rules of *negotiorum gestio* set out in the previous paragraphs are intended to distinguish the deserving intervener from the unworthy busybody and seem to have done so successfully since Roman times.

Other heads of obligation?

1.26 The SA 1998 says that the law of obligations 'includes' contract, unilateral promise, delict, unjustified enrichment and *negotiorum gestio*; in other words, the list of specific heads is not necessarily complete or definitive. When we analyse the list carefully, it is possible to see some potential gaps. Thus delict is about loss caused by another's wrongful conduct, enrichment about loss leading to another's benefit, and *negotiorum gestio* about loss caused by trying to help another, whether or not that other benefits as a result. An example not covered by the above list, but which has been much discussed, although little litigated, at least in Scotland, is when someone commits a wrongful act which causes no loss to anyone but leads nevertheless to the enrichment of the wrongdoer. For instance, a company director holds confidential information about the company which, in abuse of his position, he uses in making profitable deals with his personal shareholding in the company as well as in contributing to its management. Can the wrongdoer be made to disgorge his profit? And if so, by whom?[1] Again, there are cases where a party suffers loss with neither another's wrongful conduct nor his enrichment being involved. Is *negotiorum gestio* the only situation where such loss can be recovered? Shipping law provides two further examples known as general average and salvage. *Average* in shipping means any loss or injury to a ship or its cargo during a voyage. When one of the three interests at stake during a voyage – the ship itself, the cargo and the freight (ie the payment for the carriage which will not be due unless the cargo is delivered) – is voluntarily sacrificed, in whole or in part, for the safety of the rest (eg jettisoning the cargo to keep the ship afloat), the loss must be shared equally by the interested parties. *Salvage* is the payment due to the owner of a ship and its master and crew who successfully rescue another ship or its cargo from a situation of danger, with the parties obliged being those who own the ship or cargo and the persons entitled to the freight. The requirement of success differentiates salvage from *negotiorum gestio*[2], but the existence of these obligations along with general average has led some to ask whether there may not be another head of the law of obligations, to be denominated 'unjust sacrifice or impoverishment', where the policy of the law would support the view that a party who has incurred a loss should not be left to bear it alone or, indeed, at all[3].

1 On this see *Hogg* chapter 6; Blackie and Farlam 'Enrichment by act of the party enriched' in Zimmermann Visser and Reid (eds), *Mixed Legal Systems in Comparative Perspective: Property and Obligations in Scotland and South Africa* (2004).

2 See further Forte 'Salvage operations, salvage contracts and *negotiorum gestio'* 1993 JR 247.

3 *Hogg*, ch 5.

1.27   One other situation to be mentioned in this context is where parties are negotiating but have not yet concluded a contract. In general, since there is as yet no contract, a party who breaks off negotiations at this stage will incur no liability for doing so. There is however a controversial group of cases in Scotland, dating from the early nineteenth century on, in which a party breaking off pre-contractual negotiations has been held liable for the expenditure which the other had incurred in preparing for the performance it expected to undertake once the contract was concluded and which was wasted when the contract did not take place. The basis for this appears to be that the parties have reached an agreement which is not yet contractual – for example, because it is one of the few contracts where the agreement must be put in writing to have legal effect – and the party who broke off the arrangement had expressly or impliedly represented to the other that he regarded the transaction as settled[1]. However, other legal systems in Europe recognise a more extensive liability than this for unjustified termination of negotiations, not dependent on any requirement of informal agreement. Usually such liability is treated as part of the law of delict; but could it perhaps be another instance of 'unjust sacrifice'?

1 See below, para 2.89 ff. For further analysis of the case law, which runs from *Walker v Milne* (1823) 2 S 379 to *Khaliq v Londis Holdings Ltd* 2010 SC 432, see *Hogg* paras 3.25–3.37, 5.13–5.20; *MacQueen and Hogg*, 'Melville Monument liability: some doubtful dicta' (2010) 14 Edin LR 451.

THE INTERESTS PROTECTED BY THE LAW OF OBLIGATIONS

1.28   As we have seen, there are three major components of the law of obligations, namely contract and promise, delict and unjustified enrichment. The purpose of this section is to give specific examples of how they can interrelate in what is prima facie a contractual context. To do so, it is necessary to consider the function of each source of obligation in a little detail[1]. For ease of exposition, we shall restrict the discussion to contract rather than unilateral obligations.

1 For a lucid discussion of these issues, see Burrows *Understanding the Law of Obligations* (1998), ch 1.

1.29   In a contract, the parties voluntarily bind themselves to perform what they have agreed. As soon as the contract is formed, they are obliged to perform what they have agreed to do or refrain from doing. There is thus a fundamental theoretical distinction between formation of a contract and its performance. The importance of contract lies in the fact that as soon as agreement has been reached the law obliges the parties to perform in accordance with the terms of the contract even though performance is not due until some time in the future. For example, if A agrees to sell goods to B for £x, delivery to be made in six months from the date of the contract, then A is obliged from the date of the contract to deliver the goods to B in six months' time for that price. Conversely, from the date of the contract, B is obliged to accept the goods in six months' time and pay £x for them. The effect of the contract is to give the parties security in the sense that A knows that B will pay £x for the goods when delivered and B knows that she will obtain the goods in six months time for £x. It does not matter if, during that period, the market for these goods has risen and they could be sold for £x+y: A is bound to sell them for £x. On the other hand if, during the six-month period, the market for these goods has fallen and they could be bought for £x–y, B is still bound to buy them for £x. Because the parties are obliged to perform from the moment the contract is formed, they have in effect given up their freedom to act at a future date in a way which is contrary to the terms which they have agreed.

1.30   In other words, in theory at least, the law of contract – and also promise – looks to the future. Because the parties are bound to perform their undertakings from the moment the contract is formed, a contract creates expectations in the parties that it will be performed according to its terms. These expectations, it is submitted, constitute sufficient interests to be protected by the law in the sense that, if they are not fulfilled, the law will compel performance (specific implement) or, alternatively, award damages for the failure to do so. This explains why the measure of damages for breach of contract is prima facie to put the innocent party into the position she would have been if the contract had been performed properly. In short, *the primary function of the law of contract is to protect the parties' expectation interests created by the agreement*.

1.31 The law of delict obliges a person to compensate another whom he has harmed as a consequence of his wrongful conduct. The wrongful conduct can be intentionally caused harm or unintentional but careless conduct (negligence). The remedy available to the injured person is damages. In delict, the purpose of the award of damages is to place the victim in the position she would have been if the wrongful act had not taken place. In other words, *the function of the law of delict is to preserve the status quo position enjoyed by the victim before the wrongful act occurred*. While the law of contract looks forward to protect the parties' expectations, the law of delict looks backwards to preserve the *status quo*[1].

1 Where the victim's loss arises because she has relied on the defender, the *status quo* interest is sometimes described as her 'reliance' interest.

1.32 Why is this important? Consider the following examples:

A enters into a contract with B to purchase goods for £100. If the contract was performed properly, assume that A could sell the goods to C for £150. If B breaks the contract by delivering defective goods worth £50, A is entitled to damages which represent the loss of her expectation interest. Thus A is entitled to damages of £150 (expectation interest) minus £50 (the actual value of the goods), namely £100. But if B did not breach the contract and, owing to a fall in market values, A could only sell the goods to C for £20, A has simply made a bad bargain, and the loss lies where it falls. Now, if A had entered into the contract with B as a result of B's fraudulent or negligent misrepresentation, with the result that the goods were only worth £50, A could sue B for damages in delict as a negligent or fraudulent misrepresentation is a wrong. A is entitled to damages of £100 (*status quo* interest) minus £50 (the actual value of the goods), namely £50. This is, of course, less than the damages A would have obtained for breach of contract. But if A had made a bad bargain and had paid £100 for goods which could only have been sold to C for £20 due to a fall in market values, it would be in A's interest to sue B in delict and recover £80, namely £100 (*status quo* interest) minus £20 (the actual value of the goods).

1.33   The law of unjustified enrichment operates, inter alia, to reverse benefits wrongfully received or retained. In these circumstances, the defender will be obliged to make restitution to the pursuer to the extent that the defender has been unjustifiably enriched (*lucratus*). This obligation can arise in several situations which have a contractual context, as the following examples illustrate:

A enters into a contract with B to purchase goods for £100. A pays the price. A was induced to enter the contract as a result of a misrepresentation made by B: as a consequence, the goods are only worth £50. As we shall see, misrepresentation is a ground for having the contract reduced, ie set aside by the court with the effect that the contract is retrospectively null. Before A can have the contract reduced, A must be able to return the goods to B, ie *restitutio in integrum* must be possible. When the contract is reduced and the goods are returned to B, B can no longer retain the price, as the purpose of the payment has failed. A is therefore entitled under the law of unjustified enrichment to restitution of the £100. If A could have sold the goods to C for £200 and B was also in breach of contract, A could sue B in contract to obtain damages for her expectation interest, namely £200 (expectation interest) minus £50 (actual value of the goods), ie £150. A cannot reduce and sue for damages for breach of contract at the same time as the effect of reduction is to render the contract retrospectively null. But if A had made a bad bargain and the goods were only worth £20 owing to a subsequent fall in market values, it would be in A's interests to seek reduction on the ground of misrepresentation and restitution of the price, namely £100. If the misrepresentation was negligent or fraudulent, A could elect to sue in delict to recover her *status quo* interest, £100 (*status quo* interest) minus £20 (actual value of the goods), namely £80. In these circumstances, A should, of course, be advised to seek reduction and restitution: but the action for damages in delict could be useful if A wished to retain the goods.

A enters into a contract with B to hire a cottage in the Highlands for a fortnight's holiday. A pays B £500 rent. Before the holiday, through nobody's fault, the cottage is destroyed by lightning. As we shall see, the contract is frustrated and B is freed from performance of his obligation to provide holiday accommodation for A. B's retention of the rent is no longer justified as the condition upon which the money was advanced has failed, ie the hire of the cottage for two weeks. Since B is unjustifiably enriched, A is entitled to restitution of the £500.

A enters into a contract with B to purchase goods for £100. A pays the price. B fails to deliver the goods. As we shall see, as a result of B's material breach, A is entitled to treat the contract as terminated, ie to treat the contract as repudiated and refuse to perform any outstanding obligations. B's retention of the price is no longer justified and A is entitled to restitution of the £100 which she paid to B. If A could have sold the goods to C for £200, A should, of course, sue B for breach of contract and recover damages for her expectation interest, namely £200. But if the market value of the goods had fallen to £50 and A would have made a bad bargain even if B had not been in breach, it is a matter of controversy whether A can recover the full price under the law of unjustified enrichment, or whether A's expectation interest acts as a cap on the amount that B can be compelled to disgorge, ie £50[1].

1 See, for example, *Connelly v Simpson* 1991 SCLR 295 (rvsd 1993 SC 391).

1.34   It must always be remembered that, as a general rule, the principles of contract law take precedence over those of unjustified enrichment and – to a lesser extent – delict. Provided that the contract is validly constituted, the value of the exchange is a matter for the parties, each of whom is free to exercise his economic power and knowledge to achieve the best bargain he can. In a free market, people are entitled to make good bargains and high profits even though these can sometimes mean bad bargains and great losses for others. The point is that the adequacy of the price or remuneration as against the value of the goods or services is not a justiciable issue. In particular, a person who has made a bad bargain cannot argue that the other party should disgorge his profit on the ground of unjustified enrichment. Unjustified enrichment may have a role to play when the rules of contract render an agreement null or unenforceable or there has been a breach, but its function is not to redress any imbalance in the value of the exchange itself.

1.35   The purpose of this discussion has been to illustrate the respective roles of the three major components of the law of obligations and to show how they can interrelate in what is prima facie a contractual context. While this book is about voluntary obligations, it is important to appreciate that a particular situation may raise issues where remedies can also be found in delict and unjustified enrichment. As we shall see, the frontiers between the three sources of obligation have become fluid: in particular, it has been argued that a claim for damages in contract should include *status quo* and enrichment heads of loss. But for present purposes, we shall continue to treat them as separate – though, at times, interlocking – obligations.

INTERACTION OF OBLIGATIONS: CONCURRENT AND CUMULATIVE LIABILITY

1.36 A reason for spending some time looking at the parts of the law of obligations other than contract is because in practice they often overlap and interact with contract. In particular, many fact situations give rise to liability in both contract and delict. Thus, for example, if A and B are employer and employee, there is a contract of employment between them. Under that contract A owes B an obligation to take reasonable care for his safety; if A fails to take such care and B is harmed as a result, an action lies for breach of contract. However, independently of the contract of employment, A owes a delictual duty of care to anyone whom he could reasonably foresee would suffer injury as a probable consequence of a failure to take appropriate care. B is obviously such a person to whom the duty is owed. Accordingly, if A is negligent and B is injured in consequence, the latter can sue the former in delict. The same would apply if A was a professional person, such as a solicitor or an accountant, and B a client, the duty here being for A to take care in administering B's affairs or advising him. Advice may involve misrepresentation (untrue statements of fact) and this provides another example of overlap between delict and contract. If A is an art expert and advises B that the painting he proposes to buy from C is an authentic Rembrandt when in fact it is a nineteenth-century reproduction, and B therefore pays C much more than the painting is worth, he may be able to recover his loss from A in delict if he can prove that the latter's misrepresentation of the facts was intentional (fraudulent) or negligent. If A had been the owner of the painting and sold it to B, then in addition to his claims in delict B might have contractual remedies. B could argue that A had contracted that the painting was a Rembrandt, in which case he could have damages for breach of contract without having to prove fraud or negligence; or, if this suited him better, he could seek to have the contract undone, with the return of the painting and the payment which he had made.

1.37   In such cases the liability in contract and delict is said to be *concurrent*. B has a choice as to which branch of the law of obligations to use although he cannot recover under both heads at the same time (*cumulative liability*). In practice a party may make what are called *alternate* claims, leaving it to the court to decide under which the action will succeed. It is important, however, to note that in the first two examples given in the previous paragraph the content of the obligation – the duty to take care – is the same whether the claim is made in contract or delict. Matters become more complex where the breach of contract does not involve failure to take care (for example, the supply of defective goods); can the injured party in addition make an alternative claim in delict? The reasons for doing so might include evasion of clauses in the contract, recovery of losses which can only be claimed in delict and not in contract, or vice versa, and escape from difficulties with the rules on prescription. The general answer to the question is controversial. Some take the view that delictual duties are prior to contractual obligations and continue even after entry into the contract unless it clearly excludes or restricts them. Others hold that the mere existence of the contract precludes delictual liability unless the harm suffered is physical injury or damage to property. The reason for this is the danger of undermining the allocation of risks to which the parties have agreed in their contract. In other words, it is contract that has primacy amongst obligations: only if a contract clearly makes no provision for the injury or damage which has occurred as between two contracting parties will a delictual claim become possible[1]. The common ground between the two views is that it is possible for a contract in terms to exclude or restrict delictual liability between the parties and the best approach therefore seems to be to start with the contract and assess both what liabilities it creates and those which it prevents or limits, expressly or implicitly.

1 For more detailed discussion see *Hogg* ch 3. Key cases are *Henderson v Merrett Syndicates* [1995] 2 AC 145 and *White v Jones* [1995] 2 AC 207, discussed in Thomson *Delictual Liability* pp 93–98, and 169–170.

1.38   The basic relationship between contract and unjustified enrichment is rather easier to state. A valid subsisting contract may preclude or make unnecessary an obligation of unjustified enrichment. This is indeed implicit within the very definition of unjustified enrichment under which the retention of an enrichment may be justified if it has arisen through a legal cause such as a contract. But contract lawyers must nonetheless be constantly mindful of enrichment law. Thus enrichment law can be called into play to unwind the performance of a transaction which appeared to be a contract but turned out not to be one as the result of some defect in its formation, such as an error by one or more of the parties, or the use of fraud or force by one to make the other enter the contract, or the lack of writing where that is a requirement of validity. Again, a contract may cease to subsist before it is fully performed, for example as the result of breach by one of the parties, or through a fundamental change of circumstances rendering performance impossible or something fundamentally different in effect from what was originally intended. If the contract does not provide for what is to happen in such cases of part-performance, the law of unjustified enrichment is the means towards a solution. Finally, there may be rules within contract law itself which have the reversal of unjustified enrichment as their objective[1].

1 See further *Hogg* ch 4; *MacQueen* § 8; Miller, 'Unjustified enrichment and failed contracts' in *Zimmermann Visser and Reid* (eds).

1.39 The case of *Avintair Ltd v Ryder Airline Services Ltd*[1] illustrates the difficulty which may occur in distinguishing between an implied contract and an unjustified enrichment. Parties were negotiating a contract while at the same time carrying out the performance of the terms over which they were bargaining. In the end, performance was completed successfully, but the negotiations had produced no agreement as to the price of that performance; indeed, there was sharp disagreement on this subject. The performer was awarded what the court called a 'reasonable price', under a contract implied from the parties' conduct, holding that it demonstrated sufficient agreement to show that gratuitous performance had not been intended. However, while such an approach is valid where the parties have agreed that there will be a price but have deferred its precise determination until later[2], it is conceptually at least a little curious to hold that parties actually in disagreement about something as fundamental to a contract as the price of the agreed performance are nevertheless bound to each other in contract. The law of unjustified enrichment, applicable in cases where there is no contract, might have provided a more principled solution to this case albeit that the end result would have been similar ie payment based on the market rate for the performance rendered[3].

1 1994 SC 270.
2 *R & J Dempster Ltd v Motherwell Bridge & Engineering Co Ltd* 1964 SC 308; Sale of Goods Act 1979 (SGA 1979), s 8.
3 See Cameron '*Consensus in dissensus*' 1995 SLT (News) 132.

1.40 The existence of a contract between the parties will exclude any possibility of *negotiorum gestio*, while a salvage contract may override the common law of salvage (eg with regard to the requirement of success).

1.41 A final point concerns the relationship between contract and property law[1]. Many contracts have the purpose of transferring the ownership of things between the parties. But it must be kept in mind that the making of the contract and the transfer of ownership (the *conveyance*) are distinct in law, although in some situations (eg the sale of specific goods where the contract does not otherwise provide[2]) they can occur simultaneously. But the general principle is that ownership (a real right) is not transferred by contract alone[3], which merely creates a personal right to have the transfer made. If ownership is transferred and the underlying contract is subsequently declared null or retrospectively null, the transfer may still stand good although possibly subject to avoidance[4].

1 On the relationship between property and enrichment see MacQueen § 6 (at pp 58–59).
2 See SGA 1979, ss 16, 17 and 18, rule 1.
3 Or, in Latin: *traditionibus non nudis pactis dominia rerum transferuntur* (deliveries, not bare contracts, transfer the ownership of things).
4 See Thomson *Scots Private Law*, ch 4; *Reid* paras 606–618.

CLASSIFYING AND RECLASSIFYING OBLIGATIONS

1.42 Having considered the constituent elements of the law of obligations, we can now turn to their classification. For many centuries jurists have divided obligations into two main groups: those which are created by the parties' own free will, such as contract and promise, and which are therefore called *voluntary* or *self-imposed obligations*; and those imposed by the law regardless of the parties' will, such as delict, unjustified enrichment and *negotiorum gestio*, which are usually described as *obligations imposed by law or ex lege*. The point is that, whereas contracting parties or a promisor decide the content of their obligations, what it is that they are going to perform, in other obligations it is the law which determines what performance is required, what conduct is wrongful, which enrichments are unjustified, or the amount to be paid as damages or restoration of the enrichment[1].

1 For Scots law see, eg, Stair *Institutions* I, 3, 3, distinguishing between conventional and obediential obligations.

1.43 The argument that contract law is essentially about establishing and giving effect to what parties have agreed can be closely linked to the values of a market economy. The basis of such an economy is to allow each individual member of society to pursue his or her own interests as he or she judges them, subject to only a few basic constraints designed to preserve the peace, such as the prohibitions of the criminal law. Every contract reflects the peaceful pursuit of self-interest, the realisation of which without engaging in murder and robbery demands co-operation and compromise with others. The best way of achieving a stable and peaceful society in which none the less individuals can pursue their own paths to satisfaction and happiness is to allow its members to make any kind of agreement with each other about the exchange of things, services and money (*freedom of contract*), and to uphold those agreements once made (*sanctity of contract*). In this vision, the role of the law of contract is limited to the identification and enforcement of contracts. Otherwise it is up to the parties to look after their own interests (which anyway they know better than anyone else). Of course, in contracting they must not lie to or cheat their partners, but since each person is taken to be looking after his own interests, there is no further obligation to be concerned about the position of the party on the other side of the negotiating table. If a bargain turns out not to be a fair exchange – the goods sold were not worth the price paid, for example – that is not a matter in which the law should become involved; the party who made the bad deal will learn from the experience and be more wary and protective of his own interests when next he participates in the marketplace.

1.44 Such ideas have informed much of the content of modern contract law and remain of great importance today; indeed, arguably, they were reinvigorated in the last quarter of the twentieth century as around the world the frontiers of the state were rolled back and the process of privatisation took ever stronger hold[1]. Yet the law itself also plays a considerable role in determining the obligations of contracting parties. An obvious point is that it is the law, rather than the parties, which says when parties have done enough to have a contract and what the contract means, just as it says which conduct is wrongful and delictual or which enrichments are unjustified and must be reversed. Again, when a party goes to court to seek enforcement of a contract, the order that he asks for will often be, not performance of what the parties agreed, but rather the law's substitute for actual performance, namely damages. Thus in this situation contract law looks like delict, a set of rules determining whether and how much compensation should be paid in particular circumstances. However, it has to be noted that the idea of freedom of contract can overcome the law's control of remedies since it is accepted that (at least in non-consumer contracts) parties can provide in their contract for what the remedies are to be or indeed exclude particular remedies altogether. In other words, often the law is really a default system operating in the absence of contractual provision.

1 It is unlikely that it would be possible today to use the phrase 'death of contract' to describe the current state of the law: cf Grant Gilmore's famous work of that title, published in 1974.

1.45 Nevertheless, quite apart from remedies such as damages, the content of contractual obligations may be determined by the law rather than the parties. Probably millions of contracts are made in Scotland every day of the week, most of them by conduct with virtually no discussion between the parties as to what the terms and conditions of their obligations are. Such commonplace transactions as buying food, drink and newspapers in shops and restaurants, purchasing transport by bus, train and aeroplane, and seeking entertainment in cinemas, sports grounds and dance clubs, rarely if ever involve negotiation over what the obligations of the parties may be. The vast majority of these transactions will be consumer contracts and the rights of the consumer, should a dispute break out, will generally be determined under rules laid down not by the parties in their contract but by the law. Thus, for example, there is legislation governing consumers' rights in contracts for the supply of goods, services, and credit[1].

1 SGA 1979 as amended by the Sale and Supply of Goods Act 1994 (SSGA 1994) and the Sale and Supply of Goods to Consumers Regulations 2002 (SI 2002/3045); Consumer Credit Act 1974 (CCA 1974) as amended by the Consumer Credit Act 2006.

1.46 One feature of some of this legislation governing particular types of contract is that, like the rules on remedies, it can be overruled if the parties do make express provision to that effect in their contract. An example is provided by the buyer's rights laid down in the SGA 1979 as amended[1]. On the other hand, there is also legislation which expressly overrides any contrary contractual provision[2] or which enables the courts to do so if they find such provision to be unfair or unreasonable in some way[3]. Most of these rules result from the drive for consumer protection; but not all. Indeed, there are some rules of the common law of contract allowing the exercise of judicial control over unfair contract terms, for example penalty clauses and contracts in restraint of trade[4]. So again it is apparent that contract law is not simply about identifying the obligations agreed by parties; it is also concerned with the regulation of what the parties agree.

1 SGA 1979, s 55(1) (subject to the Unfair Contract Terms Act 1977 (UCTA 1977)).
2 See, eg, Housing Regeneration and Construction Act 1996, s 113 (pay-when-paid clauses void).
3 Eg UCTA 1977, Pt II.
4 See below, paras 6.47 ff, 7.30 ff.

1.47 Regulation of contract terms has become an ever more significant function of contract law with the rise of 'standard form contracts'. Companies whose business involves them in dealing with thousands, perhaps even millions, of consumers every day – for example, airline or railway companies – cannot afford to spend time negotiating individually tailored contracts for each and every one of them; and indeed it is very doubtful if the customers who merely want to get from one place to another would much appreciate having to take this time either. The solution is for the company to offer to contract on the same set of non-negotiable pre-prepared terms and conditions with every customer. This means greater speed and efficiency in contracting for both the company and its customers, reducing the costs all round. But since the company drafts the contract and the customer has no input, the terms tend to favour the interests of the company over those of the customer leading to unfairness, at least occasionally. Two points of importance in the discussion of how to classify obligations arise from this widespread phenomenon: one the role of contract law in policing the content of contracts; the other that much, perhaps even most, modern contracting practice does not involve detailed discussion and agreement of terms, merely agreement to enter a contract with one of the parties paying little heed to the details of the obligations thereby created. It is therefore difficult to say in cases of this kind that the essence of the contractual obligation is the agreement of the parties.

1.48 Thus, although the distinction between voluntary and imposed obligations retains validity, especially with regard to commercial contracts, it becomes somewhat blurred when we enter the territory of consumer transactions. This has led some to argue that the law of obligations should be treated as a unity under which the law imposes solutions to disputes between parties[1]. The mere fact that parties had made an agreement to perform would not of itself create obligations: instead these would be triggered by actions causing loss or conferring benefits. Agreements would have a merely evidential status, explaining why a person changed position and incurred loss by acquiring property or spending money in reliance on the arrangement made, or what if any value should be placed upon a benefit received. But in determining which losses should be compensated and which benefits paid for, the courts should have a much more active role than that of a mere mechanism for the enforcement of the agreement. While freedom and sanctity of contract would retain importance, perhaps most of all in commercial transactions, other policies of the kind familiar in the law of delict and unjustified enrichment would have an at least equal status in judicial decision-making. This would provide the means by which contracts could be subjected to social and community values in the same way as when we analyse which conduct is wrongful and which benefits are unjustified in delict and enrichment law respectively[2].

1 See above all the works of Atiyah: eg *The Rise and Fall of Freedom of Contract* (1979); *Promises, Morals and the Law* (1981); *Essays on Contract* (1986); *Introduction to the Law of Contract* (6th edn, 2005). For critical overviews of the debate generated by Atiyah, see Smith *Contract Theory* (2004) and Hogg *Promises and Contract Law* (2011).
2 See further on these themes, eg, Collins *The Law of Contract* (4th edn, 2003).

1.49 Analyses of this kind are at their most persuasive in consumer contracts where the obligations are determined as much by law as by agreement and where, in at least some instances, the law does enable the consumer to withdraw without penalty from an agreement within a certain period from its formation[1]. Indeed, in practice it is common for businesses to allow consumers to cancel freely agreements such as bookings in a restaurant or a theatre, or to return goods and obtain refunds of the purchase price without inquiry as to whether or not they were defective. Even in commercial transactions, socio-legal research has suggested that, when disputes break out in contracts between businesses, they commonly seek to resolve them informally by further negotiation rather than by standing on the strict letter of the agreement[2]. So if the parties themselves are not too concerned with what their agreement says, why should the courts confine themselves to that material when they are called upon to resolve contractual disputes?

1 Eg CCA 1974, ss 67–74; Cancellation of Contracts made in a Consumer's Home or Place of Work etc Regulations 2008 (SI 2008/1816. See also the Consumer Protection (Distance Selling) Regulations 2000 (SI 2000/2334) (amended by SI 2005/689)), and note further below para 1.56 note 1.

2 See the classic articles by Macaulay 'Non-contractual relations in business' (1963) 28 *American Sociological Review* 55, and Beale and Dugdale 'Contracts between businessmen: planning and the use of contractual remedies' (1975) 2 *British Journal of Law and Society* 45. For illustrative examples in the Scottish case law, see *British Coal v SSEB* 1991 SLT 302 and *Dawson International plc v Coats Paton plc* 1993 SLT 80.

1.50 The answer seems to lie in the pursuit of efficiency and certainty. One key difference between contract, on the one hand, and the remainder of the law of obligations, on the other, is that the latter deals, by and large, with mishaps or departures from the ordinary course of things. The attempt to collapse contract into a general law of obligations tends to focus upon the way in which contractual *disputes* are dealt with, and to overlook or minimise the importance of contract as a *planning and risk allocation device in private relationships*, commercial, consumer and others, most of which do not break down. Many contracts, including consumer and private contracts, are negotiated in great detail as a basis for transfers of considerable value and/or long-lasting relationships. What is agreed is often the basis for yet further arrangements. If the agreement is too easily unseated, many undesirable consequences may follow. To give a relatively simple example: in *Scottish Special Housing Association v Wimpey*[1], a builder was found not liable to its employer for negligently burning down the building upon which it was doing work. At first sight, this decision seems extremely unjust. But the building contract had said that the employer would be responsible for the risk of fire damaging or destroying the building during the contract, 'howsoever caused', so including the builder's negligence, and had also imposed upon the employer the burden of insuring the building against the risk which had materialised. Thus the employer had access, by way of the insurance contract, to resources permitting the reinstatement of the building. In other words, there was a plan under the contract for the risk that had occurred. The builder was therefore entitled to assume that there was no need to have resources available against the contingency of fire. Had it been found liable then in future builders would have had to take out insurance against fire despite what the contract said; the cost of buying that insurance would then have been included in the builder's charges to the employer; and so the employer would have ended up paying, not only for its own insurance under the contract, but also that of the builder. Probably it would be easier and cheaper for the employer to insure what was after all his building than for the builder who has no reason to know its exact value to the employer. In other words, if the builder had been held liable, the cost of carrying out the building work would have been increased without any significant advantage accruing to either party[2]. Of course it can be said that the result of the case is that there is no incentive for the builder to avoid negligence in its operations when there is a risk of fire; but a response to this point might be that builders who earn a reputation for negligence in these matters tend not to be employed and so to go out of business ultimately. It should not be forgotten that commercial incentives are much more significant than legal incentives.

1 1986 SC (HL) 57.
2 This did not stop the House of Lords reaching a rather different result in the similar case of *British Telecommunications plc v James Thomson & Sons (Engineers) Ltd* 1999 SC (HL) 9.

1.51 It thus seems right to continue to give the concept of agreement a central place and value in contract law[1]. It has been the basis of Scots contract law for several centuries as we shall see in subsequent chapters. A network of rules has been woven around it. The close relationship in both theory and practice between contract and the other parts of the law of obligations, and the fact that they often make use of similar ideas and principles, should not disguise the further fact that very often the detailed rules are different and lead to different results in what would otherwise be the same situations. It may be that one day in the not too distant future consumer transactions will come to be seen as distinct from what has been hitherto the general body of contract law, requiring the application of their own principles and concepts and with the notion of agreement being of relatively minor or no significance; but that day, it is suggested, has not yet dawned, and the regulation of consumer contracts is still too variable to allow it to be treated as anything more than a set of particular exceptions to the ordinary rules of contract[2]. Finally, upholding the centrality of the concept of agreement in contract law does not necessarily deny a social role for the law at the same time. Even in their heyday, freedom and sanctity of contract were given their pedestal because they were thought to promote social welfare, meaning that they could be trumped where appropriate by other social values. This is no less true today[3].

1 Hogg, *Promises and Contract Law* (2011), argues that promise rather than agreement is the central concept of contract law.
2 The 'Consumer Bill of Rights' promised by the UK Government, which will consolidate 12 consumer protection statutes and regulations (see the official announcement dated 19 September 2011 at http://nds.coi.gov.uk/content/Detail.aspx?ReleaseID=421254&NewsAreaID=2), may be a significant step towards the creation of a unified consumer contract law.
3 See further Smith, *Contract Theory* (2004); Hogg 'Perspectives on contract theory from a mixed jurisdiction' (2009) 29 OJLS 643.

SOURCES OF THE SCOTS LAW OF CONTRACT

1.52 The Scots law of contract is a product of the common law rather than of statute. This means that it is essentially based upon the decisions of the courts as rationalised and explained over the centuries by various text-writers – or, in at least some instances, upon the statements of the text-writers as rationalised and explained by the courts. The first significant writer on contract law was the Institutional writer, Stair, and his account of 'conventional obligations' (including promise) has had enormous influence since its first publication in 1681. Few of the other Institutional writers added much of significance to his analysis, although the cryptic statements of the basics contained in the opening chapters of Bell's *Principles of the Law of Scotland*, which went through ten editions between 1829 and 1899, were frequently cited by the courts in the nineteenth century. The first textbooks concentrating on contract alone did not appear until the early years of the twentieth century. Of these, much the most influential has been William Murray Gloag's *Law of Contract in Scotland* (1st edition, 1914; 2nd edition, 1929), which was indeed the only available text for half a century and was reprinted in 1984. By then, however, rival texts were appearing, notably D M Walker's *Law of Contracts and Related Obligations in Scotland* (1st edition, 1979; 3rd edition, 1995) and W W McBryde's *The Law of Contract in Scotland* (1987; 2nd edition, 2001; 3rd edition 2007). Professor McBryde's book seems now to have largely assumed Gloag's authoritative mantle as the leading text for practitioners.

But there should also be mentioned the three encyclopaedias of Scots law – *Green's Encyclopaedia*, which appeared in two editions before the First World War, the Dunedin *Encyclopaedia* of the 1920s and 1930s and, begun in 1987 and still current, the *Stair Memorial Encyclopaedia* – all of which contain valuable treatments of contract law much used in practice.

1.53 Both the courts and the text-writers have drawn not only upon each other and their predecessors but also upon the contract laws of other legal systems. Three legal systems have been of particular importance in the development of Scots contract law[1]. This chapter should have already made apparent the significance of *Roman law* for the law of obligations generally, and this holds good for contract also. While it is true that classical Roman law did not have a general law of contract, but rather a law of particular contracts such as sale and hire, the *Digest*, *Code* and *Institutes* of Justinian provided a rich source of materials out of which medieval and later jurists were able to fashion theories of contract law to be received into the developing national systems of Europe. *Canon law*, the law of the medieval church, was particularly influential here. Where Roman law held that, subject to exceptions such as sale, hire and partnership, mere agreements did not give rise to enforceable obligations (*ex nudis pactis non oritur actio*), the canonist maxim was that *pacta servanda sunt* (agreements must be kept)[2]. This had a significant impact in Scotland as is evident from the writings of Stair on contract law. In particular, his oft-quoted aphorism (and tongue-twister), 'Every paction produceth action'[3], is a direct translation of *pacta servanda sunt*.

1 See generally Reid and Zimmermann (eds) *History of Private Law in Scotland* vol 2 (2000).
2 See in general Zimmermann *The Law of Obligations: Roman Foundations of the Civilian Tradition* (1990, reprd 1996); Gordley *Foundations of Private Law* (2006).
3 Stair *Institutions* I, 10, 4.

1.54 The third system of law to have had significant effect on Scots contract law is *English law*[1]. Although there were borrowings from England before the Union of 1707, the influence has been mainly in the period since 1800. The reasons for this are complex and not yet fully understood; but it seems likely that amongst them will be found, first, the fact that in the nineteenth century there were a number of treatises on English contract law whereas, as we have seen, no contemporary Scottish writer was dealing with the subject in any depth; and, second, that when Scots lawyers encountered new contract problems they would often find that the English courts had already addressed the issue and provided an answer which, especially in a commercial context, looked practical and sensible. Thus there emerged in Scotland a number of doctrines of English origin, such as undue influence and misrepresentation, while Scottish rules on topics such as fraud and breach of contract were redrawn to become more like their English counterparts. The effects of this process should not be exaggerated: the Scots law of contract remained clearly separate from English law in many ways and there is no sign that Scots lawyers ever seriously considered the reception of such distinctively English contractual doctrines such as consideration and privity. But it remains true that whenever a Scots contract lawyer has to deal with a previously unconsidered matter the first instinct is to look to see how if at all it has been dealt with in England. Equally, Scots lawyers tend to be very aware of when the English courts adopt a new solution to a problem likely to arise north of the border and there is an understandable perception that it would be undesirable to have too radically different a solution in another part of what remains the single market of the United Kingdom[2].

1 On the background to contract law in England, see Ibbetson *A Historical Introduction to the Law of Obligations* (1999).
2 The comments in this paragraph may be illustrated by consideration of the decision of the House of Lords in *Smith v Bank of Scotland* 1997 SC (HL) 111, applying in Scotland its earlier English decision in *Barclays Bank v O'Brien* [1994] 1 AC 180. See further below, para 4.31.

1.55   When the Scottish and English Law Commissions were set up in 1965, one of their first joint projects was the preparation of a code of contract law to apply throughout the United Kingdom. A text was drawn up[1] but the project was never completed. The Commissions have continued to work jointly on some contract projects but have tended to produce legislation having distinct parts for Scotland and England[2]. A recent example of a joint project that would however lead to a unified set of rules is a report on unfair contract terms published in 2005 (so far unimplemented)[3]. In the 1970s the Scottish Law Commission produced a series of memoranda on various aspects of the formation and validity of contracts and promises[4], but only limited action, to do with liability in pre-contractual negligent misrepresentation[5], the rectification of contractual documents[6] and requirements of writing in contract[7], followed from these documents. The Commission returned to contract law in the 1990s, producing five major reports[8], of which only the second has so far been implemented in the Contract (Scotland) Act 1997. In 2010 the Commission began a review of contract law in the light of European developments by returning to its unimplemented reports, and had produced two new discussion papers by early 2012[9]. The Commission also did a lot of work on unjustified enrichment in the 1990s which had considerable influence in the courts but did not in the end lead to recommendations for substantial legislative initiatives[10]. The work of the Commission is doing much to modernise the law of obligations generally and its discussion papers and reports are a valuable source for current law as well as possible reforms.

1 The text and accompanying commentary, prepared by Harvey McGregor QC, was published in Italy in 1993 as *Contract Code drawn up on behalf of the English Law Commission*.

2 Eg UCTA 1977; SSGA 1994. The relevant reports are respectively *Exemption Clauses: Second Report* (Law Com no 69; Scot Law Com no 39) (1975) and *Sale and Supply of Goods* (Law Com no 160; Scot Law Com no 104) (1987).

3 *Report on Unfair Terms in Contracts* (Law Com no 292; Scot Law Com no 199) (2005). See further below, para 7.85. Another joint report which recommends a unified regime for Scotland and England is *Consumer Redress for Misleading and Aggressive Practices* (Law Com no 332; Scot Law Com no 226) (2012).

4 Memoranda nos 35–39, 42, 43 (1976–79).

5 *Report on Obligations: Negligent Misrepresentation* (Scot Law Com no 92) (1985); Law Reform (Miscellaneous Provisions) (Scotland) Act 1985 (LRMPSA 1985), s 10.

6 *Report on Obligations: Rectification of Contractual and Other Documents* (Scot Law Com no 79) (1983); LRMPSA 1985, ss 8 and 9.

7 *Report on Requirements of Writing* (Scot Law Com no 112) (1988); Requirements of Writing (Scotland) Act 1995.

8 *Formation of Contract: Scottish Law and the United Nations Convention on Contracts for the International Sale of Goods* (Scot Law Com no 144) (1993); *Three Bad Rules in Contract Law* (Scot Law Com no 152) (1996); *Report on Interpretation in Private Law* (Scot Law Com no 160) (1997); *Report on Penalty Clauses* (Scot Law Com no 171) (1999); *Report on Remedies for Breach of Contract* (Scot Law Com no 174) (1999).

9 Discussion Paper No 147 Interpretation of Contract (2011); Discussion Paper No 154 Formation of Contract (2012).

10 *Report on Unjustified Enrichment, Error of Law and Public Authority Receipts and Disbursements* (Scot Law Com no 169) (1999).

1.56 A source of growing significance in the modern law is European Union law. This springs initially from a widespread belief that the creation of a single market within the European Union requires, amongst other things, a harmonised basic level of consumer protection. This is in order to achieve two outcomes. The first is to ensure that no member state becomes a low consumer protection haven from which companies might trade while avoiding others with more stringent regimes. The second is to encourage cross-border consumer transactions within the European Union. So there are directives harmonising the national laws on such matters as the provision of package holidays, the sale of timeshare properties, the cancellation of contracts concluded away from business premises, and distance selling[1]. But more recently there have been directives of a much wider significance for consumer contracts generally, most notably the directive on unfair terms in 1993[2], on consumer sales in 1999[3], and on electronic commerce in 2000[4]. The directives on off-business premises and distance selling were consolidated and replaced by the Consumer Rights Directive in November 2011[5].

1 Council Directive (EEC) 90/314 (OJ L158 23.6.90 p 59), implemented in the UK by the Package Travel, Package Holidays and Package Tours Regulations 1992, SI 1992/3288; Parliament and Council Directive (EC) 94/47 (OJ L280 29.10.94 p 83), implemented by the Timeshare Act 1992 as amended by the Timeshare Regulations 1997, SI 1997/1081; European Parliament and Council Directive 2011/83/EU (OJ L304 22.11.2011 p 64 (the Consumer Rights Directive, replacing Council Directive (EEC) 85/577 (OJ L372 31.12.85 p 31, and Council Directive (EC) 97/7 (OJ L144 4.6.97 p 19). The substance of the two replaced directives is still implemented by, respectively, the Cancellation of Contracts made in a Consumer's Home or Place of Work etc Regulations 2008 (SI 2008/1816, and the Consumer Protection (Distance Selling) Regulations 2000 (SI 2000/2334, as amended by SI 2005/689, SI 2008/1277, SI 2009/209). But these may be re-implemented in the proposed UK 'Consumer Bill of Rights' (see above para 1.51 note 2).
2 Council Directive (EEC) 93/13 (OJ L95 21.4.93 p 29). On implementation in the UK, see below, para 7.71 ff.
3 Parliament and Council Directive (EC) 1999/44 on certain aspects of the sale of consumer goods and associated guarantees (OJ L171 7.7.99 p 12), implemented by the Sale and Supply of Goods to Consumers Regulations 2002 (SI 2002/3045).
4 Parliament and Council Directive 2000/31/EC on certain aspects of electronic commerce in the Internal Market (OJ L178, 17.8.2000 p 1) implemented by the Electronic Commerce (EC Directive) Regulations 2002 (SI 2002/2013).
5 European Parliament and Council Directive 2011/83/EU (OJ L304 22.11.2011 p 64).

1.57 European directives are the products of negotiation and compromise between the member states, the European Commission and the European Parliament. They are thus reflective of the various legal traditions in Europe and can be seen as an instrument whereby Continental concepts may infiltrate the Common Law and vice versa. Their impact upon Scots law is dependent on the extent to which in the area in question the law is more influenced by its Common Law or its Civilian background. The experience to date is one of change. In particular, a number of the directives affecting contract law make use of the Continental concept of good faith in contract which has not previously been an explicit concept in either Scots or English contract law[1]. Indeed in pre-directive cases English judges vigorously rejected a positive requirement of good faith as inconsistent with the values of a market economy (although this of course does not mean that either English law or a market economy promotes, or even countenances, bad faith in contracts). Probably the Scottish judiciary would have concurred with their English brethren if asked. This opposition to an active requirement of good faith is because in Continental legal systems it entails imposing external, or community, norms upon contracting parties and their agreements. The courts are thereby permitted to declare contract terms invalid, require a party to take the other party's interests into account, fill gaps in contracts, deal with unforeseen and changing circumstances and hardship, and control the unfair exercise of contractual remedies; quite contrary to the English and Scottish traditions of contract already described. But the implementation of the various directives has set the concept of good faith loose in the law of contract and in a Scottish House of Lords case in 1997 Lord Clyde made reference to 'the broad principle in the field of contract law of fair dealing in good faith'[2]. Views vary as to the desirability and scope of this emerging principle and as to whether the Scottish and English courts will ever take it as far as their European counterparts have done; but there can be no doubt that its arrival is one of the major effects of British membership of the European Union so far as contract law is concerned[3].

1 In addition to the Unfair Terms Directive, see the Commercial Agents Directive (Council Directive (EEC) 86/653 (OJ L382 31.12.86 p 17)), implemented in the UK by the Commercial Agents Regulations 1993, SI 1993/3053, the Distance Selling Directive, art 4, and the Unfair Commercial Practices Directive (Parliament and Council Directive 2005/29/EC, (OJ L149 11.6.2005 p 22), art 2(h)), implemented in the UK by the Consumer Protection from Unfair Trading Regulations 2008 (SI 2008/1277). The Regulations provide for criminal sanctions only; but see further the Law Commissions' joint report on *Consumer Redress for Misleading and Aggressive Practices* (Law Com No 332; Scot Law Com No 226, 2012).
2 *Smith v Bank of Scotland* 1997 SC (HL) 111 at 121.
3 See the essays in Forte (ed) *Good Faith in Contract and Property* (1999); MacQueen and Zimmermann (eds) *European Contract Law: Scots and South African Perspectives* (2006) ch 2; *Hogg* pp 36–40.

CROSS-BORDER CONTRACTS AND THE FUTURE

1.58 Discussion of the European Union reminds us that we cannot look at contract law only in the context of a single jurisdiction. Contracts frequently involve parties from different countries or performance of the contract in more than one country. More than one legal system is therefore potentially relevant. How do we decide which one applies? This is a matter for international private law, or conflict of laws as it is sometimes known[1]. The issue is of significance in Scotland not just because of membership of the European Union but also because the other legal systems of the United Kingdom are foreign laws for these purposes along with those of the rest of the world. In addition, the development of a global commercial and consumer economy coupled with the rise of electronic commerce on the Internet are leading to ever more cross-border transactions involving people and businesses based in Scotland.

1 In Scotland see generally Anton (Beaumont and McEleavy) *Private International Law* (3rd edn, 2011); Maher and Rodger *Civil Jurisdiction in the Scottish Courts* (2010); *McBryde* ch 27; Crawford and Carruthers *International Private Law: a Scots Perspective* (2010).

1.59 There are two critical legal questions: (1) Which court has jurisdiction to determine disputes? (2) Which of the possible laws applies? Both questions can be answered by reference to the express terms of the contract which may prorogate the jurisdiction of a particular court (or provide for arbitration) and declare that a particular law is to apply. The answer to one question need not be the same as the answer to the other. Parties might choose the Scottish courts without necessarily choosing Scots law; in one case, for example, it was found that although the parties had chosen English law this did not exclude the jurisdiction of the Scottish courts[1].

1 *Scotmotors v Dundee Petrosea* 1980 SC 851. See also *McGowan v Summit at Lloyds* 2002 SC 638.

1.60 In the absence of contractual provision about jurisdiction, the rules are to be found in the European Union Council Regulation 2001 on jurisdiction in civil and commercial matters ('Brussels I') if the contracting party to be sued is domiciled in another European Union Member State[1], and the Civil Jurisdiction and Judgments Act 1982 if that person is domiciled in Scotland or another part of the United Kingdom. Generally, defenders are to be sued in the courts of the place of their domicile/seat of business. But 'in matters relating to a contract' there may be concurrent jurisdiction in courts of the place of performance of the contract. There are also special rules for the protection of consumers and employees and (in Brussels I) for insurance contracts. Consumers and employees may be sued only in the courts of their domicile. The House of Lords has held that issues of unjustified enrichment arising following the avoidance of a contract are not 'matters relating to a contract', meaning that the enriched defender had to be sued in its 'home' court[2].

1 Council Regulation No 44/2001 of 22 December 2000 on jurisdiction and the recognition and enforcement of judgments in civil and commercial matters (OJ L12 16.1.2001 p 1). The Regulation replaced the Brussels Convention on Jurisdiction and Enforcement of Judgments in Civil and Commercial Matters 1968. Brussels II is a further Council Regulation (1347/2000) on jurisdiction on status questions.
2 *Kleinwort Benson v Glasgow DC* [1997] 4 All ER 641 HL. For subsequent proceedings in a Scottish court held to be governed by English law see *Kleinwort Benson Ltd v Glasgow City Council (No 3)* 2002 SLT 1190. See also, on 'matters relating to a contract', *Strathaird Farms v Chattaway* 1993 SLT (Sh Ct) 36.

1.61 If the contract makes no provision about which law applies, the general principle is that of the 'proper law of the contract', ie the law with which the transaction has the closest and most real connection. This may be determined from such factors as the place of execution of the contract, the place of performance, the parties' places of business, the form of the contract or the situation of the objects of the contract. In 1980 the member states of the European Communities agreed a Convention on Contractual Obligations (the Rome Convention) which was applied in the United Kingdom by the Contracts (Applicable Law) Act 1990. The Convention was replaced by a Regulation (usually known as 'Rome I') in 2009[1]. Under the Regulation, the closest connection is presumed to be the habitual residence of the party who is to effect the performance characteristic of the contract. This is the non-monetary performance, ie the supply of goods in the case of sale or hire. The presumption can be rebutted by other factors[2]. Consumers continue to enjoy the benefit of the consumer protection laws of their domicile whatever the law otherwise applicable to their contracts[3]. A European Union Regulation on applicable law in non-contractual obligations (known as 'Rome II') was enacted in May 2007[4].

1 Regulation (EC) No 593/2008
2 See eg *Ferguson Shipbuilders Ltd v Voith Hydro GmbH & Co KG* 2000 SLT 229; *Caledonian Subsea Ltd v Microperi SRL* 2003 SC 70. Difficulties in choice of law relating to the uniquely Scottish concept of the unilateral promise are explored in Maher 'Unilateral obligations and international private law' 2001 JR 317.
3 Regulation (EC) No 593/2008, art 6.
4 Regulation (EC) No 864/2007.

1.62   One of the problems of 'choice of law' is the fact that different legal systems may have distinct approaches and answers to particular issues. A solution to this difficulty has been for states to agree particular regimes of law to apply in all systems to contracts which inevitably have a cross-border character. The principal example is the international carriage of goods and passengers by air, land and sea, where we have, for example, the Warsaw Convention on Contracts of Carriage by Air 1929[1], the Geneva Convention on Contracts for the International Carriage of Goods by Road 1956 and the Convention for the Unification of Certain Rules of Law relating to Bills of Lading (the Hague-Visby Rules) 1924. In 1980 the Convention on International Sales of Goods (CISG) was established in Vienna (whence it is often known as the Vienna Convention). The United Kingdom was one of the signatories of CISG but has never ratified the Convention to make it part of the law of either England or Scotland, even although it is now in force in all the other major trading nations of the world.

1 For a Scottish case on the Warsaw Convention see *King v Bristow Helicopters Ltd* 2002 SC (HL) 59. Note also here Regulation (EC) 2027/97 (OJ 1997, L 285/1), applying to EC air carriers and raising the limits to which such a carrier may restrict liability to passengers in respect of death or injury in an air accident. This is now implemented in the UK by the Air Carrier Liability Order 2004, SI 2004/1418. A different issue is addressed by EC Regulation No 261/2004 establishing common rules on compensation and assistance to passengers in the event of denied boarding and of cancellation or long delay of flights. The obligations which this places upon airlines with regard to their passengers were well illustrated in 2010 and 2011 by what followed the mass cancellation of flights as a result of the effect upon European airspace of volcanic ash clouds emanating from Iceland.

1.63   The CISG contains a large number of rules of contract law, sale still being perhaps the prime example of a contract. Its success as an international regime for sales has therefore raised the question of whether it is possible to have such a regime for international contracts more generally, and also as to whether its structure of rules might be adopted on the domestic level as well. This led initially to two projects. The first was sponsored by Unidroit, which is shorthand for the International Institute for the Unification of Private Law, based in Rome. In 1994 it published *Principles of International Commercial Contracts* (PICC), a system of contract rules which might be used by parties to cross-border transactions but which could also be used as a model of an ideal system of contract law by national law-makers. Further, more developed editions were published in 2004 and 2010. The second project was the Commission on European Contract Law, which likewise produced a system of contract rules, *Principles of European Contract Law* (PECL), between 1995 and 2003 but with the European Union and its member states as the principal intended market rather than the global ambitions of Unidroit[1]. Both projects are unofficial in that what is produced by them does not have the character of positive law; but the PECL was taken up by the European Commission in 2004 to become one of the principal bases for what was called a 'Common Frame of Reference' (CFR) for European contract law. A Draft Common Frame of Reference (DCFR) was published in 2009, covering not only general contract law but also a number of particular contracts such as sale and lease of goods[2]. In turn this became the main source for a European Commission Proposal for a Common European Sales Law (the proposed CESL) published in October 2011[3]. This would provide an alternative law (an 'optional instrument') which parties could use instead of a domestic law when making cross-border contracts for the sale of goods and digital services in the European Union. It would be available for use in consumer sales and in business sales where one of the parties was a small or medium-sized enterprise (SME) as defined in the Proposal. Member States would have the option of making it available more widely within their respective jurisdictions. At the time of writing (May 2012) there is considerable controversy about the proposed CESL, and the prospects of its becoming law were uncertain[4]. The other aim of the CFR project was to provide a 'toolbox' for the improvement in quality and coherence of Community legislation in the field of contract by providing clear definitions of legal terms, fundamental principles and model rules; and the DCFR is now available for that purpose, albeit as a non-binding instrument. The material in the DCFR as well as the two sets of Principles and the proposed CESL have been used by the Scottish Law Commission in its work on the reform of contract law[5]. It has thus seemed right to draw upon them as well as other comparative material in the writing of this book since they may well provide pointers to future development of domestic as well as European law.

1 The first volume of the *Principles of European Contract Law* (PECL), edited by Lando and Beale, appeared in 1995 and the second, under the same editorial team, in 1999. A third volume, edited by Lando, Zimmermann, Clive and Prum, was published in 2003.
2 *Principles, Definitions and Model Rules of European Private Law: Draft Common Frame of Reference*, 6 volumes edited by Von Bar and Clive (2009).
3 Brussels, 11 October 2011, COM(2011) 635 final.

4 See MacQueen, Garland, Barekat and Boffey, 'The proposed Common European Sales Law' 2012 SLT (News) 65. Further developments may be followed on the European Private Law News blog at http://www.law.ed.ac.uk/epln/.
5 See most recently Scot Law Com Discussion Papers nos 147 and 154.

2. Creation of Voluntary Obligations: Contract, Promise and Third Party Rights

2.1 Contract is the main example of a voluntary obligation and this chapter deals principally with the requirements of the law for the formation of a contract. However, the concept of a unilateral promise, which is often closely connected with the process of forming a contract, must also be dealt with for a complete picture. The chapter then continues with an examination of the circumstances in which persons other than original contracting parties may acquire rights and duties under contracts before concluding with a discussion of the obligations arising when for some reason negotiations between parties do not lead on to a contract.

CONTRACT

Agreement – *consensus in idem*

2.2 While Scots law recognises that a voluntary obligation can arise from a unilateral declaration of will, ie a promise, the vast majority of voluntary obligations are created as a result of an agreement between the parties. A contract is formed when the parties have reached agreement – *consensus in idem* – on the essential terms of the contract always provided that they have intention to create legal obligations[1]. As a consequence, the parties are obliged to perform what they have agreed to do. In other words, the parties undertake to act or refrain from acting and are *obliged* to perform their obligations as soon as the contract is made.

1 On essential terms and intention to create legal relations, see further below, paras 2.4 and 2.64 ff respectively. Hogg *Promises and Contract Law* (2011) argues that contracts are about promises rather than agreements.

2.3 However, *performance* of the obligations may be suspended until a condition has been purified in which case, while the parties are still obliged to perform as soon as the contract is made, performance is not prestable ie enforceable until the condition is fulfilled. For example, A and B agree that A will buy goods from B at £x, delivery to be made by B six months from the date of the contract. While *both* undertake obligations as soon as the contract is made, A cannot compel B to deliver the goods until the condition has been purified, namely six months have elapsed. But, of course, B's obligation to deliver the goods timeously exists from the moment the contract is formed[1].

1 On conditions see further below, para 3.57 ff.

2.4   Agreement, therefore, is crucial to the formation of the contract. The parties need not be agreed on *all* the terms but there must be *consensus in idem* as to the *essential* terms of the purported contract. What is seen as essential may depend on the circumstances of the individual case. In contracts for the sale of goods and land (heritage) the identification of the subject matter[1] and the price have been said to be essential. The four essential terms of a lease are the parties, the subjects, the rent and the duration: but other terms such as a rent review clause or an option enabling the tenant to purchase the property may be regarded as essential in the particular circumstances. On the other hand, parties to a sale may agree that there is to be a price without fixing the amount in order, for example, to cope with fluctuating market conditions[2]. None the less the content of the agreement must also be reasonably certain; the words used may be too vague, or insufficient, or self-contradictory, to make for enforceable obligations[3]. In some cases if the parties have agreed upon the essentials that is enough for the formation of a contract even although there may be other details to be settled between them in the future[4]. As Lord Clarke explained in *RTS Flexible Systems Ltd v Molkerei Alois Muller GmbH*[5]:

'The general principles are not in doubt. Whether there is a binding contract between the parties and, if so, upon what terms depends upon what they have agreed. It depends not upon their subjective state of mind, but upon a consideration of what was communicated between them by words or conduct, and whether that leads objectively to a conclusion that they intended to create legal relations and had agreed upon all the terms which they regarded or the law requires as essential for the formation of legally binding relations. Even if certain terms of economic or other significance to the parties have not been finalised, an objective appraisal of their words and conduct may lead to the conclusion that they did not intend agreement of such terms to be a pre-condition to a concluded and legally binding agreement'.

That said, if the parties are in dispute about some matter which is not an essential term but which is an indivisible part of the whole transaction there will be no contract[6]. On the other hand, parties can be agreed on all the terms but also that there is not to be a binding contract until the agreement has been put in writing and signed by the parties: if this is not done no contract arises in spite of the parties' *consensus*[7].

1 *Bogie (t/a Oakbank Services) v The Forestry Commission* 2002 SCLR 278 (description of land to be sold merely by reference to its general area and location is not sufficient).

2 *R & J Dempster Ltd v Motherwell Bridge & Enginneering Co Ltd* 1964 SC 308; *Glynwed Distribution Ltd v S Koronka & Co* 1977 SC 1; *Miller Homes v Frame* 2002 SLT 459. The Sale of Goods Act 1979 (SGA 1979), s 8 allows the court to fix a reasonable price where the parties to a sale have agreed that there is to be a price but have provided no mechanism by which to ascertain it.

3 *McArthur v Lawson* (1877) 4 R 1134; *McBryde* para 5.14.

4 See, eg, *Westren v Millar* (1879) 7 R 173 (doubted by *Gloag* p 45, n 1 and *McBryde*, para 5–13 n 71); *Wight v Newton* 1911 SC 762; *Freeman v Maxwell* 1928 SC 682.

5 [2010] UKSC 14, [2010] 1 WLR 753 at para 45.

6 *Heiton v Waverley Hydropathic Co* (1877) 4 R 830; *Burnley v Alford* 1919 2 SLT 123; *Small v Fleming* 2003 SCLR 647.

7 *Karoulias SA v The Drambuie Liqueur Co Ltd* 2005 SLT 813. Cf *Immingham Storage Ltd v Clear plc* [2011] EWCA Civ 89 where an agreement was subject to board approval with a formal contract to follow in due course: nevertheless the court held that a binding contract arose before approval was obtained or a formal contract issued. Where the parties have begun to perform their agreement the court may infer that they have waived the need for a formal written agreement and that there is therefore a binding contract ie the need for a formal written agreement has been overtaken by events: *RTS Flexible Systems Ltd v Molkeri Alois Muller GmbH* [2010] UKSC 14, [2010] 1 WLR 753.

2.5 How, then, will the courts determine whether an agreement has been reached between the parties? Two approaches are possible. First, it could be argued that there is no *consensus* unless the parties have subjectively agreed on the essential terms of their contract. Apart from difficulties of proof, a subjective approach could open the way for a party who has made a bad bargain to try to escape from the consequences by maintaining that he had not subjectively agreed. This would lead to uncertainty, particularly for the commercial community. Instead, therefore, Scots law tests the existence of *consensus in idem* objectively. The courts ask the question whether a reasonable person, looking at the actings of the parties, would infer that they had reached agreement even although *subjectively* no agreement had been concluded.

2.6 In *Muirhead and Turnbull v Dickson*[1], for example, MT had supplied a piano to D 'at the value of £26, payable at 15/- per month'. When D failed to pay an instalment, MT sought to repossess the piano. MT claimed that the purported contract was one of hire purchase and that ownership of the piano would not pass to D until the last instalment had been paid and D had exercised an option to buy the piano for a nominal sum. If this were so, MT was entitled to possession of the piano as title had not been transferred to D. D, on the other hand, argued that the contract was one of sale. In this case, ownership had passed to him when the contract was formed although the price was to be paid in instalments. Since title had passed, MT was no longer the owner and was not entitled to possession of the piano. It is clear that subjectively there was no *consensus*: MT claimed it was a contract of hire purchase while D maintained it was a contract of sale. However, the Inner House of the Court of Session held that on objective criteria a reasonable person would infer from their actings that the parties had concluded a contract of sale, the price to be paid by instalments. As Lord President Dunedin observed: 'Commercial contracts cannot be arranged by what people think in their inmost minds. Commercial contracts are made according to what people say'[2].

1   (1905) 7 F 686.
2   (1905) 7 F at 694. See also the approach of Lord Clarke in *RTS Flexible Systems Ltd v Molkerei Alois Muller GmbH* [2010] UKSC 14, [2010] 1 WLR 753 at para 45 cited in para 2.4 above.

2.7   Sometimes the evidence is such that even on objective criteria it is clear that the parties never reached agreement. In *Mathieson Gee (Ayrshire) Ltd v Quigley*[1], it was established that one party had proceeded on the basis that the purported contract was one of hire of plant to remove silt (*locatio rei*): the other had proceeded on the basis that the purported contract was one for the removal of the silt as opposed to the hire of the machinery (*locatio operis*). The House of Lords held that from the evidence of the parties' documents the court could not infer objective *consensus*. Lord Reid explained[2]:

'No doubt, if an agreement could be spelled out from the documents, the Court in such circumstances would be inclined to do that and proceed to determine what were its terms. But, if it clearly appears to the Court that the true construction of the documents is such as to show there was no true agreement, then it is plainly an impossible task for the Court to find the terms of an agreement which never existed.'

It should be noticed that the House of Lords reached the conclusion that there was no contract by construing the documentary evidence rather than by investigating the parties' subjective intentions. Since the parties had litigated all the way to the House of Lords on the basis that there was a contract, it may be taken that subjectively they believed their relationship was contractual. But because *consensus* is tested objectively, the parties' subjective views can be set aside. But the evidence of *dissensus* must be very strong to infer that no agreement was ever reached, particularly as Scottish courts will, if the evidence is ambiguous, tend to uphold rather than cut down bargains. As Lord Guthrie once remarked, 'the object of our law of contract is to facilitate the transactions of commercial men, and not to create obstacles in the way of solving practical problems arising out of the circumstances confronting them, or to expose them to unnecessary pitfalls'[3].

1 1952 SC (HL) 38.
2 1952 SC (HL) 38 at 43.
3 *R & J Dempster Ltd v Motherwell Bridge and Engineering Ltd* 1964 SC 308 at 332. See also *R&D Construction Group Ltd v Hallam Land Management Ltd* [2009] CSOH 128 (aff'd on this point 2011 SC 286) where Lord Hodge observed at para 39 that the court should not be 'the destroyer of bargains'.

2.8   This issue raises particular difficulties where one or both parties have performed their obligations under a purported contract. For example, if A undertakes to provide services for B without A's remuneration having been agreed, what is to happen if A nevertheless goes ahead and provides the services? If the court took the view that the parties had never reached *consensus*, ie that no contract was ever formed, A could not sue in *contract* for his remuneration. To avoid this result, the Scottish courts have been prepared, where the purported contract has been performed or executed, to imply (i) that a contract was formed; and (ii) that there was an implied term that A would receive reasonable remuneration for his services. While this may be justifiable if the parties are agreed that an outstanding term should be negotiated at a future date, it is going a step too far where the evidence demonstrates that the parties cannot agree on the appropriate remuneration. An example of this situation can be found in *Avintair Ltd v Ryder Airline Services Ltd* where the court found that there was an implied contract[1]. But it is submitted that *Avintair* was a classic example of *dissensus* on an essential term preventing the formation of the contract: the evidence was strong enough to reach such a conclusion by objective criteria. Moreover, if services have been provided in the belief that a contract subsists and the contract is null because of *dissensus*, the law of *unjustified enrichment* will provide relief. If the defender has received a benefit without legal cause, under the law of recompense the defender must pay reasonable remuneration for the services obtained. Thus in the example, A's remedy lies in unjustified enrichment not for breach of an implied term in an implied contract. That said, such instances will be rare given that *consensus in idem* is objectively ascertained in Scots law.

1 1994 SC 270, discussed above, para 1.39. Performance was also an important factor in deciding that a binding contract existed in *RTS Flexible Systems Ltd v Molkerei Alois Muller GmbH* [2010] UKSC 14, [2010] 1 WLR 753.

2.9 The courts could determine whether or not agreement has been reached by consideration of all the evidence relating to the parties' negotiations. This would, of course, be time-consuming – and expensive. While such an approach may ultimately be necessary in extremely complex transactions, in most cases the courts rely on technical rules to help them determine whether or not agreement has been reached. What the courts do is to analyse the negotiations in terms of offer and acceptance and to conclude that agreement has been reached when an offer is met by an unqualified acceptance. While there is a degree of artificiality in such an analysis, it does provide a framework, albeit imperfect, upon which to proceed and produces some degree of certainty. That said, the offer and acceptance analysis is of limited value in highly complex and drawn out negotiations. It is therefore good practice in such situations for the parties to reduce their agreement to a single document setting out all the details of their bargain since this will mean that these are not left to the court's investigation should a dispute later break out. Equally, offer and acceptance analysis is of limited value when formation and performance of a contract more or less coincide, for example in such ordinary situations as picking up a newspaper and paying the retailer, or flagging down a bus at a stop. Here the virtually simultaneous exchange of performances on each side is probably sufficient evidence of agreement. With all these limitations, the offer and acceptance analysis is nevertheless useful and its technical rules remain important not least because they have often to be used by the courts. Very similar rules can be found in most western legal systems[1].

1 See *Zweigert and Kötz* ch 26; also Principles of International Commercial Contracts (PICC) ch 2 and Draft Common Frame of Reference (DCFR) Book II, chapter 4.

The offer and acceptance analysis

(1) Offers

2.10 An offer has been defined as 'a statement of terms which the offeror proposes to the offeree as the basis of an agreement, coupled with a promise, express or implied, to adhere to these terms if the offer is accepted'[1]. The crucial factor about an offer is that it contemplates binding obligations being formed as soon as it is met by an unqualified acceptance[2]. In considering whether or not a statement is an offer, it may be useful to ask whether, if the response to it was an unqualified acceptance, it would be possible to identify at least the essential terms of the contract in question such as subject matter and price.

1 15 *Stair Memorial Encyclopaedia* para 620.
2 See eg *William Lippe Architects Ltd v Innes* [2006] CSOH 182A, affd on this point [2007] CSIH 84, paras 24–26. See also DCFR II.-2:201.

Non-offers

2.11 It is important to distinguish an offer *stricto sensu* from other pre-contractual statements or conduct which do not contemplate the immediate conclusion of a contract. Whether a statement constitutes an offer is ultimately a question of construction ie would a reasonable person infer from the evidence that the statement was intended to be an offer? That said, it is well settled that statements made in certain situations are presumed *not* to be offers unless there is strong evidence to the contrary. Where for example, A inquires whether or not B would consider selling property to A, B's positive reply will generally not amount to an offer which A can then accept resulting in an immediate contract. Instead, the law will regard B's response as an answer to a request for information about willingness to enter into negotiations. In *Harvey v Facey*[1], A asked B if he would be willing to sell his estate and asked him to telegraph his 'lowest cash price'. B responded by saying that the lowest cash price was £900 and A then telegraphed his 'acceptance' of B's 'offer' to sell for £900. The court held that there was no contract. B's response was an indication of the lowest price at which he was willing to sell his estate. It was not an offer to sell at that price but a request to A to make his best offer with £900 as the minimum below which B would not be interested. A's telegram could therefore be no more than an offer which B was entitled to refuse.

1 *Harvey v Facey* [1893] AC 552.

2.12   In many situations a person will make a statement or engage in conduct demonstrating a willingness to negotiate a contract. This is known as an *invitation to treat*. Where there is an *invitation to treat*, its purpose is to invite others to make an offer which can then be accepted by the person who made the invitation. However, the latter is not obliged to accept the offer in the absence of a promise to do so. An example of such a promise might be an undertaking to sell to the highest bidder when inviting persons to bid (ie offer) for a property which you wish to sell. Even then, should you decide to sell to someone other than the highest bidder, you are liable for breach of the unilateral obligation, *not* for breach of any contract of sale[1].

1 See for this situation *Harvela Investments v Royal Trust Co of Canada* [1986] AC 207 as analysed by MacQueen 'Offers, promises and options' 1985 SLT (News) 187.

2.13   As a general rule, an advertisement is only an invitation to treat even if it calls itself an offer and quotes a price[1]. Thus for example, if A advertises a book for sale at £100, he is only making an invitation to treat. If B wishes to buy, he will make an offer to do so which A is free to accept or reject. If A accepts, a contract is formed when A's unqualified acceptance is communicated to B. The importance of analysing an advertisement as an invitation to treat is readily apparent if both B and C reply to the advertisement. A is free to choose which offer to accept or to reject both offers. If A accepts B's offer, he is not liable to C, as no contract has been formed with C. If A's advertisement was regarded as an offer, two contracts would be formed when A received acceptances from B and C. A would therefore be in breach of contract with C if he performed the contract with B and vice versa. Accordingly, to analyse an advertisement as merely an invitation to treat makes sound commercial sense. There can be exceptional circumstances when an advertisement will be construed as an offer and not an invitation to treat. In the famous case of *Carlill v Carbolic Smoke Ball Co*[2], the defendants advertised that they would pay £100 to anyone who suffered influenza after using their product. This was held to be an offer which the plaintiff had accepted when she bought and used the product only subsequently to suffer influenza. The argument that the offer was only an invitation to treat was rejected by the Court of Appeal on the ground that the defendant had deposited £1,000 in a bank as evidence of the company's intention to honour the advertisement and had stated as much in the advertisement. The presumption that an advertisement is only an invitation to treat was therefore rebutted by the evidence.

1 *Fenwick v Macdonald Fraser & Co Ltd* (1904) 6 F 850; *Partridge v Crittenden* [1968] 1 WLR 1204. Cf *Philp v Knoblauch* 1907 SC 994.
2 [1893] 1 QB 256, followed in *Hunter v Hunter* (1904) 7 F 136 and *Hunter v General Accident Corp* 1909 SC (HL) 30. For the full story of the redoubtable Mrs Carlill and her quack and faithless opponents, see Simpson *Leading Cases in the Common Law* (1995) pp 259–291.

2.14 It has long been settled in England that the display of goods in a shop window – even where the price is attached – only amounts to an invitation to treat[1]. Consequently, a potential customer makes an offer for the goods which the retailer can either accept or reject. It is thought that this analysis would be followed in Scots law[2]. More problematic is the position of goods displayed on supermarket shelves. There is English authority that this should also be regarded as an invitation to treat[3]. The potential customer makes an offer when the goods are placed in a basket or trolley and the offer is accepted by the retailer at the checkout. However, it may be that a less artificial analysis is to regard the display of the goods on the shelf as an offer which the customer accepts *not* when selecting the product but when taking them to the cashier at the checkout. This still enables the customer to change her mind by returning the goods to the shelf before she starts to place her goods on the checkout belt.

1 *Fisher v Bell* [1961] 1 QB 394.
2 See 15 *Stair Memorial Encyclopaedia* para 621.
3 *Pharmaceutical Society of Great Britain v Boots Cash Chemists* [1953] 1 QB 410.

2.15 An automatic vending machine could be considered as either a standing invitation to treat or a standing offer. If the former, the potential customer makes an offer by inserting the money which is accepted if the machine retains the money: if the money is rejected, no contract is formed. If the latter, inserting the money constitutes an acceptance and a contract is then formed: if the money is rejected, there would be a breach of contract. While there is no Scottish authority on the point, in England it has been held that the proprietors of an automatic car park made a standing offer which was accepted as soon as a driver had driven to a point where he could no longer return[1]. Since a contract was formed at this stage, the driver could not be bound by any purported terms in a ticket which was issued by an automatic machine situated beyond the point of no return! It remains to be seen whether this approach would be followed in Scotland: if it were, then by analogy, a vending machine would be regarded as a standing offer. In the age of electronic commerce, similar questions arise in relation to Internet web pages which indicate the availability of goods for sale and enable customers to order direct from a supplier by an electronically transmitted communication. Is the web page an invitation to treat? Or is it a standing offer with the customer's transmission of her desire to buy together with her credit card or electronic cash details constituting an acceptance and thereby concluding the contract? Again the significance of the choice concerns whether or not the supplier has the right to decline the customer's business[2].

1 *Thornton v Shoe Lane Parking* [1971] 2 QB 163.
2 See eg the Singaporean case *Chwee Kin Keong v Digilandmail.com Pte Ltd* [2004] SGHC 71 [2005] 2 LRC 28, where it was held that a website was an offer unless qualified by making it subject to availability of stock. But where the seller posted a mistaken price and six parties placed an order for 1,600 items, it was held that the contract was vitiated by their snatching at a bargain and taking knowing advantage of the seller's unilateral mistake.

2.16   At an auction sale, the exposure of articles for sale is merely an invitation to treat. The offer is made by the bidder and accepted by the auctioneer when the auctioneer drops his hammer. It follows that until the hammer drops, a bidder is free to withdraw his offer. Conversely, if the article does not make its reserve price, the auctioneer is free to refuse the highest bid and withdraw the property from sale.

2.17   Where tenders are invited from potential suppliers of materials or services, this constitutes an invitation to treat. The tender, giving details of the terms upon which a person is prepared to undertake the work, constitutes an offer[1]. The person inviting tenders is free to accept any of the tenders submitted. This need not be the lowest tender. Indeed, none of the tenders submitted has to be accepted[2]. But if the invitation to tender states that the lowest tender will be accepted, then there is a binding promise to accept that tender and failure to comply will at least expose the promisor to a claim of damages for breach of promise[3]. The same would probably hold good of any other statement in the invitation to tender which committed the invitor in some way, for example an undertaking about the procedure to be followed in choosing the successful tender[4].

1 *McBryde* para 6.17; 15 *Stair Memorial Encyclopaedia* para 626.
2 It is none the less quite common in practice for invitations to tender to state that there is no obligation to accept the lowest or any other tender.
3 See above, para 2.12.
4 See *Blackpool & Fylde Aero Club v Blackpool Borough Council* [1990] 1 WLR 1995, discussed further below, para 2.96.

When is an offer effective?

2.18 It has been said that an offer is nothing until it is communicated to the offeree[1]. What this means is that an offer cannot be accepted until it has been communicated to the offeree. Actual communication to the offeree is generally required. This is consistent with the principle that the approach to ascertaining agreement is objective: an uncommunicated intention is a subjective fact which cannot be known to the party whom it is intended to affect. Where the communication has not been authorised by the offeror, the offer is ineffective[2]. Because there must be actual communication of the offer to the offeree before it can be accepted, it follows that nothing said or done by the offeree prior to receipt of the offer can amount to an acceptance. Thus for example, if A offers to sell goods to B for £100 and B offers to buy the goods from A for £100, no contract is formed if B's offer was made before B received A's offer[3]. In other words, cross-offers cannot form a contract.

1 *Thomson v James* (1855) 18 D 1 per LP McNeill at 10.
2 *Burr v Bo'ness Commissioners* (1896) 24 R 148. Contrast *Atrill v Dresdner Kleinwort Ltd* [2012] EWHC 1189 (QB).
3 *Harvey v Smith (1904) 6 F 511; Tinn v Hoffmann & Co* (1873) 29 LT 271.

2.19 An offer can be made to a specific person: in this case, only the specified offeree can accept the offer[1]. However, an offer can be made to members of a particular group or, indeed, all the world: if so, it can be accepted by anyone who falls within the class or, in the latter situation, anyone! The classic case is the advertisement of a reward for performing some act such as providing information about a crime or finding a lost person or property. An unresolved question is whether in this kind of case the acceptance needs to be communicated to the offeror. In *Carlill v Carbolic Smokeball Co*[2], for example, it was held that Mrs Carlill had accepted the offer of the £100 reward by buying the smokeball from a retailer, using it and catching influenza;

she did not have to advise the Carbolic Smokeball Company of these things. The importance of this was that the company could not defeat Mrs Carlill's right by withdrawing its offer before she communicated with them.

1 See for example *Fleming Buildings Ltd v Forrest* [2010] CSIH 8 (offer made to Mr and Mrs Forrest could not be accepted by KWF Ltd, a company owned by Mr and Mrs Forrest).
2 [1893] 1 QB 256. See also *Atrill v Dresdner Kleinwort Ltd* [2012] EWHC 1189 (QB).

2.20   An offer, not being by itself an obligation, can be withdrawn by the offeror at any time before the offeree's acceptance is communicated to the offeror. Just as the offer must be communicated to the offeree before it can be accepted, so the withdrawal of the offer must also be communicated to the offeree before the acceptance has been communicated to the offeror. For example, if A offers to sell a picture to B and communicates the withdrawal of the offer to B *before* B has communicated his acceptance to A, then the withdrawal of the offer is effective. Where a contract has to be in writing – for example, a sale of land – and an appropriately written offer is on the table, there is authority that an oral withdrawal communicated to the offeree is effective so that the offeree's subsequent formal written acceptance does not conclude a contract[1].

1 *McMillan v Caldwell* 1991 SLT 325.

2.21   The offeror may give up her right of withdrawal by making a promise not to use it for a period of time: for example, by saying that the offer is open for acceptance until the end of the month or some other given date or time. The offer is then described as firm[1]. If A promises not to withdraw the offer for a period, then communicates a withdrawal of the offer during that time but before B has communicated his acceptance, it is submitted that the offer is still validly withdrawn and no contract can arise from a subsequent acceptance by B. A will, of course, be in breach of the unilateral obligation to keep the offer open until the period has lapsed and B can sue him for damages for breach of the promise.

1 *Littlejohn v Hadwen* (1882) 20 SLR 5; *A & G Paterson Ltd v Highland Railway Co* 1927 SC (HL) 32 at 38.

2.22   When an offer stipulates that it must be accepted within a time limit, an acceptance must be communicated to the offeror within that period. If no acceptance has been received during that period, the offer will automatically lapse when the time limit expires[1]. If no time limit is stipulated, an offer will lapse after a reasonable period[2]: what is reasonable will depend on the commercial environment in which the offer is made[3].

1 But note the possible effect of the postal acceptance rule, discussed below, para 2.31 ff.
2 *Flaws v International Oil Pollution Compensation Fund* 2001 SLT 897 approved 2002 SLT 270.
3 *Wylie & Lochhead v McElroy & Sons* (1873) 1 R 41; *Flaws v International Oil Pollution Compensation Fund* 2001 SLT 897, 2002 SLT 270.

(2) Acceptance

2.23 An acceptance is the final unqualified assent by the offeree to the terms stipulated in the offer. While an acceptance is usually made in words, an acceptance can be inferred from the positive conduct of the offeree. Conversely, if the offeree rejects the offer, the offer falls when the rejection is communicated to the offeror: the offer is then no longer capable of acceptance or of maturing into a contract. These positions are clear and obvious enough. The problems arise where during negotiations the parties make responses which are neither outright acceptances nor rejections.

Qualified acceptance

2.24 Acceptance is an *unqualified* assent to the offer. If an 'acceptance' purports to qualify the terms stipulated in the offer, saying in effect, 'I accept, but …', two things happen when it is communicated to the offeror. First, a qualified 'acceptance' rejects the original offer which thereupon ceases to be capable of acceptance by the offeree should she later change her mind[1]. Second, the qualified acceptance becomes a counter-offer to the original offeror which can itself be accepted by that party. In so far as the qualified acceptance 'accepts' some of the terms of the offer, these terms are in effect incorporated into the counter offer[2].

1 *Wolf & Wolf v Forfar Potato Co* 1984 SLT 100; *Rutterford v Allied Breweries Ltd* 1990 SLT 244; *Tenbey v Stolt Comex Seaway Ltd* 2002 SLT 418; *Pinecraven Construction (Guernsey) Ltd v Taddei and Taddei* [2012] CSOH 18.
2 *Howgate Shopping Centre Ltd v GLS 164 Ltd* 2002 SLT 820 per the Lord Ordinary (MacFadyen) at 826.

2.25 For example, A makes an offer (01) to B. If B purports to accept 01 but qualifies its terms, when the purported acceptance is communicated to A, it destroys 01 which is no longer capable of being accepted by B. Therefore no contract is formed if B later changes his mind and communicates an unqualified acceptance of 01. However, B's purported acceptance while destroying 01 becomes a counter-offer (02)[1] which is capable of acceptance by A. If A purports to accept 02 but qualifies its terms, when the purported acceptance is communicated to B, it destroys 02 and itself becomes a counter-counter offer (03) which is capable of acceptance by B. This process continues until there is an offer (0n) which is accepted without qualification or the parties abandon their negotiations.

1 The terms of the counter offer (02) will contain the terms of the original offer (01) which were not rejected by the purported acceptance: see para 2.24 above.

2.26   Does every qualified acceptance amount to a counter offer and trigger the process outlined above? In theory, the answer must be Yes. But where the change in terms is trivial, it is thought that a qualified acceptance will not amount to a counter-offer as a result of the *de minimis* rule. Requests for clarification of details in the offer or suggestions for variation would not per se amount to a counter-offer provided it is clear that negotiations are continuing[1]. Where it is apparent that an offeree is only prepared to accept an offer if its terms are changed, it is thought that this would constitute a counter-offer which rejects the original offer when communicated to the offeror.

1 *Stevenson Jacques & Co v Maclean* (1880) 5 QBD 346.

2.27   An area in which these rules are very important is the exchange of 'missives' which constitute a contract for the sale of land[1]. Since such contracts must be in writing, normal practice is for the prospective buyer to send a written offer which in theory is then accepted in writing by the seller. In reality, the exchange usually involves many more communications than this and as a result the legal position can become quite unclear. In *Findlater v Mann*[2] for example, F offered to buy M's house on 25 March 1988. M sent a qualified acceptance on 28 March. On 29 March F accepted M's qualified acceptance but added one further condition. On 30 March, and without reference to F's letter of the 29th, M sent one more condition. On 6 April F withdrew his extra condition of 29 March and accepted M's letter of the 30th. M by this stage wished to withdraw. The court held that since the letters of 29 and 30 March were sent without reference to each other, both fell to be treated as offers open for acceptance by either side at the same time. F had accepted before M had intimated the withdrawal of his offer and accordingly there was a contract of sale.

1 See further below, para 2.44 ff.
2 1990 SC 150.

The acceptor

2.28   As suggested above, where an offer is made to a specific person only that person, or her agent, can give a valid acceptance[1]. Where an offer is made to the world at large stipulating a method of acceptance, then anyone who performs the required act can accept the offer. In principle, it would appear that an offer can only be accepted if the offeree knows about the offer when the acceptance is communicated to the offeror[2]. So for example, if A offers £100 to anyone who finds his dog, no contract is formed if the person who finds the animal does not know about the offer at the time she delivers the dog to A. This problem does not arise if, instead of an offer, A *promises* £100 to anyone who finds his dog. A has undertaken a unilateral obligation which is prestable ie enforceable by anyone who purifies the condition: knowledge of the promise at the time the condition is purified is not necessary before it can be enforced[3].

1 *Fleming Buildings Ltd v Forrest* [2010] CSIH 8.
2 See 15 *Stair Memorial Encyclopaedia* para 633.
3 See further below, para 2.57 ff, on the requirements of writing here.

Communication of acceptance

2.29   An acceptance is only effective to conclude a contract when it has been communicated to the offeror. Where the offeror prescribes the method of communication, this must be followed. So for example, if the offer stipulates that an acceptance must be communicated to the offeror in writing, an oral acceptance will not suffice. Where an offer does not stipulate a method for communicating the acceptance, any method of communication can be used provided it is not disadvantageous to the offeror. Similarly, an offer may stipulate that acceptance must be communicated to the offeror within a prescribed period, for example 24 hours.

2.30   While an offeror is free to prescribe the way in which an acceptance is to be communicated, he cannot stipulate that the offeree's silence will constitute acceptance[1]. Thus for example, if A offers to sell goods to B for £1,000 and stipulates that if he does not hear from B within a week he will assume B wishes to buy the goods, prima facie no contract exists. The law will not allow an offeror to impose a contract upon an offeree by stipulating that a contract will exist unless the offeree positively rejects the offer. But where in such circumstances the offeree wishes to contract, he may have rights against the offeror. Because he has stipulated that the offeree's silence would constitute acceptance, the offeror will be personally barred from denying the existence of the contract on the ground that no acceptance was communicated to him. In other words, while the offeree's silence cannot be stipulated as amounting to acceptance in order to impose a contract upon the offeree, the offeror who waives the need to communicate acceptance cannot argue against the offeree that a contract does not exist due to the absence of a communicated acceptance[2]. In these circumstances, personal bar fulfils its traditional function of providing the offeree with a shield and not a sword. It should also be noted that technically the personal bar only operates between the parties to prevent the offeror raising the point that acceptance has not been communicated to him. The question could arise whether this personal bar is constitutive of a contract between the parties. The practical answer in most cases is that since the offeree is seeking performance, she will in fact have indicated to the offeror that she is intending to accept the offer. A contract will therefore be formed at least at that stage. But is a contract created earlier? In theory, the answer must be no: personal bar provides a defence, it does not create positive rights[3]. Consider the following example:

A offers to sell a racehorse to B for £10 million. A says that if he does not hear further, he will assume that B is a buyer. If B does not want the horse, A cannot impose a contract upon him in this way. If B does want the horse, A is personally barred from arguing that a contract cannot exist because B did not communicate an acceptance. When B indicates to A that he wants the horse, it would appear that a contract now exists because B's positive conduct amounts to an acceptance. But assume that before that date, B had sold the horse to C. Can C claim the horse from A relying on the fact that A could not raise the absence of acceptance point in an action brought by B? This could only happen if the personal bar is constitutive of a contract between A and B so that B obtains the title to the horse which he can then pass to C. English authority suggests that no contract would exist between

A and B unless B has actually communicated an acceptance to A[4]. It is thought that this approach would also be adopted in Scotland where a plea of personal bar is restricted to the immediate parties concerned: third parties should not be affected. Therefore it is submitted that C could not directly claim ownership of the horse from A and his remedy lies in suing B for breach of contract. Similarly, if the horse is injured by the negligence of D before B has indicated positive acceptance to A, it is A and not B who has title to sue D in delict for the harm to the horse.

1 *McBryde* paras 6.78ff. Where there have been prior dealings between the parties or prolonged negotiations including draft contracts, the circumstances may be such that the court can infer consent from the fact that the party did not respond to a communication. In *Shaw v James Scott Builders & Co* [2010] CSOH 68, while recognising that silence will not usually conclude a contract, the Lord Ordinary (Hodge) observed at para 50 that 'it is well recognised that the surrounding circumstances may occasionally cause the court to infer that a party, through his silence, has assented to be bound by a preferred contract.'
2 15 *Stair Memorial Encyclopaedia* para 639.
3 *The Advice Centre for Mortgages v McNicoll* 2006 SLT 591 per Lord Drummond Young at 595.
4 *Felthouse v Bindley* (1862) 11 CB (NS) 869.

The postal acceptance rule

2.31 Communication is crucial in the offer and acceptance analysis. An offer, withdrawal or rejection of an offer and an acceptance are only operative when they have actually been communicated to the relevant parties[1]. There is, however, a very important exception to this fundamental requirement of communication, namely the postal acceptance rule. The rule means what it says. It only applies when an acceptance has been posted and applies only to acceptances[2]. It does not apply to postal offers, withdrawals of offers or qualified acceptances which only become counter offers when actually communicated.

1 In the case of postal offers, counter offers, withdrawals or rejections, transmission of the communication takes effect when the mail is delivered viz 'by pushing the letter…through the letter box': where mail is collected, transmission of the communication takes place at the time of collection. See *Carmarthen Developments Ltd v Pennington* [2008] CSOH 139 per Lord Hodge at para 31.
2 *Carmarthen Developments Ltd v Pennington* [2008] CSOH 139 (postal acceptance rule does not apply to the exercise of an option to waive the need to purify suspensive conditions).

2.32 The rule is simple. When an unqualified acceptance is *posted*, the contract is formed when the letter is *posted* rather than when it is actually communicated to the offeror. The implications are important. For example, where an offer contains a time limit for acceptance, a contract will be formed if the acceptance is posted within that period even although it does not reach the offeror until the time limit has expired[1]. Indeed, if it can be proved that an acceptance has been posted, logically a contract is formed even although the letter never arrives; but there are dicta against this conclusion from the Scottish courts[2].

1 *Jacobsen Sons & Co v Underwood & Son Ltd* (1894) 21 R 654.
2 See *Mason v Benhar Coal Co Ltd* (1882) 9 R 883 at 890; *J M Smith Ltd v Colquhoun's Tr* (1901) 3 F 981. Contrast England: *Household Fire and Carriage Accident Ins Co v Grant* (1879) 4 Ex D 216.

2.33 The most important effect of the postal acceptance is that it will defeat the offeror's uncommunicated withdrawal. An offer can be withdrawn at any time before acceptance. If A purports to withdraw an offer to B, the withdrawal will be ineffective if B has posted an acceptance before the withdrawal has actually been communicated to B[1]. Because of the postal acceptance rule, the contract was formed before A's withdrawal reached B. It does not matter that A no longer wished to contract at the time B's acceptance was posted. But in very exceptional circumstances a court may depart from strict adherence to the logic of the rule if the result would be absurd. In *Burnley v Alford*[2], A offered to sell an estate to B. A week later, he sent a letter to B's lawyers withdrawing the offer. The letter was sent to the correct address. However, it was not communicated to the solicitors who were on a shooting expedition and had not left a forwarding address. Later, but before their return, the solicitors sent a telegram to A accepting the offer. On their return, they read A's withdrawal. The postal acceptance rule applied to telegrams – which are no longer in use. Applying the rule, there should have been a contract as the acceptance took place when the telegram was sent, ie before the solicitors saw the purported withdrawal. The Lord Ordinary (Ormidale) refused to endorse this result. Instead, he argued that the withdrawal would have been communicated to B before the acceptance was telegraphed if the lawyers had been present at their office during normal business hours or had left a forwarding address for mail. A had done everything possible to communicate withdrawal of the offer and it was the fault of the solicitors that they had not received the notice of the withdrawal before telegraphing an acceptance. In these circumstances, they were not entitled to take advantage of the rule[3]. The result would have been different if, for example, A had also been at fault for the failure to communicate the withdrawal timeously by sending it to the wrong address. Here, it is submitted, the full rigour of the postal acceptance rule would have continued to operate and there would have been a contract.

1 *Thomson v James* (1855) 18 D 1.
2 1919 1 SLT 123.
3 In *Carmarthen Developments Ltd v Pennington* [2008] CSOH 139, Lord Hodge took the view at para 31 that 'it is the task of recipients of mail to arrange for its prompt handling and the sender of a notice cannot be prejudiced by internal delays in so doing'.

2.34 Once an offeree has posted an acceptance, a contract is formed. Should the offeree change her mind after the letter has been posted, logically she should still be bound by the contract even although she attempts to terminate the contract by informing the offeror before the acceptance is actually communicated. Again, the strict logic of the application of the rule may not be followed in Scotland. In *Countess of Dunmore v Alexander*[1], the Countess wrote to her friend, Lady Agnew, to engage Betty Alexander to be the Countess' servant. The next day the Countess changed her mind and sent a letter to Lady Agnew withdrawing her acceptance of Miss Alexander's services. The two letters arrived together. The court held that Miss Alexander had not been appointed. The reasoning in the decision is not satisfactory (unless, as Gloag suggested[2], the Countess's first letter is analysed as an offer rather than an acceptance). It would appear that Lady Agnew was acting as agent or mandatory for both parties and that the second letter was treated as a postscript to the first so that when read together, Lady Agnew no longer had the authority to engage Miss Alexander on behalf of the Countess. It should be noted, of course, that this case was decided before the postal acceptance rule had been transplanted into Scots law. There is later authority that the case would not be followed in so far as it was inconsistent with the rule[3]. But at the same time it was suggested that a postal acceptance could perhaps be withdrawn if the offeree informed the offeror that there was to be no contract before the acceptance had in fact arrived: for instance, if I telephoned, faxed or e-mailed to you that a letter of acceptance from me which was on its way to you by post should be ignored once it arrived. This seems a sensible result as the offeror does not know that a contract had been formed by the posted acceptance and should not have acted on the assumption that the offer would be accepted.

1 (1830) 9 S 190.
2 *Gloag* p 38.
3 *Thomson v James* (1855) 18 D 1.

2.35 We have emphasised that it is the *postal* acceptance rule. The rule does not apply where the acceptance has been made using instantaneous forms of communication, for example telephone[1]. In these circumstances, the normal principle applies and a contract is not formed until the acceptance has actually been communicated to the offeror. The same principle would presumably apply to an acceptance left on a telephone answering machine or voicemail system, or sent by fax or email although there may be room for speculation about the position of the recipient of such a message who does not activate the means of accessing it within a reasonable time. Perhaps the rule about revocations in *Burnley v Alford*[2] could be extended to cover this situation, taking the message to have been heard or read and to have become effective when it ought to have been listened to or read in the ordinary course of business[3].

1 *Entores Ltd v Miles Far East Corp* [1955] 2 QB 327; *Brinkibon v Stahag Stahl GmbH* [1983] 2 AC 34.
2 See above, para 2.33.
3 Cf DCFR I.-1:109, III.-3:106. Note that the postal acceptance rule is not found as such in continental Europe: *Zweigert and Kötz* ch 26.

2.36 The courts may well depart from the strict application of the postal acceptance rule if otherwise there would be an absurd result. This could occur in the context of international trade where, for example, the acceptance might be received by employees with limited authority or outside the offeror's normal business hours because of time differences between the parties. Another example of a possibly unreasonable consequence of rigorous application of the postal rule is in contracts for the sale of land. The risk of destruction by fire of the buildings on the land falls on the buyer the instant the contract is concluded unless the contract otherwise provides[1]. If the contract is concluded by the seller's postal acceptance, then the buyer may have the risk without realising it and as a result may not obtain the necessary insurance until after receipt of the seller's letter. If in the meantime the building burns down, a very unfair burden could be thrown upon the unfortunate buyer. It has been judicially stated, however, that the postal rule might not be applied in such a case[2].

1 As in practice it commonly does.
2 *Sloans Dairies v Glasgow Corporation* 1977 SC 223.

2.37 Even modern forms of instantaneous communication may break down. It has been suggested[1] that where the offeree has reasonable grounds to believe that the acceptance has been communicated and the offeror was at fault in failing to notify the offeree that the acceptance has not been received, then a court would deem that a contract had been formed. In other words, the offeror is personally barred from denying the existence of a contract on the ground that the acceptance has not been communicated. However, if the offeree's belief is unreasonable or the offeror was not at fault, then no contract exists until the acceptance has actually been communicated to the offeror.

1 *Entores Ltd v Miles Far East Corp* [1955] 2QB 327 per Denning LJ at 332 ff.

2.38 The postal acceptance rule has been criticised as artificial. Its main purpose is probably to protect the offeree against the withdrawal of the offer; a policy which would be unnecessary if offers were generally irrevocable, as in Germany, or if damages could be recovered for abusive withdrawal, as in France, neither country having a postal acceptance rule as such. As we have seen, the courts are at times prepared to deviate from the rule's strict logic in the interests of business and common sense. As the offeror can stipulate the method of acceptance, the postal acceptance rule can be avoided if the offeror states that an acceptance must actually be communicated to him[1] and this seems to be quite common in practice. The Scottish Law Commission has called for the rule to be abolished and proposed its replacement with the rule in the CISG and the DCFR, namely that an offer ceases to be revocable once an acceptance is dispatched although a contract is only formed on communication of the acceptance[2].

1 *Holwell Securities v Hughes* [1974] 1 WLR 155.
2 Discussion Paper No 154 on Formation of Contract (2012). See previously *Report on Formation of Contract: Scottish Law and the United Nations Convention on Contracts for the International Sale of Goods* (Scot Law Com no 144) (1993). See also CISG arts 16 and 18(2); PICC, arts 2.4 and 2.6(2); and DCFR II.-4:202(1) and 205(1).

The utility of the offer and acceptance analysis

2.39 As suggested at the outset, there is a degree of artificiality in analysing formation of contract in terms of offer and acceptance. That said, the courts must have some tools to aid them in assessing when a contract has been formed and the terms governing the contract. There is also the importance of bringing some degree of certainty into this area of law not least for the benefit of the parties and their legal advisers.

2.40 In the commercial world, it is common for parties to contract on what are known as standard forms ie printed forms which contain the terms upon which the company is prepared to contract. These may be found in printed quotations, order forms, delivery notes or receipts. Their use in the consumer context was discussed in the previous chapter; there only one party, the supplier, will normally make use of standard terms[1]. But in the commercial context it is perfectly possible, and not uncommon, for both parties to use standard forms in attempting to contract. Where this happens and the contract is performed, a dispute may arise over whose terms have in fact been incorporated into the contract[2]. For example, A may give a quotation containing A's terms, B may place an order using a form with B's terms, A may send a receipt containing A's terms whereupon B performs the contract. Whose terms prevail? The practical importance of a solution to this 'battle of the forms' is that, because the parties tend to have different interests to protect, the terms of their forms will not match each other: therefore on an objective view, and despite the performance, there is no contract. A supplier of goods or services may have terms saying that no particular delivery time is guaranteed, that the price may be changed without prior notice, and that there is no liability for defective performance; whereas a party ordering the goods or services will have clauses saying that time is of the essence of the contract (meaning that they can cancel for late performance), imposing penalties for delay, fixing the price, and requiring the re-tender or repair of substandard performance.

1 See above, para 1.47.
2 See eg *C R Smith Glaziers (Dunfermline) Ltd v Toolcom Supplies Ltd* [2010] CSOH 7.

2.41 The courts have tended to use the offer and acceptance analysis to provide an answer to this kind of conflict[1] – even though it bears little relation to how the parties actually contract. So in the example, the court might argue that A's quotation was an offer, B's order form was a counter-offer, A's receipt a counter-counter offer – albeit on the same terms as the original offer – and B's *positive* conduct in performing the contract acceptance of A's counter-counter offer. In other words, the battle of forms will be won by the party which gets its terms in last provided there is positive conduct on the part of the other side from which acceptance of the terms can be inferred.

1 *Uniroyal v Miller & Co* 1985 SLT 101; *Continental Tyre & Rubber Co Ltd v Trunk Trailer Co Ltd* 1987 SLT 58. For England see *Butler Machine Tool Co Ltd v Ex-Cell-O Corp* [1979] 1 WLR 401; *Tekdata Interconnections Ltd v Amphenol Ltd* [2010] 2 All ER (Comm) 302 (CA).

2.42 Attempts are sometimes made to pre-empt such a battle by a party stipulating that its terms are to prevail over the other's – an 'overriding clause'. Usually such a clause will not be successful if the other party's response in its standard form contains – as it always will – clauses which are not the mirror image of those in the form which contains the overriding clause. This follows from the rule that a counter-offer kills or knocks out the preceding offer[1]. There may be some exceptional situations. In one case for example, it was stipulated in an offer that any alteration of the party's terms would only be effective if agreed in writing by that party. The other party's 'acceptance' purported to change a term in the offer. This variation was not agreed in writing by the offeror who, nevertheless, went ahead and performed the contract. On a strict offer and acceptance analysis, the original offer was met by a counter-offer which was accepted by performance: the contract should therefore have contained the altered term. The court held, however, that the contract had proceeded on the original terms as the offeror had made it clear that no performance would take place except on their terms. When the alteration was not agreed in writing, it should have been clear that the contract would have to be governed by the original terms and this was accepted by the other side when they asked for the work to begin[2]. In the final analysis, this case illustrates that while the offer and acceptance analysis is a useful guide, the ultimate issue is what the parties had agreed on an objective construction of the evidence in the particular circumstances of the case.

1 *Butler Machine Tool Co Ltd v Ex-Cell-O Corp* [1979] 1 WLR 401.
2 *Roofcare v Gillies* 1984 SLT (Sh Ct) 8.

2.43 In 1993 the Scottish Law Commission recommended that the law relating to the battle of the forms should be reformed along the lines set out in CISG[1]. Where a reply to an offer purports to be an acceptance but contains additional or different terms, it is nonetheless an acceptance concluding a contract if the new terms do not *materially* alter the terms of the offer. The offeror may escape this conclusion by objecting without undue delay to the discrepancy. If there is no such objection, the terms of the contract are those in the offer together with the modifications in the acceptance. An alteration is material if it relates, among other things, to price, payment, quality and quantity of goods, place and time of delivery, extent of liability and the settlement of disputes; exactly the matters on which standard forms tend to conflict. The change would therefore probably make little practical difference save that 'instead of inferring acceptance from the offeror's actings (for example, in sending goods) acceptance of non-material additions or variations could be inferred from the offeror's failure to object without undue delay'[2]. The Commission's proposal thus remains unimplemented. The Draft Common Frame of Reference takes a more radical approach than CISG, holding that a contract is formed if the parties reach agreement although using conflicting standard forms, with the terms being those of the forms so far as they are common in substance[3]. A party may escape this rule by a pre-contractual statement to that effect, not contained in its standard form, or by a prompt objection to the other party's form[4]. In 2012 the Scottish Law Commission published a new proposal based on this approach but it remains to be seen whether this solution will command any more support than its predecessor[5].

1 *Report on Formation of Contract: Scottish Law and the United Nations Convention on Contracts for the International Sale of Goods* (Scot Law Com no 144) (1993); CISG, art 19(2) and (3). There is a similar rule in PICC, art 2.11.
2 Scot Law Com no 144 para 4.19.
3 DCFR II.-4:209(1). Other terms would be implied in law or in fact: see further below, para 3.27 ff.
4 DCFR II.-4:209(2). See further Forte 'The battle of forms' in *MacQueen & Zimmermann* (2006).
5 See Scottish Law Commission Discussion Paper No 154 on Formation of Contract (2012) ch 5 for further discussion.

Written formalities – contracts relating to real rights in land

2.44   As a general rule, writing is not required for the constitution of a contract in Scots law[1]. Provided the parties intend to create legal relations[2], their agreement constitutes a contract as soon as it is reached. There is no need for writing and the existence of the contract can be proved by parole evidence. However, there are some important exceptions to this general rule, all created by statute. Sometimes this is for reasons of publicity, where the contract is likely to affect property rights or third parties in some way and a written record therefore makes it easier to identify[3]. In other cases, the requirement of writing is for the protection of consumers with the imposition of the formal step of applying a signature to a printed document aiding the consumer in realising that a legally significant commitment is being made[4]. Similarly requirements of writing in employment contracts ensure that employees are aware of their provisions[5].

1 Requirements of Writing (Scotland) Act 1995, s 1(1).
2 See further below, para 2.64.
3 See, eg, Policies of Assurance Act 1867, s 5; Bills of Exchange Act 1882, ss 3(1), 73, 83(1); Partnership Act 1890, s 2(3)(b); Merchant Shipping Act 1894, s 31(1) Marine Insurance Act 1906, s 22; Patents Act 1977, s 31(6); Copyright, Designs and Patents Act 1988, ss 90, 92; Civil Aviation Act 1982, s 86; Mobile Homes Act 1975.
4 Consumer Credit Act 1974, ss 61(1), 105(1).
5 Employment Rights Act 1996, ss 1 and 13(1)(b).

2.45 For lawyers, the most significant contracts which require writing are those relating to real rights in land. Section 1(2)(a)(i) of the Requirements of Writing (Scotland) Act 1995 (RWSA 1995)[1] provides that a written document subscribed by the parties is necessary to *constitute* 'a contract or unilateral obligation for the creation, transfer, variation or extinction of a real right in land'. For this purpose real rights in land include ownership of land and the lease of land when the lease is for a period of more than a year[2]. 'Subscription' means signed at the end of the page or document in question. Thus for example, a contract for the sale of a house is not formed unless and until there is a written contract of sale subscribed by the seller and purchaser (typically by way of the buyer's signed written offer and the seller's signed written acceptance, the exchange of missives)[3]. Consequently, where the parties have merely reached an oral agreement or have put their agreement in an unsigned document no legally enforceable contractual obligations arise; the agreement must now be reduced to writing and signed before it has legal effect. The same would seem to be true when there is a written offer on one side and a verbal acceptance or an acceptance by conduct on the other. Until there is signed writing on both sides, either party can withdraw from the arrangements. It should also be noted that the requirement of writing applies to all unilateral obligations relating to land even where the promise is non-gratuitous and would not otherwise require to be in writing[4].

1 As amended by the Abolition of Feudal Tenure etc (Scotland) Act 2000, s 76 and Sch 12 para 58.
2 RWSA 1995, s 1(7).
3 In practice the missives will be signed on behalf of the parties by their solicitors ie their agents.
4 RWSA 1995, s 1(2)(a)(i). See further below, para 2.54 ff.

2.46 'Writing' means 'typing, printing, lithography, photography and other modes of representing or reproducing words in a visible form'[1]. This seems apt to cover electronic or digital writing; but unless such writing is subsequently printed on paper it will not be enough for the purposes of RWSA. It is also unclear how far an electronic facsimile of a person's 'wet ink' signature, placed on a fax or an electronic version of a writing, will suffice to bind that person in a contract where formal writing is required under RWSA 1995[2]. When the Land Registration etc (Scotland) Act 2012 comes into force, however, RWSA will be significantly amended[3]. It will then be possible to constitute any obligation requiring formal writing with purely electronic writing, provided that the writing is authenticated by electronic signatures of the parties meeting the requirements for such signatures to be set out in regulations made under the 2012 Act. The overall result will be two distinct methods of constituting obligations formally: the 'traditional' method, using paper and 'wet ink' signatures, and the 'electronic', using only the digital medium and electronic signatures. The new law does not seem to permit the use of mixed media – for example, an emailed or faxed acceptance of a traditional or paper offer – and it will not remove the difficulty about whether a facsimile version of a person's 'wet ink' signature on an electronically transmitted copy of an original paper document has binding effect[4].

1 Interpretation Act 1978, Sch 1; Interpretation and Legislative Reform (Scotland) Act 2010, s 25.
2 Thus a faxed acceptance has been held not sufficient to conclude a contract for the sale of land: *Park, Petitioners* 2009 SLT 871, noted by Anderson 2010 SLT (News) 67; Gretton (2010) 14 Edin LR 280.
3 Part 10 and Sch 3 of the 2012 Act introduce a new Part 3 (Electronic Documents) to RWSA (as ss 9A–9G).
4 For further discussion see Scottish Law Commission Discussion Paper No 154 on Formation of Contract (2012) ch 7.

2.47   Because no contract relating to real rights in land is formed before it is in writing, either of the parties may withdraw from the agreement at any time before it is reduced to a written document[1]. However, under s 1(3) and (4) of the RWSA 1995, parties to an oral – and therefore prima facie unenforceable – agreement upon which one of them has acted may be personally barred from denying the existence of a contract because of the absence of writing and the contract will be treated as valid. The law thus gives protection to the party who has acted in reliance upon the informal arrangements becoming a binding contract. Section 1(3) and (4) provides as follows[2]:

'(3) Where a contract … is not constituted in a document complying with section 2 or, as the case may be, section 9B, of this Act, but one of the parties to the contract … ("the first person") has acted or refrained from acting in reliance on the contract … with the knowledge and acquiescence of the other party to the contract … ("the second person") –

(a) the second person shall not be entitled to withdraw from the contract, … ; and

(b) the contract … shall not be regarded as invalid, on the ground that it is not so constituted, if the condition set out in subsection (4) below is satisfied.

(4) The condition referred to in subsection (3) above is that the position of the first person –

(a) as a result of acting or refraining from acting as mentioned in that subsection has been affected to a material extent; and

(b) as a result of such a withdrawal as is mentioned in that subsection would be adversely affected to a material extent.'

1 Thus creating a chance to 'gazump' (seller finds another buyer willing to pay more) or 'gazunder' (buyer finds another seller willing to accept a lower price for an equivalent property).

2 The text is set out as amended by the Land Registration etc (Scotland) Act 2012, s 92(2)(b). The phrases omitted in the quotations here relate to gratuitous unilateral obligations and trusts. Sales of land will be by far the most common application of these provisions and only that example is considered here. For unilateral gratuitous obligations, see below, para 2.54 ff.

2.48 Section 1 (3) and (4) is technically complex. Nevertheless, its purpose is relatively simple. When the provisions are satisfied, there are two consequences. First, a party who was prima facie entitled to deny the existence of a contractual obligation because of the absence of writing becomes personally barred from so doing. In short, he is no longer entitled to withdraw from the informal agreement on the ground that it has not been reduced to writing. Second, the agreement is no longer treated as invalid on the ground that it is not constituted by appropriate writing[1]. In other words, s 1(3) and (4) has a constitutive effect. *As between the parties*[2], they transform agreements which are informal – and therefore unenforceable – as a result of the absence of writing into valid, enforceable contracts relating to real rights in land. Before s 1(3) and (4) can be triggered, the court must be satisfied that not only had the parties reached agreement but that they intended the agreement to have legal effect ie intention to contract must be present. Put another way, s 1(3) and (4) only applies when the agreement is unenforceable solely because of the absence of formalities[3].

1 The double negative should be noted. The contract can still be invalid on other grounds, for example defective consent: only invalidity on the ground of lack of formalities is removed.

2 As s 1(3) and (4) constitutes a form of statutory personal bar, it has been held that the provisions cannot affect third parties: see *The Advice Centre for Mortgages v Mc Nicoll* 2006 SLT 591 and discussion at para 2.30 above.

3 *Aisling Developments Ltd v Persimmon Homes Ltd* 2009 SLT 494.

2.49   When can s 1(3) and (4) be used? For the purpose of construing these provisions let us consider a simple example. A and B agree orally that A will buy B's house for £100,000. This is an agreement for the sale of land and consequently no contract is formed unless and until their oral agreement is in appropriate writing. Assume this has not been done. Because no contract has been constituted, both A and B are free to ignore their agreement: either can refuse to perform as no obligations have been created because their agreement is not in writing. Either party may withdraw from the oral agreement because the absence of written formalities makes it invalid as a *contract*. So if B changes his mind and refuses to sell to A, perhaps because C has made a better offer, he is entitled to do so as no legal obligations have been created between them. However, B may be personally barred from withdrawing from the agreement and a contract with A may be validly constituted in spite of the absence of writing if s 1(3) and (4) apply. This involves a two-stage process:

(1) The person wishing to enforce the obligation (the first person) must have acted or refrained from acting in reliance on the 'contract' (technically, only an agreement, as a contract *ex hypothesi* has not been constituted[1]) with the knowledge and acquiescence of the other party to the contract (the second person) who is now seeking to escape the obligation. In our example, A is the first person – he wishes to purchase the flat for £100,000; B is the second person – he no longer wishes to sell. If A attempts to prevent B from exercising his prima facie right to withdraw from an agreement invalid for lack of formalities, the onus rests on A to establish that s 1(3) and (4) apply. A's claim will fail unless he can show that he acted or refrained from acting in reliance on the agreement with the knowledge and acquiescence of B. So for example, A could argue that in reliance on their agreement, he entered into an onerous contract to obtain a loan or gave up a secured tenancy or did not buy cheaper alternative accommodation. Or it might be that B let A have possession of the flat in order to carry out expensive repairs or improvements. While A's

conduct has clearly been taken in reliance on the agreement, it will be irrelevant for the purpose of s 1(3) and (4) unless it occurred with the knowledge and acquiescence of B. The second person, B, must not only *know* about A's conduct but must also *acquiesce* in it, ie either assent or, at least, not oppose it. It is thought that actual knowledge by B of A's conduct will be required but that B's acquiescence will readily be inferred once knowledge has been established. The point to be emphasised is that any claim under s 1(3) and (4) cannot 'get off the ground' unless the second person *knows* that the first person is engaging in conduct in reliance on the informal agreement.

1 This is an example of the less than felicitous drafting of RWSA 1995, s 1.

2.50

(2) Before the s 1(3) personal bar applies and the obligation is constituted in the absence of writing, the condition set out in s 1(4)(a) and (b) must be established. This condition is in two parts.

First, the *first person* – A in our example – must be *affected to a material extent* as a result of his conduct. This is the conduct in reliance on the agreement *which was known and acquiesced in* by the *second party* – B in our example. The reason for this provision is to ensure that the second party's right to withdraw is not lost as a result of relatively trivial acts of the first party albeit known to the second party. It is submitted that A's conduct in the examples would clearly pass this test: taking out a loan or giving up a secured tenancy or failing to purchase another house or carrying out expensive repairs and improvements are all situations where we can safely assume that A has been 'affected to a material extent'. In short, this hurdle should not be too difficult to cross. Only when the first party's conduct has been trivial can problems be anticipated: for example, it would not be enough if A had merely informed his friends by e-mail that he was changing his address or invited them to a 'flat-warming'.

Second, the *first person* must be *adversely* affected to a material extent by the second person's withdrawal from the agreement. What does this provision mean? It would appear that the first person must show that the second person's refusal to perform as anticipated by the parties will adversely affect the first person. If for example, as a result of B's refusal to sell, A was left with servicing a loan at high interest rates or was rendered homeless because he had terminated the lease or foregone the chance to purchase an alternative house, it is submitted that this part of the condition would be satisfied. But would the condition be established if A could cancel the loan or renegotiate his lease or buy more than adequate alternative accommodation for the same price? Again, if A had bought food and drink for a flat-warming party, he could still use it elsewhere so the effects are probably not adverse here either. Clearly *de minimis* consequences are to be excluded as the first person must be adversely affected to a *material* extent. The mere loss of the anticipated benefits under the contract *per se* may not be enough[1]. Whether the adverse effect is sufficiently material is ultimately a question of degree to be inferred from the evidence[2].

1 *Caterleisure Ltd v Glasgow Prestwick Airport* 2006 SC 602 at 609.
2 For an example of a successful claim under s 1(3) and (4) in the context of a truster as trustee trust, see *McHugh v McHugh* 2001 Fam LR 30.

2.51   In our examples, A has suffered as a result of a combination of (i) his conduct in reliance on the agreement *known to* B and (ii) B's refusal to continue, ie B's withdrawal from the informal agreement. No doubt this was the situation Parliament intended to remedy. However, if the RWSA 1995 is read literally, there is no need for the first party to be adversely affected by both these factors: it is enough if he is adversely affected by the second party's withdrawal. An example will make this clearer:

A and B enter into an oral agreement for the sale of B's house. A, with B's knowledge and acquiescence, orders fitted carpets for the house. Unknown to B, A also borrows from C to finance the purchase. B withdraws from the agreement. The carpet shop agrees that it will terminate the contract of sale without penalty to A. But A has to pay a penalty to C if he wishes to withdraw from the loan. Can A utilise ss 1(3) and (4) to compel B to perform?

A's purchase of the carpets was with the knowledge and acquiescence of B. Therefore s 1(3) is satisfied. The purchase of carpets is not immaterial. But B's withdrawal does not adversely affect A in so far as the carpets are concerned so the second limb of s 1(4) is not satisfied. However, B's withdrawal does affect A adversely *vis à vis* the loan. Although the loan was undertaken without B's knowledge, unlike s 1(4)(a), s 1(4)(b) does not stipulate that any adverse effects from withdrawal must also arise from the conduct of A which satisfies s 1(3) and 1(4)(a). It is at least arguable that, always provided there are actings of the first person which satisfy s 1(3) and 1(4)(a), the adverse effect of withdrawal by the second person need not be as a result of these actings but can be caused by the first person's conduct which was unknown to the second party and which does not satisfy s 1(3). However, until the point is settled by appellate court decision, the generally accepted view is that the adverse effect of withdrawal must be consequent upon actings which satisfy both s 1(3) *and* s 1(4)(a)[1].

1 This was the view of Lord Drummond Young in *The Advice Centre for Mortgages v McNicoll* 2006 SLT 591.

2.52 It is important to appreciate that s 1(3) and (4) are concerned with actings of the first person known to and acquiesced in by the second person. Unlike the law before the RWSA 1995, the actings of the second person cannot per se give rise to the statutory bar. For example, A and B enter into an oral agreement under which B agrees to sell A a house. B withdraws from the agreement before it is reduced to writing. B's acknowledgment or affirmation of the existence of contractual obligations made before he withdrew, ie his *homologation* of the informal agreement, cannot trigger s 1(3) and (4) as A has not acted in reliance on the agreement. The doctrine of homologation in respect of contracts defective in form has expressly been abolished along with *rei interventus*, the common law precursor of s 1(3) and (4)[1]. It should be noted, however, that since s 1(3) only applies to actings of the first person, known to and acquiesced in by the second person, there is an element of homologation present in s 1(3). But in the absence of such actings, the second person remains free to deny the existence of a contract on the ground of defect in form even though he has previously acknowledged or affirmed the oral agreement.

1 RWSA 1995, s 1(5). This was confirmed in *The Advice Centre for Mortgages v McNicoll* 2006 SLT 591.

2.53 A question the answer to which RWSA 1995 arguably left unclear may be seen from an example which arose in a case before 1995:

A makes a formal written offer to buy a lease of farmland from B. B allows A to incur expense in using and improving the land for agricultural operations but never makes either a written or an oral acceptance. B then seeks to eject A on the ground that there is no contract. Can A use B's conduct to show that there was an agreement *and* that he knew and acquiesced in A's actings so that B is barred from denying the existence of a contract?

The answer under the pre-1995 common law was, controversially, Yes[1]. Under the RWSA 1995, since the actings inducing bar must *follow* the agreement[2], it would seem necessary to show that there had been conduct concluding the informal agreement and then *in addition* actings of which the second party was aware and in which he acquiesced. Again, suppose that B rather than A made the written offer, but that the facts are otherwise the same. It is suggested that A would have to show actings by himself that concluded the agreement and then *further* separate actings by him in reliance upon that informal agreement before he could prevent B arguing that there was no contract. In *The Advice Centre for Mortgages v McNicoll*[3] the Lord Ordinary (Drummond Young) confirmed that while an agreement could be inferred from the parties' conduct only actings of the first person after the agreement was made are relevant for the purposes of s 1(3) and (4). If no agreement can be inferred s 1(3) and (4) cannot be triggered. Moreover it must be established that the parties intended the agreement to be legally binding ie they had contractual intent[4].

1 *Errol v Walker* 1966 SC 93.
2 *Super (Tom) Printing and Supplies Ltd v South Lanarkshire Council* 1999 GWD 31-1496, 38–1854.
3 2006 SLT 591.
4 *Aisling Developments Ltd v Persimon Homes Ltd* 2009 SLT 494.

PROMISES

2.54 Scots law recognises that a voluntary obligation can be created by a promise provided the promisor intended to be legally bound[1]. It may however be very difficult to establish that the promisor intended the promise to be legally binding[2]. As Lord Menzies observed in *Regus (Maxim) Ltd v Bank of Scotland*[3], 'clear words are required to express the promisor's intention to bind himself by an enforceable obligation'. A promise is a unilateral obligation in that only the promisor undertakes an obligation at the time the promise is made: the promisee does not undertake to do or refrain from doing anything. Because the obligation arises from the declaration of the promisor's will, there is no need for the promisee to agree to accept the promise before she can enforce it[4]. Indeed, the promisee does not have to exist at the time the promise is made[5]. The promisee can, of course, refuse to accept performance of the promise.

1   The traditional name for such a promise was the technical Latin term, *pollicitatio*. See generally McBryde 'Promises in Scots law' (1993) 42 *International and Comparative Law Quarterly* 48; Sellar 'Promise' in Zimmermann and Reid (eds) *A History of Private Law in Scotland Vol 2 Obligations* 252 (Oxford 2000). See also James Gordley (ed*) The Enforceability of Promises in European Contract Law* (Cambridge 2001); *Hogg*, ch 2. Readers of German may also study Zimmermann and Hellwege 'Belohnungsversprechen: "pollicitatio", "promise" oder "offer"', (1998) 39 *Zeitschrift für Rechtsvergleichung* 133. For Italian perspectives, see Vagni *La Promessa in Scozia* (2008) and De Gioia-Carabellese 'The concepts of the Scottish (and Italian) unilateral promise' [2011] *European Business Law Review* 381. DCFR II.-1:103(2) also recognises promises as binding without acceptance.

2   *Cawdor v Cawdor* 2007 SC 285; *McDougall v Heritage Hotels Ltd & MH Apartments Ltd* [2008] CSOH 54 (form reserving a flat for a potential purchaser not a unilateral promise to sell her a flat: it was a statement of future intention rather than a promise); *Braes v the Keeper of the Registers of Scotland* 2010 SCLR 202 (Keeper's assertion that he would indemnify the pursuer for losses attributable to the Keeper's omission could amount to an enforceable promise); *Sim v Howat and McLaren* [2011] CSOH 115 (new partnership's implied legally binding promise to assume responsibility for the old partnership's debts); *Wylie v Grosset and Greater Glasgow Health Board* [2011] CSOH 89 (no legally binding promise to compensate participants in a clinical trial).

3   [2011] CSOH 129 at para 46.

4   In *Cawdor v Cawdor* 2007 SC 285 the Lord President (Hamilton) observed that 'Delivery to or acceptance by the promisee is not necessary to the constitution of a promise… though, in my view, the presence or absence of communication to the other party may be an adminicle of evidence in the question whether the statement amounts to a promise'.

5   Stair *Institutions* I, 10, 4; *Morton's Trs v Aged Christian Friend Society of Scotland* (1899) 2 F 82.

2.55   A unilateral obligation may be gratuitous ie A promises to act or refrain from acting for the benefit of B without B providing any benefit for A. For example, A may promise to give B £100. However, other cases may present analytical difficulties. For example, suppose that A promises to give B £100 if B finds A's dog. The obligation in this case is unilateral in that only A undertakes an obligation at the time the promise is made: B does not undertake an obligation to find the dog. However, B cannot call upon A to perform the obligation ie pay him £100 until the dog is found. Only if this condition is purified does A's obligation become enforceable. But at this stage, A has received a benefit as his dog has been found! Thus while the promise is a unilateral obligation, in this example it is not the case that the promisee is getting something for nothing. Some would argue that technically the promise in this case is nevertheless a gratuitous obligation because the promisee is not *legally bound* to do anything in return for the promisor's obligation[1]; others would say that the onerous nature of the performance to be carried out by the promisee before getting the benefit of the promise means that the promisor's obligation is not gratuitous[2].

1 See MacQueen 'Constitution and proof of gratuitous obligations' 1986 SLT (News) 1 at 2; 15 *Stair Memorial Encyclopaedia* para 613; *Hogg* paras 2.06–2.11.
2 Thomson 'Promises and the requirement of writing' 1997 SLT (News) 284. It will be apparent that the authors of this work are not *ad idem* on this topic! See also *McBryde*, para 2.03. Both sides of the argument might seek support from the difficult decision in *Royal Bank of Scotland v Wilson* 2004 SC 153.

2.56   Those adhering to the second of the above positions would accept that a conditional unilateral obligation may be gratuitous in some circumstances. For example if A promises to give B £100 on B's eighteenth birthday, the promise is not enforceable until the condition is fulfilled: yet it is still a gratuitous unilateral obligation as A does not receive any tangible benefit when B becomes 18. But a unilateral obligation is not gratuitous when it consists of a promise to enter a future contract; for example, A promises B that A will sell goods to B. This is a unilateral obligation in that B, the promisee, does not undertake that he will buy the goods. But if B does buy the goods, A receives a benefit and accordingly those holding the second position would say that the promise to sell is not a gratuitous unilateral obligation. In other words, where a promise anticipates that the promisee will act upon the promise even though he is not obliged to do so, then if the promisor would receive a benefit as a consequence, the promise is not gratuitous. It is this *potential* benefit to the promisor which renders the unilateral obligation non-gratuitous. The contrary argument says that unless the promisee is legally bound to render its performance then it is gratuitous. This would suggest that all unilateral obligations are gratuitous.

2.57   Why is this important? Under s 1(2)(a)(ii) of the RWSA 1995, a *gratuitous* unilateral obligation must be constituted in traditional writing subscribed by the promisor or in electronic writing electronically signed by the promisor unless the promise was undertaken in the course of business. Thus if there is a category of non-gratuitous or onerous unilateral obligations, it would seem that these do *not* require any form of writing in order to be constituted: s 1(1) of the RWSA 1995. If so, an onerous conditional promise can be established by any competent evidence (parole evidence); for example, such a promise if made orally might be proved by witnesses. When the promise is truly gratuitous, the promise is not *constituted* unless it is in a document[1] subscribed or electronically signed by the promisor. As a consequence, an obligation to perform a gratuitous promise does not arise until the promisor makes the promise in a document. Conversely, the promisee will be unable to *enforce* the promise unless it is in a document subscribed or electronically signed by the promisor.

1 The word 'document' here and later in this section embraces both traditional and electronic documents.

2.58 If it is right to say that all unilateral obligations are gratuitous then, whether or not the obligation is subject to an onerous condition of performance by the promisee, it must be in a formal document unless it is made in the course of a business. There is as yet no guidance from the courts as to whether gratuitous and unilateral obligations are co-terminous or distinct but overlapping categories; it is certainly unfortunate that the legislature has given no guidance on the question of what it means by 'gratuitous unilateral obligation', especially as elsewhere in the same and other Acts it has chosen to use only the phrase 'unilateral obligation'[1].

1 RWSA 1995, s 1(2)(a)(i); Contract (Scotland) Act 1997, s 1(1) ('unilateral voluntary obligation'). In the report giving rise to the RWSA 1995 (Scot Law Com no 112) (1988) the draft Bill referred only to 'gratuitous obligations' but there is no discussion of the precise scope of this phrase.

2.59 No writing in any form is required where the gratuitous unilateral obligation is undertaken in the course of business. Although at first sight it may seem unlikely that hard-headed business persons would enter into 'something for nothing' transactions, a number of examples can be identified. We have already referred in this chapter to promises made in invitations to treat and firm offers[1]. Other more specific instances are cheque cards under which banks promise to pay on cheques satisfying certain conditions, bankers' letters of credit in international sales transactions under which bankers are bound to pay sellers of goods on the production of certain documents, so-called 'requirements' transactions under which A undertakes to supply goods to B as and when the latter needs them, and 'output' transactions under which A commits himself to taking all the goods produced by B[2].

1 See above, paras 2.17 and 2.21.
2 See generally for these examples MacQueen 1986 SLT (News) 1. For an example of a possible promise undertaken in the course of business see *Morrison v Leckie* 2005 GWD 40-734 (Paisley Sheriff Court).

2.60 The absence of a formal document may also not prove fatal if s 1(3) and (4) of the RWSA 1995 applies. Where the promisee has acted in reliance of the promise with the knowledge of the promisor, then the promisor cannot rely on the lack of formalities to deny the existence of the obligation where it would be detrimental to the promisee to do so[1]. For example, A promises to give £10,000 to B. This is a gratuitous unilateral obligation and can on any view only be constituted in a formal document. If the promise is not in writing, the obligation does not exist and B cannot enforce it. But if B (the first person) acts upon the promise by spending £10,000 on a new motor car, then provided that (i) B acts with the knowledge and acquiescence of A (the second person), (ii) the acting affects B to a material extent and (iii) B will be adversely affected if A did not perform the promise, then A is barred from maintaining that he is not bound by the promise on the ground that it was not constituted in writing and the promise is not invalid in spite of the absence of writing[2]. The moral to be drawn is not only never to look a gift horse in the mouth but also to spend the gift as soon as possible *provided* this is done with the knowledge and acquiescence of the donor!

1 See above, para 2.47 ff.
2 Thus the result in the pre-1995 Act case of *Smith v Oliver* 1911 SC 103 would now be different.

2.61 For many years, the concept of an enforceable unilateral promise was little utilised in Scots law. Where a statement was ambiguous ie it could be treated as a promise or an offer to enter into a contract, the Scottish courts tended towards a contractual analysis[1]. Moreover, until the RWSA 1995, although in theory the unilateral obligation was created by the promisor's declaration of his will to be bound, proof of the existence of the promise was restricted to the promisor's writ or oath[2]. In reality, this meant that a promise could not be enforced unless it was in writing. The old law has been swept away and the 1995 Act provides a new foundation. Consider the following situations:

(1) A promises to give B £100. This is a gratuitous unilateral obligation and B can enforce the promise provided that it is constituted in writing. When B has acted upon this promise with A's knowledge, A could be personally barred from relying on the absence of written formalities and the promise treated as valid without the requirement of writing. If the promise was made in the course of business, there is no need for writing.

(2) A promises his neighbour B that he will not practise the piano after 10 pm. This is a gratuitous unilateral obligation and prima facie should be constituted in writing subject to the statutory plea of personal bar and validation.

(3) A promises B £100 if B finds A's dog. If this is a non-gratuitous promise, it does not have to be in a formal document. An analysis in terms of unilateral obligation avoids difficulties inherent in a contractual analysis such as what will constitute acceptance by B.

(4) A promises to sell a painting to B for £1,000. If this is a non-gratuitous unilateral obligation, it does not require to be constituted in writing. It is a unilateral obligation at the time the promise is made as B does not undertake to buy. If B does wish to buy the picture, A will be in breach of the promise and liable to pay damages to B if for example, A has sold the picture to C.

(5) A can give up his right to withdraw his offer to B by promising to keep the offer open for B's acceptance for a set period, for example seven days. This is a unilateral obligation as B is not obliged to accept A's offer. It may be non-gratuitous, as A has the benefit of the contract if B accepts the offer within the period. If this is right, the promise does not have to be constituted in writing. If A purports to withdraw the offer during the period, B can sue A for breach of the promise to keep the offer open[3].

(6) A can take an 'option' from B under which A can exercise a right to acquire specific rights from B at a future date[4]. For example, A might pay B £10,000 for the option of acquiring the right to film B's novel. B in effect promises A that if A exercises his right to choose during that period, B will transfer the film rights to A. On one view, as B will benefit from the promise, it is not a gratuitous unilateral obligation and does not therefore have to be in writing. Alternatively, if all unilateral obligations are gratuitous then writing must be used unless the transaction is in the course of business.

(7) When A and B enter into a contract, circumstances may arise when one party wishes to vary its terms. Usually this will be done by agreement, ie the parties will agree to change the terms. However, it is possible to vary the contract by utilising the law on promises. For example, A contracts to lease machinery from B for five years at a cost of £1,000 a month. Owing to adverse trading conditions, A discovers that he can no longer afford that rent. B could promise to reduce the rent to, say, £500 while the adverse trading conditions exist;

when conditions improve, the rent will revert to £1,000[5]. Since B is promising not to enforce the original contractual rent, it is thought that this is a gratuitous unilateral obligation and should, prima facie, be in writing – although since B is in business, writing may not be required. As a result of the promise, the contractual rights of the parties have effectively been varied though as a matter of law the original terms continue to subsist.

1 See, eg, *Malcolm v Campbell* (1891) 19 R 278.
2 Established in *Millar v Tremamondo* 1771 Mor 12395. See also *Smith v Oliver* 1911 SC 103. Proof by writ or oath has now been abolished: RWSA 1995, s 11.
3 See above, para 2.21.
4 On the characterisation of options as promises, see MacQueen 1985 SLT (News) 187 at 189–190; Hogg *Promises and Contract Law* (2011) pp 230–235. In *Miller Homes Ltd v Frame* 2002 SLT 459 it was recognised by the Lord Ordinary (Hamilton) at 464 that a valid option to purchase, whether constituted as a promise or bilateral contract, might be created without consideration ie gratuitously. That case was concerned with an option to purchase land. Such a unilateral obligation must be constituted in a formal document as it relates to a real right in land: see RWSA 1995, s 1(2) (a) (i) discussed at para 2.45 above. See further on the characterisation of options *Carmarthen Developments Ltd v Pennington* [2008] CSOH 139 per Lord Hodge at paras 13–15.
5 Example based on the English case of *Central London Property Trust Ltd v High Trees House Ltd* [1947] KB 130.

2.62   Finally, it should always be remembered that a gratuitous contract can exist in Scots law. If A offers to give B £100, the obligation does not arise until B accepts the offer. The *agreement* of the parties is the source of A's obligation[1]. In the case of a promise, the obligation to give B £100 will arise as soon as the promise is constituted in a written document since it is, of course, a gratuitous unilateral obligation. The point which should be emphasised is that in the case of the promise there is no need for B's acceptance before the obligation is created. Moreover, B is free to refuse the money as he does not undertake to receive it. However, if A and B enter into a gratuitous contract not only does A's obligation arise when B accepts A's offer but B is under an obligation to receive the gift. This may not seem important when the gift is money but it would be different if the gift was a white elephant!

1 See, eg, *Morton's Trs v Aged Christian Friend Society of Scotland* (1899) 2 F 82; *Miller Homes Ltd v Frame* 2002 SLT 459.

2.63   When parties enter into a gratuitous contract, there is no need for a written document as the need for written formalities is restricted to gratuitous *unilateral* obligations: while, in theory, the agreement can be established by parole evidence, in practice it would be advisable to have such a contract in writing.

INTENTION TO CREATE LEGAL OBLIGATIONS[1]

2.64 Before a promise or an agreement will create legal obligations, the promisor or the parties to the agreement must intend to enter into obligations which are to be legally binding. When no such intention exists, the promise or the agreement cannot be legally enforced. The question whether or not the promisor or the parties have such an intention is, theoretically, a question of fact[2]. However, it is impractical to inquire into the subjective intentions of individuals whenever a dispute arises in respect of an allegedly enforceable promise or contract. Instead, the law presumes that, in certain circumstances, the promisor or the parties to an agreement intended to enter into legal obligations. Conversely, in certain circumstances, the law presumes that they did not intend the promise or agreement to be legally binding. These presumptions can be rebutted if the promisor or the parties have expressly – or occasionally, impliedly – stipulated to the contrary. Consider the following examples:

(1) Where a promise or agreement is made in a commercial context, there is a presumption that the promisor or the parties to the agreement intend to enter legal relations. This covers the vast majority of agreements made in Scotland, since one of the parties will be acting in the course of business and the other will not (a consumer contract) or both parties will be acting in the course of their business. It is open to the parties to rebut the presumption by expressly stipulating that the agreement or promise is *not intended* to be legally binding, for example 'binding in honour only'[3]. Care must be taken to make it absolutely clear that the agreement or promise is not to be legally binding. If the phrase used is ambiguous, for example that a payment is made '*ex gratia*', the court will construe it as not effectively rebutting the presumption that the promise or agreement is prima facie legally binding[4]. Likewise, the relatively informal language of an email exchange between business parties negotiating a contract did not prevent that exchange having contractual effect[5]. Nor does the use of the phrase 'subject to contract' automatically negate contractual intent in Scotland

by contrast with the position in England[6]. However, where it is clear that the parties did not intend to be legally bound by their agreement until it was reduced to a formal written contract, the presumption will be rebutted and the agreement will have no legal effect if the contract is not drawn up[7].

(2) When the promise or agreement is made in an entirely social context, for example an invitation to dinner, the presumption is that the arrangement is not intended to be legally binding. Moreover, an agreement or promise made between members of a family or cohabitants is also presumed not to be intended to create legally enforceable obligations[8]. Once again, the presumption may be rebutted where the promisor or the parties have expressly stipulated that the promise or agreement is intended to be legally binding or such intention can be inferred from the particular facts of the case. In *Robertson v Anderson*[9] two friends had a long term agreement to divide their bingo winnings equally between them. The court held that on the facts of the case, they had intended their agreement to be legally binding albeit that it had been made in a purely social context[10]. This is extremely important when, for example, siblings enter into a partnership or spouses enter into a separation agreement. In *Hutchison v Graham's Exx*[11] the pursuers provided finance to enable their grandmother to purchase her house: it was part of the agreement that the grandmother would on her death bequeath the house to them. Because the agreement was reduced to writing in a formal minute of agreement, it was held to be legally binding and therefore the grandmother's estate was liable for breach of contract when she died leaving the house to her daughter rather than the pursuers. It has been argued that the reason why Scottish courts do not enforce social or domestic arrangements is not so much the absence of intention to create legal relations as the absence of a patrimonial interest and that where there is such an interest, or a question of status, as for example between the members of a club, then the courts will intervene to enforce the agreements[12].

(3) Sometimes an agreement does not fall into either of these categories. Here the court must determine whether or not the agreement was intended to be legally binding. Thus in spite of being negotiated in a commercial context, a collective agreement between an employer and trade union was held not to be intended as legally binding[13]. There is now a statutory presumption that a collective agreement is not

legally binding unless the parties have expressly stipulated in writing that their agreement is to have legal effect[14]. In *Percy v Church of Scotland*[15], on the other hand, the House of Lords held that there is no presumption against an intention to create legal relations in the relationship between a church and one of its ministers with the result that a contract of employment may exist between such parties.

In *Morgan Utilities Ltd v Scottish Water Solutions Ltd*[16] the Lord Ordinary (Hodge) set out four criteria which should be used in determining whether the parties intended to be legally bound:

(i)   Did the parties manifest an intention to be immediately bound 'there and then'?

(ii) The court should take an objective approach: what would reasonable and honest men in the position of the parties have intended or what would have been the reasonable expectations of sensible businessmen in the position of the parties?

(iii) The court should consider not only the events as they unfolded but also the parties' behaviour after the alleged agreement;

(iv) The court should take a neutral approach.

Nevertheless it is thought that the presumptions still provide the court with at least a starting point for what can be a difficult exercise.

1 See for debate on this topic Stewart '"Of purpose to oblige": a note on Stair I, x, 13' 1991 JR 216; *McBryde* 'The intention to create legal relations' 1992 JR 274; Stewart, 'Stair I, x, 13: a rejoinder' 1993 JR 83; Black 'Formation of contract: the role of contractual intention and email disclaimers' 2011 JR 97.

2 In the context of promises Stair *Institutions* 10.2 distinguishes three acts of the promisor's will viz 'desire, resolution and engagement'. In other words, Stair distinguishes the situations where a person wishes to make a promise, decides that he or she will make a promise and actually makes the promise: only the third, 'engagement', creates a unilateral obligation on the promisor. See *Cawdor v Cawdor* 2007 SC 285 per the Lord President (Hamilton) at para 15.

3 *Woods v Co-operative Insurance Society* 1924 SC 692; *Rose & Frank Co v Crompton* [1925] AC 445; *Kleinwort Benson v Malaysian Mining Corporation* [1989] 1 WLR 379; *McDougall v Heritage Hotels Ltd* 2008 SLT 494.

4 *Edwards v Skyways Ltd* [1964] 1 WLR 349.

5 *Baillie Estates Ltd v Du Pont (UK) Ltd* 2010 SCLR 192.

6 *Stobo Ltd v Morrisons (Gowns) Ltd* 1949 SC 184.

7 *Karoulias SA v The Drambuie Liqueur Co Ltd* 2005 SLT 813; note also *Aisling Developments Ltd v Persimmon Homes Ltd* 2009 SLT 494.

8 *Balfour v Balfour* [1919] 2 KB 571.

9 2003 3 SLT 235.

10 It is doubtful that the ladies remained friends.

11 2006 SCLR 587.
12 15 *Stair Memorial Encyclopaedia* paras 657 and 658.
13 *Ford Motor Co v Amalgamated Union of Engineering and Foundry Workers* [1969] 2 QB 303.
14 Trade Union and Labour Relations (Consolidation) Act 1992, s 179.
15 2006 SC (HL) 1.
16 [2011] CSOH 112 at para 52.

THIRD PARTY RIGHTS

Privity of contract

2.65   In general a contract creates enforceable rights and duties only between those who were party to its formation. Third parties are unaffected by the contract whether in terms of acquiring rights or being subject to obligations[1]. This is sometimes known as the principle of privity of contract: a contract is a relationship exclusive to, or private between, the parties who made the contract. This is so even if the third party's interests are affected by the contract. Thus in one case two railway companies agreed to hold down their freight charges in a particular area but eventually decided to abandon this arrangement. A customer who was now confronted with the prospect of higher charges raised an action to hold the companies to their original agreement but it was held that, while the customer had an interest in that contract, he had no rights in it as a mere third party[2].

1 See for example *Osborne v BBC* 2000 SLT 150; *Howgate Shopping Centre Ltd v GLS 164 Ltd* 2002 SLT 820; *Kenneil v Kenneil* 2006 SLT 449.
2 *Finnie v Glasgow and South-Western Rly Co* (1857) 20 D (HL) 2.

2.66   The principle of privity is important in a number of situations. Perhaps the most important in practice is where there are several contracts which involve a number of parties and are closely connected with each other in economic terms in the sense that each makes a contribution to a common goal. A good example is a construction project. An employer wants a building or work of civil engineering and for this purpose enters a contract with a building or civil engineering company (usually known as the main or management contractor). In a project of any size and complexity, however, it is unlikely that the main contractor will have all the necessary skills and experience: and so for these purposes it will turn to, and make further contracts with, specialist sub-contractors. It will also have to buy in materials and hire machinery such as cranes. Indeed, with a management contractor the main task may well be the selection and coordination of other parties to carry out the actual work. In law, the contractual relationships which result can be pictured like this:

Employer —— Main/management contractor —— Sub-contractor(s)

2.67 The significance of privity here is as follows:

(1) The employer has a contract only with the main contractor. The crucial importance of this arises if there are defects in the work done. In the absence of any other arrangement under the contract terms, the main contractor is liable to the employer for the whole job including those parts of it carried out by the sub-contractors. So far as contract law is concerned, the employer has rights only against the main contractor and none at all in relation to the sub-contractors. Equally the employer pays the main contractor for the whole job as it is completed.

(2) The sub-contractors and suppliers have contracts only with the main contractor. As we have just seen, this means that they are not directly liable to the employer for defective work although the main contractor can pass on any liability there may be through its own contractual rights against them. The issue of privity is also important here when payment is sought for the sub-contracted work and materials supplied. Privity means that the sub-contractors and suppliers can look only to the main contractor and not to the employer even although ultimately the latter will (through its payment obligation under the principal contract) provide the resources from which the main contractor will reimburse the subs and the suppliers.

2.68 Issues like these become particularly important when one or other of the various parties is unable to perform its obligations, usually as a result of insolvency. If the main contractor becomes insolvent then the employer has no one to sue for defective work and the sub-contractor has no one from whom to claim payment. As a result of this obvious risk, well-planned projects will incorporate further contractual provisions establishing remedies to deal with the situation. For example:

(1) sub-contractors may provide employers with guarantees of the quality of their work;

(2) employers may be required not to pay main contractors in full as work proceeds but to retain a percentage of the moneys due in a special fund from which if necessary the sub-contractors can claim directly.

But if the parties do not make provision in ways like this then the problem of the main contractor's insolvency may be tackled by using parts of the law of obligations other than contract. Thus the employer might sue the sub-contractor for defective work in the law of delict[1], while the sub-contractor might have a claim for work accepted by the employer under the rules of unjustified enrichment or *jus quaesitum tertio*[2].

1 See, eg, *Junior Books v Veitchi* 1982 SC (HL) 244; *British Telecommunications v James Thomson & Co (Engineers) Ltd* 1999 SC (HL) 9. But note that both these cases are highly controversial.
2 See *J B Mackenzie (Edinburgh) Ltd v Lord Advocate* 1972 SC 231 for an unsuccessful claim in *delict* by a sub-contractor.

Jus quaesitum tertio

2.69 While privity is an important principle of the law of contract, it yields to one that is even more fundamental viz that the law of contract gives effect to the intention of the contracting parties. If upon interpretation of the contract it appears that the parties intended to confer rights upon a third person, then, subject to certain further requirements, the law will give effect to that intention and allow the third person to make claims under the contract. This branch of contract law is usually known by the Latin name of *jus quaesitum tertio*[1], meaning 'right acquired by a third person', and as a result we will give it the shorthand name of 'JQT' in what follows. A JQT can only arise when two parties *contract* to confer a benefit on a third: a unilateral promise cannot confer a JQT on anyone[2]. It is not enough, moreover, that a third party benefits as the result of a contract; the contracting parties must intend to benefit the third party in this way, although the intention may be implied as well as express[3].

1 Following Stair *Institutions*, 10, 5.
2 *Smith v Stuart* 2010 SC 490.
3 *Finnie v Glasgow & South Western Railway Co* (1857) 3 Macq 75. For a modern example see *Marquess of Aberdeen v Turcan Connell* [2008] CSOH 183. See further below, para 2.80.

2.70 Three preliminary points seem worth making before turning to the detailed rules on this subject and their application.

(1) Terminology

2.71   Most contracts giving rise to third party rights involve one of the contracting parties making a payment or other performance to the third party. That contracting party is therefore usually known as the *debtor*. The other contracting party is called the *stipulator*, the person who through the contract stipulates or requires the debtor to perform to the third party.

(2) Rights, not duties

2.72   Contracting parties can only confer *rights* upon a third party. Contracts cannot impose duties upon third parties without that party's consent[1]. If such consent is given, the result seems to be the making of a second contract between the parties to the original arrangement and the third party, not a JQT. The essence of JQT is the third party's acquisition of a right under a single contract between two others. JQT is therefore often analysed by way of promise, with stipulator and debtor making promises, not only of the primary performance required of the debtor, but also, in the case of stipulator, of taking whatever steps may be needed to enable the third party to realise its rights[2]. The relations can be illustrated as follows, with the arrows flowing from the party with a right in the relationship:

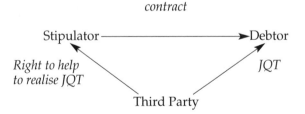

contract

Stipulator ——————————►Debtor

*Right to help
to realise JQT*   *JQT*

Third Party

1 *Howgate Shopping Centre Ltd v GLS 164 Ltd* 2002 SLT 820.
2 15 *Stair Memorial Encyclopaedia* paras 826–828.

2.73   It does seem possible to confer immunity from liability upon a third party by way of contract. Contracts often contain clauses restricting not only the liability of a contracting party but also that of others connected with him such as employees, agents, independent contractors, and subsidiary, parent or other associated companies. Here is an example:

Any exclusion or limitation of liability of carrier shall apply to and be for the benefit of agents, servants and representatives of carrier and any person whose aircraft is used by carrier for carriage and its agents, servants and representatives.

The courts have given effect to such clauses, sometimes by way of a JQT in favour of the third party, sometimes as a factor making the imposition of the duty of care in delict unjust or unreasonable[1]. It is not clear whether a clause excluding a third party's claim to damages[2] under what is otherwise a JQT is subject to the controls of the Unfair Contract Terms Act 1977 other than in cases of personal injury or death resulting from breach of delictual duty; it will certainly not be caught by the Unfair Terms in Consumer Contracts Regulations 1999[3].

1 *Melrose v Davidson and Robertson* 1993 SC 288. See also *Aberdeen Harbour Board v Heating Enterprises (Aberdeen) Ltd* 1990 SLT 416.
2 See further below, para 6.53 for the third party's claim for damages.
3 MacQueen 'Third party rights in contract: English reform and Scottish concerns' (1997) 1 Edin LR 488.

2.74 A final and not always well understood point is that the recognition in a contract of a third party right which is actually derived from another source is not an example of JQT. Thus a contract for the supply of software which incorporated a copyright licence in which the third party author of the software licensed its use by the purchaser was held to create a JQT in favour of the third party author[1]. But his rights in this situation stemmed, not from the contract of supply, but the law of copyright. The best legal analysis of the situation is that there are two contracts, one of supply, the other a licence, involving a total of three parties, not a single contract creating rights for each member of the triumvirate.

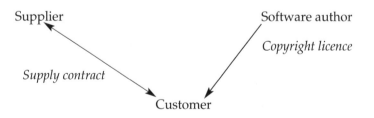

Another, slightly different, example is the case where a solicitor is instructed by a client to draw up a will with a bequest in favour of a third party. The solicitor either draws up the will negligently or, again negligently, fails to draws it before the would-be testator's death. As a result, the third party does not get the bequest on the client's death.

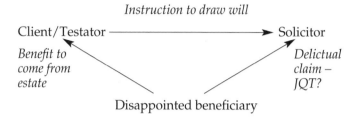

Instruction to draw will

Client/Testator ⟶ Solicitor

Benefit to come from estate

Delictual claim – JQT?

Disappointed beneficiary

The House of Lords has held that the beneficiary has a delictual claim against the solicitor[2]. This is controversial since it gives protection to the beneficiary's expectations which are normally the domain of contract rather than delict. Could the beneficiary have a JQT against the solicitor given that the latter's relationship with the testator was contractual? It would seem not. While testator and solicitor intended to confer a benefit upon the beneficiary, it was to come from the testator's estate rather than from the solicitor. The best that might be said is that the solicitor had failed to assist the beneficiary achieve his right against the estate; but it would be curious to hold that he was the 'stipulator' in this particular triangle of relationships. Further, given that the testator was free to change his will until his death, there is also some doubt about whether the intention to benefit had been made irrevocable as may be required for JQT[3].

1 *Beta Computers (Europe) Ltd v Adobe Systems Ltd* 1996 SLT 604.
2 *White v Jones* [1995] 2 AC 207; applied in Scotland in *Robertson v Watt & Co* (4 July 1995, unreported); *Holmes v Bank of Scotland* 2002 SLT 544. See further Thomson *Delictual Liability* (4th edn, 2009) paras 7.5 ff.
3 See further below, paras 2.76 ff.

(3) Comparative law

2.75 Until 1999 JQT was one of the chief features distinguishing Scots from English contract law. For English law the principle of privity prevailed over the principle of upholding parties' intentions. This may explain why the Scottish courts have tended to treat JQT narrowly as a very special exception to the ordinary rule constituted by privity. But a more global view of contract law reveals that it is the English emphasis on privity which is exceptional. Most if not all European legal systems clearly give effect to third party rights in contract if intended by the contracting parties[1]. Elsewhere in the world even those systems which are historically derived from English law have tended to abolish privity and recognise third party rights. In 1996 the Law Commission of England and Wales proposed a similar change for English law[2]. The proposals were implemented in the Contracts (Rights of Third Parties) Act 1999. It remains to be seen whether Scots lawyers will feel more prepared to develop JQT and, where possible, abandon or minimise some of the more technical rules by which its use has hitherto been restricted[3].

1 See, eg, the French *Code Civil*, arts 1121 and 1165, and the German *BGB*, § 328. See also Hogg *Promises and Contract Law* (2011) ch 5; DCFR II.-9:301-303; and PICC ch 5 section 2.
2 *Report on Privity of Contract* (Law Com no 242) (1996).
3 See further Sutherland 'Third-party contracts' in *MacQueen & Zimmermann* (2006) and earlier literature there referred to.

(4) Intention to benefit and irrevocability

2.76   A key issue is whether, in order to enable a third party right to come into existence, it is sufficient that there is a term in a contract which purports to do so or whether a further step is required of the parties. At the heart of this issue is the freedom which contracting parties normally enjoy to change the contents of the contract by agreement between themselves. Just as a contract is made by the parties' agreement so it can be unmade and remade by the same process. But if the parties create a right for a third party, it would seem elementary that that right cannot be undone merely by the agreement of the contracting parties; in addition the consent of the third party should also be necessary. The courts have therefore tended to say that before contracting parties can be held to have deprived themselves of their ordinary freedom to adjust their relations as they wish, there must be something more than just a term in favour of a third party. It must be clear that the contracting parties intended not only to confer a benefit upon a third party but also to give up the freedom to change their minds. In the technical language used by the courts, it must be shown that the intention to create a third party right was also intended to be irrevocable[1].

1 The leading case is *Carmichael v Carmichael's Exx* 1920 SC (HL) 195.

2.77 Irrevocability can be shown in various ways:

- intimation or delivery of the contract to the third party;
- putting the contract out of the power of the contracting parties;
- registration of the contract, for example in the Books of Council and Session;
- content of the term itself;
- third party's knowledge of the contract term in its favour;
- third party's reliance upon the contract term in its favour.

2.78 This list does not cover all the situations in which a JQT has been held to arise. In *Love v Amalgamated Society of Lithographic Printers of Great Britain and Ireland*[1], the society operated a scheme which provided certain benefits for the relatives of sick members but which also provided that the rules of the scheme could be changed. In other words the scheme which was constituted by a contract amongst all the members of the society was not irrevocable. But when a particular relative claimed a benefit under the scheme, the court found a JQT in her favour since the rules had not in fact been changed or revoked at the time the claim was made. In some decisions the courts seem to have placed less emphasis on the need to show irrevocability of the benefit and *Love* suggests that it is not an invariable requirement of JQT. But on present authority it is difficult to say in what kinds of case this is so[2]. The case of the disappointed beneficiary's claim against the negligent solicitor, discussed above[3], might be one instance where *Love* could be of assistance: while clearly the client's testamentary intent was revocable until death, once he was dead the will could not be revoked. A difficulty remains; inasmuch as in this case *ex hypothesi* there never was a valid will; and if an unrevoked intent was enough then the beneficiary would have a direct claim against the deceased's estate.

1 1912 SC 1078.
2 See further 15 *Stair Memorial Encyclopaedia* paras 829–832.
3 See above, para 2.74.

2.79 Under the English legislation, the contracting parties retain the right to vary or cancel the contract until the third party has acted in reliance upon it or accepted the right; while a term that the contract is irrevocable has no effect. French, Dutch and South African law all require third party acceptance before the third party right arises. The DCFR allows cancellation or modification by the contracting parties so long as the third party has not been notified of its right by one or other of the parties, or if the contract so provides, even post-notification, unless the third party has been led to believe that the right is not revocable or subject to modification and has acted reasonably in reliance upon the right[1]. This is an area in which Scots law requires review and rethinking.

1 DCFR II.-9:303(3). See national notes to this article for other legal systems' rules. PICC art 5.2.5 allows modification or revocation until the beneficiary's acceptance or acts of reasonable reliance.

(5) Identification of the third party

2.80   For a third party right to arise, the contract must identify the third party. Identification may be of a particular individual or through membership of a class of persons. The third party need not be in existence at the time the contract is made and there have been cases where the right was enforced more than a century after it was created. The identification of the third party may be express or by implication. It is not enough that a contract refers to a third party since there must also be manifest an intention to confer an enforceable benefit upon that third party. Thus for A and B to contract that A shall pay B's debts does not without more confer any right upon B's creditors as third parties[1]. But in one case guarantors of an association of underwriters were held liable to persons assured by a member of the association[2]. The relevant clause read:

'We guarantee the liabilities arising on the account of JB [the underwriter] underwritten by us in his name.'

The persons assured were therefore not identified in the guarantees and in turn their assurance policies made no reference to the guarantees. However the persons assured knew of and relied upon the existence of the guarantees and it was held that the purpose of the guarantees was to ensure the protection of their interests.

1 *Henderson v Stubbs Ltd* (1894) 22 R 51.
2 *Rose, Murison and Thomson v Wingate, Birrell & Co's Tr* (1889) 16 R 1132.

(6) Stipulator's interest

2.81   The courts have rejected two propositions put forward to limit the scope of JQT. First, it has been held that it is not necessary for the stipulator to have a continuing interest in the contract. In other words, if the debtor's only obligation is to perform to the third party, it is still JQT. So when A sold his hotel to B in a contract which included a promise by B to pay Mrs A £100 'as some compensation for the annoyance and worry of the past few days and for kindness and attention to me on my several visits to Crieff', it was held that Mrs A's claim for the £100 should succeed even though her husband's interest in the contract had been discharged by the successful completion of the sale of the hotel[1]. But it does not follow from this that a JQT can arise only when the sole substantial interest is that of the third party. This can be illustrated by the complicated case of *Mercedes-Benz Finance Ltd v Clydesdale Bank plc*[2]. Mercedes-Benz (MB) supplied cars to Glen Henderson (Stuttgart) Ltd (GH) for re-sale to customers in Scotland. When GH sold a car, the proceeds were lodged in an account held with the Clydesdale Bank (CB). GH and CB had agreed that appropriate transfers should then be made to MB. The relationships may be pictured thus, the arrows indicating the direction of the performances involved:

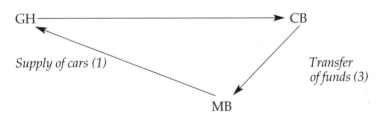

Pay in proceeds of sales (2)

GH → CB

Supply of cars (1)   *Transfer of funds (3)*

MB

GH went into receivership indebted to both CB and MB but with funds sitting in GH's account with CB which had been due to be transferred to MB. Lord Penrose found that the agreement between GH and CB could give a JQT to MB and rejected CB's argument that a JQT could only arise where the third party alone had a substantial interest in the performance whereas in this case CB clearly also had an interest in ensuring the payment to themselves of the debt which they were owed by GH.

1 *Lamont v Burnett* (1901) 3 F 797.
2 1997 SLT 905.

(7) Effect of invalidity of contract

2.82 Although there is little authority directly in point, it seems correct in principle to suppose that if there is a defect in the contract's formation rendering it invalid or potentially null (void or voidable) then the third party's right is equally invalid or potentially null. Where the original contract is illegal, the right conclusion may be less clear if part only of the contract is illegal and that does not include the conferment of the third party right. But if the third party right is dependent upon the illegality then it seems clear that it is unenforceable. If however a contract is unenforceable on grounds other than illegality (for example lack of formalities, prescription etc) then it may be that a JQT can still arise from it[1].

1 15 *Stair Memorial Encyclopaedia* para 839.

(8) Examples of third party rights in contracts: insurance

2.83   The most important practical examples of third party rights are provided by insurance contracts. Contracts of life assurance commonly provide for the benefit of the policy to go to a third party, typically a member of the assured's family such as a spouse, civil partner or child. Motor insurance is another area where third party rights are important since it is compulsory for owners of motor vehicles to take out policies of assurance which give third parties enforceable rights in respect of certain risks. Motor policies also commonly provide cover not only for the owner but also for users of the insured vehicle; such users may have a JQT under the policy. Other forms of liability insurance provide further instances of contracts in which parties other than the person paying the premiums under the policy may have a JQT[1].

1 See further 15 *Stair Memorial Encyclopaedia* para 841. The position is complicated further by statutes.

Assignation

2.84   Another way in which a third party may acquire rights under a contract is by assignation from one of the original contracting parties[1]. Assignation is a form of transfer of rights. A right arising under a contract may be transferred (assigned) by the creditor (cedent, assignor) to a third party (assignee) so as to give that third party a title to sue the debtor in the right for performance. Assignation can thus be distinguished from *jus quaesitum tertio* since the latter is a creation of the original contract whereas assignation requires a further and independent juristic act by one of the contracting parties.

1 See generally Anderson *Assignation* (2008); 15 *Stair Memorial Encyclopaedia* paras 853–864. Note also DCFR III.-5, section 1, on which see also Clive 'The assignment provisions of the Draft Common Frame of Reference' 2010 JR 275.

2.85 The contract nonetheless can control assignation in significant ways, either by way of express prohibition[1] or restriction or through the implied limitation known as *delectus personae*[2]. As a transfer of rights, assignation is completed by intimation to the debtor; this may be carried out by either party but usually by the assignee. Intimation means that the debtor cannot subsequently discharge his obligations by performance to the original creditor. An unintimated assignation is not completely without effect; there will almost certainly be a contract in place between cedent and assignee under which various rights and duties will arise between them. Intimation also gives the assignee priority over any other claimant to whom the creditor may have purported to assign the debt. But the assignee gets no better right than the cedent had before the assignation or intimation. Thus the debtor may plead against the assignee the invalidity of the original contract or pre-intimation rights of compensation or set-off. But assignation does not subject the assignee to the cedent's liabilities to the debtor[3].

1 See for example *James Scott Ltd v Apollo* 2000 SC 228; also Anderson *Assignation* ch 11C.
2 15 *Stair Memorial Encyclopaedia* paras 859 and 860. See further on *delectus personae* below, para 2.87.
3 15 *Stair Memorial Encyclopaedia* para 864; Anderson *Assignation* paras 8.25–8.27; *Binstock Miller & Co v Coia & Co Ltd* 1957 SLT (Sh Ct) 47; *Alex Lawrie Factors Ltd v Mitchell Engineering Ltd* 2001 SLT (Sh Ct) 93 (report corrected at 2001 SLT 110). Cf *McBryde* paras 12.87–12.89.

2.86 The law of assignation in Scotland suffers to some extent from a lack of conceptual clarity. While in principle it should apply only to the transfer of rights, in practice it is often used loosely to cover also the transfer of duties or liabilities under contracts. But more appropriate legal concepts exist for transfers of duties, in particular that of *delegation* by which one debtor in an obligation is substituted for another with the effect that the first debtor's liability is extinguished and replaced with that of the second. Unlike assignation, in order to be effective delegation always requires the creditor's consent[1].

1 Anderson *Assignation* ch 3; 15 *Stair Memorial Encyclopaedia* para 856 and below, para 3.80. Note the recognition in DCFR III.-5:302 of transfer of *both* rights and duties under a contract, alongside assignation (above, para 2.84 note 1) and delegation (DCFR III.-5, sections 2 and 3).

2.87 Confusion seems to arise when a contracting party is transferring to another *both* rights and duties under a contract, a situation which seems always to be referred to as assignation. The importance of this emerges from consideration of the important but confusing idea of *delectus personae* (meaning 'choice of person'). As a limit on assignation, the phrase infers that a person has been chosen as a contracting party for unique personal qualities not obtainable elsewhere and accordingly that person cannot assign. But it is hard to see why, if all that a person can assign is rights, there should be *delectus personae* for the debtor in choosing to whom to render a performance. The notion seems much more apt for the person purporting to transfer duties; one can see why a creditor might wish to choose one person rather than another to perform what is owed to him. The classic examples of contracts in which there is *delectus personae* – to paint a portrait or to write a book – and the leading modern cases on the subject are all concerned with debtor rather than creditor assignations[1]. The tendency in the cases seems to be to look at the contract as a whole, identify it as one which in some aspect or another involves *delectus personae* and then to bar assignation (or, more typically, not to do so) without consideration of whether the specific right to be transferred should be so affected. The result is an unsatisfactory and unclear body of rules.

1 15 *Stair Memorial Encyclopaedia* para 859; Anderson *Assignation* para 3.32.

2.88 That problems have not often arisen from this fuzziness is probably because assignation (in its widest sense, related to both rights and duties under contracts) is usually dealt with by express terms in the original contract. The usual approach in such terms is to prohibit assignation, delegation or any other form of transfer by either party to the contract unless the other party first gives consent. The clause may sometimes add that the consent will not be unreasonably withheld. It may be that such a provision would in any case be implied although it is settled law that this is not so in leases. The courts will give effect to prohibitions on assignation by declaring any purported transfer not in accordance with the contract to be null and void[1]. Accordingly the assignee acquires no rights to enforce the contract although a claim will exist against the cedent for failure to transfer[2].

1 It is thought that the English decision in *Linden Gardens Trust Ltd v Lenesta Sludge Disposals Ltd*; *St Martins Property Corp Ltd v Sir Robert McAlpine & Sons Ltd* [1994] 1 AC 85 would be followed on this point in Scotland: see *James Scott Ltd v Apollo* 2000 SC 228. But see Anderson *Assignation* para 11.42 (arguing that the nullity cannot prejudice creditors).

2 15 *Stair Memorial Encyclopaedia* paras 859–862. For the claims arising, especially damages, see below, para 6.54.

PRE-CONTRACTUAL LIABILITY

2.89 The general principle is that when parties are negotiating a contract they are at arms' length in the sense that each has to look after its own interests and has no obligations to the other party short of not telling lies (misrepresentation), practising deception (fraud), coercing the other party into entering the contract (force and fear), or exploiting a special relationship which one party has with the other party quite separately from the contract under negotiation (undue influence). If any of these factors is present in negotiations which lead to an apparent contract, then that contract may be either null or annullable, with obligations based upon unjustified enrichment arising in respect of any performance which may have been rendered prior to the discovery of the flaw in the lead-up to the contract[1]. In so far as the perpetration of the flaw in the negotiations may also have been a civil wrong, there can also be delictual liability of which the most important examples in practice are for negligent misrepresentation under section 10 of the Law Reform (Miscellaneous Provisions) (Scotland) Act 1985, and for fraud at common law[2]. Again, where negotiations break down but there has been some preceding transfer of value between the parties, an obligation to restore any benefits received may arise under the rules of unjustified enrichment.

1 See below, paras 4.3 ff and 4.20 ff.
2 On which see below, paras 4.27 and 4.63 ff.

2.90 Although these rules may seem quite a substantial qualification on the general statement that there is no liability for pre-contractual negotiations, closer examination suggests that they are in fact quite limited.

- First, the issue of liability tends to arise only if a contract apparently results from the negotiations. For example if there is no apparent contract, usually there is no relevant loss upon which to base a delictual claim for any misrepresentation, fraud or force which may have been used. It seems of the essence of the whole idea of contract that prior to the moment of formation and legal commitment to a set of obligations, the parties are free: and that that freedom includes the right to withdraw from negotiations ie the freedom not to contract.

Thus for example, if I invite tenders for the construction of a building on my land, I am not liable to the unsuccessful tenderers for the often quite substantial expenditure incurred in preparing their tenders while the successful tenderer must look to the contract to recoup whatever he may have spent in order to obtain it.

- Second, for most of the vitiating factors a positive action is required – a mis-statement, innocent, negligent or fraudulent; an act of force; giving advice or acting in a way which takes advantage of the trust and confidence reposed in one person by another. It is much harder to persuade a court to strike down an apparent contract or grant a delictual remedy in damages for inaction. The authorities, while by no means uniform, are on the whole against the idea of liability arising if I know that the other party is labouring under some misapprehension of which I take advantage *without* misrepresentation: the classic example is my purchase of a painting which through superior information I know is much more valuable than the price the seller is putting upon it[1]. There is no general duty in contract law to disclose material information to the other party although there are specific instances in insurance, caution and fiduciary relationships such as trustee–beneficiary, principal–agent and company–director.
- Third, claims on the basis of these rules are rare, and successful claims even rarer, suggesting that the courts are suspicious of attempts to undermine contracts by attaching significance to the preceding negotiations.

1 See below, para 4.53 ff.

2.91 What is also clear is that the real world does not quite fit into a legal model in which negotiations take place, a contract is formed and then and only then do the parties commence the performances required by the contract. In many commercial situations time does not allow for such dalliance: negotiations and performance go together with an expectation perhaps that the formal contract to be concluded in due course will have retrospective effect. Indeed, it may be that the parties never make use of formal written contracts and pursue an entirely informal relationship in which negotiations, performance and contract are almost indistinguishable. Cases of these kinds have often come before the Scottish courts and in at least some the outcome has not been consistent with the legal model so far discussed of parties at arms' length, entitled to look after their own interests only and to ignore those of the other party without incurring liability as a result. On occasions, the court has found that a contract has come into existence despite the continuation of negotiations[1]. Equally where there has been a transfer of value between the parties but there is no contract, the party suffering loss in the transfer – for example through payment or performance ahead of conclusion of the contract – may well have a claim in unjustified enrichment[2]. But some other cases, involving successful claims for wasted pre-contractual expenditure without either a civil wrong by, or enrichment of, the other party, have caused great difficulties of analysis for commentators since they do not fit easily into the traditional categories of the law of obligations.

1 See *Avintair Ltd v Ryder Airline Services Ltd* 1994 SC 270, discussed above, para 2.8.
2 For two examples of (unsuccessful) enrichment claims in respect of pre-contractual activity, see *Microwave Systems (Scotland) Ltd v Electro-Physiological Instruments Ltd* 1971 SC 140, OH; *Site Preparations Ltd v Secretary of State for Scotland* 1975 SLT (Notes) 41, OH.

2.92   The foundation authority is the Melville Monument case, *Walker v Milne*[1]. Walker owned the estate of Coates upon which he and his father carried out part of the development of the New Town in Edinburgh. The development was to include a monument to Viscount Melville, paid for by subscribers led by Milne. With Walker's permission, the subscribers entered the lands of Coates, broke it up and carried out preparatory operations which disrupted Walker's feuing plans on his estate. After some delay, the subscribers took their monument off to St Andrew Square where it stands to this day. Walker sued for breach of contract. Milne defended on the basis that as the alleged agreement related to land (heritage) and was not in writing he was not bound in contract and so could not be liable. The court held that although there was no contract and no enrichment of the subscribers, Walker was entitled to recover any of his own expenditure wasted as a result of the movement of the monument from its agreed site.

1 (1823) 2 S 379.

2.93   A number of nineteenth-century cases followed *Walker v Milne*[1]. To summarise the principles to be drawn from these cases is far from easy. In most of them it could be said that the parties had reached (or at least averred) an agreement which was not contractual only because some other legal rule about the constitution and proof of contracts stood in the way. At one level, these cases are not about anticipated contracts so much as agreements which are only non-contractual for technical reasons. Further, the cases are not about the recovery of enrichment. Instead the pursuer is reimbursed or indemnified against expenditure incurred on the faith of the non-contractual agreement although in none of the cases had this expenditure been made to the defender. The injustice of the situation of the pursuer seems to arise from the other side's unilateral withdrawal from arrangements which could reasonably have been regarded as settled.

1 *Bell v Bell* (1841) 3 D 1201; *Heddle v Baikie* (1846) 8 D 376; *Dobie v Lauder's Trs* (1873) 11 M 749; *Hamilton v Lochrane* (1899) 1 F 478.

2.94　In a number of other cases, however, the courts declared that *Walker v Milne* did not give rise to a principle of general application[1] and in this they were followed by the influential text-writer, Gloag[2]. Later cases confirm this narrow approach. In *Dawson International plc v Coats Paton plc*[3] two companies were negotiating a merger whereby Dawson would purchase Coats Paton's shares. This also included a 'lock-out' arrangement under which Coats Paton would not encourage third-party bids. Dawson incurred expense in preparing offer documentation. A third party bid materialised with which Coats Paton co-operated and which was ultimately successful. Dawson claimed unwarrantable and reckless misrepresentations by Coats and sought reimbursement of its expenditure. The claim failed. Lord Cullen held that this was an exceptional branch of the law and that any tendency to expand its scope should be discouraged. It was equitable in nature and not dependent upon contract, unjustified enrichment, or delict. He found that the law allowed reimbursement of expenditure by one party occasioned by the representations of another only when the former acted in reliance on an implied assurance by the latter that there was a binding contract between them when in fact there was no more than an agreement which fell short of being a binding contract.

1 *Allan v Gilchrist* (1875) 2 R 587; *Gilchrist v Whyte* 1907 SC 984; *Gray v Johnston* 1928 SC 659.
2 *Gloag* pp 19 and 176–177.
3 1988 SLT 854. Lord Cullen's opinion was affirmed in the Inner House (1989 SLT 655). At a later stage it was held by Lord Prosser that the negotiations had not given rise to a contract between the parties (1993 SLT 80). Lord Cullen's opinion is followed in *Bank of Scotland v 3i plc* 1990 SC 215. In *Khaliq v Londis (Holdings) Ltd* 2010 SC 432 an Extra Division cast doubt on Lord Cullen's analysis but it is thought that this is unwarranted: see Hogg and MacQueen

'Melville Monument liability: some doubtful dicta' (2010) 14 Edin LR 451. Liability for pre-contractual expenditure on the basis of *Walker v Milne* was not pled in *Aisling Developments Ltd v Persimmon Homes Ltd* 2009 SLT 494 or *Karoulias SA v The Drambuie Liqueur Co Ltd* 2005 SLT 813.

2.95 It may be that this approach is too narrow. There are cases of no agreement and no implied assurance of a contract yet with enough to suggest the likelihood of a contractual agreement in the reasonably near future after some further negotiation. The best example is provided by the 'letter of intent' which a party may use to signal to one of a group of tenderers or bidders for a contract that he now intends to enter a contract with that party although the tender/bid is not to be accepted without further negotiation[1]. The purpose of the letter of intent is to allow the chosen party to commence preparation for the contract and it is not unusual for preparation to pass on to performance before the contract is concluded. Typically, the letter of intent will provide that such work will be paid for at the contract prices once agreed. But suppose the contract is never formed because the negotiations are unsuccessful. What, if any, claims may be made by the recipient of the letter of intent? Where the performance involves a transfer of value to the party who has issued the letter of intent, the solution may well lie in unjustified enrichment[2]. If, however, there is no transfer of value but only expenditure by the recipient of the letter, enrichment solutions may not be available or appropriate to cover the loss. Scots law could here call upon its doctrine of unilateral promise to give the letter obligatory effect and imply some sort of payment for the recipient's wasted work[3]. But given that letters of intent often expressly stipulate that they are not intended to have obligatory effect, the promise analysis may not be possible.

1 For other possible examples, see *Hoffman v Red Owl Stores* (1965) 133 NW (2d) 267; *Sabemo Pty Ltd v North Sydney Municipal Council* [1977] NSWLR 880 and *Walton Stores (Interstate) Ltd v Maher* (1988) 164 CLR 387. See further Hogg *Promises and Contract Law* (2011) pp 179–203, 235–239.
2 As in *British Steel Corporation v Cleveland Bridge* [1984] 1 All ER 504.
3 See *MacQueen* 1986 SLT (News) 1 at 3–4.

2.96 Other legal systems in Europe approach the problem of pre-contractual liability through the general concept of good faith allowing recovery of loss caused by breaking off negotiations when they had reached a stage where the conclusion of a contract was probable[1]. If the concept of good faith takes root in Scots law, the law on pre-contractual liability could develop beyond its somewhat limited present scope. Another interesting situation can be illustrated from the English case of *Blackpool & Fylde Aero Club v Blackpool Borough Council*[2]. The council invited tenders for a contract in a document which set out the procedure which it would follow in considering the tenders received. The Court of Appeal held that the council was liable in damages to an unsuccessful tenderer for having failed to follow this procedure but left unclear whether this was a matter of tort (delict) or of contract. A Scots lawyer might approach this case, as neither contract or delict, but rather through the promissory route[3]. But if this is thought artificial or to involve strained construction of the invitation to tender then a wider concept of good faith might provide a better solution. This would undoubtedly go further than anything found in Lord Cullen's opinion in *Dawson v Coats Paton*[4]. There is no real question of agreements and implied assurances that a binding contract exists. The contract, if it comes into existence at all, is not assured to any particular party. Yet it seems clear that justice demands liability for the council.

1 See Cartwright and Hesselink (eds) *Precontractual Liability in European Private Law* (2008). Note also PICC, art 2.15 and DCFR II.-3:301, but observe that English law does not recognise pre-contractual liabilities of this kind: see especially *Walford v Miles* [1992] 2 AC 128 and *Regalian Properties plc v London Dockland Development Corporation* [1995] 1 All ER 1005.

2 [1990] 1 WLR 1995. The case has been followed by the Federal Court of Australia in *Hughes Aircraft Systems International v Air Services Australia* (1997) 146 ALR 1.

3 The concept of promise might also be the way in which Scots law would solve such famous 'difficult' cases as *Hoffman v Red Owl Stores* 26 Wis 2d 683, 133 NW 2d 267 (1965) and *Walton Stores (Interstate) Ltd v Maher* (1988) 164 CLR 387.

4 1988 SLT 854.

3. Contents, Effects and Performance

3.1 In this chapter, we turn away from the analysis of whether or not the parties have agreed to a consideration of what it is that they have agreed; or, to put the matter in another way, to the determination of their respective rights and duties under the contract.

3.2 Most non-lawyers think of contracts as written documents and indeed many contracts are entirely in writing. But, the one or two exceptions discussed in the previous chapter apart, the law does not *require* contracts to be in writing. It is merely an option available to contracting parties albeit one which many will take up for reasons of certainty and record-keeping. Nevertheless, contracts can be made entirely through the medium of the spoken word or can arise through actions of the parties rather than their utterances. A contract which is a mixture of writing, oral statements and the conduct of the parties is perfectly conceivable and acceptable in law.

3.3 The variety of forms which a contract may assume presents problems for which the law has to provide solutions. If a contract is not expressed in writing or is not limited to what has been written down, the question of what the terms are may well arise. In particular, how are contract terms to be distinguished from other statements which have been made in the course of negotiations leading up to the contract? How are terms not in writing to be proved should there be a dispute between the parties? If a contract has been written down, how can one be sure that other non-written exchanges between the parties do not form part of the contract?

3.4 A further issue arises about terms which the parties have not expressed in any way, whether in writing or otherwise – the so-called implied terms. Such terms fall into two main classes. First there are the terms *implied in law*. As noted in the first chapter, most contracts fall into one or other of the categories which the law has established over time: sale, hire, employment and so on. Within each of these categories there has developed a concept that certain terms will always form part of the contract unless the parties agree otherwise. Such terms are, as it were, a legal consequence of entering a contractual relationship of a particular kind. There are also some terms which may be applicable to all contracts, whatever their category. The second class of implied term, the term *implied in fact*, is the law's way of dealing with the problem of what happens when a contract does not contain any term expressly covering the situation which now requires to be resolved. A term is therefore implied: being in theory a term to which the parties would have agreed had they considered the matter during negotiations thus preserving the law from the reproach of making rather than simply enforcing the parties' contract.

3.5   Having established what the terms of the contract are, their meaning has to be determined: the process of *interpretation and construction* of the contract. Indeed this step necessarily precedes the implication of terms in fact, since that process requires first a finding that the contract contains no express provision on the matter in issue. Disputes about interpretation and construction are mainly concerned with the meaning of written documents, at least as appears from the reported cases on the subject, and the courts have evolved ways of approaching the difficulties which arise. These methods of approach are probably best seen as such rather than as legal rules but they give considerable help in the solution of problems and therefore require careful consideration.

3.6   Until quite recently, Scots law in this area was characterised above all by the very high value which it placed on writing as a final and conclusive statement of contract terms. Speaking broadly, the starting point was that the written terms were the whole terms of a contract and proof of other unwritten terms was not allowed. A written contract which did not accurately express the intention of the parties could not be rectified save through a very cumbersome procedure. A very large number of contracts either had to be constituted in writing or could only be proved by written evidence.

3.7   All these rules were changed significantly by legislation in the course of the 1980s and 1990s. It remains the law at the time of writing that in the process of interpreting a written document no evidence from outside the document (extrinsic evidence) as to the parties' intentions is allowed, another instance of the preference for written over other material; but this rule too has been reviewed by the Scottish Law Commission which has proposed that extrinsic evidence of certain relevant surrounding circumstances should be allowed for this purpose[1]. Should this reform take place, it will complete Scots law's departure from an excessive reverence for writing in favour of a more flexible approach designed to determine, as far as possible, the intention of the parties and to give that intention legal effect.

1 Discussion Paper no 147 on Interpretation of Contract (2011), which reviews and further develops proposals first put forward in *Report on Interpretation in Private Law* (Scot Law Com no 160) (1997).

EXPRESS TERMS OF THE CONTRACT

3.8   What are the terms of the contract? Where do we go to look for the terms of the contract?[1]

1 See generally Cabrelli *Commercial Agreements in Scotland: Law and Practice* (2007).

Written terms

3.9   The simplest case is where an apparently complete contract is embodied in a single written document or a set of documents. Under the law as it stood until 21 June 1997 such a document or set of documents was assumed to be a complete contract and no extrinsic evidence could be led to show that there were terms over and above those in the document. The document did not need to state that it was the sole expression of the parties' agreement and a party relying on it did not have to show that it was intended to be so.

3.10   This 'parole evidence rule' no longer applies. The starting point is that an apparently complete document will be presumed to contain all the terms of the contract but contrary evidence may be led to show that there are additional terms, written or otherwise[1]. However, if the document expressly states that it does indeed comprise the whole express terms of the contract (an 'entire contract'/'entire agreement'/'merger' clause), then that term is conclusive and no contrary evidence is allowed[2].

1 Contract (Scotland) Act 1997 (CSA 1997), s 1(1) and (2). The rule applies in proceedings brought from 21 June 1997 onwards.
2 CSA 1997, s 1(3). In *MacDonald Estates plc v Regenesis (2005) Dunfermline Ltd* 2007 SLT 791 Lord Reed suggests (at para 178) that an entire contract clause does not preclude the remedy of rectification (for which see below, paras 3.25–3.26).

3.11   Here are two examples of such a clause from a standard form contract for the supply of goods (notice however that both clauses leave open the possibility of adding more terms by a specified procedure)[1]:

'No conditions other than those specifically set forth herein shall be deemed to be incorporated in or to form part of the contract. Any alteration made by the Buyer to such conditions shall be invalid unless and until confirmed in writing by the Supplier.'

'These conditions, together with the particulars overleaf, constitute the entire agreement between the User and the Supplier and no variation on or waiver of and no addition to these conditions will be valid unless previously agreed in writing and signed by a Director of the Supplier.'

1 See also *McBryde* para 5.56.

3.12   Putting a contract in writing has many advantages. It makes clear what has been agreed and marks an end to the process of negotiation. A document creates certainty about what has to be done under the contract. It is valuable as a record and, if a dispute leads to proceedings in court or in an arbitration, as evidence. But under the current law, it does not follow that the document is the whole or the complete contract. However, it may well be to the parties' advantage to have a document as the sole source of the terms of their contract: for example, it may eliminate uncertainty as to whether points discussed in the negotiations but not included in the document, are terms or not. But the onus is on the parties to stipulate expressly that the document is to have this exclusive effect whereas under the former law the document had such an effect whatever the parties' intentions may have been.

3.13   These rules apply only where a document appears to be a complete contract. Where a document bears to be only part of a contract, then clearly we must look elsewhere for the other terms whether in another document or the oral or other exchanges between the parties. A fortiori if there is no document at all but only oral statements and/or conduct. The upshot is that, unless a document bears an 'entire contract' clause, it may well be necessary to look across the entire range of the statements, conduct and other communications of the parties in order to determine what the terms of the contract are.

Representations and contract terms (warranties)

3.14   How does the law distinguish between those parts of the exchanges between the parties which are contractual terms and those which are not? This analysis is made no easier by the existence of rules which may make a party liable for statements and activities made or carried out in pre-contractual negotiations even though these statements and activities are not contractual. Thus a pre-contractual negligent misrepresentation which induces the representee to enter a contract with the representor can give rise to a delictual claim for damages[1]. Property may be handed over, services rendered and money paid before any contract is concluded, giving rise to enrichment and other claims if the negotiations are unsuccessful[2].

1 Law Reform (Miscellaneous Provisions) (Scotland) Act 1985 (LRMPSA 1985), s 10(1). See further below para 4.63 ff.
2 See further above, para 2.89 ff.

3.15   What then is mere negotiation and what is contract? The rules on offer and acceptance, eliminating statements which are merely invitations to treat or advertising 'puffs', are clearly relevant to this distinction but have been treated already in the chapter on formation[1]. But other statements made during negotiations between the parties may not fall into any of these categories. The most important is when one of the parties makes a statement *of fact* about the subject-matter of the contract. Statements of fact should be distinguished from statements of opinion, such as forecasts about how a company is going to perform, or the expression of a view about how many animals may be grazed on a farm. The line can be rather fine: for example, what about a statement that a secondhand car is in 'good running order', which a Scottish court held to be a statement of opinion[2]? The importance of the distinction is, however, that a statement of fact may give rise to either contractual or delictual liability, which a statement of opinion does not.

1 See above, para 2.10 ff.
2 *Flynn v Scott* 1949 SC 442.

3.16 A statement of fact uttered in contractual negotiations may be treated in law as either a *representation*, possibly giving rise to *delictual* liability if untrue[1], or a *contractual* term (often known as a *warranty*). Several points should be noted:

- A misrepresentation, be it fraudulent, negligent or entirely innocent, can be used to *reduce* the contract[2], whereas breach of warranty will only permit rescission or termination of the contract if it is material. Reduction for misrepresentation is only allowed if *restitutio in integrum* (ie restoration of the parties to their pre-contractual position) is possible, whereas there is no such limitation upon termination for breach.
- If a statement is a term, damages can always be claimed if it is false, whereas a misrepresentation can only give that remedy if it is fraudulent or negligent.
- Fraudulent and negligent misrepresentations are delicts and give rise to delictual damages protecting the *status quo* interest, while breach of warranty gives rise to contract damages protecting the expectation interest. Delictual damages put the pursuer in the position he would have been if the statement had not been made, while contract damages put him in the position he would have had if the statement had been true. This distinction becomes important if, had the representation been true, the value of the subject matter of the statement would have been higher than the price actually paid.

1 See below, para 4.63 ff.
2 See below, para 4.57 ff.

3.17 What, then, determines whether a statement of fact is a representation or a term? It is difficult to state any test other than the presence or absence of contractual intention as objectively disclosed by the wording of the statement. There is almost no discussion in Scottish cases and we have been told by one judge that 'to constitute a warranty no *voces signatae* are necessary. A representation may be a warranty if it appears that it was so intended and understood'[1].

1 *Hyslop v Shirlaw* (1905) 7 F 875 per Lord Kyllachy at 881. '*Voces signatae*' means here 'technical words/terms'.

3.18 The English authorities are coloured by the use of the idea of warranty to evade the former rule that damages were not recoverable for pre-contractual negligent misrepresentation; so much so, indeed, that the Court of Appeal has held a statement about the potential throughput of a filling station was both a misrepresentation and a warranty, wholly blurring the distinction between contract and delict[1]. Thus the English courts have regarded the relative knowledge and degree of fault of the parties as a relevant consideration: if the representor has knowledge and the representee does not and has no reasonable means of checking what is said, then the statement is more likely to be taken as a warranty[2]. But it is not clear that the factors of knowledge and fault, highly relevant in issues about delictual liability, should also be relevant to questions about whether a statement is contractual in nature.

1 *Esso Petroleum v Mardon* [1976] 1 QB 801. The case also blurs the distinction between fact and opinion. In *Fortune v Fraser* 1993 SLT (Sh Ct) 68 an argument based on this decision was unsuccessful. The point was not discussed on appeal (1995 SC 186).
2 See in particular the contrasting cases of *Oscar Chess Ltd v Williams* [1957] 1 All ER 325 and *Dick Bentley Productions Ltd v Harold Smith (Motors) Ltd* [1965] 1 WLR 623, CA.

3.19   More obviously pertinent is the time at which the statement was made. If it is made around the same time that the contract is formed, as for example when a salesman successfully persuades a customer to purchase a car, the statement is more likely to be seen as contractual in nature. If however a statement was made quite separately from the process of concluding a bargain, the notion that the parties intended it to form part of the eventual contract seems much less likely unless some specific reference to it is made in that contract[1]. Where a contract has been reduced to writing and contains an 'entire contract' clause, any statement in the prior negotiations which does not appear in the document cannot be a contract term; it can, of course, amount to a representation upon which a delictual claim can be based[2].

1 *Paul v Glasgow Corporation* (1900) 3 F 119; *Malcolm v Cross* (1898) 25 R 1089.
2 See eg *Inntrepreneur Pub Co (GL) v East Crown Ltd* [2000] 2 Lloyds Rep 611; *BSkyB Ltd v HP Enterprise Services UK Ltd* [2010] BLR 267; *BSA International SA v Irvine* [2010] CSOH 78.

Bringing in terms from outside the negotiations

3.20   Terms may be brought into a contract without direct negotiation by means of signature, reference at the time of contracting, or course of dealing between the parties. These techniques are commonly used to ensure that a set of standard terms is incorporated into a contract without detailed discussion being required. If detailed discussion did take place, the speedy and efficient conclusion of the contract would be impeded. Typical scenarios include contracts of carriage, car parking contracts, software licences and on-line contracting. When I seek to travel by public transport such as bus or train, I do not want to spend time negotiating terms and conditions with the supplier of the service, but to obtain my ticket and complete my journey. But the supplier, much better aware of the many and varied hazards of travel, ranging from delays to fatal accidents, will want to ensure that the contract defines precisely what the parties' rights and duties are. Standard terms perform precisely that function and hence the need for some means to make these contractual without impeding my access to the service.

3.21   So typically my ticket will contain a printed statement saying something like 'Issued subject to conditions of carriage' and advising me where a copy of these conditions can be obtained or inspected. Similarly, car parks usually have brightly lit or painted signs outside declaring that use of the facility is subject to terms and conditions and the tickets issued at the point of entry will carry a statement to the same effect. Again, computer software is commonly sold in transparent 'shrink-wrap' packaging through which is visible a tag or sign saying that the sale is subject to terms and conditions about the copyright in the material and that the customer will accept these by tearing open the packaging[1]. Further, when the customer loads the software into a computer for the first time, it will often not run until the customer has transmitted assent to the manufacturer's terms and conditions of use, copies of which are included within the actual programme. Commercial websites such as Easyjet and the bookseller Amazon will require customers to click on screen-boxes saying they accept the supplier's terms and conditions (also usually available in full by way of a link from the acceptance box) before their transactions are completed; this is sometimes known as 'click-wrap' contracting.

1 See, eg, *Beta Computers (Europe) Ltd v Adobe Systems Ltd* 1996 SLT 604.

3.22   All these techniques for bringing the existence of terms and conditions to the attention of the customer are attempts to invoke the rules which give contractual effect to unnegotiated terms. The conditions for successful incorporation include the following:

- A party who signs a contractual document will generally be held to have assented to terms and conditions written thereon, even though he has not read or understood them[1]. In the software example given above, there might be an interesting issue as to whether an online transmission of assent to the terms and conditions has an equivalent effect. It is however hard to imagine that tearing open a shrink-wrap packaging to gain access to goods already purchased can be seen as assent to the terms and conditions of the copyright licence to use the software.

- A document which refers to but does not contain the text of terms and conditions will only bring these terms into the contract if the document itself is understood to be contractual in nature. Tickets in contracts of carriage are understood to be contractual in nature[2], but invoices, receipts and acceptance notes for goods supplied, documents which tend to be issued after the contract has been concluded and indeed substantially performed, are not[3].

- Notices containing the text of the terms and conditions which are displayed in such a way that they can be easily seen at the time and place of contracting may bring these terms into the contract[4]. It is possible for such notice to be given in documents which might otherwise appear to be invitations to treat, for example in brochures, circulars and catalogues[5]. In the context of construction works, invitations to tender commonly state that the contract to be made will be subject to one or other of the building and engineering standard forms. Again, the software and other transactions carried out online provide an interesting situation inasmuch as the software and websites give the customer the opportunity to scan the terms and conditions on the computer screen prior to the transmission of assent.

- In the absence of a signature, the document making reference to, or the notice embodying further terms and conditions must do so in a way that serves to draw the existence of the terms and conditions to the notice of the customer. Thus reference on the back of a ticket[6], or a sign in very small print hung on a wall difficult for the customer to reach[7], may not be enough. Very prominent notice can be required of particularly onerous terms: Lord Denning once remarked that 'some clauses I have seen would need to be printed in red ink on the face of the document with a red hand pointing to it before the notice could be held to be sufficient'[8]. Hence perhaps the bright lighting which is often a feature of the notices outside car parks giving tariffs and reference to the terms and conditions of use. An example of a particularly onerous clause requiring special notice to be part of the contract is found in *Interfoto Picture Library Ltd v Stiletto Visual Programmes Ltd*[9], where a photographic lending library included in the standard terms printed on its delivery notes a clause imposing upon a borrower, who had not previously dealt with the supplier, daily accumulating charges for late return of material.

- The reference should be made or the notice given at the time of contracting. Consequently a reference or notice provided after the contract is concluded is ineffective as a means of incorporating terms and conditions[10]. This is why commercial websites will not allow the customer to proceed unless the acceptance box is clicked.

- However, where there is a course of dealing between the parties, terms may be incorporated in a particular transaction even though the reference or notice was given after the contract was concluded. For this to happen, there must have been a series of transactions from which objectively the knowledge and assent of the parties to the conditions is apparent[11]. It is therefore not enough to show that the parties have had previous dealings, nor is it a matter of counting the number or frequency of such dealings to get 'a sufficiently high score'; it must also be shown that the dealings gave notice of the existence of terms and conditions[12]. Thus the fact that I go to and from work by bus every day does not of itself signify that the bus company's terms and conditions are incorporated into each contract I make with it. Knowledge can be shown if in the course of dealing reference has always been made to the terms, or copies always sent, or if the parties are in the same trade and each uses similar conditions; assent may be taken from actings following the conditions or from failure to object to them.

1 See *McCutcheon v MacBrayne* 1964 SC (HL) 28.

2 *Gray v London and North Eastern Railway Co* 1930 SC 989.

3 See, eg, *Taylor v Glasgow Corporation* 1952 SC 440 (ticket for entry to public baths); *McCutcheon v MacBrayne* 1964 SC (HL) 28 (receipt issued on payment of freight); *Buchanan & Co v Macdonald* (1895) 23 R 264 (invoice).

4 *W N White & Co Ltd v Dougherty* (1891) 18 R 972 (notice in front of auctioneer's rostrum part of sale contract); *Wright v Howard Baker & Co* (1893) 21 R 25 (notices at work places part of employment contract).

5 *Jarvis v Swan Tours* [1973] 1 QB 233 (holiday brochure).

6 *Henderson v Stevenson* (1875) 2 R (HL) 71.

7 *McCutcheon v MacBrayne* 1964 SC (HL) 28.

8 *Spurling Ltd v Bradshaw* [1956] 1 WLR 461 at 466.

9 [1989] QB 433. The approach taken in *Interfoto* has been accepted as representing Scots law: *Montgomery Litho Ltd v Maxwell* 2000 SC 56. 'The question really is whether a particular term is of such an unusual nature that it should specifically be drawn to the attention of the other party rather than being left simply as part of a large collection of other terms and conditions which are of a fairly standard nature'; per Lord Sutherland at 59. It was irrelevant that the defender had signed the contract which contained a statement that he had read and accepted its terms.

10 *McCutcheon v MacBrayne* 1964 SC (HL) 28.

11 See generally *McBryde* paras 7.21–7.32; 15 *Stair Memorial Encyclopaedia* para 707.

12 *Grayston Plant v Plean Precast Ltd* 1976 SC 206.

3.23 Many of the rules just described were developed in the context of cases about exemption clauses in standard form consumer contracts enabling the supplier of goods or services to avoid any liability to the consumer for defective performance. As a result, the rules were often used to find that the clause in question had not been incorporated into the contract, meaning that the consumer was entitled to full recovery. In the 1970s, legislation was passed to allow more direct challenges to exemption clauses as unfair[1]. But the common law approach remains important, since the courts have declared that the statutory controls are only necessary if the clause is otherwise incorporated into the contract[2].

1 Ie Supply of Goods (Implied Terms) Act 1973; supplanted by the Unfair Contract Terms Act 1977. See also the Unfair Terms in Consumer Contracts Regulations 1999. The whole subject is discussed in more detail in ch 7.

2 *Boomsma v Clark & Rose Ltd* 1983 SLT (Sh Ct) 67.

3.24 The common law rules on incorporation are also significant in many commercial situations. In building and civil engineering contracts for example, it is common for parties to contract on the basis of standard terms and conditions in use throughout the construction industry. An employer's invitation to tender will contain the first reference to the terms and conditions to be applied and this process will continue throughout the subsequent negotiations. Another example arises where there is a main contract and a sub-contract: it is common for the sub-contract to incorporate the relevant terms and conditions of the main contract by appropriate reference in its text and indeed for the main contract to require that this be done. The aim is to ensure that the liabilities of the contractor in the main contract are matched by those of the sub-contractor so that all parties involved in the project are working towards the same goal under the same conditions.

RECTIFICATION

3.25   A problem which may arise with a written contract is the failure of the writing to express accurately what the parties have agreed. Under the law as it stood until the end of 1985, Scots law dealt with this problem in two ways. If the mistake in the document was obvious (*patent*), then it would be corrected as a matter of interpretation. If the mistake was not obvious (*latent*), the party seeking to correct it had to raise an action of reduction and declarator in the Court of Session. Reduction got rid of the mistaken document and declarator stated the terms that had actually been agreed[1]. Following consideration of the issue by the Scottish Law Commission, a new remedy of rectification was introduced by statute in 1985[2]. The remedy, which is available in either the Court of Session or the sheriff court[3], can be used in two circumstances:

(a) when a document intended to express or to give effect to an agreement fails to express accurately the common intention of the parties to the agreement at the date when it was made[4];
(b) when a document intended to create, transfer, vary or renounce a right, and other than one caught by (a) above (for example unilateral rather than bilateral), fails to express accurately the intention of its grantor at the date the document was executed[5].

The intention of the parties under (a) must amount to an agreement prior to the creation of the document, while under (b) the intention of the grantor must be something more than a wish, belief, indication or general understanding[6]. Knowledge is not agreement[7]. The intention and failure to express it accurately may be proved by any relevant evidence, written or oral[8], and is determined on the balance of probabilities[9]. Although the court is concerned with the actual intentions of the parties, these are assessed objectively[10]. The court may order the document to be rectified in any manner to give effect to the intention[11], but the use of the word 'may' here indicates that the court has a discretion as to whether or not to grant the application even if the grounds for rectification are made out[12]. The rectification has retrospective effect[13], although the statute contains provisions for the protection of third party interests against the possible adverse consequences[14]. The court's discretion as to whether or not to order rectification may also have a role to play here. The retrospective effect means that even where the parties are not in dispute that the writing is inaccurate it may still be worth their while seeking rectification by court order[15].

1 The old law remains in force and is applied in *Aberdeen Rubber Ltd v Knowles & Sons (Fruiterers) Ltd* 1995 SC (HL) 8, affg 1994 SLT 662 (First Division, rvsg Lord Cameron of Lochbroom in the Outer House, 1994 SLT 177).

2 LRMPSA 1985, ss 8 and 9; implementing *Report on Rectification of Contractual and Other Documents* (Scot Law Com no 79) (1983). In *Rehman v Ahmad* 1993 SLT 741 Lord Penrose held that it was legitimate to have regard to the preceding Scottish Law Commission documents in interpreting the 1985 Act. See generally Reid 'Rectification of deeds' (2009) 103 Property Law Bulletin 1.

3 LRMPSA 1985, s 8(9).

4 LRMPSA 1985, s 8(1)(a).

5 LRMPSA 1985, s 8(1)(b). This would presumably cover a unilateral promise, but it expressly does not extend to wills (s 8(6)). See further on the distinction between (a) and (b) *Royal Bank of Scotland v Shanks* 1998 SLT 355; and for other cases on (b) see *Bank of Scotland v Graham's Tr* 1992 SC 79; *Bank of Scotland v Brunswick Developments (1987) Ltd* 1995 SLT 689, affg 1994 SLT 623; *Bank of Scotland v Brunswick Developments (1987) Ltd (No 2)* 1999 SC (HL) 53, rvsg 1998 SLT 439, affg 1997 SLT 48.

6 *Shaw v William Grant (Minerals) Ltd* 1989 SLT 121 (note); *George Thompson Services Ltd v Moore* 1993 SLT 634; *Rehman v Ahmad* 1993 SLT 741. *MacDonald Estates plc v Regenesis (2005) Dunfermline Ltd* 2007 SLT 791.

7 *Baird v Drumpellier & Mount Vernon Estates* 2000 SC 103; *Delikes v Scottish & Newcastle plc* 2000 SCLR 163.

8 LRMPSA 1985, s 8(2).

9 *Shaw v William Grant (Minerals) Ltd* 1989 SLT 121 (note); *Rehman v Ahmad* 1993 SLT 741.

10 *Shaw v William Grant (Minerals) Ltd* 1989 SLT 121 (note); *Rehman v Ahmad* 1993 SLT 741; *Oliver v Gaughan* 1990 GWD 22-1247; cf *Angus v Bryden* 1992 SLT 884. *MacDonald Estates plc v Regenesis (2005) Dunfermline Ltd* 2007 SLT 791; *Brown v Rysaffe Trustee Co (CI) Ltd* [2011] CSOH 26.

11 LRMPSA 1985, s 8(1), concluding words.

12 *Bank of Scotland v Brunswick Developments (1987) Ltd* (No 2) 1998 SLT 439 (First Division); *Norwich Union Life Assurance Society v Tanap Investments UK Ltd (in liquidation) (No 2)* 2000 SLT 819.

13 LRMPSA 1985, s 8(4).

14 LRMPSA 1985, s 9. See *Sheltered Housing Management Ltd v Cairns* 2003 SLT 578; *Co-operative Wholesale Society Ltd v Ravenseft Properties Ltd (No 3)* 2003 SCLR 509; *Jones v Wood* 2005 SLT 655.

15 See eg, *Belhaven Breweries v Swift* 1996 SLT (Sh Ct) 127; *Beneficial Bank plc v Wardle* 1996 GWD 30-1825.

3.26 The courts have adopted a fairly broad approach to these provisions. Mistakes in the expression of a document or in filling out a form can be rectified as can ambiguities and omissions; the line will be drawn, however, when the court is asked to cure fundamental defects such as the absence of a signature where that means that the document could not be said to be executed at all[1], or to engage in wholesale restructuring of the contract[2].

Nor can it be used to change retrospectively the character of a document to something other than was intended by the relevant party at the time of execution[3], or to make the document better or more effective[4]. Missives which have 'expired' under a clause providing for their supersession by the implementation of a disposition may nonetheless be rectified[5]. But at least two points seem to require further clarification:

(1) The statute does not say who is entitled to bring an application for rectification and it may therefore not be limited to the parties to the document. This could be of benefit, for example, to a third party claiming that a document failed to express the original parties' common intention to confer a *jus quaesitum tertio*.

(2) Rectification is available in respect of a document 'intended to express or to give effect to an agreement'. The aim of the remedy here is to give effect to the common intention of the parties. But with whose intention should the court be concerned when it is considering whether the document was intended to express an agreement?[6] Is it the intention of the parties to the agreement only, or is the intention of the person executing the document relevant? That person might well be someone other than the parties – a solicitor, for example – especially where the parties are not natural persons; or it could be that one only of the parties draws up the embodiment of what the parties have agreed[7]. A similar question arises with regard to the unilateral document that fails to express accurately 'the intention of the grantor'; if the grantor is a company, is the intention of the person actually signing on behalf of the company relevant or not to enable rectification to take place? The House of Lords has held that the relevant intention is that of the company rather than that of the signatory without saying how the former's intention is to be determined[8].

---

1 *Bank of Scotland v Graham's Tr* 1992 SC 79.
2 *Huewind v Clydesdale Bank plc* 1995 SLT 392; 1996 SLT 369.
3 *Bank of Scotland v Brunswick Developments (1987) Ltd (No 2)* 1999 SC (HL) 53.
4 *Baird v Drumpellier & Mount Vernon Estates Ltd* 2000 SC 103.
5 *Reyana-Stahl Anstalt v MacGregor* 2001 SLT 1247.
6 See *MacDonald Estates plc v Regenesis (2005) Dunfermline Ltd* 2007 SLT 791, paras 166–176.
7 See *MacDonald Estates plc v Regenesis (2005) Dunfermline Ltd* 2007 SLT 791, paras 177, 181.
8 *Bank of Scotland v Brunswick Developments (1987) Ltd (No 2)* 1999 SC (HL) 53.

IMPLIED TERMS

3.27   A contract may include terms and obligations that have not been expressly stated by the parties. Such terms and obligations are said to be *implied*[1]. The standard modern analysis of implied terms divides them into two broad categories, namely, terms *implied in law* and terms *implied in fact*[2]. As already noted, the distinction is essentially that terms implied in law apply to all contracts, either generally or within the categories developed by the law, such as sale, insurance, partnership and employment, while terms implied in fact occur in individual contracts, the express terms of which do not deal with a problem requiring solution. What links the two categories as implied terms is that both are seen as dependent upon the parties' agreement: terms which are inconsistent with or excluded by express terms in the contract cannot be implied[3], while through the cases there runs the thread that the terms to be implied are those which the parties would have agreed as reasonable persons[4]. An important distinction remains that, while terms implied in law are included unless the parties otherwise intend, terms implied in fact are only included if the parties' intention to do so can be made out in accordance with the rules on the subject.

1 Implied terms are recognised in DCFR II.-9:101 and PICC ch 5.
2 See *McBryde* paras 9.01–9.07; 3 *Stair Memorial Encyclopaedia* para 29, and 15 *Stair Memorial Encyclopaedia* para 711.
3 See, eg, *Cummings v Charles Connell & Co (Shipbuilders) Ltd* 1968 SC 305; *G M Shepherd v North West Securities Ltd* 1991 SLT 499; *Morrish v NTL Group Ltd* 2007 SC 805. An implied term can however deal with the same subject area as an express term: *Scottish Power plc v Kvaerner Construction* 1999 SLT 721; *E & J Glasgow Ltd v UGC Estates Ltd* [2005] CSOH 63. In *Johnson v Unisys Ltd* [2003] 1 AC 518, Lord Hoffmann observed at para 37 '[A]ny terms which the courts imply into a contract must be consistent with the express terms. Implied terms may supplement the express terms of the contract but cannot contradict them.'
4 See *William Morton & Co v Muir Bros & Co* 1907 SC 1211 per Lord M'Laren at 1224; *Crawford v Bruce* 1992 SLT 524; *J & H Ritchie v Lloyd Ltd* 2007 SC (HL) 89.

Terms implied in law

3.28   Four sub-categories can be identified within this category of implied terms:

Terms implied by statute

3.29   There are numerous examples of statutes laying down terms to be implied into particular types of contract. The best-known are those under sections 12–15A of the Sale of Goods Act 1979 (SGA 1979) as amended by the Sale and Supply of Goods Act 1994 (SSGA 1994) and those under the Supply of Goods and Services Act 1982 (SGSA 1982) (extended to Scotland by the same 1994 Act). Thus under these Acts, a supplier of goods in the course of business has an implied obligation to provide goods of satisfactory quality. But the customer's obligation to accept and pay for the goods, which arises under the same Act, is not an implied term of the contract of supply. If the parties agree that the customer is not obliged to accept and pay, the transaction is probably not a contract for the supply of goods at all.

Terms implied at common law

3.30   The courts have also developed terms to be generally implied in particular categories of contracts. Examples include the implied duty of care owed by professionals such as solicitors and accountants to their clients[1], the duty of builders to execute their work in a good and workmanlike fashion using the skill and care of a builder of ordinary competence[2], the duty of care owed by a custodian of another's property to the owner[3], and the duty of mutual trust and confidence in the employment contract[4]. The basis on which such implied terms develop was stated thus by Lord McLaren:

'If the condition is such that every reasonable man on the one part would desire for his own protection to stipulate for the condition, and that no reasonable man on the other part would refuse to accede to it, then it is not unnatural that the condition should be taken for granted in all contracts of the class without the necessity of giving it formal expression'[5].

1 Thomson *Delictual Liability*, Ch 7.
2 3 *Stair Memorial Encyclopaedia* para 35; see also *McBryde* para 9.37.
3 *McBryde* paras 9.52–9.58.
4 See Brodie *The Contract of Employment* (2008) ch 8.
5 *William Morton & Co v Muir Bros & Co* 1907 SC 1211 at 1224.

Terms implied by custom[1]

3.31   Custom or commercial usages and practices which are certain, uniform, reasonable and notorious (in the sense that they are well known in the place where they are to apply and capable of ready ascertainment) are to be regarded as being 'a term so well known in connection with the particular transaction that it was nothing but waste of time and writing to introduce it into the contract'[2]. Today on this basis customs might be inferred from such things as industry codes of practice or standard forms of contract in widespread use in a particular sector such as the construction industry.

1 *McBryde* paras 9.60–9.64; 15 *Stair Memorial Encyclopaedia* para 717.
2 *Strathlorne Steamship Co v Baird & Sons* 1916 SC (HL) 134 per Lord Buckmaster at 136.

3.32 There are few examples of the implication of terms on this basis in the modern law reports[1]. In *William Morton & Co v Muir Bros & Co*[2], which arose from a dispute between two companies in the lace industry in the Irvine valley, Morton supplied Muir with designs from which to manufacture lace curtains. Muir later used the designs in the manufacture of curtains for another company. The court found that there was a custom of the lace trade in the Irvine valley that designs should only be used to manufacture goods for the owner of the design and that this custom was an implied term of the Morton/Muir contract, putting Muir in breach[3].

1 For one, failed attempt see *McGowan v Readman and Ritchie* 2000 SCLR 898.
2 1907 SC 1211.
3 The case also illustrates that a custom may be local in nature.

3.33 However a custom was found not to be implied into a contract in *Strathlorne Steamship Co v Baird & Sons*[1] even though there was express reference to it in the contract, a charterparty of a ship providing for discharge of the ship's cargo 'according to the custom of the port of discharge'. It was shown that there was an established mode of discharging cargoes of grain at the port of Leith but this existed mainly for the convenience of the receivers of grain and the evidence showed a history of protest against it by shipowners. It was therefore not a term on which the parties were clearly (if implicitly) agreed.

1 1916 SC (HL) 134.

Terms implied generally in contracts

3.34 It has been suggested that there are some terms which are to be applied generally in all types of contract (absent, of course, express contrary provision in a given contract, or particular implications and rules in certain categories of contract)[1]. The particular example given is an implied term requiring parties to co-operate to ensure that the contract is carried out[2]. Other instances might include implications that contractual performance be carried out within a reasonable time[3]; that one party does not do anything to prevent the completion of performance by the other or otherwise derogate from the contract[4]; and that discretionary powers given by a contract are exercised reasonably[5]. But such concepts may be so general and so far from any notion of the parties' agreement that they are better regarded not as implied terms but as rules of law about contracts or about their interpretation and construction. A more radical suggestion still would be to see them as examples of a general principle of good faith in contracts[6].

1 15 *Stair Memorial Encyclopaedia* para 714.
2 Based on a dictum of Lord Blackburn in *Mackay v Dick and Stevenson* (1881) 8 R (HL) 37 at 40.
3 *McBryde* para 9.13.
4 15 *Stair Memorial Encyclopaedia* para 714 (citing English authority); see further *Gloag* pp 296–301, and *Barr v Lions Ltd* 1956 SC 59. See also *Scottish Power plc v Kvaerner Construction* 1999 SLT 721; *E & J Glasgow Ltd v UGC Estates Ltd* [2005] CSOH 63; *Coranta Corporation Ltd v Morse Business Applications Ltd*, (Glasgow Sheriff Court, 11 July 2007) http://www.scotcourts.gov.uk/opinions/CA581-04.html
5 See cases cited in 15 *Stair Memorial Encyclopaedia* para 861, n 2; cf *Gloag* pp 302–308.
6 See further below, para 4.30 ff. The duty to co-operate is immediately preceded by the general obligations of good faith and fair dealing in DCFR III.-1:104.

Terms implied in fact

3.35 For a variety of reasons contracts are often incomplete. It may be that parties did not foresee all the situations which might arise to affect their relationship; or that they decided not to deal with a particular point in the contract because it was thought unlikely to arise; or because they could not agree on how the point should be dealt with and left it, hoping for the best. The result is the occurrence of events giving rise to some question between the parties but for which the express terms of the contract make no provision. An example is found in *Crawford v Bruce*[1] where a ten-year lease of a shop provided for rent review every three years but said nothing about how the rent was to be assessed. In *J & H Ritchie v Lloyd Ltd*[2] the seller of defective agricultural machinery offered orally to investigate the problem and took the goods back to do this; but the parties said nothing about what was to happen when the seller identified the cause of the difficulties: for example, was the buyer entitled to information about it before repair was carried out?

1 1992 SLT 524. For how the court dealt with this case, see below, para 3.37.
2 2007 SC (HL) 89. See further below, paras 3.37, 5.39.

3.36 Another more complex example is the English case of *Trollope & Colls v NWMHB*[1]. A building contract provided for completion of the work in three phases, each with its own fixed date of completion and its own conditions, including provisions for extensions of time in certain circumstances. Phase 1 was to run from 1 February 1966 to 30 April 1969. Phase 3 was to start six months after the completion of Phase 1 and to be complete by 30 April 1972. Unfortunately Phase 1 overran by 59 weeks and was completed on 22 June 1970. Thus Phase 3 had to start by 22 December 1970 and work for which 30 months had been allowed had to be completed within 16. None of the express provisions for extension of time on Phase 3 dealt with delayed completion of Phase 1. What was to be done, given that no express term covered the situation[2]?

1 [1973] 1 WLR 601, HL.
2 For the result of this case, see below, para 3.38.

3.37 The approach of the courts to the solution of this kind of problem has been influenced by a number of ideas which often interact and overlap:

- First, since a court cannot impose contractual obligations upon the parties, it must be satisfied that the term to be implied is one that would have been agreed by the parties. But because the very existence of the dispute before the court indicates that the parties would most probably have not agreed a term[1], the term to be implied is that which any reasonable person would wish to have for his protection and which no reasonable person would refuse[2]. In *Ritchie v Lloyd*[3], for example, the House of Lords held that no reasonable seller already in breach of contract could have refused a term that the buyer was entitled to information about the cause of the defect in the goods as revealed by the seller's investigation. This was balanced by another implied term that the buyer would not exercise its right of rejection under the main contract of sale while the investigation was carried out. Similarly in *Scottish Power plc v Kvaerner Construction*[4], a sub-contractor SP recovered damages from a main contractor K for disruption and delay to its work caused by the latter, on the basis of implied terms that K would not hinder or prevent SP from performing in a regular and orderly manner, that K would take all reasonable steps to enable SP to do this, and that K would provide the information needed to let SP do this. Scots law thus appears to adopt an objective approach in this area[5]. This however is not the same as implying any reasonable term in the circumstances. In *Crawford v Bruce*[6] for example, the landlord argued that the term to be implied was one making the current market rent payable but this was rejected because it would have been disadvantageous to the tenant and it would not have been unreasonable for him to refuse to accede to such a term. Similarly in *Lothian v Jenolite*[7], a principal argued that his agent was bound under an implied term not to sell goods manufactured by the principal's competitors. The argument failed, amongst other reasons, because the court took the view that the agent would have charged a higher commission to give up the other business which was coming his way.

- Second, the term to be implied must be one which is necessary to make the contract work, or, in another phrase picked up from the English authorities, to give it business efficacy[8]. The idea is that a further term is needed to make the contract complete and that without such a term it lacks point or sense. This approach is found in Lord Rodger's explanation of the terms implied in *Ritchie v Lloyd*[9]. In *North American and Continental Sales Inc v Bepi (Electronics) Ltd*[10], a Scottish company held an exclusive licence to distribute an American company's software in the United Kingdom, its remuneration being dependent on the number of sales made. The Scottish company did not market the software, alleging that it was defective, and the American company claimed breach of contract on the basis of an implied term that best endeavours would be used to market the software. The term was implied on the basis of necessity since sales of the software in the United Kingdom would otherwise be stultified; an exclusive licence to distribute which imposed no obligation to distribute would be a pointless exercise. In the leading English case of *Liverpool City Council v Irwin*[11], written contracts of lease between the council and its tenants stated only the obligations of the tenants; the House of Lords held that it was necessary to imply terms giving the obligations of the council in order to complete the contracts. On the other hand, in *M'Whirter v Longmuir*[12] a term was not implied where it had been considered by the parties in negotiation but not expressly included in the contract. In *Lothian v Jenolite*[13], the contract was workable with the agent acting for competing principals, the business world abounding in such contracts, and no term to prevent such actings was necessary. An instructive contrast with the *Bepi* case is provided by *Thomson v Thomas Muir (Waste Management) Ltd*[14], where a farmer leased land to a tenant for the tipping of waste. Payment was to include a royalty based on the income of the tenant above a certain level. The tenant did not charge a commercial rate to some of its customers for tipping. The farmer contended that this was in breach of an implied term that the contract would be operated in good faith as a commercial venture. The implied term was rejected on the basis that the contract was not unworkable without it. Unlike the *Bepi* case, where the royalty was the sole source of return for the licensor, the farmer also received a 'not insubstantial' fixed rent for the land and the maximisation of his return was not necessary to make the lease a reasonable business proposition. Again, it has been said that implied terms which impose obligations in matters over which the party to be bound has no control – in the particular case where the question arose, failure to provide access to a building site caused by the actings of any party whatsoever – would not have business efficacy for that party[15].

- Third, the content of the term to be implied must be clear, certain and obvious. This is perhaps most strikingly put in the words of Mackinnon LJ:

'Prima facie that which in any contract is left to be implied and need not be expressed is something so obvious that it goes without saying; so that, if while the parties were making their bargain, an officious bystander were to suggest some express provision for it in the agreement, they would testily suppress him with a common "Oh, of course!".'[16]

1 And indeed that is very often the reason why there is no express provision in the contract in the first place.
2 *Gloag* p 289; approved in *M'Whirter v Longmuir* 1948 SC 577.
3 2007 SC (HL) 89 per Lord Hope at para 16 and per Lord Rodger at para 37. On the buyer's right of rejection, see further para 5.39 below.
4 1999 SLT 721.
5 *Lothian v Jenolite* 1969 SC 111 per Lord Milligan at 121.
6 1992 SLT 524.
7 1969 SC 111.
8 The leading case in Scotland accepting the 'business efficacy' test is *M'Whirter v Longmuir* 1948 SC 577. But 'business efficacy' points to a commercial context, and terms can be implied in fact in non-commercial contracts as well: see *Crawford v Bruce* 1992 SLT 524 per LP Hope at 531D–E.

9 2007 SC (HL) 89 para 37.
10 1982 SLT 47.
11 [1977] AC 239.
12 1948 SC 577.
13 1969 SC 111.
14 1995 SLT 403.
15 *Ductform Ventilation Ltd v Andrews-Weatherfoil Ltd* 1995 SLT 88.
16 *Shirlaw v Southern Foundries (1926) Ltd* [1939] 2 KB 206 at 227 (affd [1940] AC 701). This test is referred to with approval in *McCutcheon v MacBrayne* 1964 SC (HL) 28 per Lord Reid at 35; but cf Lord Hoffmann's comments in *Attorney General for Belize v Belize Telecom Ltd* [2009] 1 WLR 1988 (PC) para 25.

3.38   In the *Trollope & Colls* case, the facts of which were given above[1], four or five possible implied terms were put forward in argument as solutions to the problem that had arisen. The House of Lords held that, since there were all these plausible alternatives, no term could be implied since it could not be said which one would have been chosen by the parties. It may be that this decision is affected by the slightly more subjective approach to the implication of terms adopted by the English courts, but the difficulty in this case even with the more objective Scottish approach can be seen when we note that it was actually the employer rather than the building contractors who wanted to have a term implied extending the time for the contract. The contractors were quite happy with the 16-month completion time, probably because under the measure and value arrangements typical of such contracts they would get paid more, while the employers had to find sub-contractors who would probably charge very high rates given the very short period within which the work was to be done. To determine what two 'reasonable' persons would have agreed in this situation is probably not possible.

1 See above, para 3.36.

3.39   The opinion of the Privy Council in *BP Refinery (Westernport) Pty Ltd v Hastings Shire Council*[1] has often been referred to in modern implied term cases for its summary of the approach to be taken. It was said there that the term to be implied must (1) be reasonable and equitable; (2) be necessary to give business efficacy to the contract so that no term will be implied if the contract is effective without it; (3) be so obvious that it goes without saying; (4) be capable of clear expression; and (5) not contradict any express term. In *Attorney General of Belize v Belize Telecom Ltd*[2], however, Lord Hoffmann sought to relate the process of implying terms to that of construing or interpreting contracts which in his view (as will be elaborated more fully later in this chapter[3]) is about what the contract language would mean to the reasonable person. If a contract fails to provide for a particular eventuality, the answer may often be that any resultant loss must be left to lie where it falls. But if the reasonable person would understand from the contract, read against the relevant background, that something is to happen should the eventuality occur, then the court will imply the term needed to fulfil that understanding as part of the process of construing the contract. 'In every case,' said Lord Hoffmann, 'the question for the court is whether such a provision would spell out in express words what the instrument, read against the relevant background, would reasonably be understood to mean.'[4] On this view, it is wrong to ask what the actual parties would have agreed, even casting them as two reasonable people, since the matter is pre-eminently a matter of the objective construction of the express agreement. The list in the *BP Refinery (Westernport)* case 'is best regarded, not as a series of independent tests which must each be surmounted, but rather as a collection of different ways in which judges have tried to express the central idea that the proposed implied term must spell out what the contract actually means, or in which they have explained why they did not think that it did so.'[5] This approach should not be read, however, as extending the power of a court to introduce a term into a contract simply because it would be reasonable to do so[6]. It is submitted that, if understood in this way, Lord Hoffmann's approach is consistent with the generally objective approach to implied terms that has been taken hitherto by the Scottish courts, even if it is wrong to ask what two reasonable people would have agreed on the matter in issue[7]. A term should only be implied in fact when it is reasonably clear from the contract's express terms read against the background of relevant surrounding circumstances what that term should be. This probably means that the courts will imply terms only very occasionally.

1 (1977) 180 CLR 266, cited eg in *DFR Properties Ltd v Glen House Properties* 2007 SC 74.
2 [2009] 1 WLR 1988 (PC), paras 16–27.
3 See below, paras 3.40–3.46.
4 [2009] 1 WLR 1988 (PC), para 21.
5 [2009] 1 WLR 1988 (PC), para 27.
6 See *Mediterranean Salvage & Towage Ltd v Seamar Trading & Commerce Inc (The Reborn)* [2009] 2 Lloyd's Rep 639 per Sir Anthony Clarke MR at para 15. See further *McKendrick*, pp 171–4.
7 The *Belize* case has so far only been mentioned in passing in Scottish cases: see *Wyman-Gordon Ltd v Proclad International Ltd (No 3)* 2011 SC 338 para 31; *Maurice McNeill Iona Ltd v McLean* 2011 GWD 23-514 (Haddington Sheriff Court).

INTERPRETATION AND CONSTRUCTION

The traditional, objective approach

3.40 Having identified the terms of the contract, the next question is, to what obligations do the terms give rise? This is a matter of construing and interpreting the contract. The purpose of the law of contract is to enforce what the parties have agreed or their common intention. But just as the process of asking *whether* the parties have agreed is detached from their actual state of mind[1], so is the process of determining *what* they have agreed. The basic approach is objective: to determine the meaning of what the parties have said, rather than asking what did they intend to say? Lord President Dunedin's much-quoted words in *Muirhead & Turnbull v Dickson*, already referred to in a previous chapter, bear one more repetition: 'Commercial contracts cannot be arranged by what people think in their inmost minds. Commercial contracts are made according to what people say'[2]. And the nature of this objective approach as elaborated by Gloag has won judicial approval: 'The judicial task is not to discover the actual intentions of each party; it is to decide what each was reasonably entitled to conclude from the attitude of the other'[3].

1 See para 2.5 ff.
2 (1905) 7 F 686 at 694, cited above, para 2.6.
3 *Gloag* p 7; approved in *McCutcheon v MacBrayne* 1964 SC (HL) 28 per Lord Reid at 35. See also *McBryde* paras 8.02–8.04. On the development of interpretive approaches in Scots law see Clive, 'Interpretation' in *Reid and Zimmermann*.

3.41 The justification for the objective approach to interpretation is the protection from unfair surprise of all those whose rights and duties are liable to be affected[1]. Parties should be able to assume that the words used have their usual or reasonable meaning rather than being affected by a meaning of which the parties could not be aware: those charged with resolving disputes about the meaning of the words also need to adopt 'the position of a reasonable and disinterested third party'[2]. The general approach is however qualified for the case where in negotiations one party makes known its understanding of a particular phrase or clause in the contract and the other party makes no objection; then the first party's meaning is the one to be used. So in one case B purchased 'the estate of Dallas' from S who during negotiations had made clear that the estate for sale was of lesser extent than that shown by the title registered under that name. It was held by the House of Lords that S's meaning of the phrase was to be used for the interpretation of the contract's subject-matter[3].

1 *Report on Interpretation in Private Law* (Scot Law Com no 160) (1997) para 2.6.
2 *Gloag* pp 398–399.
3 *Houldsworth v Gordon Cumming* 1910 SC (HL) 49. For another possible example, see *Bank of Scotland v Dunedin Property Investment Co Ltd* 1998 SC 657 (meaning of 'in connection with').

3.42   The main consequences of the objective approach may be listed as follows:

- The starting point is the words used by the parties, placed in the context of the contract as a whole.
- Words are to be given their ordinary grammatical meaning unless it is clear from the contract that some other meaning is intended; if a word is a technical term and is used as such, it should be given its technical meaning, as to which evidence may be led.
- If the words are capable of more than one meaning, it is permissible to look at some (but not all) surrounding circumstances to determine their meaning. 'You see what is the intention expressed in the words used as they were with regard to the particular circumstances and facts with regard to which they were used. The intention will then be got at by looking at what the words mean in that way, and doing that is perfectly legitimate.'[1]
- In general, negotiations *prior* to the formation of the contract are circumstances that cannot be examined to explain the meaning of the contract[2].
- Nor, it seems, are the conduct of the parties and other circumstances *since* the formation of the contract to be used to explain the meaning of the contract[3].

1 *Inglis v Buttery & Co* (1878) 5 R (HL) 87 per Lord Blackburn at 103.
2 *Gloag* p 367; *McBryde* paras 8.28–8.29; 15 *Stair Memorial Encyclopaedia* para 761; Scot Law Com no 160, para 2.21.
3 *Gloag* pp 375–376; *McBryde* paras 8.30–8.33; 15 *Stair Memorial Encyclopaedia* para 761; Scot Law Com no 160, paras 2.25–2.27.

A change in approach?

3.43   The objective approach of the Scottish courts to ascertaining the meaning of the contract is shared with English law but contrasts to some extent with the more subjective approach adopted in Civilian systems. Thus, the civil codes of France and Germany both emphasise that the common intention of the parties is to prevail over the grammatical sense of the words used[1]. The Italian Civil Code allows the court to take into account the general course of the parties' behaviour, including that subsequent to the conclusion of the contract[2]. Both these rules are followed in the Unidroit Principles, the DCFR and the proposed CESL, which also allow reference to preliminary negotiations[3]. Both Scots and English law have begun to move a little way in this direction.

1 *Code civil*, art 1156; BGB § 133.
2 Article 1362.
3 See PICC ch 4; DCFR II.-8:101-202; CESL arts 58–65.

3.44 A key concept in the current objective approach to interpretation is *'admissible* surrounding circumstances'. As negotiations prior to, and circumstances since, the formation of the contract are excluded (ie inadmissible), the focus is on the circumstances surrounding the making of the contract. 'In order for the agreement ... to be understood it must be placed in context. The time has long passed when agreements ... were isolated from the matrix of fact in which they were set and interpreted purely on linguistic considerations.'[1] The relevant circumstances can include the nature of the parties' business or the field of activity to which the contract relates, the commercial purpose of the contract, the history of previous dealings (as distinct from negotiations) between the parties, and the conduct and statements of the parties at the time the contract was made[2]. While this might require examination of the parties' negotiations the courts have generally stressed that the aim is not the prohibited one of determining the meaning of the terms from the negotiations but rather to find the factual background explaining the genesis and objective aim of the contract or the circumstances in which it was intended to apply[3]; possibly a rather fine distinction. But, before the court could hear evidence of such circumstances, which clearly add a degree of subjectivity to the process of construction, the contract had to be found ambiguous; that is, the words used in the contract had to be unclear or capable of more than one meaning.

1 *Prenn v Simmonds* [1971] 1 WLR 1381 per Lord Wilberforce at 1383–1384.
2 See *Reardon Smith Line Ltd v Yngvar Hansen-Tangen* [1976] 1 WLR 989 per Lord Wilberforce at 995.
3 See, eg, *British Coal Corp v South of Scotland Electricity Board* 1991 SLT 305; *Bovis v Whatlings* 1994 SLT 865, affd 1995 SLT 1339, HL.

3.45 In a number of English cases, however, the House of Lords, led by Lord Hoffmann, has argued that the very process of interpretation must *always* involve examining the context in which words are used: 'the background of facts … plays an indispensable part in the way we interpret what anyone is saying'[1]. Accordingly, admissible surrounding circumstances should always be examined whether or not the words appear to be ambiguous. Indeed, 'the background may not merely enable the reasonable man to choose between the possible meanings of words which are ambiguous but even (as occasionally happens in ordinary life) to conclude that the parties must, for whatever reason, have used the wrong words or syntax'[2]. In effect, the actual words used are subject to the context in which they are articulated. This is a radical shift in approach to contractual interpretation, since it means that the actual words used do not necessarily govern the meaning to be given to the contract[3]. It has not, however, led as some expected to the overthrow of the exclusion of prior negotiations as admissible evidence of parties' intentions as to the meaning of their contract[4]. While these decisions have been cited in many subsequent Scottish cases, it remains unclear whether the English approach is to be adopted in its entirety[5]. 'Commercially sensible' constructions are favoured by the courts along with resistance to meanings which seem to give rise to absurd results; interpretations giving the contract reasonable effect or fulfilling its commercial purpose are preferred[6]. Extensive investigation into background circumstances is not encouraged; but it has been said in the First Division that ambiguity is not a prerequisite for consideration of admissible surrounding circumstances[7]. However, it is not certain whether the Scottish courts would go as far as the House of Lords in *Bank of Commerce and Credit International v Ali*[8]. Here a release clause in a redundancy agreement, stated to be 'in full and final settlement of all or any claims of whatsoever nature that exist or may exist', was read not to prevent a subsequent claim against the former employer which was of a kind only approved by the House of Lords itself in another decision made after the redundancy agreement was concluded. Lord Hoffmann, it should be noted, dissented in this case!

---

1 *Mannai Investments Co Ltd v Eagle Star Life Insurance Co Ltd* [1997] AC 749 per Lord Hoffmann at 774. See also *Charter Reinsurance v Fagan* [1997] AC 313 and *Investors Compensation Scheme Ltd v West Bromwich Building Society* [1998] 1 All ER 98, HL.

2 *Investors Compensation Scheme v West Bromwich Building Society* [1998] 1 All ER per Lord Hoffmann at 115. The Scottish Law Lords, Lords Hope and Clyde, concurred with Lord Hoffmann's speech.

3 For a survey of the English cases on the Hoffmann approach down to the end of 2010 see Scot Law Com Discussion Paper no 147 on Interpretation of Contract (February 2011), ch 4.

4 See *Chartbrook Ltd v Persimmon Homes Ltd* [2009] 1 AC 1101 (especially the speech of Lord Hoffmann; followed in Scotland in *Luminar Lava Ignite Ltd v Mama Group plc* 2010 SC 310).

5 See *Bank of Scotland v Dunedin Property Investment Co Ltd* 1998 SC 657; *Bank of Scotland v Junior*, 1999 SCLR 284; *Project Fishing International v CEPO Ltd* 2002 SC 534; *Simmers v Innes* [2007] CSIH 12. See also Scot Law Com Discussion Paper no 147, ch 5, and Cabrelli, 'Interpretation of contracts, objectivity, and the elision of the significance of consent reached through concession and compromise', 2011 JR 121.

6 See in particular *Multi-Link Leisure Developments Ltd v North Lanarkshire Council* 2011 SC (UKSC) 53; *Aberdeen City Council v Stewart Milne Ltd* 2012 SLT 205 (UKSC), where Lord Clarke at para 33 holds the case to be one of an implied term and, following his earlier judgment in *Rainy Sky SA v Kookmin Bank* [2011] 1 WLR 2900 (UKSC), states that the commercial sense approach should only be used when the words to be interpreted may reasonably bear more than one meaning, ie there is ambiguity.

7 *Luminar Lava Ignite Ltd v Mama Group plc* 2010 SC 310, para 38; cf Lord Hope in *Multi-Link Leisure Developments Ltd v North Lanarkshire Council* [2010] UKSC 47, 2011 SC (UKSC) 53, para 11.

8 [2002] 1 AC 251. Cf in Scotland *Lloyds TSB Foundation for Scotland v Lloyds Banking Group plc* [2011] CSIH 87.

3.46 In 2011 the Scottish Law Commission consulted about a modification of the strongly objective approach of Scots law, as follows[1]. While the general principle of construction would remain objective, the aim would be to determine the parties' common intention. There would be no need for ambiguity before surrounding circumstances could be taken into account; and in contracts an expression used by one party in a particular sense (whether or not also used in that sense by the other party) would be given that sense if at the time of contracting the other party knew or could not have been unaware that it was being used in that sense. The concept of admissible surrounding circumstances would be extended to include prior negotiations and parties' subsequent conduct so far as relevant to show their common intention. This follows in modified form the rules set out in the DCFR and the Unidroit Principles[2]. The Commission also points out that evidence of prior negotiations to help determine the parties' common intention is allowed in rectification actions, and that it appears to be common practice in interpretation cases to run a claim for rectification alongside the other arguments, thus enabling the court to see the evidence to which it would otherwise be denied access[3]. The Commission's final recommendations have however yet to appear.

1 Scot Law Com Discussion Paper no 147, chs 6 and 7.
2 See above, para 3.43 note 3. See further Clive, 'Interpretation', in *MacQueen and Zimmermann.*
3 See above, para 3.25, on the rectification rules.

Rules of preference

3.47   There are a number of other rules of interpretation to which the courts make reference from time to time but they are less general and less absolute than the rules so far discussed. In its discussion of reform in this area the Scottish Law Commission has referred to them as 'rules of preference'[1], which seems a helpful way of demonstrating their character as guidelines often found useful but not invariably applied. The Commission has also shown how many of these canons of construction are found in some shape or form in all Western legal systems. Some of the more significant of them are as follows:

— The court will resist meanings which seem to give rise to an absurd result or to be contrary to common sense, and prefer those which seem to give the contract reasonable effect.

This rule has significant links to the issue of exploring the context and purpose of the agreement. An example of its use is *Eurocopy (Scotland) Ltd v Lothian Health Board*[2]. This case was about the hire of photocopiers, the charge for which was calculated on the basis of the amount of paper used in the operation of the machines. The customer attempted to argue that this meant that the contract was one for the supply of unused paper rather than for the hire of the copier! The court rejected this argument, quoting a well-known dictum of Lord Diplock: 'If detailed semantic and syntactic analysis of words in a commercial contract is going to lead to a conclusion that flouts business common sense, it must be made to yield to business common sense.'[3] There are, however, pitfalls in arguments based on common sense and absurdity. In *Scottish Special Housing Association v Wimpey Construction UK Ltd*[4], it was argued that certain clauses allowed building contractors, whose negligence had led to the destruction by fire of the property on which they were working, to insist that reinstatement was nonetheless at their employers' expense. This seemed an absurd result to the Second Division. But the interpretation was upheld in the House of Lords where it was pointed out that the clauses in question were intended to apportion risk and the consequent insurance burden. To make the contractors liable for the fire would lead to wasteful double insurance.

— Negotiated terms will be taken as the better indicator of the parties' intention.

This rule would apply where a contract is a mixture of pre-printed standard terms and terms drawn up specifically for the particular bargain – as will often be the case in construction contracts, for example – and there is discrepancy or uncertainty as to the overall meaning[5].

1 Scot Law Com Discussion Paper No 147 (2011) paras 2.11–2.12, 3.20–3.22, 7.36–7.40. See also Scot Law Com no 160, Pt 6, and the preceding Discussion Paper no 101 (1996), Pt VI, where the rules are referred to as 'canons of construction'. An Extra Division perhaps added to these by holding that, where the general common law imposes obligations upon a party, the contract will not be read as excluding them unless this was clearly the parties' intention: *Mars Pension Trs Ltd v County Properties and Developments Ltd* 1999 SC 267. See, eg, *Redpath Dorman Long Ltd v Cummins Engine Co Ltd* 1981 SC 370, discussed below, para 5.20.
2 1995 SC 564.
3 *Compania Naviera SA v Salon Rederierna AB* [1985] AC 191 at 201.
4 1986 SC (HL) 57. See also discussion of this case above, para 1.50.
5 *Gloag* p 399; *McBryde* para 8.21.

3.48 Next come rules about the relationship between general words, capable of covering a wide range of subject matter, and more specific words when used in relation to each other in some way:

— Vague general terms are limited by more precise ones (*specialia generalibus derogant*). The scope of general words may be limited by the *ejusdem generis* rule of construction.

Contractual provisions sometimes take the form of a list of specific things but conclude with general words. These general words will be limited in their scope to things of the same class, or *genus*, as those specifically listed.

A leading example is *Abchurch Steamship Co v Stinnes*[1]. A clause in a charterparty made allowance for delay in loading the ship caused by 'holidays, strikes, stoppage at the colliery at which the ship is booked to load first, detention by railway or cranes, stoppage of trains, accidents to machinery, or any other unavoidable cause'. Delay was caused by shipping congestion in the port. It was found that neither the specific nor the general words of the clause applied to this delay because the specific causes which it mentioned all related to breakdowns of normal arrangements in the port and therefore delay arising from the fact that in its ordinary operations the port could only take a certain number of ships at a time was not covered by 'any other unavoidable cause'.

Before the *ejusdem generis* rule can apply, however, the specific things listed must form a *genus* or have a generic identity. Contract draftsmen frequently seek to avoid the *ejusdem generis* rule by opening (rather than finishing, as in the *Abchurch* case) a list of specifics with general words and stating that the list is 'without prejudice to the generality of the following' or some such formula. This makes it clear that general words are intended to have very general scope and the courts' first concern is with the intention of the parties not the application of artificial rules of interpretation.

— The *contra proferentem* rule

Although there has been some debate about the precise nature of this rule[2], the best view is that it applies to ambiguous terms contained in contract documents which have been prepared by one of the parties rather than being the outcome of negotiation between the parties. The court will prefer the construction which is least favourable to the party putting the term forward (the *proferens*) or which is against (*contra*) that party's interest. The classic examples of such construction have concerned clauses excluding liability for a supplier's negligence (unless the word 'negligence' is used, the clause may not be taken as going so far) and insurance contracts, but the rule is not only applicable in such cases.

1 1911 SC 1010.
2 See the varying views expressed in *Gloag* pp 400–401; *McBryde* paras 8.38–8.43; 15 *Stair Memorial Encyclopaedia* para 758; Scot Law Com Discussion Paper no 101, para 6.13.

3.49 Finally:

— The expression of one specific thing may be taken as excluding another which is not mentioned or where there are no general words (*expressio unius est exclusio alterius*)[1].

1 See Scot Law Com Discussion Paper no 101, paras 6.10–6.11; *Gloag* pp 404–405.

3.50 In its most recent discussion of these 'rules of preference', the Scottish Law Commission has taken the view that they should not be enacted in statutory form[1]. It has been judicially suggested that the rules may need reconsideration in the light of the modern approach to interpretation discussed earlier[2].

1 See Scot Law Com Discussion Paper no 147, paras 7.36–7.40.
2 *Credential Bath Street Ltd v Venture Investment Placement Ltd* [2007] CSOH 208, para 38 (Lord Reed).

ANALYSIS OF TERMS

Different types of term

3.51   In Scots law there is generally no substantive significance in the different types of contract term. There is nothing, for instance, to parallel the English classification of terms into 'conditions' (important terms breach of which, however minor, entitles the aggrieved party to terminate the contract) and 'warranties' (less important terms for any breach of which damages is the only remedy)[1]. It is true that in some cases the Scottish courts have made a similar distinction, also affecting the right to terminate for breach, between material and non-material terms of the contract[2], but this has not ossified so that there are legal rules specifying which terms may be regarded as material and which not. Scots law retains flexibility by leaving the materiality of a term to be determined according to its construction in the circumstances of the individual case, and has therefore not had to follow English law's introduction of the category of terms intermediate between condition and warranty where the availability of the remedy of termination for breach is dependent upon whether or not the failure to perform is substantial[3]. There is no magic under Scots law in the use of the word 'condition' to describe a contractual term. However, the flexibility inherent in the concept of 'materiality' lacks the certainty offered by the English rules unless the parties choose to make the matter explicit themselves in the contract. For it remains open to the parties to stipulate expressly that *any* breach of a particular term – however trivial – is to be treated as a material breach of contract[4].

1 For this see *McKendrick* ch 10.
2 See, eg, *Wade v Waldon* 1909 SC 571.
3 There may however be some parallel with termination for material breach (as distinct from breach of a material term) in Scots law, for which see further below para 5.25 ff. On the English intermediate or innominate term, introduced in *Hongkong Fir Shipping Co Ltd v Kawasaki Kisen Kaisha Ltd* [1962] 2 QB 26, see *McKendrick* para 10.5.
4 *Dawsons v Bonnin* 1922 SC (HL) 156 per Viscount Cave at 169; *Bell Bros (HP) Ltd v Aitken* 1939 SC 577 per LP Normand at 588.

3.52   This is not to say that the words 'condition' and 'warranty' are meaningless in Scots law. We will return to 'conditions' later in this chapter, and we have already touched upon 'warranties' as contractual terms which are *statements of fact about the subject matter of the contract.* In this sense the word 'warranty' commonly turns up as a descriptor of terms in contracts of insurance (usually concerned with statements about the subject insured), charterparties (in connection with the seaworthiness of ships), sales of property and businesses (terms about the state and condition of the property or business), and leases (with regard to the general fitness for purpose of the lease-subjects). However, no inference should be drawn from the mere use of the word 'warranty' in these or any other contexts that, if the statement turns out to be untrue, the remedy of termination is unavailable.

3.53 What may be difficult with a pure warranty is obtaining a decree of specific implement – that is, a court order for the performance of the contract[1]. A statement that something is the case is either true or untrue: the business sold did or did not earn profits of £100,000 last year; the seller of a piece of land did or did not obtain planning permission before the sale; the roof of the leased property does or does not require repair. No court order can change these facts. So the only remedies are likely to be termination and/or damages representing the loss suffered as a result of the untruth, working on the basis of the difference in value between things as they are and things as they should have been, that is, as if the warranty were true. This may be enough but both termination and damages claims are potentially costly and time-consuming. Accordingly, the contract draftsman is likely to seek to add to the warranty an obligation on the appropriate party to make the statement good should it prove to be untrue. Thus for example, a warranty in a house sale to the effect, 'The seller warrants that the central heating system is in good working order', might be re-cast as 'The seller will ensure that the central heating system is in good working order', thereby providing the buyer with a right which he can compel the seller to perform[2]. But such tricks of draftsmanship will not always be possible as for example in a warranty about the profitability of a business in the past or at the time of a sale.

1 On specific implement see further below, para 6.6 ff.
2 Example derived from Gretton and Reid *Conveyancing* (1st edn, 1993) 74 (not found in subsequent editions).

3.54 It follows from this that it is sometimes necessary to distinguish between warranties and other terms, but as a matter of practicality rather than as one of substantive law. Further, given that a draftsman may mix together warranty-type statements of fact together with obligations to make the statement good, it can become difficult to determine whether or not the term actually is a warranty or some other obligation. The reason why this can be important is because a warranty is actionable as soon as its statement of fact is shown to be false, whereas an obligation to make good grounds a claim only when there is failure to do so. Thus for example, a common clause in leases imposes upon the landlord an obligation to repair defects in the subjects of the contract; but this is not a warranty that the subjects will never need repair and the emergence of defects in the property is therefore not by itself a breach of contract.

3.55   An additional observation would be that just as warranties can be distinguished from positive obligations to do something, so also they should be distinguished from negative obligations not to do something, for example in the sale of a business that the vendor will not set up again in competition with the purchaser. Such obligations are enforced by interdict rather than specific implement[1]. Again, it is not always easy to draw the distinction between positive and negative obligations: to give a simple example, the positive obligation to perform the contract can also be expressed as the negative obligation not to breach the contract. But the courts have drawn this distinction in order to define what remedies are available for breach[2] and it is therefore of some practical importance to know the nature of the obligation which a party may be seeking to enforce through court action.

1 See McBryde 'Remedies for breach of contract' (1996) 1 EdinLR 43 at 53–54.
2 *Church Commissioners for England v Abbey National plc* 1994 SC 651 (Five Judges).

3.56   Warranties should be distinguished from 'warrandice'. The latter is a guarantee of title implied in contracts for the sale of heritable property: either simple (that the granter will do nothing subsequently to prejudice the grantee's title), fact and deed (that the granter has done and will do nothing to prejudice the grantee's title), and absolute (against any defect or limitation in the title, whether the granter's fault or not). In addition, in the assignation of incorporeals, there is warrandice *debitum subesse*, namely that the debt assigned is at that date payable to the cedent. At common law there was also implied warrandice of priceworthiness in the sale of goods, which has now been superseded by the implied terms of the sale and supply of goods legislation. Warrandice is usually enforced by way of an action for damages: the loss is the market value of the property at the time in the case of total eviction[1], or the diminution in market value if the defect in title is a lesser one (eg the emergence of an unexpected servitude).

1 Should there be restitution of the price, however?

Conditions and contract terms

3.57 Just as the word 'warranty' is found in Scottish legal usage with regard to contracts, so is the word 'condition'. However, 'condition' is used not to characterise a type of contract term but rather to describe the circumstances or events upon the occurrence of which a contract term will become, or cease to be, enforceable; or, to put it another way, when a party to a contract has to perform or stop performing its obligations under the term[1]. It is not necessarily the case that contractual obligations require immediate performance and it is equally clear that parties can provide for their obligations to end before complete performance. Some examples will make the point clear:

(1) Parties reach agreement but provide that their agreement will not come into effect until it is embodied in a formal written document, or subject to the approval of some third party (eg the full board of a company)[2].
(2) A sale of land is subject to the purchaser obtaining satisfactory planning permission[3].
(3) A sale of a house is subject to a satisfactory report on the property's condition by a surveyor appointed by the buyer[4].
(4) Payment of a monthly rent is to be made on the last day of each month. TIME CLAUSE
(5) In a sale of shares, the transfer of the shares is to take place on the buyer's demand for them[5].
(6) An agency agreement will be terminated if a certain level of turnover is not achieved by a given date[6].
(7) A contract will be terminated by the insolvency of either party.

1 See *Gloag* ch XVI; 15 *Stair Memorial Encyclopaedia* paras 5–6; Thomson 'Suspensive and resolutive conditions in the Scots law of contract' in Gamble (ed) *Obligations in Context: essays in honour of Professor D M Walker* (1990) pp 126–140. There is some but not a complete parallel with the English concepts of 'condition precedent' and 'condition subsequent', as to which see *McKendrick* para 10.2. See also DCFR III.-1:106.
2 See eg *W S Karoulias SA v The Drambuie Liqueur Co Ltd* 2005 SLT 813, discussed above, paras 2.4, 2.64.
3 *Ellis Properties Ltd v Pringle* 1974 SC 200.

4 A common provision in buyer's missives to ensure that the buyer only has to pay survey fees for a property to which he has a contractual right rather than before merely submitting an offer to buy.

5 *Connelly v Simpson* 1993 SC 391.

6 *Dowling v Methven Sons & Co* 1921 SC 948.

3.58 When performance of an obligation is made conditional in ways like these examples, various issues arise. The first is, is there a contract at all? The proper interpretation of the exchange between the parties may be that the *formation or conclusion* of the contract and not just its performance is dependent upon the fulfilment of a condition. A familiar example is where parties agree to embody their arrangements in a formal written contract, as in example (1) above[1]. In such a situation the parties usually do not have a contract and are therefore free to withdraw (resile) from the arrangement until the condition is fulfilled (*locus poenitentiae*). The courts have also held that when parties make arrangements 'subject to contract', the effect may be that no contract exists until further formal steps are taken[2]. But there are no hard and fast rules to this effect, as is clear from the following dictum of Lord President Cooper:

'[I]t is perfectly possible for the parties to an apparent contract to provide that there shall be *locus poenitentiae* until the terms of the arrangement have been reduced to a formal contract; but the bare fact that the parties to a completed agreement stipulate that it shall be embodied in a formal contract does not necessarily import that they are still in the stage of negotiation. In each instance it is a matter of the construction of the correspondence in the light of the facts, proved or averred, on which side of the border line the case falls.'[3]

1 *Van Laun & Co v Neilson Reid & Co* (1904) 6 F 644; *W S Karoulias SA v The Drambuie Liqueur Co Ltd* 2005 SLT 813.

2 *Stobo v Morrison (Gowns) Ltd* 1949 SC 184. *Contrast Erskine v Glendinning* (1871) 9 M 656.

3 *Stobo v Morrison (Gowns) Ltd* 1949 SC 184 at 192.

3.59 In contrast, where a contract is made and it is merely performance that is dependent upon the fulfilment of a condition, the parties are not free to withdraw. That would be a breach of contract[1]. However, performance of the obligation itself may not be enforceable (for example, by way of specific implement) until the condition is fulfilled, as in example (2) above, the buyer of land obtaining planning permission. It may be that the conditional obligation never becomes enforceable because the condition is never fulfilled, or because the condition, when it is fulfilled, is one upon the occurrence of which the obligation comes to an end, as in example (6) above, the agency agreement which was to be terminated if a certain turnover was not achieved.

1 At least as repudiation, as to which see below, para 5.28 ff.

3.60 There is a somewhat technical distinction between *future* and *contingent* obligations. The difference is that with a future obligation the condition is certain to happen, whereas with a *contingent* obligation it is not. All the examples of conditions given above are contingent except that of the obligation to pay the rent due under a lease on a particular day each month, which is future because the day in the month is certain to occur. The obligation to pay under a life insurance contract might also be future in nature, because the event upon which payment depends, the death of the assured, is certain to happen. The main practical significance of the distinction is in relation to debt enforcement processes such as diligence, bankruptcy and liquidation of companies, and will not be dealt with in greater detail here.

[handwritten margin note: Time clause ≠ condition]

3.61 Conditions that are contingent, that is, about uncertain events relative to the performance of a contract, are commonly distinguished into the categories of *suspensive* and *resolutive*. The basis of the distinction is that with suspensive conditions performance of the obligation is delayed or suspended until the condition is fulfilled, whereas the fulfilment of a resolutive condition brings the obligation to an end. Thus the condition requiring a satisfactory survey of the house to be sold before the buyer is obliged to pay for it is a suspensive condition, while the provision for the termination of the agency agreement on failure to achieve a certain turnover is resolutive.

3.62 Applying the distinction of suspensive and resolutive to particular terms is sometimes difficult and may be a question of perspective. Thus in the obligation to sell land subject to the buyer obtaining planning permission (example (2) above), it may appear that the obligation to sell is suspended until the planning permission is obtained but it might also be said that the obligation is resolved when the buyer fails to obtain planning permission. A contract for the sale or return of goods (for example, a supply of wine for a party) provides a classic example: is the buyer's obligation to pay for the goods suspended until he consumes or otherwise disposes of them or is it resolved by his returning them to the seller?[1] Here and elsewhere, the distinction will be of little importance but at least some practical consequences may follow.

1 *Brown v Marr, Barclay & Ors* (1880) 7 R 427.

3.63 If a condition is resolutive, attempts by the parties to prevent fulfilment of the condition are perfectly acceptable: in the agency agreement example, for instance, the agent is entitled to seek to achieve the required level of turnover. But with a suspensive condition the debtor in the obligation may at the least be bound not to impede its purification. Again, if a condition is suspensive but unfulfilled, the debtor is not necessarily bound indefinitely since it can be implied that the condition must be fulfilled within a reasonable time if there is no express time-limit[1]; but this doctrine cannot be applied to resolutive conditions such as, for example, a provision that a contract will terminate upon the insolvency of a party.

1 *McBryde* para 5.39; Thomson in Gamble (ed) *Obligations in Context* at 132–133; *T Boland & Co Ltd v Dundas's Trs* 1975 SLT (Notes) 80.

3.64 The nature of the condition may perhaps be best determined by asking whether or not performance by the debtor in the obligation is taking place prior to the fulfilment of the condition; if not, the condition is suspensive, and if it is, the condition is resolutive. Thus the planning permission condition (example (2) appears suspensive of the obligation to sell rather than resolutive of the obligation to buy: the obligation to sell is not performed until fulfilment of the condition, the buyer is bound to seek planning permission and failure to obtain the permission within a reasonable time or as the result of rejection by the planning authority results in the discharge of the obligation to sell.

3.65 Any condition, suspensive or resolutive, may be either *potestative, casual* or *mixed*. Potestative conditions are those which it is entirely within the power of a party or the parties to fulfil, while casual conditions are those dependent on third parties or on chance. Mixed conditions are those dependent on a combination of the potestative or casual. Thus a condition that the contract will come into effect when the parties have created and signed a formal written document is potestative, while a provision that a contract will be brought to an end in the event of an outbreak of war is clearly casual. An example of a mixed condition is provided by the planning permission clause, under which the buyer has to act to bring the condition into play but fulfilment is also dependent upon the actions of the planning authority.

3.66 The importance of this distinction lies in the duties falling upon the parties with respect to potestative elements in conditions. The basic rule is that if a party prevents fulfilment of a suspensive condition within his own power, the condition will be held fulfilled. If the contract is capable of being performed independently of the condition, the court will compel performance. In *Mackay v Dick and Stephenson*[1], it was a condition of the buyer's acceptance of a 'steam navvy' that the machine perform to a certain standard in tests. The machine failed two tests conducted in an improper manner by the buyer who refused to perform any further tests. The court held that the requirement of a satisfactory trial was fulfilled and ordered the buyer to pay the price.

1 (1881) 8 R (HL) 37.

3.67 Similarly, a debtor will be personally barred from relying on the purification of a resolutive condition to free him from further performance of his primary obligations under a contract if the condition was purified as a result of the debtor's actions. Thus in *Dowling v Methven Sons & Co*[1], an agent had to achieve a specified turnover to prevent termination but his failure to meet the target was because the principal chose not to furnish him with sufficient goods to fulfil orders. The court held that the principal could not terminate the agency.

1 1921 SC 848.

3.68 Is a party bound to do everything possible to ensure that a potestative condition is realised? In *Mackay v Dick and Stephenson*[1] Lord Blackburn stated:

'As a general rule, where in a written contract it appears that both parties have agreed that something shall be done which cannot effectually be done unless both parties concur in doing it, *the construction of the contract is that each agree to do all that is necessary to be done on his part*, though there may be no express words to that effect' [emphasis supplied].

Gloag suggests that it is 'by no means a general rule' that there is an implied obligation to purify a potestative condition, citing cases where the proper construction of the contract is that the fulfilment of the condition is an option of the party: for example, in a hire purchase transaction, where the buyer has a choice between paying the price for goods and becoming owner or not paying and returning the goods to the supplier[2]. Perhaps, however, the underlying principle of good faith would suggest that parties should seek the fulfilment of suspensive conditions or the avoidance of resolutive ones within their power unless the contract clearly points in another direction.

Rodger 1991 SLT (N) 253
Murray 1991 SLT (N) 185.

1 (1881) 8 R (HL) 37 at 40.
2 *Gloag* pp 279–281. See further *Coranta Corporation Ltd v Morse Business Applications Ltd* (Glasgow Sheriff Court, 11 July 2007) http://www.scotcourts. gov.uk/opinions/CA581-04.html

3.69   The party for whose benefit a condition exists may waive compliance and seek implement of the contract[1]. But the courts are reluctant to find that a condition exists solely for the benefit of one party and even when it is, will not allow it to be waived unless it is clearly severable from the rest of the contract[2]. If performance of a condition is impossible, illegal or immoral, the condition will be ignored[3]. There is, however, no rule in contract law that, if a party has done everything in its power to fulfil a condition which none the less remains unfulfilled, the condition is taken as purified. Otherwise the condition in example (2) above would be satisfied if the buyer sought planning permission but was unsuccessful[4].

1 *Dewar & Finlay Ltd v Blackwood* 1968 SLT 196.
2 Thomson in Gamble (ed) *Obligations in Context* at 133–134.
3 Thomson in Gamble (ed) *Obligations in Context* at 131.
4 See *Gloag* p 279, criticising the contrary view in Erskine *Institute* III, 3, 85. *Gloag* is supported by *McBryde* para 20.19; Thomson in Gamble (ed) *Obligations in Context* at 131; and 15 *Stair Memorial Encyclopaedia* para 6. The principle may apply with regard to conditions in wills.

3.70   These rules about the obligations of performance which may arise from potestative conditions in contracts make it important to distinguish the situation where each party has express obligations under the contract – for example, one is to supply goods and the other the price – but there are provisions about the *order of performance* or the sequence in which acts of performance are to take place. Thus for example, goods may be due to be delivered on the first day of the month with payment to be made on the last. Although it might be said that performance on one side was a condition of performance on the other, the initial non-performance of the obligation to deliver the goods would clearly be a breach of contract entitling the other party not only to withhold its own performance but perhaps also to terminate the contract and make other claims in respect of the breach such as damages.

SOME TYPICAL CLAUSES

3.71   In this section we give some examples with comments of 'boilerplate' contract clauses, that is terms commonly included in contracts in order to deal with problems regularly arising either in fact or in law.

Assignation

3.72 'The Contractor shall not assign the contract or any part thereof or any benefit or interest therein or thereunder without the written consent of the Employer.'

'The Supplier shall be entitled in its absolute discretion to assign the whole or any part of this agreement.'

These clauses are responses to the rules affecting the ability of a party to assign (transfer) its side of the contract to a third person. A contract may be assigned unless there is *delectus personae*. The first clause comes from a civil engineering contract in which it might be doubtful whether there is *delectus personae* but the employer is very keen to ensure that its chosen contractor continues as such. None the less flexibility is retained because the employer may consent to an assignation if it wishes. Very often in practice, the phrase 'which consent will not be unreasonably withheld' is added in such clauses although it might be implied in at least some cases. In the second contract a freedom to assign is being asserted in a hire contract probably for the avoidance of doubt. The phrase 'absolute discretion' is an attempt to avoid any implied limitations of reasonableness.

Interpretation clauses

3.73 'Every provision set out in a separate paragraph will be construed as a separate and independent provision severable from all or any of the other provisions. The headings are for convenience only and will not affect the validity or construction thereof.'

This clause seeks to avoid the rule of interpretation to the effect that the particular words of a contract must be read in the context of the whole contract.

Choice of law and jurisdiction

3.74 '(1) This contract shall be governed and construed in accordance with the Laws of Scotland and the parties submit to the non-exclusive jurisdiction of the Courts of the said country.

(2) If the Works are situated in Scotland the Contract shall in all respects be construed and operate as a Scots contract and shall be interpreted in accordance with Scots Law.'

Where the parties to a contract come from different jurisdictions or where performance is to take place in more than one country, there are rules to determine which system of law applies to the contract and which court will have jurisdiction to determine disputes arising out of the contract. But these rules may not suit the parties or, since they are cast in fairly general terms, their application may not be sufficiently clear and certain. The contract may therefore contain explicit provision on the matter along the lines of the clauses given above. The first clause is a fairly typical example of its kind, although by not making the jurisdiction of the Scottish courts exclusive it leaves open other possibilities should that prove more convenient for the parties at the time the dispute actually breaks out. The second clause chooses a law but makes no reference to jurisdiction. Although this sometimes happens by oversight, in this case it was because the contract provided for the resolution of disputes by private arbitration rather than through the courts.

Exemption clauses

3.75   '(1) Delivery dates are given in good faith but no liability is accepted for damage or loss caused by delay in delivery.

(2) If the goods are defective in quality or state, the Company will, if duly notified in writing within 7 days after the delivery thereof, replace them as soon as may be reasonably practicable. This provision is accepted by the customer in lieu of any other legal remedy and is agreed by the parties to be reasonable.

(3) If part of the goods are defective in quality or state, the seller undertakes to allow a return of such goods and to replace them as soon as may be reasonably practical.

(4) The parties accept these conditions as fair and reasonable for inclusion in any agreement of this nature.

(5) Any exclusion or limitation of liability of the carrier to the passenger shall apply to and be for the benefit of agents, servants and representatives of the carrier and any person whose aircraft is used by the carrier for carriage and its agents, servants and representatives.'

The first of these clauses is a classic exemption – or exclusion – clause declaring that the supplier of goods is not liable in damages for breach by late or non-delivery. This is precisely the kind of clause at which controlling legislation like the Unfair Contract Terms Act 1977 and the Unfair Terms in Consumer Contracts Regulations 1999 is aimed and such a clause may well be challengeable as unfair and unreasonable. Contract draftsmen are therefore now adopting a different approach exemplified in the second and third clauses. These state what the customer's remedy is if the goods supplied are defective in some way: return and replacement. But these too are in fact exemption clauses since under the supply of goods legislation the customer has the right to return the goods and to be refunded the price. The clauses are therefore offering less than the general law and are challengeable under the unfair terms legislation. The commercial reason for having such a clause is that the general legal remedy leads to the loss of a sale whereas the business is kept if the customer can only seek a replacement. The provision in the second clause and the more general one in the fourth are the draftsman's further attempts to head off challenge under the unfair terms legislation. The effectiveness of such declarations of reasonableness has yet to be tested in the context of unfair terms; in a restraint of trade case it was said that such a clause was 'an illegitimate attempt to oust the jurisdiction of the court'[1]. It may be, however, that if such a clause is negotiated, or notified and accepted, then it should be accepted as at least prima facie evidence of what it says. The final clause shows an attempt to extend the benefit of an exemption clause to third persons. This might be effective under the doctrine of *jus quaesitum tertio* although it is not clear whether it could be challenged under the unfair terms legislation[2].

1 *Hinton & Higgs v Murphy* 1988 SC 353 per Lord Dervaird at 355.
2 See above, para 2.73.

Indemnity

3.76 'During the continuance of the hire period the Hirer shall fully and completely indemnify the Owner in respect of all claims by any person whatsoever for injury to person or to property caused by or in connection with or arising out of the use of the plant and in respect of all costs and charges arising in connection therewith whether arising under statute or common law.'

This is a fairly typical indemnity clause in the standard form of a plant hire company. The scenario to which it relates is where the company supplies both plant and an operator who is one of its employees. If the employee's negligent operation of the plant injures a third person, the plant hire company may be vicariously liable as the employer. By this clause, the hirer assumes that liability[1]. An indemnity arises where one party to a contract must pay the other the amount of a loss suffered by that other as a result of another transaction. The effect is the transfer of the loss. Since indemnity clauses shift loss away from the party primarily liable, their function is rather akin to that of exemption clauses[2].

At first sight indemnity may appear somewhat akin to cautionary obligations or guarantees under which the cautioner or guarantor promises to pay the beneficiary if the beneficiary's debtor does not pay. But the distinction between an indemnity and a guarantee should become apparent immediately from the preceding sentence because in an indemnity the person indemnified is one who was a debtor to a third party and has suffered loss through having to pay that creditor; or was a loser in some other way rather than being a creditor who has suffered loss through non-payment of his debt. Further, caution is trilateral in that the obligation is accessory to the principal obligation, while an indemnity is a principal or primary obligation in its own right, existing even though the beneficiary has no enforceable rights in the transaction under which loss is suffered. An example of indemnity is the promise to pay another's debt if the creditor will release the debtor. Insurance can provide another example of indemnity as for example in fire, liability and third party accident insurance, under which losses suffered and no more are covered; but not all insurance is for indemnity as for example in life and endowment insurance where a sum is payable to the creditor on the fulfilment of certain conditions regardless of the loss he has actually suffered.

1 See eg, *Lindsay Plant Ltd v Norwest Holst Group plc* 2000 SC 93.
2 Several significant cases about indemnity clauses have arisen from operations in the North Sea oil industry: see eg, *Caledonia North Sea Ltd v London Bridge Engineering Ltd* 2000 SLT 1123, affd 2002 SC (HL) 117 (Piper Alpha); *Farstad Supply AS v Enviroco Ltd* 2010 SC (UKSC) 87.

Frustration and *force majeure*

3.77   '(1) The Landlord shall be under no liability to the Tenant in respect of anything which, apart from this provision, may constitute breach of this Agreement arising by reason of *force majeure*, namely, circumstances beyond the control of the Landlord which shall include (but shall not be limited to) acts of God, war, fire, flood, drought, explosion (howsoever caused), sabotage, accident, embargo, riot, civil commotion, acts of local government and parliamentary authority, breakdown of equipment and labour disputes of whatever nature and for whatever cause arising including (but without prejudice to the generality of the foregoing) work to rule, overtime bans, strikes and lockouts, and whether between either of the parties hereto and any or all of its employees and/or any other employer and any or all of its employees and/or between two or more groups of employees (and whether of either of the parties hereto or any other employer).'

The effect of supervening events upon a contract is governed by the rules on frustration which are on the whole restrictive. A contract will only be discharged prior to complete performance if its further performance becomes impossible, illegal or radically different; tests not easily satisfied. Thus a party confronted with a situation where performance has become much more difficult or onerous may still find that at common law non-performance will give rise to liability for breach. A *force majeure* clause may therefore be included to specify the circumstances in which the parties will cease to be bound to perform. The clause comes from a contract for the lease of premises for commercial purposes when the landlord would also be conducting its own business on the premises in question. It also illustrates techniques for avoiding the application of the *ejusdem generis* canon of construction: it twice opens lists of events with general words ('circumstances beyond the control of the landlord', 'labour disputes of whatever nature and for whatever cause arising'), and after each of the general words, it indicates that they are not restricted by the specifics which follow ('shall not be limited to', 'without prejudice to the generality of the foregoing').

Insolvency

3.78 'In the event of the customer (being a company) going into liquidation or a receiver or administrative receiver or administrator judicial or other similar officer being appointed over the whole or any part of the assets of the customer or in the event of the customer (being an individual or partnership) becoming bankrupt or committing an act of bankruptcy or being the subject of a Receiving Order or being sequestrated or become apparently insolvent, or granting any trust deed or entering into any composition or similar arrangement with his creditors, this agreement will be thereon terminated.'

Insolvency is the inability to meet obligations as they fall due because total liabilities exceed total assets. There are several processes in law to deal with this problem, the aim in general being to realise the debtor's assets, pay off the creditors and enable the debtor to start again. Because liabilities exceed assets, it is inevitable that some, perhaps most, creditors will not be paid in full and will thereby suffer loss. Further, a party who is contractually bound to render a performance to a party involved in an insolvency process may not be able to recover payment for that. Accordingly, it is common for contracts to provide that, if a party becomes subject to insolvency processes, the other party is released from performance and the contract is terminated. The example given here also illustrates how the draftsman of a standard form contract of the type from which the clause is taken has to cover the various types of persons with whom the user of the form may deal. Thus the supplier of the services under this contract may have companies, partnerships and individuals as customers and there has to be provision covering the different forms of insolvency process to which each of these may be subject.

PERFORMANCE AND EXTINCTION

3.79 Scots law has very few rules on the performance of contracts. In particular, there are no general rules about the order of performance except, perhaps, that the parties' contract governs the matter. In sale of goods, delivery by the seller and acceptance and payment by the buyer are concurrent conditions unless the contract otherwise provides[1]. In carriage of goods by sea, freight is payable only on completion of the voyage; but the parties may agree that freight will be paid in advance[2]. There are some rules about payment of money: a creditor may demand payment in legal tender and a debtor is bound to pay at the creditor's residence or place of business. Finally, performance of an obligation (of course) extinguishes it, ie performance can no longer be demanded by the other party through legal process. However, it is for the party who claims to have performed to prove it. The extinction of the obligation may be conditional, as for example with payment by cheque where if the cheque is dishonoured the original debt revives and becomes enforceable again[3].

1 SGA 1979, s 27.
2 *Gloag & Henderson* paras 23.10 and 23.11.
3 *Leggatt Bros v Gray* 1908 SC 67. Payment by credit card is, however, an absolute discharge of the obligation: *Re Charge Card Services Ltd* [1987] Ch 150; [1989] Ch 497. See further Hugo 'Payment' in *MacQueen and Zimmermann*, pp 231–240.

3.80 An obligation may be extinguished if performance or payment is rendered by a third party rather than by the debtor. This can arise through *delegation* where the debtor with the consent of the creditor authorises the third party to perform; but there is a presumption against delegation which means that clear evidence of both intention and consent is needed for the third party's performance to discharge the debt[1]. However, there may also be discharge even if the third party is unauthorised by the debtor. The creditor may only decline the unauthorised third party's tender of performance where he is entitled to claim personal performance by the debtor and even that may be overcome if the third party has a legitimate interest to protect by making the performance. The third party who discharges a debt in this way has a claim against the debtor either by way of *negotiorum gestio* or of a claim of recompense so far as the debtor is enriched (*lucratus*)[2]. In *Whitbread Group plc v Goldapple Ltd (No. 2)*[3] a third party payment was held to discharge the debt on the basis of 'ad hoc' agency but this seems to have been decided without the court being made aware of all the relevant authorities on the matter.

1 See, eg, *W J Harte Construction Ltd v Scottish Homes* 1992 SC 99 (a case later settled at the door of the House of Lords). Delegation should be distinguished from sub-contracting which does not discharge the obligation of the original contracting party. See also DCFR III.-5:201-209 (substitution of new debtor).
2 See MacQueen 'Payment of another's debt' in Zimmermann and Johnston (eds) *The Comparative Law of Unjustified Enrichment* (2002) for discussion of the Scottish authorites. DCFR III.-2:107 allows discharge by unauthorised third party performance as does South African law (see Hugo 'Payment' in *MacQueen and Zimmermann*, pp 240–242).
3 2005 SLT 281. See further Macgregor and Whitty 'Payment of another's debt, unjustified enrichment and *ad hoc* agency' (2011) 15 Edin LR 57.

3.81 Performance (or payment, in the case of money obligations) is not the only way in which an obligation may be extinguished. Just as the parties created the obligation by agreement or promise, so may they unmake or discharge it before full performance (*acceptilation*). The parties may also decide to replace their existing unperformed obligations with new ones (*novation*), in which case the previous ones are discharged. Novation, which is essentially about *new obligations*, should be distinguished from *assignation* under which a party transfers to another its *existing* rights under a contract which are otherwise unaffected, although the assignor or cedent drops out of the picture[1]. Likewise novation should be distinguished from delegation under which obligations of performance are placed upon a *new debtor*, the old one being discharged. In practice, these lines can be rather hard to draw and probably most of the time they do not matter very much; but it should be kept in mind that there are strong presumptions against both novation and delegation so that clear words will be needed to achieve them, whereas the law is less strict about assignation unless the contract involves *delectus personae*.

1 See above, para 2.84 ff. For examples of novation/delegation see *Blyth & Blyth Ltd v Carillion Construction Ltd* 2002 SLT 961; *MRS Distribution Ltd v DS Smith (UK) Ltd* 2004 SLT 631.

3.82   A number of other rules about the extinction of obligations are dealt with elsewhere in this book: for example, compensation under the Compensation Act 1592, frustration and termination for material breach[1]. There are still others of which space allows only the briefest of mentions[2]. A word should, however, be said about *prescription*, the effect upon an obligation of the lapse of time without either a relevant claim by the creditor or acknowledgment by the debtor being made towards the enforcement of an obligation[3]. If from the date an obligation becomes enforceable a continuous period of five years elapses without such a claim or acknowledgment, then it ceases to be enforceable and is said to have prescribed[4]. If a claim or an acknowledgment interrupts the running of time, the prescriptive clock is wound back to the beginning and the whole process begins again. It may be useful in the pursuit of clarity to distinguish between the primary obligations of performance arising directly under the contract and the secondary obligation to pay damages for its breach, in particular since it is provided that obligations of reparation (ie to pay damages) become enforceable not at the date of the wrong (ie the breach of contract) but at the date the resultant loss, damage or injury occurred[5]. Where the damage is latent, ie not immediately apparent, the prescriptive clock starts to run only when the injured party becomes aware of it or could with reasonable diligence have become so[6]. For example, where a contractor negligently installed a drainage system on a golf course, it was held that prescription only began to run when the defects manifested themselves in flooding on the course[7]. The law can be represented by way of the following diagrams:

---

1 Obligation ———————————————— 5 years = prescription
to perform   (*non-performance, no claim/acknowledgment*)

2 Breach _x_ Loss, damage, ——————————— 5 years = prescription
of contract injury (patent)   (*no claim/acknowledgment*)

3 Breach _x_ Loss, damage, _y_ Discovery / ——— 5 years = prescription
of contract injury (latent) discoverability
                             (*no claim/acknowledgment*)

In this diagram, the firm horizontal lines represent the period during which time has to run continuously, ie without a relevant claim by the creditor or relevant acknowledgment by the debtor; the dotted lines x and y represent the indeterminate periods of time, ranging indefinitely upwards from zero, which may intervene between breach, the occurrence of loss and, finally, its discovery/discoverability. It will be appreciated that, especially in cases of latent damage, this means that the prescriptive period is much longer than five years.

---

1 See below, paras 4.67 ff (frustration), 5.20 ff (compensation) and 5.24 ff (termination for material breach).
2 Eg confusion (creditor and debtor become the same person, acting in the same capacity).
3 See Prescription and Limitation (Scotland) Act 1973 (PLSA 1973) as amended and in general Johnston *Prescription and Limitation* (1999). See also DCFR III.-7 and Zimmermann *Comparative Foundations of a European Law of Set-Off and Prescription* (2002)
4 PLSA 1973, s 6. For the obligations to which s 6 applies (including those arising from contract, promise, unjustified enrichment and *negotiorum gestio*), see Sch 1.
5 PLSA 1973, s 11. See *Dunlop v McGowans* 1980 SC (HL) 73.
6 PLSA 1973, s 11(3).
7 *Renfrew Golf Club v Ravenstone Securities Ltd* 1984 SC 22.

3.83   The potential indeterminacy of the five-year prescriptive period, especially in cases of initially latent damage, explains the existence of a second 'long-stop' prescriptive period of 20 years which runs from the date of the enforceability of the obligation as defined above except that the provisions about discoverability are omitted[1]. It may therefore be represented like this diagrammatically:

> Breach___x Loss, damage, ──────────── 20 years = prescription
> of contract injury   (*no claim/acknowledgment*)

Consequently, it is possible for an obligation to prescribe before the creditor becomes aware that she had a right to enforce[2]. In *K v Gilmartin's Executrix*[3], the court held that it was not possible to 'read down'[4] the statutory provisions on the 20 years prescription to prevent it operating where the pursuer had been abused as a child over 40 years before the action. This may seem unjust: but one of the purposes of a regime of prescription is to ensure that cases come to court when the evidence is still reasonably fresh. The further away in time the case is from the basic events of the dispute, the poorer the recollection of the witnesses will be; some will have died; and documentary evidence will more likely than not be incomplete or non-existent. The chance of perpetrating an injustice by hearing cases after such long intervals is that much greater as a result.

1 PLSA 1973, s 7.
2 For an example see *Beard v Beveridge Herd & Sandilands WS* 1990 SLT 609.
3 2004 SC 784.
4 Under section 3 of the Human Rights Act 1998.

3.84 The 20-year prescription also applies to contractual obligations relating to land (which will usually arise in the context of land sales by way of missives)[1]. However, claims for damages for breach of such contracts still fall under the five-year prescription[2], as do obligations to make periodical payments in respect of land (eg rent)[3].

1 PLSA 1973, Sch 1, para 2. See eg *Barrett Scotland Ltd v Keith* 1993 SC 142 (obligation to give good and marketable title by delivery of valid disposition); also *Glasgow City Council v Morrison Developments* 2003 SLT 263 (building obligations in lease). The category of 'obligations relating to land' is treated narrowly by the courts: see *Gloag & Henderson*, para 4.17 note 93; eg not applicable to a unilateral written undertaking to enter an agreement to sell land (*Smith v Stuart* 2010 SC 490).
2 *Lord Advocate v Shipbreaking Industries Ltd* 1991 SLT 838.
3 PLSA 1973, Sch 1, para 1(a).

4. Getting Out of the Contract

4.1 In this chapter we turn to consider how parties who wish for some reason to escape from, or not to continue with, the performance of a contract may do so without incurring liability for breach. There are several avenues of approach in this situation. Some of them arise from the fundamental idea of contract as a voluntary obligation created by acts of individual will coming together to form an agreement. Some persons are treated as *lacking legal capacity* to perform such acts, for example as being too young; or lacking full understanding of what they are doing as a result of mental weakness or intoxication of some kind; or, in the case of legal persons such as companies and public bodies, because the law does not give them the powers (*vires*) to carry out the transactions in question. In some other cases, the agreement of a party is procured through the other *party's improper negotiating techniques*: for example, the use of force (extortion or duress), fraud (deception) or some abuse of the trust which the first party feels for him. Again, if a party makes an *error* about some matter of significance in relation to the contract, the outcome may not be that to which she agreed and the law may then say that the agreement is not binding.

4.2 All these issues are traditionally seen as affecting the *essential validity* of the contract. We have decided also to include within the scope of this chapter another set of rules which in effect allow the parties to give up the performance of the contract. After formation a contract which *becomes impossible, illegal,* or, very exceptionally, *radically different in nature through change of external circumstances* may be treated as discharged. The general name for this branch of contract law is *frustration*; what it and the other subjects mentioned in this paragraph have in common is that they are means by which parties who have gone through the process of forming a contract as described in Chapter 2 may be released from their obligations to carry through the transaction[1].

1 A party may also be released, temporarily or permanently, from its obligation
to perform by the other party's breach; this is dealt with in ch 5.

DEFECTIVE CONTRACTS

Introduction

4.3   Where A and B are parties to an apparent contract, one or
both of them may be entitled to be released from performance of
their obligations. Because *consensus in idem* is tested objectively
in Scots law, there are exceptional cases where it might follow
that no contract has been formed even although each party
considered subjectively that an agreement had been reached.
In this situation the apparent contract is *null*, ie *it has never been
formed*[1]. Scots law also holds that, before contractual obligations
are created, the parties must have reached agreement as a result
of their voluntary consents to be bound. Where a party's consent
is defective, the apparent contract may be null if, for example,
he had no rational capacity to consent. But where the defect in
consent is not so fundamental, the contract will be held to subsist
if the objective criteria for determining *consensus* are satisfied. A
party may nevertheless be released from his obligations under
the contract if his consent has been improperly obtained. In other
words, the contract can be *annulled*, ie *set aside and treated as if it
was null*. Until this is done, the contract exists as if it was valid[2].
Similarly, where a party purports to contract but does so under
error, the party's consent to the apparent contract may be so
fundamentally flawed that even on objective criteria no contract
was in fact formed. It is more likely, however, that the error does
not prevent the formation of the contract but may be a ground for
having the contract set aside, ie annulled[3]. Because it is important
for third parties to be able to rely on apparently valid contracts,
Scots law is reluctant to hold that such contracts are null: this is
done by testing *consensus* objectively. For the same reason, the
grounds upon which a contract can be set aside – reduction –
are kept within a narrow compass although the precise scope of
these grounds is a matter of controversy.

1 Sometimes in this situation the contract is said to be *void*.
2 Sometimes in this situation the contract is said to be *voidable*.
3 See further on error, below, para 4.35 ff.

4.4   The distinction between a null and an annullable contract
is of the utmost importance. A null contract does not and never

has existed: it has never been formed. Therefore it cannot create *contractual* obligations. Suppose A and B enter into an apparent contract under which A sells B a horse for £1,000. It is held that for some reason the contract is null. A has no *contractual* obligation to transfer the ownership of the horse to B: likewise B has no *contractual* obligation to pay the price to A. If A has delivered the horse to B, A cannot sue B in *contract* for the price. Moreover, because the contract is null, the transfer of ownership of the horse to B may also be null[1]; even if B has paid the price, A is still the owner and can recover the horse from B (vindication). B cannot sue A in contract for A's failure to transfer the ownership of the horse because the contract is null and A never had an obligation to transfer ownership. If B obtained the possession of the horse and sold it to C, and if A is still the owner, A can recover the horse from C. C's remedy would be to sue B for breach of their contract[2].

Since *ex hypothesi* no contract exists, any remedy to re-adjust the parties' positions must be found in the law of unjustified enrichment. If in our example, B has paid the price and A refuses to deliver the horse, B can recover the price in an action of repetition since otherwise A would be unjustifiedly enriched. When the apparent contract is for the sale of goods which the buyer has used up, for example food, since the contract is null if the seller has not been paid he cannot sue in contract for the price. Instead, the seller must use the law of unjustified enrichment and bring an action in recompense where he will recover the value of the benefit the buyer received to the extent that the buyer was enriched (*lucratus*). This might well be the same as the price 'agreed' in the contract but it could be less if the seller had made a good bargain, ie the agreed price was more than the market value of the goods at the date of the transaction[3].

1 See above, para 1.41, and Reid *The Law of Property in Scotland* (1996) paras 607 and 613–618.
2 Note, however, *Reid* para 617, and *Morrisson v Robertson* 1908 SC 332.
3 See Rodger 'Recovering payments under void contracts in Scots law', in Swadling and Jones (eds) *The Search for Principle: Essays in Honour of Lord Goff of Chieveley* (2000).

4.5 Where a contract is annullable, it subsists until it is reduced. Once it is reduced, it is treated as though it never existed, ie reduction has the effect of rendering the contract retrospectively null. Suppose A and B enter into a contract under which A agrees to sell a car to B for £10,000. The contract is annullable by A but has not been annulled. Ownership of the car is transferred to B. If B fails to pay the price, A can sue him in contract for it. Alternatively, provided that *restitutio in integrum*[2] is possible, A can seek reduction. The contract will then be treated as null with retrospective effect. A will be able to recover the car from B as B has no longer a legal basis for retaining it and would be unjustifiedly enriched if he were to do so. If the contract was annullable by B and A decides to sue B in contract for the price, B can plead the ground of reduction as a defence (*ope exceptionis*[1]) and the contract will be annulled. A could then claim the car if the ground on which the contract has been annulled has also affected the transfer of ownership to B[2]. If B has paid the price and the contract is annullable by B, provided *restitutio in integrum* is possible B can seek reduction. The contract will then be treated as null with retrospective effect. B will be able to recover the price from A because A has no longer a legal basis for retaining the money and would be unjustifiedly enriched if he were to do so. But because he has no legal basis for retaining the car after the contract has been reduced B must return the car to A for otherwise B would be unjustifiedly enriched.

1 Literally, 'by way of exception'; 'exception' is an old word for a defence in law.
  See for example *Vaughan Engineering Ltd v Hinkins & Frewin Ltd* 2003 SLT 428
2 Literally, 'restoration to original position'.
3 See *Reid* para 607.

4.6   Where a person has a choice either to reduce the contract or sue for breach, the election will be dependent on whether or not he has made a good bargain. Suppose that A agrees to buy goods from B for £5,000. In breach of the contract, B delivers defective goods worth £3,000. If the market value of these goods has fallen so that if the contract had been properly performed they would only be worth £2,000, A should reduce the contract and recover the price, having of course to return the goods. If the market value of these goods has risen so that if the contract had been properly performed they would be worth £10,000, A should sue for breach of contract and recover his expectation loss, ie £10,000 (expectation interest) minus £3,000 (actual value) = £7,000. It should be emphasised that a party cannot reduce a contract *and* sue for breach of contract. This is because if the contract is reduced, it is treated as being retrospectively null, ie treated as if it had never existed. Therefore the two remedies are mutually exclusive: for if the contract is reduced, there has never been a contract to breach[1].

1 See discussion above, para 1.36 ff.

4.7 Because an annullable contract exists until it is reduced, it can operate to support the transfer of ownership. In the example of the car[1], since the contract is only annullable the ownership of the car will prima facie pass to the purchaser, B, as soon as the contract is formed. Until the contract and transfer are reduced, B has a good title to pass to a third party, C. Provided that C bought the car in good faith, ie did not know that B's contract with A was defective, and for value, then A cannot claim the car from C as A has been effectively divested of the ownership of the car[2].

1 Para 4.5 above.
2 See *MacLeod v Kerr* 1965 SC 253; Sale of Goods Act 1979 (SGA 1979), s 23; and further below, para 4.42 ff.

4.8 Where a contract is annullable, reduction takes place in two ways. The party entitled to reduce the contract can do so simply by intimating the fact that the contract is annulled to the other party[1]. If the other party disputes the annulment, a declarator may have to be obtained from a court to establish that the contract has been annulled. Alternatively, the party entitled to reduce the contract may bring an action of reduction in the Court of Session. This may well be necessary if the contract is in the form of a deed upon which third parties could rely. As we have seen, reduction may also be pled as a defence *ope exceptionis*: such a defence is competent in the sheriff court.

1 *MacLeod v Kerr* 1965 SC 253; note that this differs from the very similar English case of *Car & Universal Finance v Caldwell* [1965] 1 QB 525 on the point as to whether in cases of fraud intimation to the police is sufficient: it is not enough in Scots law.

4.9 The right to have the contract reduced may be lost by the party seeking reduction. This would occur in the following situations:

(1) if there has been unnecessary delay in seeking reduction;
(2) if the party entitled to reduction has at any time before seeking reduction affirmed the validity of the contract: before affirmation operates as a bar the party must know about the defect which renders the contract annullable;
(3) if *restitutio in integrum* is not possible at the time reduction is sought. What this means is that the party seeking reduction must be in the position to restore *both* parties to their pre-contractual positions[1]. For example, A buys goods from B. The contract is annullable. Before the contract can be reduced, A must be in a position to return the goods to B in

the same state as they were before the contract was made. If this is not possible, A is barred from obtaining reduction and cannot therefore recover the price. In other words, *restitutio in integrum* is a *pre-condition* of entitlement to reduction: if it is not possible, the remedy of reduction is barred[2]. While this can be defended where the property rights of bona fide purchasers have intervened, as in the example of the car[3], it is difficult to see why *restitutio in integrum* should be a pre-condition of reduction in other situations. If A has used the goods so that they are no longer in their pre-contractual state, it is thought that nevertheless he should still be entitled to reduction. Since reduction renders the contract retrospectively null, while A can claim the price back from B in an action of repetition, the law of unjustified enrichment obliges A to make restitution for benefits received. Thus B could bring an action in recompense against A for the benefit he enjoyed in using the goods[4]. Be that as it may, it is clearly the current law that A will lose his right to have the contract annulled if *restitutio in integrum* is not possible. Although the House of Lords held in 1939 that the requirement of *restitutio in integrum* need not be taken too literally[5], the courts have not followed this lead and the Scottish Law Commission has recommended its replacement with a more flexible approach[6].

1 *Western Bank v Addie* (1867) 5 M (HL) 80; *Houldsworth v City of Glasgow Bank* (1880) 7 R (HL) 53.
2 *Boyd & Forrest v Glasgow & South-Western Railway Co* 1915 SC (HL) 20.
3 Paragraph 4.5 above.
4 For full discussion, see Thomson 'Obligations ordinary' in Lomnicka and Morse (eds) *Contemporary Issues in Commercial Law* (1999) at pp 198 ff.
5 *Spence v Crawford* 1939 SC (HL) 52.
6 *Defective Consent and Consequential Matters* (Scot Law Com Memorandum no 42) (1978), Vol 2, pt IV. No report has followed upon this proposal.

4.10   As we have seen, the distinction between an apparent contract which is null and a defective contract which is annullable is important, particularly in the context of the rights of third parties. With the consequences of the distinction always in mind, we shall now consider the situations when a contract is null or annullable.

Lack of capacity

4.11   An apparent contract or unilateral obligation will be null if either of the parties did not have capacity to create voluntary obligations[1]. This could be as a consequence of mental incompetency. A person who is insane cannot enter into voluntary obligations if the mental illness prevents him from understanding the nature of the obligation although a mentally ill person can contract during a lucid period. Similarly, a person will lack the ability to contract if he has been deprived of the exercise of reason as a result of intoxication induced by alcohol or the abuse of other drugs. The degree of intoxication required before capacity is lost is substantial. Merely because a person has had a few drinks will not usually deprive him of the ability to reason even if his judgment is not as sharp as it would have been if he had been sober[2]. Where capacity is lost for these reasons, any purported contract is null.

1 McBryde *The Law of Contract in Scotland* (3rd edn 2007) ch 3.
2 See *Taylor v Provan* (1864) 2 M 1226; *Pollok v Burns* (1875) 2 R 497.

4.12 Where we are concerned with artificial legal entities such as a company, the capacity to contract will be determined by the powers given to the entity by its constituent documents. If it purports to act beyond these powers, *ultra vires*, any purported contract will be null[1]. An unincorporated association, such as a club, has no legal personality and therefore cannot make contracts on its own behalf: instead, office holders contract on behalf of the membership under the rules of the club which in themselves form a contract between all the members[2]. A trade union has the power to contract by virtue of statute[3].

1 However, the effect of the *ultra vires* doctrine with regard to corporations has been significantly modified: see the Companies Act 2006, s 39. Note also the Local Government (Contracts) Act 1997, enacted to prevent the *ultra vires* doctrine impeding public/private partnership schemes.
2 2 *Stair Memorial Encyclopaedia* paras 801–819.
3 Trade Union and Labour Relations (Consolidation) Act 1992, s 10.

4.13 The capacity of children and young persons to enter into voluntary obligations is governed by the Age of Legal Capacity (Scotland) Act 1991 (ALCSA 1991). As a general principle, a young person below the age of 16 has no capacity to enter into legal transactions[1]. When a child under 16 purports to contract, the apparent contract is null. Instead, any contract must be made on the child's behalf by the child's legal representative who will usually be the child's parent. When such a contract is prejudicial to the child's interests, the child's remedy will be against the parent[2]; the child has no right to reduce the contract made on her behalf by the parent and the third party. For example, A, a child aged ten, owns a house which was bequeathed to A by her grandmother. Suppose that B, the child's parent, sells the house to C on behalf of A. If the house was sold for less than its market value, A cannot have the sale between B and C set aside. Instead, A is entitled to call upon B to account for his intromissions with A's property when B ceases to be the child's legal representative. As this example illustrates, although a child below the age of 16 has no *active* legal capacity, ie cannot enter into legal transactions on her own behalf, the child does enjoy *passive* legal capacity, ie can have rights such as ownership of property.

1 ALCSA 1991, s 1(1)(a).
2 Children (Scotland) Act 1995 (CSA 1995), s 10.

4.14   There are important exceptions to the general rule that a child below the age of 16 has no active legal capacity. For our purposes, the most important exception is that a child below the age of 16 has the capacity to enter into a legal transaction provided (a) the transaction is of a kind commonly entered into by persons of the child's age and circumstances, and (b) the transaction entered into is one whose terms are not unreasonable[1]. Both limbs of the provision must be fulfilled if the transaction is to be treated as valid and not null. First, the contract must be of the kind *commonly* entered into by children of that age and circumstances. So for example, when a child of eight purchases a soft drink or sweeties or cinema tickets or a local bus ticket, the contract is prima facie valid as children of eight commonly enter into such transactions. Contrast these contracts with, for example, the purchase of a music centre or a plane ticket to the USA or a holiday in the Bahamas. These transactions are not commonly entered into by eight-year-olds! Second, even if the first limb is satisfied, the terms of the particular contract must not be unreasonable: for example, if the eight-year-old child is charged £100 for an ice cream cone. In that situation, the apparent contract is still null and the child – or his legal representative – can seek repayment of the £100 under principles of unjustified enrichment. If a child has received goods or services under a null contract and has not paid for them, he cannot be sued in contract for the price. But the other party may have a claim in recompense or restitution of the property again under principles of unjustified enrichment.

1 ALCSA 1991, s 2(1).

4.15 When a young person reaches the age of 16, she has full legal capacity to enter into legal transactions[1]. Nevertheless, special protection exists when the young person makes a contract between the ages of 16 and 18[2]. When such a contract is made, the young person can apply to a court to have the contract set aside on the ground that it was a prejudicial transaction. The young person can do so at any time before she reaches the age of 21. A prejudicial transaction is defined as a transaction which (a) an adult, exercising reasonable prudence, would not have made if he had been in the circumstances of the young person at the time the young person entered into the transaction; and (b) has caused or is likely to cause substantial prejudice to the young person[3]. For example, a young person aged 17 buys a second hand car for £5,000. It breaks down. The repairs will cost £2,000 and the car is worth only £1,000. The young person can have the contract set aside since an adult, exercising reasonable prudence, would not have bought such a car for that price and the contract has caused substantial prejudice to the young person. In effect, this provision allows a court to reduce the contract. In these circumstances, it is thought that the contract cannot be set aside if *restitutio in integrum* is not possible. So if in the example the car had been 'written off' by the young person before he applied to have the transaction set aside, the court could not do so as *restitutio in integrum* is not possible.

1 ALCSA 1991, s 1(1)(b).
2 ALCSA 1991, s 3(1).
3 ALCSA 1991, s 3(2).

4.16 Because of the possibility of having a contract set aside until the young person reaches 21, *all* the parties concerned can make an application to the court to have the proposed transaction ratified[1]. The court *must* ratify the proposed transaction unless satisfied that an adult exercising reasonable prudence would not have entered into the transaction if the adult was in the same circumstances as the young person. If the court ratifies the transaction, it can no longer be set aside as a prejudicial transaction[2]. In practice, ratification proceedings are most likely to be used when a young person between the ages of 16 and 18 purports to sell land, for example a house she has inherited from a deceased grandparent. Then the purchaser would be advised to have the purported sale ratified so that the contract cannot be reduced before the young person reaches the age of 21. It is ironic that a purchaser of land is in a stronger position if he buys a house owned by a child under the age of 16 from the child's legal representative than from a child aged 17 who prima facie has full legal capacity. For as we have seen, in the case of a child under the age of 16, the contract of sale cannot be reduced *vis a vis* the purchaser even if the sale was prejudicial to the child; instead, the child's only recourse is against her legal representative.

1 ALCSA 1991, s 4.
2 ALCSA 1991, s 3(3)(j).

4.17 Apart from contracts which have been ratified, certain other transactions made when a young person is between the ages of 16 and 18 cannot be set aside as a prejudicial transaction. These include the exercise of testamentary capacity, agreement to adoption orders, consent to medical procedures and taking steps in civil proceedings[1]. If a young person lied about his age or affirmed the transaction on reaching 18, he is barred from bringing an action to set aside the transaction[2]. Where a young person between the ages of 16 and 18 is engaged in a trade, business or profession, any contract made in the course of his trade, business or profession cannot be set aside as a prejudicial transaction[3]. For example, a young person aged 17 sets up in business as a cleaner. He buys a second hand van for £5000 and it breaks down frequently. Even if the van is useless and he could have purchased an adequate van for £500, he cannot have the contract set aside as a prejudicial transaction as the contract was made in the course of his business.

1 ALCSA 1991, s 3(3)(a), (c), (d) and (e).
2 ALCSA 1991, s 3(3)(g) and (h).
3 ALCSA 1991, s 3(3)(f).

4.18 The current regime on legal capacity of children and young persons can be criticised on several grounds. It is complex and unlikely to be understood by adults, let alone children and young persons. In relation to children below the age of 16, it is surely a serious defect that they have no recourse against third parties who have made contracts with their legal representatives which are prejudicial to the child. This is particularly unfortunate, given that a ratification procedure exists to protect *both* the young person and the third party when a contract is proposed between the third party and a young person between the ages of 16 and 18. Moreover there are important exceptions to the general rule that a child below the age of 16 has no legal capacity. It should be noticed that in these cases 12 often becomes the relevant age or, at least, the age when a presumption applies that the child has sufficient understanding of the implications of the legal transaction[1]. It could be argued, therefore, that 12 rather than 16 should be the general rule. Moreover, given the paucity of case law concerning young persons between the ages of 16 and 18, it is doubtful whether the extra layer of protection in respect of legal transactions entered into at that age is necessary.

1 Eg in relation to the exercise of testamentary capacity. See also CSA 1995, s 6(1).

4.19 In spite of the fact that the ALCSA 1991 was a measure introduced by the Scottish Law Commission after elaborate consultation[1], it is submitted that the law is not satisfactory and should be the subject of further reform.

1 Report on the Legal Capacity and Responsibility of Minors and Pupils (Scot Law Com no 110) (1987).

Improper negotiations and abuse of position

4.20 Civilian systems classically know three grounds of challenge to contracts: force, fraud and error[1]. This was true of Scots law until the nineteenth century when further grounds of invalidity were developed partly borrowed from English law. In this section, we will deal with force, then with fraud and its progeny, facility and circumvention, before turning to undue influence. These may be grouped together because they involve the use of improper negotiating techniques or the abuse of a position of trust to obtain the other party's consent to an agreement. Error, which raises rather different issues, is treated in the next, separate section.

1 *Zweigert and Kötz*, ch 38; Sefton-Green (ed) *Mistake, Fraud and Duties to Inform in European Contract Law* (2005). Note also DCFR Book II ch 7 (invalidity for mistake (including misrepresentation), fraud and threats). See also Du Plessis and McBryde, 'Defects of consent', in *Zimmermann Visser and Reid* (2004); Du Plessis 'Threats and excessive benefits or unfair advantage' in *MacQueen & Zimmermann* (2006).

(1) Force and fear (extortion or duress)[1]

4.21 When a person's rational exercise of his will has been totally excluded as a result of force exerted against him and consequent fear then any purported voluntary obligation entered into while in that state is null. The situation envisaged is that a person's will has been completely overborne as a result of torture or physical coercion or having been put into an hypnotic trance. The purported voluntary obligation amounts to enforced simulation of consent and is consequently null. Apart from terrorist activities, in modern times such situations are, we trust, rare. More common is the situation where a person's will is not completely overborne but as a result of improper pressure consent is given, albeit reluctantly ie it is not 'free and untrammelled'. In these circumstances, the contract can be annulled. It has been held in one case that the pressure need not come from the other contracting party but from a third person[2]; and the threat may likewise be to a third person, for example a close relative of the victim[3].

1 See generally Du Plessis, *Compulsion and Restitution* (Stair Society vol 51 2005).
2 *Trustee Savings Bank v Balloch* 1983 SLT 240.
3 *Priestnell v Hutcheson* (1857) 19 D 495.

4.22 Force and fear may not be the best term for this ground of challenge since it is not the law that both elements are essential. It has been suggested that 'or' should replace 'and' in the phrase, which reflects the Roman *vis ac metus* or that it should be replaced altogether by the word 'extortion' (for which there is the authority of Stair)[1]. The English term is 'duress'. However, we will follow the customary usage in what follows.

1 *McBryde* para 17.01; see Stair *Institutions* I, 9, 8.

4.23 It has been contended that before force and fear can be operative, the pressure exerted must be such that a person of reasonable fortitude would have submitted to the duress. In our view, the test should not be entirely objective. The question should not be whether a reasonable person could withstand the pressure but rather whether a reasonable person would infer from the evidence that the *victim's* consent has been involuntarily obtained. Thus the particular characteristics of the victim will be relevant, for example age, sex or state of health. The more trivial the actings alleged to constitute extortion, the less likely that a reasonable observer would conclude that the consent was involuntary.

4.24 What kind of conduct constitutes duress? First, if the victim is threatened with unlawful conduct, duress can be established: for example, if A threatens to assault B[1] or A threatens to defame B, then B may plead force and fear. Where the threatened conduct is lawful, prima facie there is no ground upon which to plead duress: for example, to threaten to take court proceedings to enforce a debt which is due. Second, if the threat of lawful conduct is used to obtain money which is not due or to compel the victim to enter into an obligation he would otherwise not have undertaken, then the pressure becomes illegitimate and duress can be pleaded[3]. For example, if A discovers that B had once committed a crime, a threat to tell the police unless B pays £100 *which he owes to* A is not illegitimate and does not constitute duress: but if A threatens to tell the police unless B pays A £100, then the threat is illegitimate and constitutes extortion[4]. Indeed, A is guilty of the crime of extortion![5]

1 *Earl of Orkney v Vinfra* 1606 Mor 16481; see also *Barton v Armstrong* [1976] AC 104.
2 *Priestnell v Hutcheson* (1857) 19 D 495.
3 *Hislop v Dickson Motors (Forres) Ltd* 1978 SLT (Notes) 73; *Euan Wallace & Partners v Westcot Homes plc* 2000 SLT 327 (not an illegal or unwarrantable act to report to the prosecution authorities actings which were genuinely believed to be criminal even if the actings, viewed correctly, were not criminal).
4 This was the situation in the *Hislop* case above. Put another way, force and fear arise if the threat itself is illegitimate or the threat is imposed to achieve an illegitimate result.
5 There may also have been a delict: see Du Plessis, *Compulsion and Restitution*, para 4.4. Cf *McBryde* para 17.01.

4.25 Where these problems become acute is when the threat amounts to economic pressure to enter into an obligation. A person is entitled to use their full economic power to strike the best possible bargain when negotiating a contract. In other words, A is entitled to put economic pressure on B to conclude a contract which is favourable to A. If for example, A knows that B is having cash flow difficulties, A can use that knowledge to force B to contract on terms which are advantageous to A: A, of course, runs the risk that because of his financial difficulties, B might go bankrupt before the contract is performed. Similarly, A can threaten to undercut B's prices and put B out of business unless B is prepared to contract on A's terms. In a capitalist society, A's methods are not considered illegal as they encourage competition in a free market economy[1]: since the pressure is merely economic, it does not matter that B agrees to contractual terms which he would not otherwise have undertaken.

1 See above all *Allen v Flood* [1898] AC 1.

4.26 However, the economic pressure induced by A must not involve unlawful means. Consider the following examples:

- A threatens B that unless B contracts on A's terms, A and C will combine together to put B out of business. If their predominant motive is to harm B, then A and C are guilty of conspiracy which is a civil wrong (delict)[1]. The threat is therefore of unlawful conduct and B can plead economic duress[2].
- A has a contract with B. A threatens to break the contract unless B agrees to a variation to A's advantage or enters into a new, less favourable, contract with A. As A has threatened to breach an existing contract with B, this amounts to unlawful means and B can plead economic duress[3].
- B has a contract with C. A threatens to induce C to breach his contract with B. Since it is a civil wrong (delict) to induce a breach of contract[4], A is threatening unlawful means, and B can plead economic duress in respect of any contract he concludes with A while under that pressure[5].

Accordingly, where one party contracts under economic pressure induced by the other party's threat of unlawful conduct – an economic civil wrong or breach of an existing contract – then the contract can be annulled on the ground of economic duress. In taking up this position Scots law would be following in the path of the English authorities.

1 On which see Thomson *Delictual Liability* (4th edn, 2009) paras 2.6–2.8.
2 *Universe Tankships Inc of Monrovia v International Transport Workers Federation and Laughton* [1983] AC 366.
3 See *Occidental Worldwide Investment Corp v Skibs A/S Avanti* [1976] 1 Lloyds Rep 293; *North Ocean Shipping Co Ltd v Hyundai Construction Co Ltd* [1979] QB 705; *Pao On v Lau Yiu Long* [1980] AC 614 (PC).
4 See *Thomson* para 2.2 ff. The law in this area has been recast by the House of Lords in *OBG Ltd v Allan; Douglas v Hello; Mainstream Properties Ltd v Young* [2008] 1 AC 1.
5 *B & S Contracts & Design Ltd v Victor Green Publications Ltd* [1984] ICR 419.

(2) Fraud

4.27   Traditionally, fraud has been regarded as a ground of annulment in Scotland. Fraudulent conduct was widely defined; most famously, perhaps, by Erskine, as 'a machination or contrivance to deceive'[1]. The concept was given quite a broad meaning in Scots law until, under the influence of English law[2], it was restricted to cases where the fraudster clearly *intended* to deceive his victim[3]. In our view, the reason in modern law why fraudulent conduct may render a contract null is because the innocent party has been induced to enter the contract under error[4]. Put another way, the law on error induced by misrepresentation has overtaken the old-fashioned concept of annulment of a contract on the ground of fraud per se. Fraud remains important for two reasons. First, liability for fraudulent conduct cannot be excluded by an exemption clause[5]. Second, when a party has been induced to enter a contract as a result of a fraudulent misrepresentation, not only can the contract be rendered null but the innocent party can also claim damages in delict[6]. Reduction is not a prerequisite for an action in damages.

1 *Institute* III, 1, 16.
2 In particular, *Derry v Peek* (1889) 14 App Cas 337.
3 *Wright v Cotias Investments Inc* 2001 SLT 353; *McBryde* ch 14; *Defective Consent and Consequential Matters* Scot Law Com Memorandum no 42 (1978), Vol 2, Pt III.
4 See further below, paras 4.40 and 4.57 ff.
5 *H & J M Bennett (Potatoes) Ltd v Secretary of State for Scotland* 1988 SLT 390.
6 See *Thomson* paras 2.10 ff; 11 *Stair Memorial Encyclopaedia* paras 701–789.

(3) Facility and circumvention

4.28 A contract can be annulled on the ground of what is known as facility and circumvention. The doctrine developed out of the wider concept of fraud in the nineteenth century and took on its own life as fraud was progressively narrowed down. A person is facile when owing to age, bodily infirmity, distress or mental health, she is in a weak state of mind and thus liable to be influenced by persuasion or intimidation to act against her own interests[1]. Where the weakness is a result of mental illness, it must not amount to insanity: as we have seen, if a person is insane, she has no legal capacity and any purported contract or promise is null[2]. When a contract is to be reduced on this ground not only must the party be shown to have been facile at the time the contract was made but also it must be proved (i) that the contract was to her disadvantage (lesion) and (ii) she was induced to enter into the transaction as a result of fraud and circumvention. While lesion will be readily apparent, it may be difficult to establish circumvention. The gist of circumvention is that a person has taken dishonest advantage of the facile person's condition to induce her to enter into a disadvantageous contract or unilateral obligation. This can be done by persuasion; for example when an avaricious relative persuades an old lady to sell him her house at a very low price by smooth talking and smarmy charm. It can also be done by intimidation; for example if the relative threatens to send the old lady to a home unless she sells him her house for a modest sum. When the degree of facility and lesion is great, the easier it will be to infer circumvention and vice versa[3]. When the contract has been entered into at arms' length, it will be necessary to establish deceitful and dishonest conduct from which circumvention can be inferred, particularly if it is alleged that a person was facile because of a physical injury such as a broken leg[4].

1 See for example *Anderson v The Beacon Fellowship* 1992 SLT 111.
2 See above, para 4.11 ff.
3 See, eg, *MacGilvary v Gilmartin* 1986 SLT 89.
4 *Mackay v Campbell* 1967 SC (HL) 53, criticised by *McBryde* para 16.20.

(4) Undue influence

4.29 A contract can be annulled where a party's consent was obtained as a result of undue influence, a doctrine partially received into Scots from English law in the later nineteenth century[1]. The gist of undue influence is that one party has assumed a position of dominant or ascendant influence over the other and has abused this position of confidence and trust by entering into a contract with the subservient party. It differs from facility and circumvention where advantage is taken of some weakness because here it is trust or affection which is exploited. While there is no presumption of undue influence arising from particular relationships in Scots law[2], a dominant or ascendant position will be readily inferred where the parties are parent and child, lawyer and client or doctor and patient. In *Honeyman's Executors v Sharp*[3], it was held that such a relationship could arise between a professional adviser and a client who over a period had placed her trust in his professional judgment. It must then be shown that the dominant party received a substantial benefit from the contract. This could be a gift (a gratuitous benefit) or a benefit obtained for a grossly inadequate consideration. Finally, if the subservient party did not receive independent advice, undue influence will be inferred unless the dominant party can show that the subservient party's position was as good as if she had had such advice. For example, A sells her house to her solicitor for £20,000. In fact the house is worth £200,000. The contract can be annulled on the ground of undue influence if (i) the solicitor had a dominant position of influence over A – which will be readily inferred from their relationship of law agent and client; (ii) the price of £10,000 is grossly inadequate – which at

10 per cent of the market value it is; and (iii) A did not receive independent advice. Because the contract is only annullable, it cannot be reduced if *restitutio in integrum* is not possible; for example, if the property had been sold to a bona fide purchaser for value before A sought reduction.

1 See *McBryde* paras 16.22–16.36; Winder 'Undue influence in English and Scots law' (1940) 56 LQR 97. Modern Civilian systems are introducing kindred doctrines: see, eg, Dutch NBW art 3:44(4) (abuse of circumstances). See also DCFR II.-7:207 (excessive benefit or unfair advantage).
2 Unlike English law.
3 1978 SC 223.

(5) Abuse of good faith

4.30   When the parties to a contract are married or in a civil partnership or cohabiting, there is no *presumption* of undue influence between them. It is, of course, open to a husband (H), for example, to prove that his wife (W) had assumed a dominant position over him which she abused when he entered into a contract with her for grossly inadequate consideration and without independent advice. Then the contract could be reduced on the ground of undue influence. It will be noticed that if such a plea was successful, it is the contract *between* the spouses which will be annulled.

4.31   But consider the following situation. H and W own the matrimonial home in common. H's business is in financial difficulties. H's bank (B) will not make any further advances unless H provides further security. W agrees with B that she will act as cautioner for H's debts, ie she enters into a contract with B to pay H's debts to B if H fails to do so. In addition, she grants a standard security to B over *her* one half *pro indiviso* share of the house. If H fails to pay his debts to B, can B call up the standard security over W's share of the house and enforce her cautionary obligation? In *Smith v Bank of Scotland*[1], the House of Lords applied its earlier decision in the English case of *Barclays Bank v O'Brien*[2] and held that the security could only be called up if B had acted in good faith towards W throughout the transaction. Where a reasonable creditor (B in our example) would believe that, because of the personal relationship between the debtor (H) and the potential cautioner (W), W's consent to the transaction was not fully informed, B was under a duty to act in good faith towards W. At the very least, B would be under a duty to warn W of the consequences of the transactions and to suggest she seeks independent advice before undertaking the cautionary obligation. As B had fulfilled none of these duties in *Smith*, W was entitled to have the cautionary obligation and the standard security reduced.

1 1997 SC (HL) 111.
2 [1994] 1 AC 180.

4.32   It is now established that the creditor's obligation of good faith does not arise unless the debtor has *in fact* acted under the undue influence of her partner or under an error induced by the partner's misrepresentation[1]. If a reasonable person in the position of the creditor would have inferred from her relationship that the debtor's consent might not have been freely given, the contract between the debtor and creditor can be set aside on the ground of such undue influence or error unless the creditor has fulfilled the obligation of good faith. Moreover the obligation of good faith does not arise if the debtor receives any benefit from the transaction, for example an increased borrowing facility from the creditor[2]. In this way the principle in *Smith v Bank of Scotland*[3] has been kept within the narrowest of limits. That said, within its limited sphere there is no reason why it should be confined to spouses and civil partners and should at least extend to opposite sex and same sex cohabitants. Indeed, there is no reason why it should not be even wider; for example, a parent or grandparent who is prepared to act as cautioner for a child or grandchild's debts[4].

1 *Clydesdale Bank v Black* 2002 SC 555 approving *Braithwaite v Bank of Scotland* 1999 SLT 25 and *Wright v Cotias Investments Inc* 2001 SLT 353.
2 *Royal Bank of Scotland v Wilson* 2004 SC 153.
3 1997 SC (HL) 111.
4 *Wright v Cotias Investments Inc* 2001 SLT 353.

4.33   It appears settled that the creditor can fulfil his obligation of good faith by advising the potential debtor of the nature of the transaction and suggesting that she obtains independent legal advice[1]. When the potential debtor has a solicitor who appears to represent her interests, the creditor can assume that she was properly advised even though the solicitor was also acting for her partner[2].

1 *Clydesdale Bank v Black* 2002 SC 555: the detailed duties under the analogous doctrine in English law laid down in *Royal Bank of Scotland v Etridge (No 2)* [2002] 2 AC 773 do not apply in Scots law.
2 *Forsyth v Royal Bank of Scotland* 2000 SLT 1295; *Ahmed v Clydesdale Bank* 2001 SLT 423.

4.34 It will be clear that the obligation of good faith laid down in *Smith* has received a very subdued welcome in Scotland. In these circumstances it is perhaps very unlikely that a duty to contract in good faith will be extended beyond cautionary obligations[1]. Some of the doctrines we have already examined, in this chapter and elsewhere[2], could be treated as aspects of a good faith doctrine, for example force and fear, undue influence and implied terms. Yet a general duty to contract in good faith rests uneasily with the principle of freedom of contract, ie a party's right to negotiate the most favourable bargain *provided* he does not contravene certain well-established rules which constitute grounds to have the contract set aside. As we have seen, these grounds are narrow given the law's predilection to uphold rather than strike down contracts which are apparently valid ie where a reasonable person would conclude that *consensus in idem* had prima facie been reached.

1 See above, para 1.57. For varying views see Forte (ed) *Good Faith in Contract and Property* (1999), especially the contributions of the editor and the present authors; and note MacQueen 'Good faith' in *MacQueen & Zimmermann* (2006).
2 See above, paras 2.89 ff, 3.34, 4.21 ff and 4.29 ff. See also below, para 4.53 ff.

Error

(1) Introduction

4.35 It is well recognised that an apparent contract may be null or annullable because the consent of the parties or one of the parties was vitiated or flawed as a result of error. The theoretical basis of the doctrine of error and its scope have been the matter of much academic controversy. It is not proposed in this introductory text to discuss the historical development of the doctrine of error or engage in a critical analysis of the literature on the subject[1]. Instead, an attempt will be made to give as simple an account of the current law as the state of the authorities will allow[2].

1 For these see *McBryde* ch 15; and the same author's 'A note on *Sword v Sinclair* and the law of error' 1997 JR 281 and 'Error' in *Reid & Zimmermann* (2000). See also 15 *Stair Memorial Encyclopaedia* paras 680–694; Gloag & Henderson (13th edn, 2012), paras 7.21–7.33; MacLeod 'Before Bell: the roots of error in the Scots law of contract' (2010) 14 EdinLR 385.
2 See, however, Thomson 'The effect of error in the Scots law of contract' [1978] *Acta Juridica* 135, and 'Error revised' 1992 SLT (News) 215.

4.36 There is no doubt that at one time the scope of error as a ground for annulment of a contract was, in theory at least, potentially wide. Stair boldly stated that 'Those who err in the substantials of what is done, contract not'[1]. But Stair also recognised that a person seeking relief on the ground of error faced great difficulties: 'But the exception upon error is seldom relevant, because it depends upon the knowledge of the person erring, which he can hardly prove'[2]. So even in the seventeenth century, in practice error was of limited utility as a ground of annulment. From the nineteenth century onwards, the doctrine received a further set back when the Scottish courts accepted that *consensus in idem* should be tested objectively. This meant that where agreement had been inferred from an objective assessment of the parties' acts, a party's *subjective* error could not be used to deny the existence of a contract. Yet justice demanded that when a party had contracted under error, *sometimes* he should be entitled to be freed from performance of his obligations. This led to the recognition that when a party's error had been induced as a consequence of a misrepresentation made to him by the other party or his agent this constituted a ground to have the contract reduced[3].

1 Stair *Institutions* I, 10, 3.
2 Stair *Institutions* I, 10, 3.
3 See in particular the classic cases of *Stewart v Kennedy* (1890) 17 R (HL) 25 and *Menzies v Menzies* (1893) 20 R (HL) 108.

4.37   The difficulty with any exposition of the doctrine of error is that while the parameters of the doctrine are relatively easy to determine, there remains a tension in the case law between the earlier, arguably more liberal, application of the doctrine and the more restrictive approach evident in more recent times. An important factor is that as a result of the development of other principles, a person who has contracted under error may not be able to obtain reduction on that ground but will, nevertheless, have an alternative remedy, for example to obtain damages[1]. The discussion falls into three parts, namely:

• error that prevents the formation of the contract;
• uninduced error as a ground of annulment; and
• error induced by an operative misrepresentation as a ground of annulment.

1 See further above, para 3.16 ff and below, para 4.63 ff.

(2) Error that prevents the formation of the contract – *dissensus*

4.38   It has been emphasised throughout this book that in Scots law *consensus in idem* is objectively ascertained. Nevertheless, parties can enter into a contract under an error which is so fundamental that a reasonable person examining the evidence of their acts cannot infer that agreement was reached, ie on objective criteria there was no *consensus in idem* because as a result of the parties' error there is – objectively – no congruence of offer and acceptance. In other words, there is *dissensus* and no contract has been formed. In these circumstances, the purported contract is null.

4.39   We have already seen an example of *dissensus* in the case of *Mathieson Gee (Ayrshire) Ltd v Quigley*[1]. Here one party's offer contemplated a contract of hire while the other party's 'acceptance' contemplated a contract of services: after construing the documentary evidence, the House of Lords held that an objective observer could not infer that an agreement had been reached. As a result of their error as to the nature of the purported contract, the offer and acceptance were incongruent and no *consensus in idem* had been reached. *Raffles v Wichelhaus*[2] provides another striking illustration of the operation of the principle, albeit that it is an English decision. Here the purported contract was for the sale of the cargo on board the good ship, *Peerless*, which was due to set sail from India. In fact, two ships named *Peerless* were due to set sail within a few months of each other. It was established that the offer was made on the assumption that the ship concerned was *Peerless I*, while the acceptance was made on the premise that the ship was *Peerless II*. The court held that on objective criteria the parties had never reached agreement as a result of their error as to the subject matter of their purported contract. The purported contract had never been formed because the offer and acceptance were not congruent. In Scots law, this is a case of *dissensus* where the purported contract is null.

1   1952 SC (HL) 38; discussed above, para 2.7.
2   (1864) 2 H&C 906. On the factual background to this case, in particular the total of 11 ships called *Peerless* sailing the seven seas in the 1860s, see Simpson *Leading Cases in the Common Law* (1995) pp 135–162.

4.40   In these examples, both parties were under error as to the nature of the contract in the first case and the subject matter of the contract in the second. *Dissensus* can also arise where only one of the parties is in error, at least when that error has been induced by the misrepresentation of the other party. In *Morrisson v Robertson*[1], a rogue, Telford, fraudulently misrepresented to Morrisson that he was the son of Wilson of Bonnyrigg, a dairyman of good credit. Telford then purported to buy two cows from Morrisson, on behalf of Wilson. When he obtained the cattle – without, of course, paying – Telford sold them to Robertson, a bona fide purchaser for value. The Inner House held that no contract had been formed between Morrisson and Telford, acting as agent for Wilson. As a result of Telford's fraud, Morrisson made an offer to sell the cows to Wilson, an offer which could only be accepted by Wilson or his genuine agent. Since Telford was not Wilson's agent, he could not accept the offer on his behalf. Accordingly, owing to Morrisson's error as to Telford's identity, induced by Telford's misrepresentation, Morrisson's offer had – on objective criteria – never been accepted. Any purported contract was null and Telford was a thief. Consequently, Morrisson retained the ownership of the cows and could vindicate them from Robertson. This case shows that an error as to the identity of a party can prevent the formation of a contract, ie give rise to a case of *dissensus* when the purported contract is null. It also illustrates that such an error can be induced as a result of a misrepresentation – which in this case was, of course, fraudulent[2].

1 1908 SC 332.
2 On fraud, see above, para 4.27.

4.41   Because *consensus* is tested objectively, cases of *dissensus* are rare: nevertheless they do arise. In *Shogun Finance Ltd v Hudson*[1] a car dealer agreed a price for the sale of a motor car on hire purchase to a fraudster who produced a stolen driving licence as proof of his identity. The dealer faxed to the finance company a copy of the licence and a draft hire purchase agreement that the rogue had signed forging the signature on the licence. Having completed a satisfactory credit check of the person named on the licence, the finance company approved the sale. At this stage a contract of hire purchase should have been formed between the finance company and the customer under which the company hires out the car to the customer until all the instalments have been paid when the company transfers the ownership of the vehicle to the customer. Although the hirer is not the owner of the car until the end of the period of hire, statute provides that if in breach of the contract of hire purchase the hirer purports to sell the car to a bona fide private purchaser, the latter is to have a good title[2]. The day after he had got possession of the car, the fraudster in *Shogun* sold the car to a bona fide private purchaser. By a majority of 3–2 the House of Lords held that the bona fide private purchaser could not have the benefit of the 1964 Act. Before the Act applied there had to be a valid contract of hire purchase between the hirer and the finance company.

The rogue had lied about his identity and it was clear that the finance company had only intended to contract with the person identified in the driving licence. The contract with the rogue was therefore null and the 1964 Act did not apply. As the owner of the car the finance company could therefore recover it from the bona fide private purchaser.

1 [2004] 1 AC 919. While this is an English case it is thought that it would be followed in Scotland.
2 Hire Purchase Act 1964 ss 27–29.

4.42 One of the reasons why *Shogun* is such an interesting case is that the House of Lords ultimately upheld the interests of a finance company rather than those of a bona fide transferee for value. This is surprising as the interests of bona fide third party purchasers make courts generally reluctant to treat apparently valid contracts as null. Instead, where it is alleged that there has been an error as to the identity of a contracting party, the courts have argued that a contract has nevertheless been formed in spite of the error albeit that the contract may be subject to reduction, ie it is annullable. For instance, in *McLeod v Kerr*[1], Mr Kerr advertised his car for sale. A rogue answered the advertisement. After negotiations, Mr Kerr agreed to sell the car for £385. The rogue paid by cheque. In fact the cheque book had been stolen and the cheque was subsequently dishonoured. Meanwhile the rogue had sold the car to a bona fide purchaser for value. In these circumstances, the Inner House of the Court of Session held that a contract had been formed even although the rogue had used a false name throughout the negotiations. Why? In Lord President Clyde's opinion, 'there was no dubiety in the present case as to the identity of the purchaser, namely, the man who came in answer to the advertisement'[2]. In other words, the seller's offer was made to the person in front of him who had answered the advertisement and who, therefore, unlike Telford in *Morrisson v Robertson*, *had* capacity to accept the offer. A contract of sale had been formed, even though the seller was acting under an error as to the creditworthiness of the purchaser which had been induced by his misrepresentations. Consequently, until the contract and his title were reduced on the ground of misrepresentation, the rogue had title to the car which he could pass to a bona fide purchaser. As this had happened *before* Mr Kerr had sought reduction, it was too late to have the contract set aside as *restitutio in integrum* was no longer possible.

1 1965 SC 253.
2 1965 SC 253 at 256.

4.43   There is little doubt that the court in *McLeod* was anxious to reach a decision which protected the interests of a bona fide third party purchaser for value. Yet it is submitted that the court's reasoning can be defended on the grounds that in *Morrisson* the seller would not have made the offer except to an agent of Mr Wilson: while in *McLeod* the seller was prepared to make an offer to anyone who answered the advertisement. Accordingly, on objective criteria, no contract was made in *Morrisson* while a contract – albeit annullable – was formed in *McLeod*. In the *Shogun* case, again, the finance company clearly intended to contract with an identified person other than the rogue, with whom accordingly no contract was made.

4.44   Whatever difficulties exist in reconciling the decisions, it is unarguable that error – whether or not induced by a misrepresentation – will only prevent the formation of a contract in very exceptional circumstances. The reason is, of course, that *consensus in idem* is tested by objective criteria under the law of Scotland.

(3) Uninduced error as a ground of annulment

4.45   Where a reasonable person would infer that *consensus in idem* has been reached in spite of both parties or one of the parties acting under error, it is submitted that the error can, at best, constitute a ground for reduction, ie the effect of the error is to render the contract annullable. In other words, a contract has been formed but it may be reduced as a result of the error and treated as null. However, unless the error has been induced by a misrepresentation made to one party by the other, the scope of error as a ground of reduction is limited. The traditional exegesis proceeded on the theory that before a contract was annullable, the party's error had to be *in substantialibus*, ie go to the root of the contract. In particular, the discussion has been dominated by Bell's classification of error in substantials into five categories, namely error in relation to (i) the subject of the contract or obligation; (ii) the person who undertakes the obligation; (iii) the price; (iv) quality of thing bargained for; and (v) the nature of the contract[1]. But the classical analysis fails adequately to distinguish when the error results in the contract being null or merely annullable. It will therefore not be followed in the present account. What is accepted, is that uninduced error will not be operative unless it does in fact go to the root of the contract. It is also submitted that uninduced error has no effect unless it is related to provisions of the contract – an *error in transaction*. Where a party enters into a contract under an *error in motive*, the law provides no relief unless that error was induced by the other party's misrepresentation[2]. An example will bring out the distinction:

- A is an avid collector of the art of Picasso. B agrees to sell a 'Picasso' print to A for £10,000. The print is not by Picasso. Since the subject matter of the contract is a 'Picasso', the error goes to the root of the contract. Moreover, it is a provision of the contract that the print is by Picasso. The error is an error in transaction which goes to the root of the contract so that A can reduce the contract and recover the price while, of course, having to return the print. Alternatively, A could sue B for breach of contract if it was a term of the contract that the print was by Picasso.
- A is an avid collector of the art of Picasso. A sees a print which he believes is by Picasso. B agrees to sell the print to A for £10,000. The print is not by Picasso. Since the subject matter of the contract is a print and it is not a provision of the contract that the print is by Picasso, A's error is not in transaction but in motive. A cannot reduce the contract on the ground of uninduced error. Only if the error was induced by B's misrepresentation that the print was by Picasso could the contract be reduced on the ground of error.

1 Bell, *Principles* § 11.
2 This distinction originates in German law: see *Zweigert and Kötz* pp 413–417. The Scottish Law Commission deployed it in Consultative Memorandum no 42 (1978), para 3.49. It is applied in *Angus v Bryden* 1992 SLT 884. See further 15 *Stair Memorial Encyclopaedia* para 686.

4.46 Why does an uninduced error in transaction, if serious enough, constitute grounds for annulment? It is suggested that in many contracts the parties' performance is suspended until certain implied conditions are purified[1]. A condition will only be implied if its purification goes to the root of the contract. If these conditions cannot be purified, the parties are freed from their obligations to perform the contract. If one or both have performed, the contract can still be reduced with the law of unjustified enrichment coming into play to redress any resulting imbalances. It is therefore submitted that where the parties contract under the misapprehension that one or more of these implied suspensive conditions have been purified, the contract can be reduced and treated as retrospectively null if the conditions have not *in fact* been purified. Usually the purification of the condition operates for the benefit of both parties so that either can have the contract annulled if it has not been purified. Sometimes the purification of the condition operates for the benefit of only one of the parties; in this situation, if the condition has not in fact been purified, only that party can seek reduction on the ground of error. Alternatively, he can affirm the contract and sue for damages for breach.

1 On conditions, see above, para 3.57 ff.

4.47   Thus in the first example above, it is an implied condition that the print is by Picasso: this is because the subject matter of the contract is a 'Picasso' which happens to be a print. The fact that it is not by Picasso therefore goes to the root of the contract. If the purification of the condition is only for the benefit of A, A can elect to reduce the contract since he has contracted under the misapprehension that the condition was purified. As the purification of the condition was only for A's benefit, A could affirm the contract in spite of the non-purification and sue for damages if it was a term of the contract that the painting was by Picasso. However, if the purification of the condition was for the benefit of *both* A and B then B is also entitled to seek reduction if the condition was not purified. This would be useful for B if the print was not by Picasso but by Matisse and worth £50,000 rather than £10,000. It is a matter of construction whether the purification of the condition is for the benefit of one or both parties. It could not, for example, be for the benefit of B if B had exempted himself in the contract from any liability for errors as to the authentication of the print.

4.48   Many situations where the courts have given relief for an error in transaction can be analysed in this way. Consider the following example[1]:

A agrees to sell B a picture for £1,000. Prima facie, there is a contract of sale of specific goods. At the time they contract, unknown to A and B, the picture has been accidentally destroyed. The existence of the picture goes to the root of the contract. There is, therefore, an implied suspensive condition that at the time of the contract the picture exists. The purification of the condition is for the benefit of both A and B. Because of their error that the condition was purified when *in fact* it was not, both parties are freed from performance of their obligations and the contract is treated as null[2]. If B has paid the price, he can recover the money from A in an action of repetition as A has no legal basis for retaining the money and would be unjustifiably enriched if he does not return it to B.

If in this example, A had expressly stipulated that the picture existed, ie its existence was a term of the contract, then the purification of the implied suspensive condition that the picture exists only operates for the benefit of B. B's error that the condition is purified renders the contract null. B is therefore freed from his obligation to pay the price. If he has paid, the contract can be reduced and B can recover the price on principles of unjustified enrichment. Alternatively, as it is an express term of the contract that the picture does exist, A can sue B for breach of contract and recover damages for his expectation interest[3].

1 Based on analogy with the English case of *Couturier v Hastie* (1865) 5 HLC 673.
2 There is now a statutory basis for this result: see SGA 1979, s 6.
3 Cf *McRae v Commonwealth Disposals Commission* (1951) 84 CLR 377. In this case McRae recovered the costs of his expedition to salvage a wreck which was not to be found on the reef where the Commission had warranted it would be.

4.49   Of course, it is open to the parties in a contract of sale to stipulate that the risk of the non-existence of the subject matter is to be assumed by the buyer. In these circumstances, a suspensive condition that the goods exist at the time of the contract cannot be implied for the benefit of the buyer (and, indeed, the seller). This is an example of an *emptio spei* (purchase of a hope, as distinct from an expectation). If in our example, A agreed to sell B the picture for £100 but stipulated that he did not know whether it existed, B cannot reduce the contract if the painting does not exist. The subject matter of the contract is not the picture but the *chance* of a bargain for B if the painting exists. The risk that the painting has been destroyed has been assumed by B and so there is no room for an *implied* suspensive condition that it exists: the operation of the doctrine of error is accordingly excluded.

4.50   It is important to emphasise that the implied suspensive condition is that the subject matter exists at the date of the formation of the contract. The condition is purified if the goods exist at that time. If the goods are destroyed *after* the contract has been formed, there is no room for the operation of the doctrine of error. Indeed, the subsequent destruction of the painting in our example would have no effect on the parties' obligations. As the goods are specific, prima facie the ownership of the picture would have passed to B as soon as the contract was formed. B accordingly takes the risk that it might be accidentally destroyed before delivery[1]. If destruction occurs after the contract is formed, B is still therefore obliged to pay the price.

1 SGA 1979, ss 16, 17, 18, rr 1, and 20. However where there is a contract of sale of goods and the buyer is a consumer, the goods remain at the seller's risk until they are delivered to the consumer: SGA 1979, s 20(4). This provision does not apply when both parties are private persons or both are businesses.

4.51   It has been argued that an uninduced error in transaction going to the root of the contract may render a contract annullable. This has been illustrated by the situation where the error related to the *existence* of the subject matter of the contract where there is usually an implied suspensive condition of performance that the property to be sold exists. However, where as in the case of the Picasso print, some quality of the goods is of the essence of the contract, there will be an implied suspensive condition that that quality exists and the doctrine of error will apply if *in fact* it does not[1]. Error as to quality – in the sense of a particular quality related to the subject matter of the contract – is not restricted to contracts of sale. In *Great Peace Shipping Ltd v Tsavliris Salvage Ltd*[2] the defendant hired the plaintiff's ship to go and stand by a vessel in distress. The defendant believed that the plaintiff's ship was only 45 miles from the distressed vessel: in fact she was 410 miles away. After the defendant had hired the services of another vessel which was closer to the distressed ship, he cancelled the contract with the plaintiff. When the plaintiff sued for the cancellation fee stipulated in the contract, the defendant refused to pay arguing that the contract had been formed under the fundamental mistake that the plaintiff's vessel was in close proximity to the distressed vessel. Having construed the contract, the Court of Appeal held that it was not a fundamental condition of the contract that the vessels were in close proximity and at the time the contract was formed it was therefore possible for the plaintiff to perform the contract in the way anticipated by the defendant. The defendant would have expected the plaintiff's ship to continue on her way to the distressed vessel but for the fortuitous discovery of another ship which was closer to her. Accordingly, the plaintiff was entitled to the cancellation fee. It is thought that a Scottish court would have reached a similar conclusion. In the absence of an express provision in the contract, the fact that the ship was 45 miles from the vessel in distress was not an implied suspensive condition whose purification went to the root of the contract. Consequently, in the absence of an operative misrepresentation, the error in relation to the actual location of the ship would not free the parties from performance of their contractual obligations. But it is submitted that the fact that the ship could reach the distressed ship before she sank was an implied suspensive condition so that error would have been operative if the ship had been 4,100 instead of 410 miles away at the time the contract was formed[3].

1 *Wemyss v Campbell* (1858) 20 D 1090.
2 [2003] QB 679.
3 See also *Kyle Bay Ltd v Insurers* [2007] EWCA Civ 547 where the court emphasised that before a mistake would be operative, what the parties believed the subject matter of the agreement to be had to be "essentially and radically" different from what it actually was.

4.52 Similarly, an error as to the extent of property purportedly bought in a contract of sale of land may be sufficiently serious for the court to allow reduction[1]. It will be remembered that a contract for the sale of a real right in land must be constituted in writing. If A agrees to sell land to B, no contract is constituted until the contract is formed in a written document subscribed by the parties. In the written contract (missives of sale), the property described in the contract may be greater or less than the parties intended in their negotiations. If the difference is substantial, the court may be prepared to imply a suspensive condition that the extent of the property in the written contract should correspond to that agreed in the oral negotiations. In these circumstances, the written contract can be reduced on account of the error. An error may also occur when the property is described in the disposition which conveys the ownership of the land to the purchaser when it is registered. In these circumstances, the disposition can also be reduced[2]. But because the written contract and the disposition are only annullable, reduction will be lost if the property has been bought by a bona fide purchaser for value who has relied on the apparently valid written contract or disposition.

1 *Anderson v Lambie* 1954 SC (HL) 43; *Hamilton v Western Bank* (1861) 23 D 1033; *Parvaiz v Thresher Wines Acquisitions Ltd* 2009 SC 151 (purchaser bought shop premises under error that the subjects included toilets which the purchaser had seen when he inspected the property before the sale). In *McLaughlin v Thenew Housing Association Ltd* 2008 SLT (Sh Ct) 137 both parties were in error as to the price of the property sold (a housing association home) as a result of different understandings of the statutory calculation required, and the contract was reduced. Cf *Woods v Tulloch* (1893) 20 R 477.
2 See *Anderson v Lambie* 1954 SC (HL) 43; note also the possibility of rectification, discussed above in para 3.25 ff.

4.53 Where an uninduced error in transaction is unilateral, further difficulties can be experienced by the party who is under the misapprehension should she seek reduction of the contract.

As a general rule, when A enters into negotiations with B, B is entitled to assume that A intends to contract on the terms of her (ie A's) offer. In other words, B is entitled to assume that A means what she says and it is irrelevant that B knows A is making a bad bargain. In so far as there is a principle of good faith in Scots law, it does not prevent one party making a contract at the expense of another. Consider the following example:

A offers a painting for sale at £1,000. B knows that the painting is worth £50,000. B is perfectly entitled to purchase the picture for £1,000 even though B knows that A is under an error as to the value of the picture. Because A offered the painting for sale at that price and because B is entitled to assume that A was prepared to contract on these terms, A cannot rely upon her unilateral, uninduced error in order to have the contract reduced[1].

Contrast the following example:

A and B enter into negotiations for the sale of A's painting. During these negotiations, A maintains that she will only consider a price around £10,000. A decides to sell the picture to B for £9,500. By mistake, she sends B a letter in which she offers to sell the picture for £950. B purports to accept the offer at the price of £950. In these circumstances, A *can* rely on her unilateral, uninduced error as to the price in order to have the contract set aside. Why? Because of their prior negotiations, B knows that A is only prepared to sell at around £10,000. B therefore knows that A's offer to sell at £950 is the result of A's error in expression. B is no longer entitled to assume that A intended to be bound by the terms of her offer. A is therefore not prevented from relying on her error in order to reduce the contract[2].

1   See *Brooker-Simpson Ltd v Duncan Logan (Builders) Ltd* 1969 SLT 304 and *Spook Erection (Northern) Ltd v Kaye* 1990 SLT 676.
2   *Steuart's Trs v Hart* (1875) 3 R 192; *Angus v Bryden* 1992 SLT 884. See also the explanations of *Sword v Sinclair* 1771 Mor 14241 in *Steel v Bradley Homes (Scotland) Ltd* 1972 SC 48 and in McBryde 'A note on *Sword v Sinclair* and the law of error' 1997 JR 281.

4.54   To this extent Scots law will not allow a party 'to snatch at a bargain'. But the scope of the doctrine is kept within the narrowest of limits. The onus rests on the party who made the error in expression to show why the other party is not entitled to assume that she meant what she said: in other words, to demonstrate why she should not be prevented from pleading her unilateral, uninduced error in expression.

4.55 Where the contract relates to the sale of land or other heritable property, no contract is constituted unless there is a written document subscribed by the parties. In such contracts, the parties are assumed to be selling according to the titles. Consequently, a seller cannot plead her unilateral, uninduced error as to the legal effect of the titles in order to set aside the contract. But if it is clear from the evidence that during the negotiations the buyer is aware that the seller was labouring under error as to the legal effect of the titles, then the seller will be allowed to plead her error[1]. This is because the particular purchaser knew and took advantage of the seller's error and does not merit the protection which the purchaser of land usually enjoys. Again, it should be noted that the onus rests on the party under the error to show why in the circumstances the normal rule that she cannot plead uninduced, unilateral error in relation to the titles should not apply. Such cases are very rare. In *Parvaiz v Thresher Wines Acquisitions Ltd*[2], Lord Brodie took the view that if it could be established that the seller's solicitors knew that the purchaser was contracting under the belief that the toilets which he had seen when he inspected the shop were part of the shop premises, then the purchaser would be able to plead his error as the solicitors were not acting in good faith: this was the 'added extra' which made the purchaser's uninduced unilateral error operative. *Parvaiz* is similar to the error in expression cases where it must be shown that during the negotiations the purchaser *in fact* knew that the seller was labouring under an error as to the legal effect of the titles and this error was serious enough to go to the root of the contract.

1 *Steuart's Trs v Hart* (1875) 3 R 192; *Angus v Bryden* 1992 SLT 884 See also the Singaporean website offer case, *Chwee Kin Keong v Digildmail.com Pte Ltd* [2004] SGHC 71, [2005] 2 LRC 28, discussed above para 2.15 n 2.
2 2009 SC 151; noted by Hogg, (2008) 14 Edin LR 286.

4.56 When a person enters into a contract under an error as to the legal effect of the transaction, it is now settled that the contract cannot be reduced unless the error was induced by the misrepresentation of the other party or his agent[1]. For example, if A signs a deed with B under which her property is transferred to B, A cannot obtain reduction merely because she was under error as to the legal effect of the transaction or, indeed, thought that she was entering a completely different contract with B. It is only if A can prove that the error was induced by a misrepresentation made by B as to the legal effect of the transaction that it can be reduced. Moreover, A will lose her right to have the transaction set aside in such circumstances if *restitutio in integrum* is not possible because, for example, bona fide third parties have relied upon A's deed.

1 *Ellis v Lochgelly Iron and Coal Co Ltd* 1909 SC 1278; *McCallum v Soudan* 1989 SLT 523; *Royal Bank of Scotland v Purvis* 1990 SLT 262.

(4) Induced error as a ground of annulment: misrepresentation

4.57   Because an uninduced error must be in transaction and *in substantialibus*, the scope of the doctrine of error as a ground of annulment is kept within the narrowest of limits. However, if an error is induced by a misrepresentation, the contract can be reduced even although the error is in motive and does not go to the root of the contract, ie it is not *in substantialibus*[1].

1 *Ritchie v Glass* 1936 SLT 591.

4.58   Consider the following examples:

- A buys a car from B under the misapprehension that the car will do 50 miles to the gallon. The car only does 25 miles to the gallon. This is not an error in transaction nor does it go to the root of the contract. Accordingly, the contract cannot be reduced on the ground of *uninduced* error.
- B tells A that the car does 50 miles to the gallon. A is induced by B's statement to purchase the car. The car only does 25 miles to the gallon. A can have the contract reduced on the ground that he entered into the contract under an error induced by B's misrepresentation. It does not matter (i) whether or not the error is in transaction or (ii) whether or not the error so induced goes to the root of the contract.

4.59   Before a contract can be reduced, the pursuer must show that the error was induced by what we shall describe as an operative misrepresentation. To be operative, the following criteria must be satisfied[1]:

(1) The misrepresentation must have been made to the pursuer by the other party to the contract or his agent.
(2) The misrepresentation must be an inaccurate statement of fact[2].
    Because of this, certain statements are not regarded as misrepresentations. These include:
    (a) Trade puffs: *verba jactantia*[3].
    (b) Statements of pure opinion: If B tells A that in his opinion

the car does 50 miles to the gallon, prima facie that is not a misrepresentation as it is not a false statement of fact. But if B is lying to A and B knows or does not believe the car does 50 miles to the gallon, the false statement is a misrepresentation since B has misrepresented to A his true state of mind. A person's state of mind is as much a fact as the state of his digestion[4]. If B is in a better position than A to have access to the facts upon which B's opinion is based, in exceptional circumstances the courts have been prepared to hold that B has misrepresented the facts upon which his opinion is based[5].

(c) Statements of future intention: If B tells A that B will do X in the future that is not a misrepresentation as it is not a false statement of fact. But if B lies to A, ie at the time he made the statement B has no intention of doing X in the future, that is a misrepresentation as B has misrepresented his state of mind[6].

(3) The misrepresentation must take the form of a statement or positive misleading conduct made *prior* to the conclusion of the contract. Consistent with the right to negotiate as good a bargain as possible, silence does not usually constitute a misrepresentation.[7] In certain situations, however, the law does recognise a *duty to disclose*; then, a failure to do so will amount to a misrepresentation. A duty of disclosure arises:

(a) if there is a *fiduciary or quasi-fiduciary* relationship between the parties so that they are not at arms' length and are bound to put the other party's interests before their own, for example parent and child, trustee and beneficiary, solicitor and client;

(b) if a statement is made which is believed at the time to be true but which the maker learns is false before the contract is formed (*fraudulent concealment*);

(c) when a person tells a *half-truth*. For example, if A tells B that a nineteenth-century reproduction of a thirteenth-century Italian painting is 'old': A is under a duty not to allow B to conclude the contract under the misapprehension that it is in fact a thirteenth-century Italian painting;

(d) when the transaction is a contract *uberrimae fidei*, ie of the utmost good faith, for example a contract of insurance or partnership[8].

(4) The misrepresentation must in fact have induced the misrepresentee to enter into the contract. The onus rests on the alleged misrepresentee to prove, as a matter of fact, that he was induced to enter into the contract as a result of the

misrepresentation. The misrepresentation does not have to be the only reason the party entered into the transaction but there must be some causative link between the misrepresentation and the fact that the misrepresentee entered into the contract. When a misrepresentee tests the accuracy of the statement himself, the law presumes that he trusted his own judgment and the misrepresentation loses its causative effect[9].

(5) The error induced by the misrepresentation does not have to go to the root of the contract, ie it does not have to be *in substantialibus*. Nevertheless the error has to be material in the sense that the matter misrepresented was sufficiently important that it would have been a factor which would have induced a reasonable person to enter the contract[10].

1 See also on representations above, para 3.14 ff.
2 *Brownlee v Miller* (1880) 7 R (HL) 66; *McGhie v Morrison* 2010 SCLR 652.
3 As to which see above, para 2.13.
4 *Edgington v Fitzmaurice* (1885) 29 Ch D 459 per Bowen LJ at 483.
5 *Brown v Raphael* [1958] Ch 636; *Esso Petroleum v Mardon* [1976] QB 801.
6 *Harvey v Seligmann* (1883) 10 R 680; *Ferguson v Wilson* (1904) 6 F 779; *Bell Bros (HP) Ltd v Reynolds* 1945 SC 213. One of the difficulties facing the pursuer in *Hamilton v Allied Domecq Plc* 2004 SLT 191, rvsd 2006 SC 221, affd 2007 SC (HL) 142, was to establish that an operative misrepresentation had taken place as the defenders had merely explained their reasons for entering into the transaction. But even if the defenders had said that they would have distributed the pursuer's product this would have been a statement of future intention and would not have amounted to a misrepresentation unless fraud had been proved ie it could be established that the defenders were lying to the pursuer at the time.
7 *Hamilton v Allied Domecq plc* 2007 SC (HL) 142. A defender's failure to speak can however give rise to liability in delict if the defender has voluntarily assumed responsibility for the pursuer's financial interests knowing that the pursuer will rely on that assumption: ibid. In these circumstances it could be said that the parties were in a quasi-fiduciary relationship: discussed below.
8 See for discussion of the concept of *uberrima fides* and as to whether it differs from *bona fides*, Forte 'Good faith and utmost good faith: insurance and cautionary obligations in Scots law' in *Good Faith in Contract and Property* (1999).
9 *McLellan v Gibson* (1843) 5 D 1032; *Burnett v Burnett* (1859) 21 D 813.
10 *Menzies v Menzies* (1893) 20 R (HL) 108 per Lord Watson at 142–143, as explained in *Ritchie v Glass* 1936 SLT 591. However, a fraudulent misrepresentation may not have to be material in this sense.

4.60 Because of these complex criteria, it may be difficult to establish that a misrepresentation is operative[1]. But if a party can prove that she entered into a contract under an error induced by an operative misrepresentation then she is entitled to reduction of the contract. This widens the scope of error as a ground of annulment since the error can be an error in motive as well as an error in transaction and, in either case, does not have to be *in substantialibus*. So for example, when a party enters into a transaction under error as to its legal effect, the error does not give rise to reduction if it was uninduced: people should not enter into contracts without taking legal advice! If on the other hand, the error was induced by an operative misrepresentation, the contract can be set aside[2]. In this way a compromise is reached in Scots law between the need for certainty in contractual relations and the desire that sometimes, at least, a party should be able to withdraw from a contract entered into under error.

1 See for example *Hamilton v Allied Domecq Plc* 2006 SC 221.
2 *Stewart v Kennedy* (1890) 17 R (HL) 25; *Menzies v Menzies* (1893) 20 R (HL) 108; cf *Royal Bank of Scotland v Purvis* 1990 SLT 262; *Wright v Cotias Investments Inc* 2002 SLT 353.

4.61 The extent of the compromise is apparent when we consider that a misrepresentation is operative even although it was made innocently ie even although the misrepresentor believed what he was saying was true. If for example, A buys a painting from B as a result of B's statement that the painting was by Bellany, A is entitled to reduce the contract as a result of B's misrepresentation if in fact the painting is not by Bellany. It is irrelevant that B honestly believed that Bellany was the artist. But it should be noted that in this situation, *both* parties are labouring under the error. Because the error was induced by an operative misrepresentation, A is entitled to reduction even though the quality that the picture was by Bellany was not the gist of the contract since an error induced by an operative misrepresentation does not have to go to the root of the contract, ie does not have to be *in substantialibus*.

4.62 When the misrepresentation is *innocent*, ie unintentional and not negligently made, the misrepresentee's only remedy is reduction and restitution of the price: and, as always, *restitutio in integrum* must be possible. Where, however, the statement which forms the basis of the misrepresentation has been incorporated as a term of the contract[1], the misrepresentee can elect to sue for breach of contract as an *alternative* to reduction. In this way, the misrepresentee can recover his expectation interest if that would be greater than the enrichment claim which he can recover if the contract is annulled. So for example, if A had paid £10,000 for a fake Bellany worth £100, he will recover the price if the contract was reduced on the ground of misrepresentation. But if it was a term of the contract that the painting was by Bellany, A should sue for breach of contract if the price for a comparable painting by Bellany has risen to £15,000: then he would obtain £14,900, ie the difference between the value of the painting if the contract had been performed properly (£15,000) and its actual value (£100).

1 See above, para 3.14 ff on this.

4.63 When a misrepresentation is not innocent, the misrepresentee *in addition* to reduction may be entitled to sue for damages in delict. This will arise if the misrepresentation was made *fraudulently or carelessly*. The difficulty in the former case is that the misrepresentee must prove the *mens rea* of fraud, ie that the misrepresentor knew that his statement was false or believed it was false or was recklessly indifferent to whether it was true or false[1]. The difficulty in the latter case is that the misrepresentee must establish (a) that the misrepresentor owed him a duty of care and (b) that that duty was broken as a result of the misrepresentor's carelessness in making the false statement, ie the misrepresentor was negligent. It is submitted that a duty of care arises between parties to a potential contract if one party assumes responsibility for the economic interests of the other, knowing that the other will rely on his expertise[2]. These criteria are most likely to be satisfied when the misrepresentor is in a better position than the misrepresentee to assess the accuracy of the information provided in the pre-contractual statement. The duty will, of course, only be broken if the misrepresentee can prove that the misrepresentor was negligent in making the false statement, for example that he did not check the facts before making the statement when a reasonable person in his position would have done so.

1 *Lees v Todd* (1882) 9 R 807; *Derry v Peek* (1889) 14 App Cas 337. In *Wright v Cotias Investments Inc* 2002 SLT 353, the Lord Ordinary (MacFadyen) laid down the criteria which must be established in an action based on fraudulent misrepresentation. He said at p 366, "In the present case the pursuer must in my opinion aver clearly (i) the representation or representations which she claims were made to her; (ii) that that representation was, or those representations were, untrue; (iii) that the maker of each representation knew at the time when he made it that it was false; (iv) that she was induced by that representation or those representations to enter into the contracts which she now seeks to have reduced; and (v) that there existed at the time each representation was made a relationship between the maker of the representation and the defenders which in law justifies holding the defenders responsible for the representation". See also Thomson *Delictual Liability* paras 2.10 ff. Where there has been a fraudulent misrepresentation, the misrepresentor cannot rely on a entire agreement clause in the contract: accordingly the misrepresentee could still seek rescission of the contract. See *Peart Stevenson Associates Ltd v Holland* [2008] EWHC 1807.

2 *Esso Petroleum v Mardon* [1976] QB 801; *Henderson v Merrett Syndicates Ltd* [1995] 2 AC 145. Scots law has allowed for such development as a consequence

of the Law Reform (Miscellaneous Provisions) (Scotland) Act 1985, s 10: see *Palmer v Beck* 1993 SLT 485; *Clelland v Morton Fraser Milligan* 1997 SLT (Sh Ct) 57. In *Hamilton v Allied Domecq plc* 2001 SC 829 the Lord Ordinary (Carloway) suggested that s 10 equated a negligent misrepresentation with a fraudulent misrepresentation and therefore there was no need to establish a duty of care between the parties. *Hamilton* was followed on this point in *BSA International SA v Irvine* [2010] CSOH 78. Nevertheless it is thought that this is wrong. The purpose of s 10 was merely to abolish the rule in *Manners v Whitehead* which had restricted a right to damages to fraudulent misrepresentation. However where the pursuer and defender are parties to the same contract a duty of care should not be too difficult to establish. See Thomson 'Misrepresentation' 2001 SLT (News) 279.

4.64 It is not a pre-condition of suing in delict that the misrepresentee should seek reduction of the contract. Therefore the misrepresentee can affirm the contract and sue in delict to recover his *status quo* (ie reliance) interest. Consider the following example:

A purchases a sports car from B for £10,000. A was induced to buy the car as a result of B's fraudulent or negligent misrepresentation that the car was once owned by Marilyn Monroe. This is not true. Without the film star connection, the car is only worth £1,000. A could reduce the contract, return the car and recover the price. But if A likes the car, A could sue B in delict and recover his *status quo* (or reliance) interest, namely what he paid for the car (£10,000) less its current value (£1,000) = £9,000. This way, A recovers his out-of-pocket expenses but keeps the car. If the statement that the car belonged to Miss Monroe was also a term of the contract and if it had been true the car would now be worth £15,000, A should sue for breach of contract rather than reduction or in delict. By suing for breach of contract, A recovers his expectation interest, namely the value of the car if the contract had been properly performed (£15,000) less its current value (£1,000) = £14,000.

4.65 This discussion illustrates how important it is to remember that contract is only one part of a unified law of obligations[1]. The principles of the law of contract are also interlinked. It is true that misrepresentation has been used to extend the doctrine of error as a ground of annulment in Scots law. Once the contract has been reduced and is retrospectively null, the way is open through principles of the law of unjustified enrichment to redress any economic imbalances that have occurred. But because of developments in the law of delict, misrepresentation may also give rise to claims for reparation in the way we have described. The misrepresentee can sue in delict whether or not the contract is reduced. Finally, the statement which constitutes a misrepresentation may also have been incorporated as a term of the contract in which case the misrepresentee can sue for breach of contract as an *alternative* to reduction and restitution. Although a contract is defective and annullable, it still subsists as a contract until it is reduced. The decision to seek reduction is entirely a matter for the misrepresentee, ie the misrepresentor cannot compel the misrepresentee to have the contract reduced. When it is in the misrepresentee's interests to do so, he can therefore elect to sue for damages for breach rather than reduction. But the onus lies on the misrepresentee to show that the pre-contractual statement which constitutes the misrepresentation has in fact been incorporated as a term of the contract. This may be difficult[2].

1 In turn, the law of obligations and the law of property form the foundations of private law: see Thomson *Scots Private Law* (2006).
2 Above, para 3.14 ff.

4.66   It should be emphasised that before a misrepresentation is operative it must be a statement which has been made by a party to the contract or her agent. So for example, when A is induced to contract with B as a result of B's misrepresentation, A can seek reduction of the contract on the ground of induced error. But what if A is induced to enter into a contract with B as a result of C's misrepresentation? There is no difficulty if C is acting as the agent of B. But if C is not B's agent, then A cannot reduce the contract with B as a consequence of the error induced by C. While A cannot escape from the contract with B nevertheless A may have a remedy in delict against C for the economic loss sustained by A as a result of the contract with B. If C's misrepresentation was made fraudulently, A can sue C for fraud. If C was careless, A can sue C in negligence if C has assumed responsibility for A's financial interests knowing that A will rely on C's expertise. C will then owe a duty of care to A to prevent A suffering economic loss[1]. This duty will be breached if C's statement was made without the care that the law expects from a reasonable person in C's position. If A has a remedy for breach of contract against B, A must elect whether to pursue an action against B in contract or sue C in delict: this will depend upon whether A's expectation interest which is recoverable in contract against B is greater than the reliance or *status quo* interest which is recoverable in delict against C. If they are the same, A must decide to sue B or C as he cannot be compensated twice for the same loss[2].

1 See for example *Bank of Scotland v Fuller Peiser* 2002 SLT 574; *IFE Fund SA v Goldman Sachs Int* [2007] EWCA Civ 811.
2 Erskine *Institute* III, 1, 15, For full discussion of these delictual issues, see Thomson *Delictual Liability paras* 4.11 ff.

FRUSTRATION

Introduction

4.67 As we have seen, an apparent contract may be null or annullable as a consequence of the doctrine of error. Error is concerned with the parties' misapprehensions *at the time* the purported contract is formed. But as a general rule, events which occur *after* the formation of the contract are irrelevant to the parties' obligations to perform what they have undertaken.

For example, A agrees to sell goods to B for £x. If the market falls so that B could purchase similar goods for £x–y, B is still obliged to buy the goods from A at the contractually agreed price of £x. Conversely if the market rises so that B could sell the goods for £x+y, B is still obliged to sell the goods to A at the contractually agreed price of £x. The expectations of the parties that their contract will be performed according to the agreed terms is, after all, the essence of contractual obligation.

4.68 In exceptional situations, however, an external event may occur which will relieve the parties of their obligation to perform what they have contractually undertaken. In these circumstances, the contract is said to be *frustrated*[1]. At the outset it is important to grasp what happens when a contract is frustrated. A contract has been formed. When a frustrating event occurs, it does not affect the contract. Instead, the parties are automatically freed from their obligation to perform any contractually agreed undertakings which were due to be performed *after* the frustrating event.

1 See generally *McBryde* ch 21; 15 *Stair Memorial Encyclopaedia* paras 880–889.

4.69 Consider the following example. A hires a holiday cottage from B for four weeks in the summer. The rent is £100 per week, payable at the end of each week. Before the holiday is due to begin, the cottage is destroyed by lightning. Prima facie the contract is frustrated. A is relieved from the obligation to pay the rent: B is freed from the obligation to make the cottage available. Suppose, however, that the cottage was destroyed by lightning after A had enjoyed two weeks' holiday. Again, prima facie the contract is frustrated. A is freed from the obligation to pay rent for a further two weeks: B is relieved from the obligation to make the cottage available during that period. Since the parties are only freed from performance in respect of undertakings due to be performed *after* the date of the frustrating event, ie *de futuro* performance, A is not relieved from having to pay rent for the first two weeks of the holiday. If the rent for that period has not been paid before the cottage was destroyed, A is still obliged to pay and if he does not, B can sue him for breach of contract. Conversely, if the cottage was not in a habitable condition prior to the fire, A could sue B for breach of contract.

4.70   Because the contract exists in spite of a frustrating event, its terms remain enforceable. This is important if, for example, the parties had agreed that any dispute should go to arbitration or there was an exemption clause excluding or limiting liability for breach. In particular, the parties may have made express provision in respect of what is to happen if such an event occurs: a *force majeure* clause[1]. In our example, it might have been agreed that in the event of the accidental destruction of the cottage by fire, B should make alternative accommodation available to A and that A should pay rent at the same weekly rate. These clauses operate because the contract continues to subsist in spite of the prima facie frustrating event.

1 For examples see above, para 3.77 and below, paras 4.86 ff.

4.71   How can a subsequent event operate to free the parties of further performance of their contractual undertakings? While the matter is controversial, it is our view that an answer can be found by considering the effect of resolutive conditions[1]. It will be remembered that parties can expressly stipulate that they will be relieved of further performance of their contract if a condition is purified. So for example, A and B may contract that A will hire his car to B for £1,000 a year until B graduates from University. When B graduates, the resolutive condition is purified and A and B are freed from further performance of the contract, ie A is no longer obliged to make his car available to B and B is relieved from his obligation to pay £1,000 a year to A. It is submitted that in the absence of express contractual provisions, the law will imply certain resolutive conditions into contracts. For example, it is an implied resolutive condition that a contract is not incapable of performance. If as a result of a subsequent event, performance of a contract becomes impossible then the implied resolutive condition is purified and the contract is frustrated. Similarly, it is an implied resolutive condition that performance of a contract is not illegal: if as a result of a subsequent event, performance of a contract becomes illegal then the implied resolutive condition is purified and the contract is frustrated. Finally, it is an implied resolutive condition that performance of the contract will not be radically different from that anticipated by the parties at the time of formation: if as a result of a subsequent event, performance of a contract would be radically different from that originally envisaged then the resolutive condition is purified and the contract is frustrated. We shall now consider these situations in more detail.

1 For conditions generally, see above, para 3.57 ff.

When does frustration arise?

(1) Supervening impossibility – *rei interitus*

4.72 When performance of a contract becomes impossible following the destruction of the subject matter of the contract, the contract will be frustrated in the absence of express contractual provisions to the contrary. For example, A agreed to let a music hall to B. When the hall was destroyed by fire before the date of the concert, the contract was frustrated[1]. Both parties were therefore relieved of their obligation to perform. The destruction of the subject matter can be constructive as well as actual. In one case, the parties had leased a furnished mansion for nineteen years. When war broke out, the house was requisitioned by the government and the furniture was put into store. The tenant could no longer use the house as a furnished dwelling. In these circumstances, the court held that the contract was frustrated and the tenant was relieved of the obligation to pay rent for the remaining period of the lease[2].

1 *Taylor v Caldwell* (1863) 3 B & S 826. For a somewhat similar case in Scotland, see *Cantors Properties (Scotland) Ltd v Swears & Wells Ltd* 1978 SC 310. In the latter decision the relevant provision about reinstatement in the event of fire should possibly have been applied.
2 *Mackeson v Boyd* 1942 SC 56.

4.73 A resolutive condition can only be implied if the parties to a contract have not expressly stipulated to the contrary. This is ultimately a question of construction of the terms of the contract. When the parties have clearly undertaken to perform in any event, the doctrine of frustration cannot operate. In *Gillespie v Howden*[1], a shipbuilder agreed to build a ship to certain specifications and warranted that she would carry 1,800 tons of cargo. When the ship was built according to the specifications, she could only carry 1,600 tons. The shipbuilder argued that the original contract had been frustrated because it was physically impossible to build a ship that would carry 1,800 tons of cargo and also meet the specifications. The court held that, since the shipbuilder had expressly warranted that a ship built to those specifications would carry 1,800 tons of cargo, he had undertaken an absolute obligation and, accordingly, there was no room for the operation of the doctrine of frustration. The shipbuilder was therefore liable for breach of contract.

1 (1885) 12 R 800. For another example see *Scottish Coal Co Ltd v Fim Timber Growth Fund III Trustees* 2009 SCLR 630.

(2) Supervening illegality

4.74   When performance of a contract becomes illegal *after* the contract has been formed, the contract will be frustrated. In the leading case of *Cantiere San Rocco SA v Clyde Shipbuilding & Engineering Co*[1], an Austrian firm entered into a contract with the defender, a Scottish company, under which the defender would build a set of marine engines. The price was to be paid in instalments, the first instalment to be paid when the contract was signed. This was duly done. Before the work was begun, the First World War broke out and it became illegal to trade with an Austrian company as it had become an enemy alien. The contract was therefore frustrated and both parties were relieved of further performance of the contract. Frustration would not have operated if the parties had expressly stipulated what was to occur in the event of war between Austria and the United Kingdom: for example, they might have agreed that while performance should be suspended during hostilities, the parties should continue with performance as agreed once peace was restored[2].

1 1923 SC (HL) 105.
2 It should be noted that if a state of war had existed between the United Kingdom and Austria at the time the contract was formed, it would have been an illegal contract and unenforceable from the outset. Frustration only operates when an event, *subsequent to the formation of the contract*, renders *further* performance illegal. In *Robert Purvis Plant Hire Ltd v Farquhar Brewster* [2009] CSOH 28 the Lord Ordinary (Hodge) held that a lease was not frustrated owing to the absence of a supervening event after the lease had been concluded, Lord Hodge provides a useful summary of the law of frustration at paras 10–14. Contracts illegal from the outset are discussed below: paras 7.1–7.24.

(3) Commercial frustration

4.75 A contract may be frustrated if a subsequent event destroys some basic, albeit tacit, assumption upon which the parties have contracted. Put another way, a contract will be frustrated when a subsequent event occurs which goes to the root of the parties' contract in that performance would be radically different from that originally envisaged by the parties when they made the contract. In other words, it is an implied resolutive condition that performance will not be radically different from what, as a matter of construction, the parties intended: if a subsequent event renders performance radically different, the condition is purified and the parties relieved of future performance of the contract. An example will illustrate the point. Suppose A charters a sailing ship from B to sail around the Western Isles during the summer. The ship is damaged in February and she will not be repaired until November. The charterparty will be frustrated and A will no longer be obliged to charter the ship. The parties envisaged the ship being available for the summer months. A winter voyage is radically different from a summer voyage. Consequently, an implied resolutive condition that the ship should not be unavailable during the summer is purified and the parties are freed from further performance of their contract[1].

1 Compare *Jackson v Union Marine Insurance Co* (1874) LR 10 CP 125.

4.76 Before the courts will imply such a condition, they must be satisfied that the subsequent event does indeed render performance *radically* different. It is not sufficient that performance has become less profitable or, indeed, unprofitable for one of the parties: economic hardship *per se* is not frustration[1]. This can be illustrated by the leading case of *Tsakiraglou & Co v Noblee & Thurl GmbH*[2]. The parties had entered a cif contract[3] for the purchase of Sudanese groundnuts. Under the contract, the price included the cost of transport. The seller undertook responsibility for the carriage of the nuts from East Africa to Hamburg where the buyer was located. In determining the price of the nuts, the parties had anticipated that the nuts would be shipped via the Suez canal. After the sale had been agreed, the canal was closed as a result of war. The nuts had to be shipped via the Cape of Good Hope. This increased the transport costs that would still have to be paid out of the agreed price thus lowering the seller's profits. In these circumstances, the seller argued that the contract for the sale of the nuts had been frustrated.

Contract of carriage

The House of Lords held that the contract of sale had not been frustrated. While the voyage around the Cape of Good Hope was longer than via the Suez canal, the nuts would still be fit for human consumption when they arrived in Hamburg. The performance of the contract of *sale* was therefore not radically different from that anticipated by the parties. The only difference was that the seller would make less profit and this was a risk which he undertook in a cif contract where it was his responsibility to arrange for the transport of the goods. It should be noted that the increase in transport costs was not astronomical and the seller would still have made a profit on the sale, albeit a smaller one.

1 *Hong Kong and Whampoa Dock Co v Netherton Shipping Co Ltd* 1909 SC 34; *Robert Purvis Plant Hire Ltd v Farquar Brewster* [2009] CSOH 28 per Lord Hodge at para 14. See further Forte 'Economic frustration of commercial contracts: a comparative analysis with particular reference to the United Kingdom' 1986 JR 1.

2 [1962] AC 93. See also *The Sea Angel* [2007] EWCA Civ 547 (A 20 day charter of a vessel to a salvor to trans-ship oil from a casualty had not been frustrated where before redelivery the vessel had been unlawfully detained for three months by port authorities); *The Mary Nour* [2008] EWCA Civ 856.

3 ie a cost, insurance, freight contract under which the seller's price includes the freight of the goods to their destination and their insurance during transit; the seller's obligations are to ship the goods and transmit to the buyer the shipping documents enabling him to claim the goods.

4.77 Parties may make express provision in their contract on the course of action to be taken if certain events occur. In charterparties for example, it is common to find a clause which stipulates that the owner of the ship should pay the charterer a sum of money for every day that the ship is not ready to load cargo after a specified date. It is a question of construction of the clause whether it is intended to cover all delays *howsoever caused* or whether the clause only applies to delays arising from events commonly occurring in international trade. In the former case, the doctrine of frustration will not operate even if the delay is for a very long period as the owner has expressly undertaken that risk. In the latter, there is room for the operation of the doctrine of frustration if the delay is due to a subsequent event to which the clause was not intended to apply, for example if the ship was not ready to load because she had been requisitioned by the government in time of war[1].

1 *Bank Line v Capel & Co* [1919] AC 435.

4.78 Before frustration can operate, the subsequent event must not have been caused by one of the parties to the contract. In the example of the hall not being available for hire because it had burnt down, the contract would not have been frustrated if the owner of the hall was responsible for the fire. In these circumstances, the owner is guilty of a material breach of contract. In *Maritime National Fish v Ocean Trawlers Ltd*[1], the appellants hired a trawler from the respondents. It was illegal to use the trawler without a licence. The appellants applied for licences for five vessels but were only granted three. They chose to use the licences for vessels other than the trawler they had hired from the respondents. Although performance of the contract had become illegal because the trawler had no licence, the Privy Council held that the contract was not frustrated. The reason why the contract could not be performed was because the appellants had elected not to use one of the licences for that ship. In other words, the non-performance was a result of the appellants' conduct in choosing not to use one of the licences for the respondent's vessel. Accordingly, the contract was not frustrated and the appellants were liable to pay the hire charges.

1 [1935] AC 624. For another possible example see *Scottish Coal Co Ltd v Fim Timber Growth Fund III Trustees* 2009 SCLR 630 per Lord Hodge at para 26.

4.79 In England, frustration may not operate if the subsequent event was caused by the negligence – as opposed to the deliberate acts or omissions – of one of the parties to the contract, but there is contrary authority in Scotland[1].

1 *Joseph Constantine Steamship Ltd v Imperial Smelting Corp Ltd* [1942] AC 154; *The Eugenia* [1964] 2 QB 226; cf *London and Edinburgh Shipping Co Ltd v The Admiralty* 1920 SC 309.

Consequences of frustration

4.80 Where a contract is frustrated, *both parties* are relieved of further performance of the obligations they have undertaken, ie they are freed from performing those obligations which were due to be performed *after* the date of the frustrating event. Frustration operates in respect of *de futuro* performance: it has no retrospective effect on the contract. Where a contract is executory (ie neither side has performed any part of the contract) at the time of the frustrating event, neither party will suffer any loss as a consequence of the doctrine. For example, A hires a holiday cottage from B for four weeks during the summer. The rent is £100 per week payable at the end of each week. Before the holiday is due to begin, the cottage is destroyed by lightning. Prima facie the contract is frustrated. A is relieved of the obligation to pay the rent: B is freed from the obligation to make the cottage available.

4.81   But what would happen if A was contractually obliged to pay a deposit of £100 at the time the contract was formed in addition to the rent at the end of each week? Assuming A has paid the deposit, she loses £100 if the contract is frustrated. Moreover, what would happen if in anticipation of the performance of the contract, B has redecorated the cottage at a cost of £200? Should these losses lie where they have fallen or should the law provide a mechanism to readjust the losses equitably?

4.82   Scots law has attempted to find a solution to these problems through the law of unjustified enrichment[1]. It will be remembered that in *Cantiere San Rocco SA v Clyde Shipbuilding & Engineering Co*[2], the purchasers of the engines had paid the first instalment of the price before the contract was frustrated. After the war, the purchasers[3] sought recovery of the money. The House of Lords held that they were entitled to recover. Because the purchasers had received nothing in return for the payment, the sellers were unjustifiably enriched. The enrichment was reversed on the basis of the *condictio causa data causa non secuta*, ie the action to recover what has been given when the cause of giving it has failed. Put another way, the money transferred was the first instalment of the price. After the contract was frustrated, the transferee was freed from performance of his contractual obligation to deliver the engines. At this stage the transferee has no longer a legal basis to retain the money. Accordingly, the transferee is obliged to return the money since otherwise he would be unjustifiably enriched.

1 *Robert Purvis Plant Hire Ltd v David Farquhar Brewster* [2009] CSOH 28 per Lord
  Hodge at para 14: 'In Scotland the law of unjustified enrichment is available
  in appropriate cases to give a remedy for enrichment at another's loss as a
  consequence of the frustration....Whether the court has a wider power to

apportion losses between the parties is a matter of academic controversy.' In *Lloyds TSB Foundation for Scotland v Lloyds Banking Group plc* [2011] CSIH 87 it was held that the courts have no general power of 'equitable adjustment' of a contract to meet changed circumstances. It is understood that this case is now under appeal to the UK Supreme Court.

2 1923 SC (HL) 105; above, para 4.74.

3 The action was actually brought by assignees of the original purchasers.

4.83 Frustration operates in respect of *de futuro* performance: it does not affect the contract retrospectively. In this, frustration is quite different from, for example reduction. When a contract is reduced, it is retrospectively annulled. Because the contract is treated as null, principles of unjustified enrichment can be used to reverse any enrichments which have arisen as a result of the parties having performed under the misapprehension that the contract was valid. This misapprehension provides the factor which renders the enrichment unjustified: there never was a legal basis for having the benefits the parties may have received. But as the House of Lords clearly recognised in *Cantiere*, frustration does not affect the validity of the contract which continues to subsist in spite of the frustrating event: the parties are only *relieved of future performance* of their obligations. Because the instalment in *Cantiere* was made on the basis that the pursuer would receive the machinery in due course, its retention no longer had a legal basis and the enrichment became unjustified when the sellers were relieved of further performance of their obligations under the contract.

4.84 *Cantiere San Rocco* is authority that principles of unjustified enrichment may operate after partial performance of a contract which has become frustrated. This is because the enrichment was not intended to be absolute but conditional on the contract being performed: when this condition could not be fulfilled as a consequence of the frustrating event there is no longer a legal basis for retaining the benefit and it must be returned since its retention is now unjustified. So in the example of the holiday cottage, A could recover the £100 deposit using the *condictio*. The deposit was made in the expectation that A would have the cottage for four weeks. When the cottage is struck by lightning, B is relieved from performing his contractual obligation to make the cottage available to A. B's retention of the deposit now has no legal basis and must be returned to A as otherwise B would be unjustifiably enriched.

Before these principles are applicable, one of the parties has to have enriched the other. In the example of the cottage, B redecorated the cottage in anticipation of the contract at a cost of £200. B cannot recover any of the expenditure from A as A has not been enriched as a result B's expense. As Lord President Inglis observed in *Watson & Co v Shankland*[1]:

'If a person contracts to build me a house, and stipulate that I shall advance him a certain portion of the price before he begins to bring his materials to the ground, or to perform any part of the work, the money so advanced may certainly be recovered back if he never performs any part ... of his contract. No doubt, if he perform a part and then fail in completing the contract, I shall be bound in equity to allow him credit to the extent to which I am *lucratus* by his materials and labour, but no further; and if I am not *lucratus* at all, I shall be entitled to repetition of the whole advance, however great his expenditure and consequent loss may have been.'

And so in the holiday cottage example, while A can recover the £100 deposit, B is not entitled to any compensation from A for his expenditure in redecorating the cottage since A is not *lucratus*. Nor can B set off any of the cost of redecoration against the £100 deposit even if the deposit was demanded by B in order to enable him to paint the cottage.

1   (1871) 10 M 142 at 152.

4.85   It is submitted that the law of unjustified enrichment is not a suitable basis for redressing losses which occur as a consequence of frustration. Even in situations where relief is given – as in *Cantiere San Rocco* – the solution is doctrinally suspect[1]. Moreover principles of unjustified enrichment cannot accommodate losses arising from one party's expenditure in expectation of performance of a contract if this expenditure has not resulted in a benefit to the other party. In these circumstances, it is thought that a legislative regime is required to provide an equitable readjustment of any losses which the parties have sustained because their contract has been frustrated[2].

1   Evans-Jones *Unjustified Enrichment* (2003) vol 1 ch 6.
2   Compare in England the Law Reform (Frustrated Contracts) Act 1943, applied in *BP Exploration Co (Libya) Ltd v Hunt* [1979] 1 WLR 783 and *Gamerco SA v ICM/ Fair Warning (Agency) Ltd* [1995] 1 WLR 1226.

Force majeure clauses

4.86   In order to avoid some of the difficulties which we have discussed in the preceding section, parties may expressly stipulate in their contract what is to happen if performance becomes impossible as a result of specified, external events: for example, war, acts of nature, strikes, acts of terrorism, falls in the value of currency. These are known as *force majeure* clauses. Because the contract subsists in spite of frustration, these clauses continue to regulate the post-frustration situation. In particular, the clause can provide a mechanism to redress the losses which have occurred as a consequence of partial performance of the contract. Indeed, the clause can go further and provide for renegotiation of the contract in the light of the changed circumstances. In other words, the parties can contract out of the rather rigid regime relating to frustration which Scots law would otherwise provide. An example of a *force majeure* clause is given below:

'In the event of the Contract being frustrated whether by war or by any other supervening event which may occur independently of the will of the parties the sum payable by the Employer to the Contractor in respect of the work executed shall be as follows ... [*the clause then goes on to give details of payment mechanisms*].'

4.87 This clause deals with the consequences of frustration that would otherwise be dealt with by the law of unjustified enrichment. The clause is based on one found in a civil engineering standard form. If for example, a reservoir is left unfinished because the contract for its construction is frustrated, no one may be benefited in a way which enrichment law can recognise[1]; and, if the contract was one under which the contractor was to be paid only on completion, the problem would be without answer. For these reasons the contract provides a mechanism by which the contractor will be paid for the incomplete work.

1 Example based on *Metropolitan Water Board v Dick Kerr & Co Ltd* [1918] AC 119.

Conclusion

4.88 Like many of the other ways for getting out of contracts considered in this chapter, frustration is a restrictively applied doctrine. It may be that the widespread use of *force majeure* clauses in contracts liable to be affected by changing circumstances – shipping, long leases and construction contracts come to mind – indicates some dissatisfaction with the narrowness of the frustration doctrine and that a slightly broader approach, possibly allowing judicial revision of the contract in response to the changing context[1], or enabling an adversely affected party to require the other to renegotiate the terms of the contract in the new circumstances[2], would be welcomed. Frustration is an all-or-nothing solution to the problem of change: either the contract is discharged or it is not. On the other hand, such a black-and-white approach is conducive to certainty which is also much desired by people in business and they are free both to write appropriate terms in their contracts and to renegotiate if they wish. The debate typifies the central issue of contract law: should justice be left to the parties or the judges?

1 As in Germany, following the hyperinflation of the 1920s, and in the USA: see Dawson 'Judicial revision of frustrated contracts' 1982 JR 86. It seems unlikely that the Scottish courts will move in this direction: see *Lloyds TSB Foundation for Scotland v Lloyds Banking Group plc* [2011] CSIH 87 (although this is understood to be subject to an appeal to the UK Supreme Court).

2 As in DCFR III.-1:110. See further Schanze 'Failure of long-term contracts and the duty to re-negotiate' in Rose (ed) *Failure of Contracts* (1997); Macgregor 'The effect of unexpected circumstances on contract in Scots and Louisiana law' in Palmer and Reid (eds) *Mixed Jurisdictions Compared; Private Law in Louisiana and Scotland* (2009) pp 244–280; Hondius and Grigoleit (eds) *Unexpected Circumstances in European Contract Law* (2011); Uribe, *The Effect of a Change of Circumstances on the Binding Force of Contracts: Comparative Perspectives* (2011).

5. Breach of Contract and Self-Help Remedies

5.1 The definition of contract discussed in Chapter 1 speaks of contracts as being those agreements that the law will enforce. In this and the next chapter we discuss the enforcement mechanisms provided and recognised by the law. Before these enforcement mechanisms are needed, however, one of the contracting parties must have ceased to adhere to what the contract requires – that is, there must be a breach of contract.

BREACH OF CONTRACT

5.2 Scots law has a basically unified concept of breach as non-performance of the contract in some respect. This means that all breaches of contract potentially have the same effect in terms of the remedies to which they give rise. It does not generally matter whether the breach is by total or partial non-performance, delayed or late performance, defective performance or refusal to perform. In this Scots law is like English law and the 'Romanistic' systems of France and the Netherlands; but unlike German and South African law which distinguish sharply between the consequences of two types of breach, namely non-performance arising through delay (*moradebitoris*) or through impossibility. Scots law also has no requirement of fault or negligence on the part of the contract-breaker before liability can arise (save in the case where the term broken is one requiring the party to take care or act without negligence). This again aligns Scots law with English law but distinguishes it from many of the continental Civilian systems[1].

1 On the comparative position generally see *Zweigert and Kötz* ch 36, Treitel *Remedies for Breach of Contract: a comparative survey* (1988), and Clive and Hutchison 'Breach of contract' in *Zimmermann Visser & Reid*.

5.3 There are perhaps two inroads upon the unity of the concept of breach. First, with regard to the defensive or self-help remedies available to an aggrieved party, there are requirements of materiality in relation to the breach. A non-material breach will not give rise to these remedies although others may be available. These remedies and the requirements of materiality will be elaborated further later in this chapter[1]. Second, as will also be discussed in more detail below[2], a party's refusal to perform is not by itself a breach of contract; breach only arises when the other party accepts the refusal. This is the only category of breach in which the actions of both parties are relevant.

1 See below, para 5.26 ff.
2 See below, para 5.28 ff.

REMEDIES FOR BREACH OF CONTRACT: GENERAL

5.4 What can a contracting party confronted with a breach do about it? What remedies are available? In the absence of contractual provision on the matter, the remedies available fall into two main categories. One involves going to court, seeking judicial assistance either to compel payment or performance (specific implement or interdict) or to obtain a substitute for performance (damages). The other can be described as self-help or defensive measures, exercisable without the assistance of a court. The essence of these defensive measures is that the aggrieved party does nothing in a situation where the contract calls upon him to do something. There are two possibilities: either *retention* under which performance is withheld until the contract-breaker repairs his breach (ie the contract is suspended pending resolution of the dispute) or *rescission* under which the contract is terminated altogether.

5.5 In theory, the approach of the Scots law of remedies for breach of contract is to favour performance of the contract. This is most obvious given the basic premise that the primary judicial remedy for breach of contract is *specific implement*, an order for performance. In this Scots law is like most Civilian systems but contrasts with English law in which specific performance is an equitable remedy awarded only if damages are not adequate compensation[1]. A cynic might say that in effect this means that a contracting party has a choice between performing and paying damages[2]. Again, in Scots law the aim of an award of *damages* for breach is to put the aggrieved party in the same position as if the contract had been performed or to protect the performance or expectation interest of the aggrieved party. The leaning towards performance can also be detected in the availability of retention as a remedy which brings pressure to perform to bear upon the contract-breaker, while even a party aggrieved by the other's breach can only free itself from the contract if that breach has been material.

1 *Zweigert and Kötz* ch 35; *Treitel* ch III.
2 See Holmes *The Common Law* (1881) at 301. See also de Wolfe Howe *The Pollock-Holmes Letters* (1942) vol 1 at 177.

5.6 In Scots law remedies for breach of contract are *cumulative*. This means that more than one can be exercised in respect of any breach provided the remedies are not inconsistent with each other. Take for example, a contract for the sale of goods under which I am due to pay the seller for the goods in instalments which fall due on the first of the month. The seller does not deliver the goods; I withhold payment on the first of the following month. Still the seller does not deliver the goods. I terminate the contract. The non-delivery has meant that I have lost an opportunity to resell the goods at a profit. I can now go on to sue for damages in respect of that loss. But having terminated the contract, I could not now turn round and seek specific implement of the seller's obligation to deliver the goods. That would be a cumulation of inconsistent remedies. It may be possible to cumulate judicial remedies. I might seek specific implement of a contract to sell a house to me plus damages for the loss caused to me by the delay in delivering it to me; or I might obtain interdict against my former employee continuing to break his restrictive covenant and seek damages for the losses which I have suffered as a result of his breach.

SELF-HELP REMEDIES

5.7 As already explained[1], the self-help (or defensive) remedies of retention and rescission are exercisable by the aggrieved party without the assistance of a court[2].

1 See above para 5.4.
2 See generally *McBryde* ch 20; 13 *Stair Memorial Encyclopaedia* paras 1–95; 15 *Stair Memorial Encyclopaedia* paras 779–781.

Mutuality of contract

5.8   In modern Scots law, the self-help remedies rest upon the concept of the *mutuality* of contract, sometimes also described as the interdependence or unity of contract. Several ideas can be found within the concept of mutuality. A crucial one is that where both parties have rights and duties under the contract, these rights and duties are interdependent or reciprocal and the enforceability of one party's rights is conditional upon the same party performing its own duties. This has two major consequences:

- if one party does not perform, the other need not perform;
- a party which has not performed or is not willing to perform its obligations cannot compel the other to perform.

In this section we will be mainly concerned with the first of these consequences as the underpinning of the remedies of retention and rescission; but the second needs to be kept in mind throughout and will be specifically referred to on occasion. It is also highly relevant to the claims that may be made by a contract-breaker, a topic dealt with at the conclusion of the next chapter[1].

1 See below, para 6.56 ff.

5.9   An important limitation upon mutuality is that, before its consequences come into play, it must be shown that the obligations in question are indeed interdependent or, in Erskine's phrase, 'are the causes of one another'[1]. Accordingly, there cannot be withholding of performance under one contract for claims arising under non-contractual relationships between the parties (eg a delictual claim for fraud inducing the contract under which payment is now withheld). There is sometimes said to be a presumption that a contract is to be regarded as a whole and that all the stipulations on either side are interdependent for the purposes of mutuality[2]. In complex contracts, however, it will not necessarily be the case that each and every obligation on the one side is to be treated as the counterpart of each and every obligation on the other side[3]. The difference can be illustrated by way of the following diagrams where X and Y are the contracting parties, the boxes listed as a, b, c, and so on are their respective obligations, and d-1 is the obligation on which X has defaulted:

(i) All obligations on either side interdependent

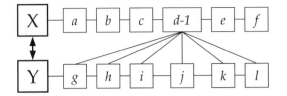

In theory Y can withhold performance of all its obligations if X's breach at d-1 is sufficiently significant. But if Y has performed, say, obligations g and h before d-1 occurs, then only obligations i-l can be withheld.

(ii) Each obligation on one side has its specific counterpart on the other

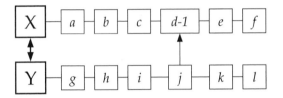

Here, however, Y can withhold only performance of the obligation which is the counterpart of X's obligation d-1 (that is, in the diagram, obligation j).

1 *Institute* III, 3, 86.
2 *Gloag*, 592, deployed, for example, in *Hoult v Turpie* 2004 SLT 308 and *Forster v Ferguson & Forster* 2010 SLT 867. But *McBryde* rejects any presumption: see para 20.55. In *Inveresk plc v Tullis Russell Papermakers Ltd* 2010 SC (UKSC) 106 Lord Hope avoids the word 'presumption' but says at para 42 that 'the analysis should start from the position that all the obligations that [the transaction] embraces are to be regarded as counterparts of each other unless there is a clear indication to the contrary.'
3 See further para 5.15 below

5.10 While typically mutuality applies within the confines of a single contract, it may also do so where two or more contracts form part of a single transaction between the parties, with the obligations in each being inter-related as a result. So in one case buyers of two ships under two separate contracts for which only a single price was payable were allowed to refuse to pay the whole price in respect of a breach in relation to only one of the contracts[1]. Where one business (A) sold assets to another

(B) with two agreements giving effect to the transaction – one the asset transfer, the other a services agreement under which A undertook to continue production, sale and distribution for a period post-sale to ensure business continuity – it was held that there could be mutuality between the obligations under the two contracts so that B could withhold payments due under the asset transfer agreement in respect of A's defective performance under the services agreement[2].

1 *Claddagh Steamship Co v Steven & Co* 1919 SC (HL) 132.
2 *Inveresk plc v Tullis Russell Papermakers Ltd* 2010 SC (UKSC) 106. This decision leaves doubtful the correctness of *Donaldson v Dodds* 1996 GWD 29-1723, cited on this issue in previous editions of this work.

Materiality of breach

5.11   The application of the mutuality principle may also be limited by the requirements of materiality in relation to the initial non-performance. In a number of Outer House cases Lord Drummond Young has developed a theory that for a breach to justify a party in withholding performance it must be such as to threaten the future performance of the contract[1]; but this over-states the position. At least two levels of materiality of breach have been identified in Scots law: that required for the less drastic remedy of withholding performance or suspension of the contract (retention) being lower than that for the more far-reaching action of terminating it altogether (rescission)[2]. A party may therefore choose only to withhold or suspend performance in respect of a material breach for which she could terminate; but not the other way around. The exact nature of the difference between these two levels of materiality has not been much explored nor has there been identification of the level at which not even retention is allowed. The courts have sometimes talked of 'trifling' breaches for which the defensive remedies cannot be used[3] but the category cannot be illustrated from the cases. There is, however, a number of cases in which it has been held that breaches were not sufficiently material to justify rescission and these will be discussed below in the section dealing in detail with that remedy[4].

1 See *Hoult v Turpie* 2004 SLT 308; *Purac Ltd v Byzak Ltd* 2005 SLT 37; *Wyman-Gordon Ltd v Proclad International Ltd* 2006 SLT 390.
2 Gloag, 623; *McBryde* paras 20.57–20.60, 20.88. This seems to be accepted by Lord Hope in *Inveresk plc v Tullis Russell Papermakers Ltd* 2010 SC (UKSC) 106, para 43. In *EDI Central Ltd v National Car Parks Ltd* 2011 SLT 75 at para 111 Lord Glennie speaks of a need for the party retaining to have suffered materially adverse effects from the other's breach.

3 Eg *Barclay v Anderston Foundry Co* (1856) 18 D 1190 per Lord Wood at 1198.
4 See below, para 5.26 ff.

5.12 It is quite possible that the concept of materiality is truly only relevant to rescission and that there is no need to show materiality in relation to retention for which the only requirement would be that the breach is more than trivial[1]. It is worth noting that the mutuality principle has been part of Scots law for a very long time, probably finding its origin in the *exceptio non adimpleti contractus* (defence of the unperformed contract) of medieval canon law. The *exceptio* also survives in the codes of modern Continental systems and in South African law; but in these systems it is used only to explain the equivalents of retention by withholding performance and not to justify outright termination of the contract[2]. The Institutional writers also use mutuality only in the context of retention[3] and it would appear that the linkage with rescission and termination was a late nineteenth-century development[4]. The importance of this may be that not all the consequences of mutuality necessarily apply in cases of rescission. An example might be the need to look for interdependence between the term broken and the aggrieved party's response since by definition rescission brings the whole of that party's outstanding obligations of performance to an end and not just those which might be said to be the counterparts of those which the contract-breaker has failed to carry through. Equally, it may be that the concept of materiality, developed mainly in the context of rescission, is not relevant to retention which is based exclusively on the concept of mutuality.

1 MacQueen 'Remedies for breach of contract: Scots law in its European and international context' (1997) 1 EdinLR 200 at 207.
2 *Treitel* pp 245–317. See also DCFR III.-3:302, PICC art 7.1.3.
3 Stair *Institutions* I, 10, 17; Bankton *Institute* I, 11, 69; Erskine *Institute III*, 3, 86; Hume, *Lectures* vol 3 p 46; Bell, *Commentaries* vol 1, 454–5; *Principles* §§ 70–71.
4 See especially *Turnbull v McLean & Co* (1873) 1 R 730. See further Johnston 'Breach of contract' in *Reid and Zimmermann*; McBryde 'The Scots law of breach of contract: a mixed system in operation' (2002) 6 EdinLR 5.

Hazards of self-help

5.13 The obvious danger in using a self-help remedy and stopping performance, whether by way of retention or rescission, is that the step turns out not to be justified either because there was no breach or because the breach was not material enough. If so, then the non-performance intended to be a remedy for breach itself turns out to be a breach. The best-known illustration is *Wade v Waldon*[1], where the manager of the Glasgow Palace and Pavilion Theatres engaged a well-known artiste to appear under a contract which required the latter to send in 14 days ahead of his performance what was described as 'bill matter' giving details of his performance which would be used for advance publicity. The bill matter was not sent and the manager terminated the contract. But in the subsequent litigation it was held that the artiste's breach did not justify termination and that the manager was guilty of breach and liable in damages in consequence. Many of the leading cases on the self-help remedies have arisen in similar circumstances. The party who wishes to invoke the remedies of retention or, more especially, rescission can seek some protection by obtaining a judicial declaration of entitlement to act, the remedy in Scotland being known as a declarator. Such a remedy requires no action from the defender. The practical problem may be the need for a speedy decision which a court may not always be able to give especially in a complex commercial case. It is worth noting, however, that in some European countries (e.g. France) termination of the contract is a judicial rather than a self-help remedy[2].

1   1909 SC 571.
2   *Treitel* pp 323–324, noting that this 'can lead to commercially inconvenient results'; DCFR III.-3, sections 4 and 5, and PICC, arts 7.1.3 and 7.3 allow self-help in these matters.

Retention (suspension or with-holding of performance)

5.14   On the views about the mutuality principle expressed earlier in this chapter, the principal consequence of the mutuality principle is the right of a contracting party confronted with a breach by the other party to withhold performance of its own obligations under the contract. The general name for this remedy is retention and its effect is to suspend or postpone the aggrieved party's obligations to perform until such time as the contract-breaker cures its breach. Retention can thus be contrasted with the other major self-help remedy, rescission, under which the aggrieved party's obligations of performance under the contract are terminated altogether. Retention is an effective way of bringing pressure to bear upon a contract-breaker to carry out the contract and is thus consistent with the emphasis which Scots contract law places upon performance as the entitlement of a contracting party. The typical example of retention is when a party withholds a price due for goods or work done because of defects in those goods or services. Another common case is the tenant in a lease who withholds payment of the rent because the landlord has not complied with his obligations. It used to be said that there could be no retention by the employer in a building contract where payment was made in stages but this is no longer the law (if it ever was). Rather, the position seems to be that a staged payment can only be withheld in respect of defects in the work to which that staged payment relates. If for example, there are six staged payments under a building contract, the third payment cannot be withheld for defects in the work done at the first stage unless that breach continues to have effect through the subsequent stages[1].

1 *Redpath Dorman Long Ltd v Cummins Engine Co Ltd* 1981 SC 370.

5.15 As noted above[1], the principle of mutuality requires that there be interdependence of the obligation withheld by the aggrieved party and the obligation that has been broken on the other side. Within a contract or set of contracts forming a single transaction the interdependence of obligations is in the end a matter of construing the contract or contracts in question. The requirement of interdependence was confirmed by the House of Lords in *Bank of East Asia v Scottish Enterprise*[2], but found in the particular circumstances not to mean that every obligation on one side of the bargain was dependent upon all the obligations on the other side. The Scottish Development Agency (SDA, predecessors of Scottish Enterprise) contracted with Stanley Miller (Scotland) Ltd for construction works. The parties recognised that SDA would be unable to make payments under the contract as they fell due. Millers arranged finance through the Bank of East Asia to which were assigned Millers' rights to payment from the SDA.

Scottish Development Agency————Millers Construction

assignation

Bank of East Asia

An instalment of the price, some £416,964.72, had been due from the SDA to Millers (and hence to the assignee bank) on 15 May 1990. Millers went into receivership around 29 May 1990 with the works admittedly incomplete and the part completed defective. The loss and damage to the SDA as at 15 May was worth £168,512.40. The SDA suffered further loss after 29 May through having to remedy the defects and complete the works using another, more expensive contractor, and through delay in letting the finished works. Could the SDA retain or withhold the payment due on 15 May in respect of the breaches of contract by Millers both before and after 15 May?

Contract	15 May 1990	29 May 1990
	payment of £416,964 due	*SM receivership*
breaches worth £168,512.40		
		further breach

The House of Lords held that, while there could be retention of the £416,964 in respect of the breaches up to 15 May 1990, the defence was not available for breaches after that date ie the bulk of the consequential losses. The bank was therefore entitled to payment of the sum due on 15 May with a deduction for the damage suffered at that date. The losses arising after 29 May did not depend upon the breaches in existence at 15 May. It is not the law that each and every obligation of one party to a contract is necessarily and invariably the counterpart of each and every obligation on the other side.

1 At para 5.9.
2 1997 SLT 1213 (HL). For the unusual background to this case in the English courts, although being decided according to Scots law, see McBryde 'Mutuality retained' (1996) 1 EdinLR 135.

5.16   The difficulties of analysis to which this gives rise were clearly demonstrated in *Macari v Celtic FC*[1]. M, manager of Celtic, was dismissed following his failure to obey the instructions of the club board as to a residence requirement in his contract. M argued that the board had previously undermined his position thereby breaching the implied obligations of 'mutual trust and confidence' in the employment contract[2] and entitling him to withhold performance under the residence requirement. It was held that the employee's duty to obey his employer's lawful instructions under the contract was not the counterpart of the duty of mutual trust and confidence especially when the employee was otherwise carrying out his duties and drawing his (substantial) salary. So M was in material breach rather than lawfully retaining performance. There is an air of artificiality in this judgment since the implied obligation is one which goes to the very basis of the employment relationship and can indeed be seen as counterpart to all the obligations undertaken by the employee. The decision can be defended perhaps on the basis that, faced with such a breach by the employer, the employee cannot be allowed to pick and choose which of his obligations he will or will not perform[3]. A contrasting decision is *Forster v Ferguson & Forster*[4], in which a partner in a law firm who had been convicted of embezzlement from the firm was held unable to sue it and the partners for a pension due to him under the partnership agreement. His breach of the duty of utmost good faith incumbent between partners, which went to the root of the whole partnership contract, disabled him from enforcing any of the obligations under the agreement.

1 1999 SC 628.
2 For which see *Malik v Bank of Commerce and Credit International* [1998] AC 20; Brodie *The Contract of Employment* (2008) ch 8.
3 See further Thomson 'An unsuitable case for suspension?' (1999) 3 EdinLR 394.
4 2010 SLT 867.

5.17 Another form of retention, involving the aggrieved party in retaining some item of property otherwise due to be delivered to the contract-breaker, is usually known as *lien*[1]. The property is often moveable but there seems no reason in principle why lien cannot be exercised over heritage – for example, by a tenant against a landlord who has failed to pay for improvements made by the former during the lease or by a contractor against the employer on whose land or buildings he has carried out construction work[2]. In the classic example of lien, however, a person who gains possession of another's goods in order to carry out repairs or other works upon them may retain those goods until paid for the work[3]. Such a lien is an example of a *special lien*, the right to withhold the property only existing in respect of the correlative obligation arising under the contract by which the aggrieved party gained possession of the property. This may be contrasted with a *general lien* in which possession of the property may be retained for all debts due by the other party under this and other transactions. General lien arises only in certain relationships: examples include solicitor and client, banker and customer, factor (or mercantile agent) and principal, and innkeeper and guest. In the case of the two latter relationships, the aggrieved party may go on to sell the subject of the lien to meet his claim provided that certain conditions are met. The extent to which this power of sale applies in special liens is not clear.[4]

1 See generally Steven *Pledge and Lien* (2008), chs 9–17.
2 Steven *Pledge and Lien*, para 12.04 (see however para 9.03 where it is said to be 'misguided to use "lien" to refer to retention of incorporeal property because retention of incorporeal property would seem to be based upon ownership and not upon a subordinate real right [of security].')
3 *Harper v Faulds* 1791 Bell's 8vo Cases 440, 1791 Mor 2666.
4 Steven *Pledge and Lien* paras 15.01–15.03.

5.18 Lien, whether special or general, is the child of possession; if possession is lost so is the right of lien. Possession is a legal concept rather than just a factual question. Mere custody of another's property under a contract is not enough for lien; for example, an employee cannot retain the computer on her office desk against non-payment of her salary. Finally, special lien is a right to retain property against the other contracting party and it may not be possible to exercise it against a third-party claim to the subjects. Thus in *Lamonby v Foulds*[1], a garage claimed a lien over a lorry which it had repaired but the defaulting customer held the goods under a hire-purchase contract which contained a provision forbidding the customer to create liens for repairs. The supplier under the hire-purchase contract was successful in reclaiming the lorry from the garage. However, an innkeeper's lien and, in some cases, a solicitor's lien may be exercised over material owned by third parties or to which they are in some way entitled[2].

1 1928 SC 89.
2 *Bermans and Nathans Ltd v Weibye* 1983 SLT 299; Steven *Pledge and Lien* (2008), paras 13.35–13.50, 16.82–16.84, 17.87–17.89.

5.19 Both retention and lien are subject to equitable control by the court[1]. An example of when such control might be exercised is where it is thought that the plea of retention is put forward merely as a means to delay payment. However, the law does not appear to require that the amount retained should bear any very close relation in value to the amount of the claim, although probably the party retaining should have suffered some materially adverse effect from the breach in question[2]. Sometimes in cases where there is dispute as to whether or not retention is justified, the party withholding performance will be ordered to consign the sum retained in court pending a final outcome. When lien is claimed over perishable goods, they may be sold and the sale price consigned in court before judgment is given on the claim.

1 *McBryde* para 20.77; Steven *Pledge and Lien* (2008) paras 15.04–15.07.
2 *EDI Central Ltd v National Car Parks Ltd* 2011 SLT 75 para 111 (Lord Glennie); affd on other issues [2012] CSIH 6.

5.20   The parties can exclude retention by contractual provision. But the language of any such exclusion will have to be clear to receive effect. In *Redpath Dorman Long Ltd v Cummins Engine Co Ltd*[1], a case about a construction contract, the employer's right of retention was held not to be excluded by the following clause:

'Whenever under the Contract any sum of money shall be recoverable from or payable by the Contractor, such sum may be deducted from or reduced by the amount of any sum or sums then due or which at any time thereafter may become due to the Contractor under or in respect of the Contract.'

The purpose of this clause is clearly to avoid the cash flow problems which may arise for a building contractor if the employer, thinking he has a claim for defective work, withholds payment as a result. In that situation the employer is required to quantify his claim and deduct that amount from the payment due. Of course, there may still be a dispute as to whether or not that deduction is justified and, if it is, what the right amount should be; but the contractor will still receive some money under which the expense of having carried out the work to date may be met. Why did the court in *Redpath* not think that this clause excluded the common law right of retention? The reasoning was that the clause did not *exhaust* retention in that it did not go as far as retention. The logic of this position is not entirely clear (how can the clause co-exist meaningfully with a right of retention?), but the lesson would seem to be that if parties wish to exclude the common law they should do so in very plain and direct words, for example 'The common law remedy of retention is hereby excluded'. In a more recent Outer House case, however, it was held that the remedy might be excluded where that was the 'necessary implication' of what the parties had actually said in the contract[2].

1 1981 SC 370.
2 *Melville Dundas Ltd v Hotel Corporation of Edinburgh Ltd* 2007 SC 12. Cf *Forster v Ferguson & Forster* 2010 SLT 867 para 16 per Lord Clarke. Note that in construction contracts under the Housing Grants, Construction and Regeneration Act 1996 s 111 a party must give an effective notice of intention to

withhold payment, specifying the amount to be withheld and the grounds for doing so, not later than the prescribed period before the final date for payment. Parties may prescribe the period but otherwise it is that provided under the Scheme for Construction Contracts. See further the *Melville Dundas* case and also *SL Timber Systems Ltd v Carillion Construction Ltd* 2002 SLT 997, *Melville Dundas Ltd v George Wimpey (UK) Ltd* 2006 SC 310, revsd 2007 SC (HL) 116.

5.21   A final point on which there is much confusion is the interaction between retention and the closely related concepts of 'counterclaims', 'set off' and 'compensation' under the Compensation Act 1592. As we have seen, retention is a means of suspending or postponing performance due under a contract until breach on the other side is made good. As well as being a self-help remedy for breach, it can also be a defence to an action by the other party for performance. But the claim of breach which triggers the remedy of retention can also give rise cumulatively to other remedies such as an action of damages. If these remedies require a court order and action from the other party, they are not merely defences but counterclaims meeting the claims of that other party. Thus for example, a party sued for non-payment on a certain date may say that his non-payment was justified as a retention and go on to counterclaim damages for the loss suffered as a result of the breach. If the damages are paid, the breach is made good and the retention no longer justified. The position then is that each party has an obligation to pay the other: the two claims may be set off against each other with a balance actually payable by whichever of the parties has the larger debt.

5.22   'Compensation' under the Compensation Act 1592 is a means of discharging contractual (and, indeed, other) obligations.[1] Compensation arises whenever each of two parties has a claim against the other and these two claims are for identified amounts currently due and payable. The sums involved are then described as 'liquid' in contrast to 'illiquid' sums which are either unquantified in amount or not yet payable. The effect of compensation is that each debt discharges the other with only the balance left payable to whichever of the parties has the lesser debt.

1 Compensation in this sense is familiar throughout Europe: see Zimmermann, *Comparative Foundations of a European Law of Set-Off and Prescription* (2002). Note also DCFR, III.-6, PICC ch 8.

5.23   Compensation is thus distinct from retention on at least three major points. First retention can be, and commonly is, exercised in respect of an illiquid claim which cannot be quantified until there is a judicial decree, for example damages[1].

Second, whereas compensation brings obligations to an end by discharging both debts up to the amount of the lesser, retention merely suspends or postpones performance and does not discharge the obligation. Finally, retention can only be exercised in respect of a performance otherwise due under a contract which has been broken by the other party. With compensation, the debts may arise from wholly separate transactions, the only requirement being that each of the parties is debtor and creditor in the same capacity (*concursus debiti et crediti*).

1 In *Inveresk plc v Tullis Russell Papermakers Ltd* 2010 SC (UKSC) 106 paras 57–107 Lord Rodger of Earlsferry argues obiter that the court has an equitable power to allow retention for purposes of compensation where the illiquid claim will shortly become liquid, and that this form of retention is distinct from retention by withholding performance until the other party proves that it has fully performed.

5.24   A final twist is provided by the concept of balancing of accounts in bankruptcy. Where a party claiming payment of a liquid debt is bankrupt, the defender may use a presently illiquid claim to off-set his liability. Where the claim cannot be made liquid, an estimate of its value must be undertaken.

Rescission (termination)[1]

5.25   Rescission is the termination of the aggrieved party's future obligations of performance under the contract. There may be other questions requiring resolution such as the effect of rescission upon performances already rendered or begun to be rendered by the aggrieved party; the performances rendered and still to be rendered by the contract-breaker; the availability of other remedies against the contract-breaker such as damages; and the effect of terms in the contract dealing, not with the primary obligations of performance under the contract, but with the resolution of disputes, remedies, and other obligations arising only after the contract has otherwise been discharged (for example restrictive covenants).

1 See generally DCFR III.-3, section 5; PICC ch 7 section 3; and Rowan *Remedies for Breach of Contract* (2012) ch 2 for the comparative position.

(1) Material breach of contract

5.26   The party wishing to rescind a contract for breach must show that the breach is material. What breaches are material for these purposes? The emphasis can fall either on the nature and consequences of the breach itself[1] or upon the nature of the term broken. The classic definition of materiality highlights the latter:

'It is familiar law, and quite well settled by decision, that in any contract which contains multifarious stipulations there are some which go so to the root of the contract that a breach of those stipulations entitles the party pleading the breach to declare that the contract is at an end. There are others which do not go to the root of the contract, but which are part of the contract, and which would give rise, if broken to an action of damages[2]'.

This formulation has been criticised because it seems to align Scots law in this area with the rather rigid English division of contract terms into *conditions* (important terms breach of which, however trivial, will entitle the aggrieved party to rescind) and *warranties* (less important terms for breach of which the aggrieved party can only recover damages, no matter how serious the breach)[3]. However, Scots law has retained the flexibility necessary to meet the justice of the individual case by avoiding sharp definitions of what are material and non-material terms while at the same time examining the nature and consequences of the breach in such light as is thrown by metaphors like 'the root of the contract'. The courts are usually able to reach just results on the facts of cases but a party considering rescission will often be uncertain about whether or not the breach is of the required level of materiality[4].

1 As for example in the Sale of Goods Act 1979 (SGA 1979), ss 12–15, as amended by the Sale and Supply of Goods Act 1994 (SSGA 1994).
2 *Wade v Waldon* 1909 SC 571 per LP Dunedin at 576.
3 See *McKendrick*, ch 10.
4 As in *Wade v Waldon*: see above, para 5.13, for the facts.

5.27   What breaches then are material? The following sections consider breach by refusal to perform, lateness, and defective performance and the possibility of contractual provision to remove uncertainty on the matter.

(2) Refusal to perform (repudiation)[1]

5.28   A clear example of a material breach of contract is when a party indicates that it is not going to perform its obligations under the contract *and* this is accepted by the other party. Such a refusal to perform is generally known as a *repudiation* of the contract and it plainly goes to the root of the contract to say that you will not do what the contract requires. Repudiation differs from other breaches of contract, material or otherwise, inasmuch as both parties are involved in the constitution of the breach: namely, the refusal of the one to perform and the acceptance thereof by the other. Before acceptance, the refusal has an inchoate character. It can be withdrawn or performance can actually be commenced or carried out despite the initial refusal; in which case, it would seem, there is no breach and no remedy at all for the other party. Acceptance therefore converts refusal to perform into breach. This also means that, when the aggrieved party does not accept the refusal, but affirms and seeks specific implement or payment, the breach for which a remedy is sought is not the refusal to perform but the actual non-performance which has followed thereupon. Acceptance of a refusal to perform also fixes the point of time at which the acceptor's obligations under the contract come to an end giving it the same effect as rescission for other material breaches of contract.

1 See generally *McBryde* paras 20.03, 20.22–20.43.

5.29 The doctrine of repudiation first developed in English law[1] and was imported from there into Scotland. Such a development also occurred in South Africa and equivalent ideas have begun to develop in many of the European systems[2], reflecting its general utility in not compelling a party confronted with advance intimation of non-performance to wait and see if the notice is made good.

1 The key case is *Hochster v De La Tour* (1853) 2 E & B 678.
2 *Treitel* pp 380–381. See also its acceptance in DCFR III.-3:504; PICC, art 7.3.3.

5.30 The refusal to perform must be clearly such, rather than, say, a threat not to perform or mere non-performance or a dispute about the manner or timing of performance, or a proposal to vary the contract[1]. However, the question of whether or not there is a refusal to perform is to be answered objectively, from the point of view of the reasonable person's understanding of the statement: it is no defence for the refusing party to say that it thought its refusal justified by the contract so that in fact the refusal to perform was upholding rather than repudiating the obligations of the contract[2].

1 *GL Group v Ash Gupta* 1987 SCLR 149; *Edinburgh Grain Ltd (in liquidation) v Marshall Food Group Ltd* 1999 SLT 15; *Wyman-Gordon Ltd v Proclad International Ltd* 2011 SC 338.
2 *Blyth v Scottish Liberal Club* 1982 SC 140.

5.31 The repudiation may occur before the due date for performance. Speaking very strictly, in the case of a refusal to perform intimated in advance, it might be said that there was no breach until there was non-performance on the due date; but that could lead to great uncertainty for the other party during the interim period and the law enables it to treat the refusal as a breach straightaway. Such breaches are often described as 'anticipatory'.

5.32 By itself, non-performance on the due date does not amount to repudiation (although it is a breach of contract) because the party due to perform may still intend to do so late and therefore cannot be said to have abandoned the contract. But failure to commence performance on the due date coupled with a contemporaneous or later indication of intention never to perform will be repudiation.

5.33 Repudiation does not terminate the aggrieved party's obligations of performance automatically. Instead, it gives the aggrieved party a choice:

(1) to accept the repudiation and treat the contract as terminated;
(2) to affirm the contract and insist upon performance, if necessary by specific implement or action for payment[1].

Acceptance of repudiation requires no particular form and may be made by communication or conduct. Formal notice or intimation to the contract-breaker is not required, only that the acceptance comes to its attention. Non-performance of contractual obligations by the aggrieved party may be sufficient[2].

1 *White & Carter (Councils) Ltd v McGregor* 1962 SC (HL) 1.
2 See, eg, *Vitol SA v Norelf Ltd: The Santa Clara* [1996] AC 800; *Edinburgh Grain Ltd (in liquidation) v Marshall Food Group Ltd* 1999 SLT 15.

5.34 Affirmation of the contract also requires no particular form. Further, there is no requirement that the decision to affirm the contract rather than to accept the repudiation be reasonable. In *White & Carter Councils v McGregor*[1] a contract to place advertisements was repudiated by the customer but the advertising company affirmed the contract, placed the unwanted advertisements and sued for payment. The House of Lords held by three to two that even though the performance was wasteful the aggrieved party was entitled to be paid. The case may have been exceptional in that the aggrieved party could perform its side of the bargain without the co-operation of the other party;

had co-operation been necessary, it might have been much more difficult to affirm the contract. Although the decision in *White & Carter* has been heavily criticised in England,[1] it has been followed in Scotland in a case where a landlord refused to accept the tenant's repudiation of its lease and sued successfully for rent falling due after the repudiation[2]. There may be extreme cases where the aggrieved party is bound to accept that the contract is at an end; and a dictum by Lord Reid in the *White & Carter* case that the non-breaching party must have a 'legitimate interest' in the performance rather than the termination of the contract has sometimes been seen as a possible limitation upon unreasonable behaviour[3]. In *AMA (New Town) Ltd v McKenna*[4] the buyer of a house refused to go ahead with the transaction and pay the price to the seller but it was held that the latter could not sue for the price until it had performed its side of the bargain in full, ie handed over a disposition and given entry with vacant possession of the property. The Scottish Law Commission has recommended that the law of *White & Carter* be changed so that a party will not be entitled to recover payment for performance occurring after intimation that further performance is unwanted if (i) that party could have entered into a reasonable substitute transaction without unreasonable effort or expense, or (ii) proceeding with the performance was unreasonable[5].

1 1962 SC (HL) 1.
2 *Salaried Staff London Loan Co v Swears & Wells*1985 SC 189.
3 1962 SC (HL) 1 at 14.
4 2011 SLT (Sh Ct) 73; commented upon by McBryde and Gretton 'Sale of heritable property and failure to pay' 2012 SLT (News) 17.
5 Report on Remedies for Breach of Contract (Scot Law Com no 174) (1999) Pt 2. The proposal is based upon PECL, art 9:101(2) (now DCFR III.-3:301(2)).

Societe Generale, London Branch v Geys [2012] UKSC 63 elective theory of breach applied is employment contract

(3) Performance or payment not made at due date

5.35 Many contracts will lay down a date or dates upon which performance or payment is to be made. Is non-performance or non-payment on the due date a material breach of contract or not? In many cases, the question will not arise as a practical issue. For example, in many contracts payment is the last step of performance. It will not be worthwhile for the payment-creditor to claim that non-payment is a material breach entitling him to rescind since that brings payment no closer. The only practical remedy is to sue for payment. Again, if a building contractor starts to fall behind schedule, rescission by the employer will probably only increase the resultant problems inasmuch as he will have to find at his own expense a replacement contractor who will almost certainly charge a higher price than the original contractor for the completion of the contract. The employer's interests in timeous completion are probably best protected through other remedies against the contractor such as damages or, more probably, damages liquidated by the contract itself[1].

1 On liquidated damages, see further below, para 6.47 ff.

5.36   But there can be cases where rescission is a useful response to lateness in breach of contract. For example, where a contract requires payment in advance of performance and the money is not forthcoming, rescission might be an appropriate remedy especially if the funds to be made available by the advance were actually to be deployed in rendering the subsequent performance. Again, where a purchaser of goods wants them on a particular date to catch a rising market for resale, the ability to rescind if delivery is not timeous may be of great importance to free the buyer to obtain substitutes.

5.37   Unfortunately, the cases provide little specific guidance as to when non-performance on the due date is a material breach justifying rescission. There is no general rule. Where the background to a contract for the supply of goods is a fluctuating market in those goods, a term about the date of delivery will probably be material as will a term in a charterparty about the arrival of a ship. In a conveyancing transaction, the seller's failure to provide a marketable title at the time fixed by the contract may justify the buyer's immediate rescission. But failure to pay on time or failure to carry out work to schedule will not generally have this effect without other circumstances being present[1]. The position may change as a delay in performance continues, making material an initially non-material breach. A not uncommon example is provided by the domestic conveyancing transaction in which the buyer's continued failure to pay the price of a house can put the seller in a very difficult position with regard to funding his own acquisition of a new property. But it is impossible to say with precision the length of delay which will have this effect. The question is one of what is reasonable in the circumstances.

1 See for a recent example *East Dunbartonshire Council v Bett Homes Ltd* [2012] CSIH 1.

(4) Defective performance

5.38 Defective performance occurs where performance is tendered but is not of the standard required by the contract. Probably the commonest example in practice is the supply of goods which are not of satisfactory quality under the implied terms of the SGA 1979, s 14. Since 1994, satisfactory quality has included freedom from minor defects such as, for example, an easily repairable fault in the power steering unit of a new car[1].But under the statute it is only in consumer contracts that the existence of such minor defects would immediately entitle the customer to rescind the contract of supply. In commercial contracts it would have to be demonstrated that the breach was material before rescission became an available remedy[2]. This can be illustrated by *The Hansa Nord*[3], where a consignment of citrus pulp pellets was sold for use to make cattle feed but upon delivery was found to be partially defective. The buyer purported to reject the goods; the seller, under reservation of rights, resold the pellets on the open market, where they were purchased by the original buyer for rather less than half the initial selling price. The buyer then used the pellets for the purpose for which he had first bought them. It was held that the buyer had not been entitled to reject and had to pay the initial contract price: the breach was minor in relation to the performance required under the agreement and the buyer was only entitled to damages representing the difference in value between the pellets as they should have been and as they were at the time of delivery[4].

1 Cf *Millars of Falkirk v Turpie* 1976 SLT (Notes) 66, the case which led ultimately to the reforms in the SSGA 1994.
2 SGA 1979, s 15B.
3 [1976] QB 44.
4 On damages for difference in value, see further below, para 6.20 ff.

5.39 In practice, when a defective performance is brought to the attention of its provider, he may offer to repair or replace it. The purchaser is of course entitled to accept such an offer which will often be the most satisfactory solution to the problem. The legal question which arises is whether either provider or purchaser is entitled to insist upon this solution against the wishes of the other party (sometimes dubbed a 'right of cure'). Scots law seems on the whole to answer the question in the negative[1], although there have been suggestions that an aggrieved party may not always be able to rescind without giving the party in breach a second chance to perform[2]. But this may simply be another way of saying that the breach in question is not material, at any rate until the attempt at cure has also failed. In the context of sale of goods, it is provided that the buyer does not lose his right to reject defective goods merely because he asks for, or agrees to, their repair by the seller[3]. Indeed, the House of Lords has held that the buyer may still reject after full repair, if the seller does not respond to requests for information about what was the problem and how it was repaired[4]. But the provision of a buyer's *right* to cure to supplement the right of rejection, found for example in the Uniform Commercial Code of the USA, was itself rejected by the Law Commissions[5]. The Unidroit Principles, the DCFR and the proposed CESL provide the supplier of a defective performance with a right to insist upon cure in certain limited circumstances[6], but the Scottish Law Commission has taken the view that this approach shifts the balance of power too much against the aggrieved party[7]. However in the case of consumer contracts for the sale of goods, SGA was amended in 2002 as a result of the Consumer Sales Directive[8]. Consequently a consumer buyer has the right to demand repair or replacement at the seller's expense and within a reasonable time of goods which do not conform to the contract[9]. The buyer's right to rescind under these provisions is suspended until the seller has had a reasonable opportunity to repair or replace[10]. The choice between repair or replacement is the buyer's. In *Wittmer v Gebr Weber GmbH; Putz v Medianess Electronics GmbH* the European Court of Justice held that replacement in relation to goods installed in good faith by the buyer rather than the seller (eg tiles put into a shower) extends to reinstallation of the goods in question, or meeting the costs of removal and reinstallation[11]. The seller's only excuses are that repair or replacement are impossible or disproportionate given the value of the goods, the significance of the lack of conformity and whether any other remedy could be effected without significant inconvenience to the buyer[12]. As we have said, the buyer also has a right to rescind under these provisions[13]. Accordingly, a buyer in a consumer contract for the sale of goods now has two distinct rights of rescission, this one (which can be suspended, as noted above) and that available for breach of the implied terms about title, description and quality of the goods under sections 12–15 of SGA[14].

1 But note the special rules on leases in Law Reform (Miscellaneous Provisions) (Scotland) Act 1985, ss 4–7, discussed in Hogg 'To irritate or to rescind: two paths for the landlord?' 1999 SLT (News) 1 and Scot Law Com Discussion Paper no 109 (1999), para 4.10.
2 *Lindley Catering Investments v Hibernian FC* 1975 SLT (Notes) 56; *Strathclyde Regional Council v Border Engineering Contractors Ltd* 1998 SLT 175.

3 SGA 1979, s 35(6)(a). This was introduced in 1994 following the recommendation of *Report on the Sale and Supply of Goods* (Law Com no 160; Scot Law Com no 104) (1987), paras 5.26–5.29.

4 *J & H Ritchie Ltd v Lloyd Ltd* 2007 SC (HL) 89. See further on this case paras 3.35, 3.37 above.

5 See *Report on the Sale and Supply of Goods* paras 4.11–4.14. For the USA, see Uniform Commercial Code (UCC), s 2–508(2).

6 DCFR III.-3:202-203(a); PICC, art 7.1.4. See also CISG, art 48. Note the limited seller's right of cure in English law discussed in Atiyah Adams & MacQueen, 497, 503. Whether this also exists in Scots law is unclear.

7 Scot Law Com no 174 (1999), para 7.21. See further V Mak *Performance-Oriented Remedies in European Sale of Goods Law* (2009), ch 6.

8 Parliament and Council Directive (EC) 1999/44 on certain aspects of the sale of consumer goods and associated guarantees (OJ L171 7.7.99 p 12), implemented in the UK by the Sale and Supply of Goods to Consumers Regulations 2002 (SI 2002/3045).

9 SGA 1979, s 48B (added by the Sale and Supply of Goods to Consumers Regulations 2002 (SI 2002/3045).

10 SGA 1979, s 48D.

11 Cases C-65/09, C-87/09, *Wittmer v Gebr Weber GmbH*; *Putz v Medianess Electronics GmbH* [2011] 3 CMLR 27.

12 SGA 1979, s 48B(3), (4). In many ways the consumer buyer's right to repair or replacement is a form of specific implement: see further MacQueen, Dauner-Lieb and Tettinger 'Specific performance and rights of cure' in Vogenauer and Dannemann (eds), *The Draft Common European Sales Law and its Interaction with English and German Law* (forthcoming).

13 SGA 1979, s 48C(1)(b). Note also the price reduction remedy available under s 48C(1)(a), and see further below, paras 6.16, 6.58.

14 Ie SGA, s 15B. See Hogg, 'The consumer's right to rescind under the Sale of Goods Act: a tale of two remedies' 2003 SLT (News) 277; *Douglas v Glenvarigill Co Ltd* 2010 SLT 634, noted by MacQueen 'Faulty goods, rejection and connected lender liability' (2011) 15 Edin LR 111; and further, *Report on Consumer Remedies for Faulty Goods* (Law Com No 317; Scot Law Com No 216, 2009).

(5) Contractual provision

5.40 The previous section has shown the uncertainty inherent in the common law about when there is material breach justifying rescission. Some of this uncertainty can be removed by appropriate contractual provision. As Lord President Normand has observed, 'Parties can always agree in a contract to treat any breach as justifying rescission'[1]. A simple example is a clause making time 'of the essence of the contract' which would mean that failure to adhere to the contractually stipulated deadlines entitled the other party to rescind. Another example, familiar in practice, is the irritancy clauses found in leases under which in certain circumstances the landlord may terminate the contract for breaches by the tenant.

1 *Bell Bros (HP) Ltd v Aitken* 1939 SC 577 at 588. See also *Dawsons v Bonnin* 1922 SC (HL) 156 per Viscount Cave at 169; *Schuler AG v Wickman Machine Tool Sales Ltd* [1974] AC 235.

5.41   But contractual provision does not eliminate all problems; indeed, new ones may be introduced by the drafter. Versions of the following clause dealing with the situation of non-payment of a price at the due date in a conveyancing transaction have been considered by the courts:

'Payment of the purchase price in full on the date of entry is of the essence of the contract. In the event of the purchase price or any part thereof remaining unpaid as at the date of entry, the purchaser will be deemed to be in material breach of contract. The seller shall have the option to rescind the contract upon prior written notice if the purchase price is not paid in full within 21 days of the date of entry.'

This clause is not ideal on a number of grounds, which explains why it has been the subject of litigation. It is not clear when the seller can rescind. The general principle is that material breach entitles the innocent party to rescind, so the first two sentences of the clause suggest that the seller may rescind as soon as there is non-payment on the date of entry. However, the third sentence gives the seller an option to rescind 21 days later: does this exclude the common law principle apparently underlying the first two sentences or supplement it by giving two chances to rescind? Then there is the requirement of 'prior written notice'. It seems that this notice is distinct from the notice of rescission itself. Does this mean that the seller has to wait 21 days and then give his prior notice before giving notice of actual rescission? Or does it mean that the seller can rescind on the twenty-first day if he has already given notice during the intervening period? In *Charisma Properties Ltd v Grayling (1994) Ltd*[1] Lord Penrose held that the first interpretation was correct. This was overruled on appeal when an Extra Division found that 'prior' was mere surplusage and that the seller could rescind by giving notice thereof on the twenty-first day after non payment. Plainly the clause requires redrafting to make clear exactly when the seller is entitled to rescind and what steps must be taken to do so.

1 1996 SLT 791, OH; 1996 SC 556, Ex Div.

(6)   The ultimatum procedure

5.42   If the contract does not define what breaches are material justifying rescission, the uncertainty of the common law may be avoided to some extent by the use of the 'ultimatum procedure'. The leading case is *Rodger Builders Ltd v Fawdry*[1], in which the purchaser of heritable property did not pay the price on the due date of 11 November 1947. On 25 November the seller gave the purchaser three days within which to pay, intimating that if he did not pay the seller would regard the contract as void and himself as free to resell. On expiry of the three-day period, the seller resold. The purchaser sought reduction of the resale. It was held that unless time was made of the essence of the contract, failure to pay was not a material breach entitling the seller to rescind. But if payment was delayed, the seller could limit the time to pay to a reasonable period after which failure to pay would become a breach of a material condition entitling the seller to rescind.

1 1950 SC 483.

5.43 The procedure is in common use in conveyancing transactions with respect to failures to pay the price but there seems no reason why it cannot be deployed in relation to other types of contract. Indeed, in conveyancing transactions it has not been confined to breaches of payment obligations[1]. The ultimatum procedure is closely akin to the 'cure' procedure discussed earlier, but in fact serves a different purpose. The ultimatum procedure converts a non-material into a material breach to justify rescission while the 'cure' procedure would prevent rescission in response to a breach which may or may not be material[2].

1 See *McLennan v Warner & Co* 1996 SLT 1349; *McBryde* paras 20.128–20.131.
2 For 'assurance of performance' mechanisms in the DCFR and the Unidroit Principles, see DCFR III.-3:103, 401(2), 505, PICC art 7.1.5.

(7) Mode of rescission

5.44 What steps must be taken to effect rescission? The 'belt and braces' approach is to notify the other party of rescission, and the courts have recognised various informal as well as more formal notifications for this purpose[1]. But is such notice always necessary? Further, must the notice be given as soon as the right arises or only within a reasonable time? Professor McBryde suggests that in some circumstances conduct showing that the contract is regarded as rescinded may be enough; but if there is no positive action by a party in response to a material breach, the right to rescind may be lost by personal bar[2]. Action can of course be dangerous as it will be interpreted objectively and thus potentially inconsistently with the actual intention of the party concerned. In *GL Group plc v Ash Gupta Advertising Ltd*[3],

AG became doubtful of GL's ability to pay for services rendered under a contract and sought immediate payment, also stating that if GL failed to make payment by a certain deadline, AG 'would have no alternative but to resile from the contract'. The upshot was that AG were found to have repudiated the contract rather than to have sought an assurance of performance and were held liable in damages as well[4].

1 See eg *Durkin v DSG Retail Ltd* 2008 GWD 14-254 (taking defective goods back to the seller's shop); *MacDonald v Pollock* 2012 SLT 462 (telephone call to seller).
2 *McBryde* paras 20.107 and 20.121. But see *Lamarra v Capital Bank plc* 2007 SC 95, where the purchaser's rejection of a car in March 2001 was upheld although he continued to use the vehicle until the following June. See also *Fiat Auto Financial Services v Connelly* 2007 SLT (Sh Ct) 111.
3 1987 SCLR 149.
4 For a formal mode of seeking assurance of performance, see DCFR III.-3:505 and PICC, art 7.3.4.

5.45   Another intermediate position between inaction and notice of rescission may be negotiation between the parties over the dispute. Does negotiation bar subsequent rescission? A difficult case is *Cumming v Brown*[1]. Buyers under missives failed to pay the price on 15 May, which under an express term gave the seller a right to rescind on 12 June; but this was not used. The buyers were in a position to settle on 31 July, but the seller purported to rescind on 11 August. It was held that the seller could no longer rescind apparently on the basis of personal bar. The message seems to be that rescission should be effected promptly, if not forthwith. Under the SGA 1979, the buyer's right to rescind for breach of the implied terms as to quality is lost by 'acceptance', which includes intimation of acceptance and lapse of a reasonable time (which is not usually very long)[2]. But, as already noted, seeking 'cure' is not 'acceptance' barring rejection[3]. The would-be rescinder therefore has to tread a fine line after the material breach.

1 1994 SLT (Sh Ct) 11.
2 SGA 1979, s 35.
3 See above, para 5.39.

(8) Effect of rescission

End of the contract

5.46   The effect of rescission is often said to be the ending or the termination of the contract. This is an inaccurate way of describing the legal effects of the remedy. The party exercising the remedy frees itself from performance of obligations arising under the contract in the future. The basic idea can be illustrated through a return to the diagrams used above to illustrate the mutuality principle:

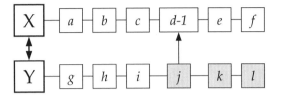

If X's d-1 performance is a material breach justifying rescission by Y, then the latter is free from obligations to perform arising after X's breach, these being shown here as the greyed-out obligations j-l. But Y remains bound to perform the obligations which arose before the rescission (here g-i) insofar as X has performed their counterparts (here a-c).

5.47 A further twist may arise where there is a gap in time between breach and rescission. Under the principle of mutuality, which prevents a party in breach seeking the counterpart performance from the other party, the contract-breaker X may be barred from action in relation to its performance of post-breach obligations. Thus in *Graham v United Turkey Red*[1] a commission agent was dismissed for material breach of contract but was able to recover from his principal what he was owed under the contract in respect of his performances up to the breach, although the mutuality principle disabled him from contractual action in respect of commission earned between the initial breach and the principal's rescission two years later when he found out about the agent's misconduct[2].

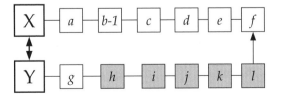

In the terms of our diagram, the agent's breach is b-1 but the principal does not rescind until the time for its performance under obligation l. The agent's performance of pre-breach obligation a must be met by performance of the principal's counterpart obligation (g in the diagram); but if the agent goes on to perform obligations c and d before Y rescinds, the principle of mutuality will prevent X enforcing any corresponding obligations otherwise owed but not yet performed by Y (greyed-out h-l in the diagram).

1 1922 SC 533.
2 But the court decided that the agent would be entitled to the *unjustified enrichment* remedy of recompense for the services he had rendered even although he was in breach of contract. See further below, para 6.56 ff.

5.48   Rescission is thus basically prospective, or forward-looking, in its effects; unlike reduction, rescission for breach generally does not involve putting the parties back into the position they would have been if there had never been a contract[1]. The contract may also contain clauses dealing with what is to happen upon rescission and consistently with the prospective principle these will be given effect. For example, after rescission the aggrieved party may also go on to seek damages for the breach; but the contract-breaker can plead any exemption clauses in the rescinded contract. Arbitration and other choice of forum clauses should also continue to have effect. The aggrieved party may wish to take action under a liquidated damages clause and again this should survive rescission. A difficult case with which the English courts have grappled is the restrictive covenant in a contract of employment which is expressly to take effect upon termination of the contract, 'howsoever caused'. If the employee is in material breach and the employer rescinds the contract as a result by dismissing him, the restrictive covenant presumably remains enforceable against the employee. But if the employee is *wrongfully dismissed* by the employer and accepts this repudiation, the House of Lords has suggested in an English appeal that the employer can no longer enforce the covenant[2]. It would be more consistent with principle, however, to say that if upon construction the covenant goes this far, termination will not affect its enforceability since the parties clearly intended the clause to have effect in this event. It is another question again whether such a clause is reasonable under the restraint of trade doctrine[3].

1 But see further below, para 5.50 ff. This is why *restitutio in integrum* is not a prerequisite of rescission.
2 *General Billposting Co Ltd v Atkinson* [1909] AC 118.
3 See further *Rock Refrigeration Ltd v Jones* [1997] 1 All ER 1 and below, para 7.38.

5.49   Rescission for breach only has effects upon the contractual relationships of the parties. It cannot affect rights arising apart from the contract. For example, real rights in property may be transferred under a contract which is subsequently rescinded for breach. The mere rescission of the contract will not give rise to a retransfer of the property. The contract-breaker who is disabled by the mutuality principle from suing on the contract may be able to make claims in unjustified enrichment[1].

1 See below, para 6.56 ff.

Restitution

5.50 As noted above, rescission is essentially prospective in effect and does not involve unwinding what has happened to restore the parties to their pre-contractual position. None the less there are circumstances in which rights of restoration or restitution arise.[1]

1 See generally MacQueen 'Unjustified enrichment and breach of contract' 1994 JR 137 at 139–149; Miller, 'Unjustified enrichment and failed contracts', in *Zimmermann, Visser & Reid*. Note also DCFR III.-510-514, PICC art 7.3.6.

5.51 The principal example in practice is probably the mutual restitution which follows rescission of a supply of goods contract when the goods are not of satisfactory quality. The customer is entitled to be repaid the price and the goods should be returned to the supplier. This right is limited, however, by the requirement that the remedy be exercised within a reasonable time after the supply[1].

1 See *Atiyah Adams & MacQueen*, 503–504; and see *Douglas v Glenvarigill Co Ltd* 2010 SLT 634.

5.52 Another example of restitution is when a seller of goods or land turns out not to be the owner of the subjects of the sale with the result that there is breach of the express or implied term that the buyer will receive a good title. Here the buyer appears to be entitled to be repaid the price and there is no restriction as to the time within which the remedy must be exercised[1]. This may appear unfair at first sight as the buyer gets the use of the goods or land, possibly for a substantial period, without having to pay for it; but the seller has actually supplied him with nothing. The buyer may be liable to the true owner of the property, whoever she may be, under the law of unjustified enrichment.

1 MacQueen 1994 JR 137 at 139–142. Note that when a buyer rescinds under SGA s 48C any reimbursement to that party may be reduced to take account of the use made by her since she took delivery of the goods (s 48C(3)).

5.53   A third example of restitution following termination concerns advance payments where the payer does not receive the performance which was due to him under the contract. For instance, I pay for my theatre ticket when I book it but the performance does not take place. It seems clear that if I do not receive the counterpart performance to which my advance payment entitles me under the contract, there must be restitution of that payment[1]. Difficult questions can arise about the exact counterpart performance to which the advance payer is entitled. In *Connelly v Simpson*[2], C paid S £16,000 for shares in S's company with delivery to be delayed until C requested it. Two years later, with the shares still undemanded by C and now worth only £400, the company went into insolvent liquidation. C claimed restitution of the £16,000 from S but was unsuccessful, one ground being that he had got what he paid for, namely a right to delivery of the shares on demand. The result also shows that the courts will not allow the right of restitution to become a means of escaping from contracts that have turned out badly for the party seeking the remedy.

1 MacQueen 1994 JR 137 at 144–146. Note the special rules there discussed, making advance freight irrecoverable. Similarly, if the payment is a non-returnable deposit under the contract, restitution on the basis of unjustified enrichment is excluded: *Zemhurst (Holdings) Ltd v Central Securities plc* 1992 SC 58.
2 1993 SC 391. On this case see additionally Dieckmann and Evans-Jones 'The dark side of *Connelly v Simpson*' 1995 JR 90; Scot Law Com Discussion Paper no 109 (1999), paras 4.36–4.47, and note *McBryde* paras 20.142–20.143.

5.54   At least two other difficult situations can be identified. First, the advance payer may receive part of what was bargained for, as in the Australian case of *The Mikhail Lermontov*[1], where a lady booked and paid for a cruise in advance, but the ship sank half-way through the voyage. The lady survived and sought restitution of her whole advance payment. Her claim was refused on the grounds that there was no 'total failure of consideration' for the payment. Scots law has no similar limitation upon the right of restitution for breach; but it would seem extreme to allow her full restitution yet very difficult to determine any partial restitution to which she might be entitled. One approach might be to set off against the claim for restitution the amount by which she was enriched. A second difficult situation concerns the party who, in a contract under which a single lump sum payment is due in return for a complete performance by her, provides part of the performance due under the contract, be it supply of land, goods or services or a combination of these, and is then confronted with a repudiatory refusal to pay the price when the task is completed. Under the doctrine of *White & Carter Councils* discussed above[2], she is of course entitled to complete the performance and sue for payment; but what is the position if she accepts the repudiation and terminates the contract? There is a claim for damages but is there an alternative claim for restitution? The courts have allowed the innocent party in somewhat similar circumstances to make a claim described as *quantum meruit* (ie payment under an *implied* contract)[3]. This looks to the worth of the work done as opposed to its value in the hands of the recipient or the restoration of what has been transferred. The basic approach seems fair: the value to the recipient of a part performance (eg a half-built house) may be very limited; restoration of materials supplied will probably not reflect the worth of the work done; and if only services have been supplied they cannot be returned. A possible objection is that the price mechanism of the contract is being replaced by another under an implied contract and that the appropriate remedy is in fact that of recompense, with *quantum lucratus* the defender being the measure of recovery not *quantum meruit*[4]. The practical difference may be small, however.

1 (1993) 11 ALR 289.
2 At para 5.34.
3 See *ERDC Construction Ltd v H M Love & Co* 1994 SC 620.
4 Wolffe 'Contract and recompense' (1997) 1 EdinLR 469.

5.55 The advance payer's right to restitution cannot be exercised against the assignee of the original creditor of the advance even where the payer has in fact made payment directly to the assignee. The latter is not subjected to the assignor's liabilities[1]; and if the contract between the assignor and the advance payer in fact dealt with the situation where advance payment was made but the assignor's performance was not completed, then in any event a claim in unjustified enrichment was excluded even against one who was a third party to that contract[2].

1 See above, para 2.85.
2 *Compagnie Commerciale Andre SA v Artibell Shipping Co Ltd (No 2)* 2001 SC 653; *Pan Ocean Shipping Co Ltd v Creditcorp Ltd (The Trident Beauty)* [1994] 1 WLR 161 (HL).

6. Breach of Contract and Judicial Remedies

6.1 Judicial remedies for breach of contract are those which may be obtained through court action by the aggrieved party. Two main subdivisions of such remedies can be discerned. First, there are remedies which compel the contract-breaker to perform in accordance with the contract; second, there are the remedies which compel the contract-breaker to provide a substitute for performance.

6.2 There are three remedies which compel a contract-breaker to perform in accordance with the contract: actions for *payment* of a debt; actions of *specific implement*; and actions of *interdict*. In general, the first of these is appropriate to enforce obligations to pay liquid sums of money while the second and third are only appropriate for non-monetary obligations.

REMEDIES LOOKING TO PERFORMANCE

Actions for payment

6.3 Probably the most common breach of contract is failure to pay money due under the contract. There are literally thousands of actions of this kind every year in Scotland, most of them undefended. The figure below seeks to illustrate this.

DEBT ACTIONS IN THE SCOTTISH COURTS 2010–11[1]

Court of Session

Outer House

(1) 4 debt actions initiated (out of 5,081 cases begun in OH); 2 disposed of.
(2) 299 damages actions excluding personal injury cases initiated (almost 6 per cent of all actions in OH), 292 disposed of.

---

(3) 157 commercial cases were initiated and 147 disposed of, with 12 being undefended and disposed of for the pursuer, 87 decrees of absolvitor being pronounced, 20 defended actions dismissed, and 16 defended actions disposed of for the pursuer.

Sheriff Court

(1) 16,135 *ordinary causes* (ie causes for over £5,000) were initiated; 9,200 were for debt and 630 for damages (excluding personal injury). 6,282 and 119 of these respectively were undefended; 798 and 100 respectively were defended; 664 and 47 were dismissed; and in 578 and 368 respectively decree of absolvitor was pronounced.

(2) Of 458 ordinary cause commercial procedure cases initiated, 223 were for debt and 163 for damages; 75 and 2 of these respectively were undefended; 39 and 6 respectively were defended; 23 and 7 respectively were dismissed; and in 51 and 9 respectively decree of absolvitor was pronounced.

(3) 23,729 *summary causes* (ie causes for £5,000 or less) were initiated, 4,337 debt actions and 457 damages actions were disposed of by decree for the pursuer, while 3,853 and 174 respectively were undefended.

(4) Of 34,386 *small claims* (ie claims of up to and including £3,000) initiated, 31,533 were for debt and 2,586 for damages, and 17,767 undefended debt claims were disposed of for the pursuer, as were a further 353 which were defended.

1 Source: *Civil Judicial Statistics 2010–11* (the latest available at the time of writing, accessible at http://www.scotland.gov.uk/Resource/Doc/933/0122575.pdf). Figures for initiations and disposals do not necessarily refer to the same cases.

6.4 The key points to note from the data above are that most debt actions are undefended and are really the first step to further processes, known as diligence, to recover the monies[1]; that debt actions are many times more frequent than actions for damages (not all of which will be in respect of breach of contract since the category includes delict damages claims in non-personal injury cases). It can also be seen that the sheriff court is the forum for debt enforcement in Scotland, not the Court of Session. The special procedures in both the Court of Session and some sheriff courts for commercial cases, most if not all of which will involve contracts, are quite commonly not followed through to formal disposal, ie they are settled by the parties out of court[2].

1 See generally *Gloag & Henderson* ch 50. But in an important contrast with specific implement (see below, para 6.8), civil imprisonment for debt is not allowed.
2 Only eight sheriff courts – at Aberdeen, Dingwall, Duns, Glasgow, Inverness, Jedburgh, Portree and Selkirk – use a commercial procedure.

6.5 Two other points are of significance. The Late Payment of Commercial Debts (Interest) Act 1998 grants, by way of an implied term, rights to businesses to claim simple interest at rates fixed by order on late payments of debt by other businesses and the public sector. Parties may contract out of the regime *after* the debt has been created but any attempt to do so *before* the debt is created is void unless a substantial remedy is provided for late payment. Terms providing for *postponement* of payment must be reasonable. Other statutes enable a debtor, in very exceptional circumstances, to argue that he is the victim of an 'extortionate credit bargain' and to seek judicial revision of the contract accordingly[1].

1 Consumer Credit Act 1974, ss 140A–140D (inserted by Consumer Credit Act 2006 in place of the previous extortionate credit bargain provisions); Bankruptcy (Scotland) Act 1985, s 61 (as amended); Insolvency Act 1986, s 244 (as amended).

Specific implement[1]

[handwritten annotation: Interest + wrongful withholding at common law?]

6.6 Specific implement is the appropriate remedy when a positive act of performance other than the payment of money is sought from the contract-breaker such as delivery of goods or other property or the rendering of services. A common use of specific implement is to compel performance of missives by the seller in a transfer of heritage. It is conventionally said that implement is the primary right of the creditor on breach but this is hard to reconcile with the situation in practice where implement is sought comparatively rarely and is even more rarely granted. In the late nineteenth century, the creditor's right to specific implement was subjected to the discretion of the court and this has since been further elaborated into a set of rules about when the remedy will be refused. These are as follows:

- when performance is impossible or otherwise unenforceable or would cause hardship to the defender out of all proportion to the benefit to the pursuer;

- where the subject matter is of no particular significance and money compensation would be adequate (eg when the breach is non-delivery of goods for which there is a readily available, albeit more expensive, alternative source of supply: the extra cost should be sought as damages);
- where the contract involves personal relationships (eg employment contracts or partnerships).

1 *McBryde* ch 23; 13 *Stair Memorial Encyclopaedia* paras 8–10, 13 and 14. Cf DCFR III.-3:302, PICC art 7.2.2 (grounds for refusal of order of specific performance).

6.7   Moreover, these rules do not confine the general equitable discretion of the court. The uncertainty as to whether or not an order will be granted explains why in practice it is common (although not essential) when seeking specific implement to include in the pleadings an alternative crave for damages. It remains important to see specific implement as the creditor's right, however qualified and however little used in practice, since otherwise there is cross-over into the 'bad man's' view of contract as essentially a choice between performance and the payment of damages[1]. In English law, the equivalent remedy of specific performance has its origins in the courts of equity and is only granted where damages does not provide an adequate remedy. This has given rise to the theory of 'efficient breach' under which a party should not be compelled to perform where his reason for breaking the contract is that he has found a third party prepared to pay more for the performance, leaving the contract-breaker able to make his profit *and* pay the damages of the aggrieved party. The theory is that because the performance goes to the party who values it most highly while the aggrieved party, through his damages, gets his economic return, the outcome produces the most efficient result economically. Be that as it may, Scots law does not go as far as this and is closer to the Continental and South African systems under which an order for performance is a right of the creditor[2].

1 Note that according to an Outer House decision the fact that a party has obtained a damages award in respect of one breach of a contract does not preclude the same party obtaining an order for specific implement of another obligation in the same contract: *Douglas Shelf Seven Ltd v Co-operative Wholesale Society Ltd (No 2)* [2009] CSOH 3.
2 *Zweigert and Kötz* ch 35; Rowan *Remedies for Breach of Contract: A Comparative Analysis of the Protection of Performance* (2012) ch 1. Performance is also a right of the creditor in DCFR III.-3:302 and PICC art 7.2.2.

6.8   One of the reasons for the general reluctance to grant specific implement in Scotland is that the basic sanction for non-compliance with the order of the court is the imprisonment of the contract-breaker provided that the refusal to comply is wilful. The maximum term of imprisonment is six months[1]. Given that the sanction is relatively severe and perhaps even an infringement of the European Convention of Human Rights[2], and that it may be difficult to frame an order for implement with enough precision to enable the defender to know what it must do in order to avoid imprisonment, reluctance to use the remedy is understandable. But courts, practitioners and text-writers have perhaps been slow to realise the flexibility of response created by statute in 1940, allowing the court a wide discretion based upon 'justice and equity' to make orders in lieu of imprisonment when enforcing decrees of specific implement[3]. Express mention is made of orders for the payment of money, in effect the imposition of a fine for breach, and of the power to order searches for moveables. There could also perhaps be orders for performance by third parties, to be paid for by the contract-breaker, or the provision of further opportunity to perform, for example by way of replacement or repair of faulty goods or services. These additional powers of the court have been particularly useful when the contract-breaker is a company or other association where the sanction of imprisonment may be of little or no coercive value.

1 Law Reform (Miscellaneous Provisions) (Scotland) Act 1940 (LRMPSA 1940), s 1(1).
2 Fourth Protocol, art 1. The Protocol is not incorporated into domestic law under the Human Rights Act 1998. Meanwhile, therefore, see Article 5(1)(b) of the Convention: 'No one shall be deprived of his liberty save in the following cases and in accordance with a procedure prescribed by law: ... (b) the lawful arrest or detention of a person for non-compliance with the lawful order of a court or in order to secure the fulfilment of any obligation prescribed by law'.
3 LRMPSA 1940, s 1(2).

6.9 An important development in the law of specific implement, which underlines the nature of the remedy as the aggrieved party's right, is to be found in the case of *Retail Park Investments Ltd v Royal Bank of Scotland plc (No 2)*[1]. RPI, the landlord of commercial premises under a 25-year lease which still had seven years to run, sought specific implement of a clause under which the tenants, RBS, were obliged to keep open and use the premises for the purposes of retail banking. RBS proposed to vacate the premises leaving in place only cash-dispensing machines. At first instance, Lord Coulsfield held that mere provision of cash-dispensers was insufficient compliance with the terms of the lease, relying on the parties' understanding at the time of entry into the lease in 1977 and on the express reference to keeping the premises open during normal business hours. However, a good objection to a decree of specific implement is impossibility of enforcement. Given the changing nature of retail banking, in Lord Coulsfield's view it was not possible to frame the order in such a way that RBS would know precisely what compliance required; it would also not be possible for the court to police compliance over the lengthy remaining period of the lease[2]. On appeal, this view was rejected. An Extra Division considered that precise specification of what compliance required was not necessary in an order of specific implement: imprisonment or other penalty only followed wilful breach of the order. With a non-wilful breach the court could give the defender a further opportunity to comply. The court could therefore specify the end to be achieved but leave open the precise means of doing so. Nor was it fatal to the granting of an order that compliance would require several actions over a period of several years.

1 1996 SC 227.
2 1996 SLT 52 (opinion not reported in 1996 SC).

6.10 The decision may be contrasted with the subsequent decision of the House of Lords in the English case of *Co-operative Insurance Society Ltd v Argyll Stores (Holdings) Ltd*[1]. In this case, the Court of Appeal granted landlords decree to hold tenants to their lease although the latter's operations from the premises were running at a growing loss. There was a vigorous dissent from Millett LJ (as he then was), asserting the traditional English principle that damages were the primary remedy for breach of contract; but the majority equally vigorously pointed out that bargains should be kept, that the parties had been free to contract that failure to keep open should sound only in damages but had not done so, and that the tenant had acted with unmitigated commercial cynicism rather than keep an unambiguous promise[2]. The House of Lords overturned the Court of Appeal and its move away from established English principles. Lord Hoffmann's leading speech noted that 'specific performance is traditionally regarded as an exceptional remedy'[3], while observing that 'by contrast, in countries with legal systems based on civil law, such as France, Germany and Scotland, the plaintiff is prima facie entitled to specific performance'[4]. He drew attention to the problems of supervision by the court, the heavy-handed nature of the supporting sanctions, the imprecision of the order and the need to bring litigation to an end, although also distinguishing between cases where the order was to continue an activity (in which the difficulties were greatest) and those in which a result was to be achieved (in which they were less)[5].

1 [1998] AC 1.
2 [1996] Ch 286 (CA).
3 [1998] AC at 11.
4 [1998] AC at 11.
5 The Scottish Lords of Appeal (Lord Hope and Lord Clyde) both concurred in the decision, although Lord Clyde commented that he would 'wish to reserve [his] opinion on the approach which might be adopted by civilian systems': [1998] AC at 19.

6.11 Given the possible hardship to the defendant a Scottish court might have refused specific implement even after *Retail Parks*. But against this conclusion, the effect of ordering continued performance of the contract in cases like this is not necessarily to condemn the defendant to continue trading at a loss and so, ultimately, to insolvency. Absent contractual provision to the contrary, the tenant can assign or sublet to a third party[1] or enter into negotiations with the landlord to buy out the remaining term of the lease. The effect of the court's decree is to set a baseline for such actions or negotiations and to prevent what would otherwise be the freedom of the tenant to throw up its contract and leave the landlord with the burden of proving and quantifying a damages claim. For this reason, the apparent expansion of the scope of specific implement seems well founded[2]. The Scottish approach to implement of 'keep open' clauses in commercial leases was reaffirmed by the First Division of the Court of Session in *Highland and Universal Properties Ltd v Safeway Properties Ltd*[3], full account having been taken in the opinions of the court of the *Co-operative Insurance case*.

1 This is what happened in the *Co-operative Insurance* case after the decision of the Court of Appeal.
2 For discussion and further cases see MacQueen and Macgregor 'Specific implement, interdict and contractual performance' (1999) 3 ELR 239.
3 2000 SC 297. See further Macgregor 'Specific implement in Scots law' in Smits, Haas and Hesen (eds) *Specific Performance in Contract Law: National and Other Perspectives* (2008); MacQueen, Dauner-Lieb and Tettinger 'Specific performance and rights of cure' in Vogenauer and Dannemann (eds) *The Draft Common European Sales Law and Its Interaction with English and German Law* (forthcoming).

Interdict[1]

6.12 Interdict is a preventative remedy by which the court forbids or prohibits the carrying out or continuation of some action. An interdict may be permanent or interim (that is, temporary). A perpetual interdict will follow a full consideration of the facts and the rights of the respective parties and like most litigation may take some time to obtain. An interim interdict can however be obtained extremely quickly and is designed as a temporary remedy preserving the *status quo* and preventing prejudice to a party pending later and fuller investigation. The court has to be persuaded (1) that there is a prima facie case (that is, an arguable case and an issue to try), and (2) that the balance of convenience between the parties favours the grant of the remedy. An interim interdict can be recalled almost as quickly as it is granted if the interdicted party can show grounds why it should be discharged. Breach of interdict is contempt of court and invites the appropriate sanctions.

1 13 *Stair Memorial Encyclopaedia* paras 17–23.

6.13 Clearly interdict can be used to prevent an anticipated breach of contract of any kind. Interim interdict in particular is extremely useful in many cases, notably the enforcement of restrictive covenants. But interdict must be kept distinct from specific implement. The courts have clearly affirmed that interdict cannot be used as an indirect way to compel a party to perform some positive act and if this will be the effect of a grant of the remedy, it should be refused[1]. A party may be compelled to perform only by a decree of specific implement. In slightly misleading shorthand, interdict cannot be used to enforce positive as opposed to negative obligations. Contractual obligations may be negative in character in that they require a party not to do something or to refrain from action, for example a restrictive covenant. The general obligation not to breach is another instance. The distinction is most clearly illustrated by the cases about tenants in commercial leases who quit in breach of obligations to keep the premises open and use them for business purposes. If the tenant notifies the landlord of its intention to quit before actually doing so, then interim interdict can certainly be obtained immediately to prevent the occurrence of the abandonment, while a permanent interdict might if necessary be obtained later[2]. However, specific implement would probably be needed if the tenant continued to occupy but simply failed to use the premises: for example, by having business signs and equipment there but no staff or stock[3]. Again, if the tenant leaves and the landlord only finds out afterwards, interdict is incompetent because compliance would force the tenant to the positive action of resuming occupation and use[4]. That requires the procedure of specific implement and there is no such thing as interim specific implement at common law[5]. Fortunately for the landlord, what would otherwise be a lacuna in his remedies encouraging the tenant not to give notice of an intention to quit is filled by ss 46 and 47 of the Court of Session Act 1988[6]. It is worth remembering that in all these cases the landlord's entitlement to the tenant's rent continues unabated, regardless of whether or not the tenant is in occupation, and is enforceable by way of an action for payment[7]. In some cases, this is all that will be required. The questions about interdict and specific implement have tended to arise most often in cases where the tenant holds a crucial prestige or 'flagship' position in a shopping or other commercial centre, such as that of a bank or a building society in a shopping mall providing cash and other facilities for shoppers and other tenants on the premises, or where the centre as a whole is in decline and the landlord is concerned therefore to prevent a haemorrhage of his tenants.

1 *Church Commissioners for England v Abbey National plc* 1994 SC 651.
2 *Highland & Universal Properties Ltd v Safeway Properties Ltd* 1995 GWD 23–1261.
3 *Retail Parks Investments Ltd v Our Price Music Ltd* 1995 SLT 1161.
4 *Grosvenor Developments (Scotland) plc v Argyll Stores Ltd* 1987 SLT 738.
5 However, *Report on Remedies for Breach of Contract* (Scot Law Com no 174 (1999)) recommends the introduction of such a remedy in both the Court of Session and the sheriff court.
6 See further below, para 6.15 ff.
7 *Salaried Staff London Loan Co v Swears & Wells* 1985 SC 189.

6.14 The questions have also arisen in two employment cases where employees were seeking to prevent employers following redundancy or disciplinary procedures against them other than those laid down in the contract of employment. Although the effect of the interdict sought was to compel performance of employment contracts which otherwise would have come to an end, in both cases the court held for the employee[1]. The cases are also significant because in both the court overcame the traditional reluctance to enforce employment contracts specifically.

1 *Anderson v Pringle of Scotland* 1998 SLT 754; *Peace v City of Edinburgh Council* 1999 SCLR 593.

Interim remedies under the Court of Session Act 1988

6.15 Sections 46 and 47 of the Court of Session Act 1988 (CSA 1988) provide as follows:

'46. Where a respondent in any application or proceedings in the Court, whether before or after the institution of such proceedings or application, has done any act which the Court might have prohibited by interdict, the Court may ordain the respondent to perform any act which may be necessary for reinstating the petitioner in his possessory right, or for granting specific relief against the illegal act complained of.

47 ... (2) In any cause in dependence before the Court, the Court may, on the motion of any party to the cause, make such order regarding the interim possession of any property to which the cause relates, or regarding the subject matter of the cause, as the Court may think fit.'

These provisions have been used to provide temporary enforcement of contracts in a number of cases, particularly the type of situation already discussed in connection with both specific implement and interdict, namely the long commercial lease where the tenant in breach of a 'keep open' clause seeks to abandon the premises. The landlord who has been notified in advance of the tenant's intention to quit can obtain interim interdict but the landlord who only discovers the tenant's intention when it has been put into effect has only specific implement at common law. In *Church Commissioners for England v Abbey National plc*[1], however, Lord President Hope pointed out that ss 46 and 47 of the CSA 1988 could provide the landlord with an interim remedy to get the tenant back into business occupation of the premises. The remedies are discretionary ('the Court *may*') and, like interim interdict, there has to be a prima facie case of breach and consideration of the balance of convenience[2]. The grant of such an interim order does not prevent a later court from concluding that a permanent order cannot be granted[3].

1 1994 SC 651.
2 *Overgate Centre Ltd v William Low Supermarkets Ltd* 1995 SLT 1181.
3 *Retail Parks Investments Ltd v Royal Bank of Scotland plc (No 2)* 1996 SC 227 at 240 per Lord McCluskey.

REMEDIES PROVIDING A SUBSTITUTE FOR PERFORMANCE: DAMAGES[1]

6.16 The principal example of a remedy for breach of contract providing a substitute for performance is that of damages[2]. Lord President Inglis once stated that it was 'impossible to say that a contract can be broken even in respect of time without the party being entitled to claim damages'[3]. It thus appears that although the remedy began as an alternative where specific implement would not be granted, damages may now generally be obtained for breach of contract. One constraint on the remedy which the courts created for themselves despite the dictum – the rule that a party could not retain defective property supplied and claim by way of damages diminution of the price (*actio quanti minoris*) – has been removed by the legislature[4].

1 *McBryde* ch 22; 15 *Stair Memorial Encyclopaedia* paras 891–940.
2 Strictly speaking, one might add cases where the court orders that there be performance by a third party rather than the contract-breaker, treated briefly above (at para 6.8) in the context of specific implement.
3 *Webster v Cramond Iron Co* (1875) 2 R 752 at 754. But see further below para 6.30.
4 Sale of Goods Act 1979 (SGA 1979), ss 15B and 53A; Contract (Scotland) Act 1997, s 1. For the background see Evans-Jones 'The history of the *actio quanti minoris* in Scotland' 1991 JR 190. Note however the introduction of a price reduction remedy in SGA 1979 s 48C, implementing the Consumer Sales Directive (above, para 5.39; see also below, para 6.58), and note also similar remedy in DCFR III.-3:601 (no equivalent in PICC).

6.17   The aim of an award of damages for breach of contract is to provide monetary compensation to the aggrieved party for the losses suffered as a result of the breach. Thus damages cannot be punitive or exemplary nor in general can they be based upon the gains which are earned by the contract-breaker through his breach. In *Teacher v Calder*[1], the defender, a timber merchant, broke his contract by investing in a distillery business money lent to him by the pursuer to invest in the timber business. It was held by the House of Lords that the damages were to be based on what the timber business would have made with the additional capital rather than on the defender's much larger gains from his distillery investment. English law has however begun to develop a concept of 'gain-based' as distinct from 'compensatory' damages; the former concentrates upon the contract-breaker's gain as the basis of recovery rather than upon the aggrieved party's loss. The leading case is the decision of the House of Lords in *Attorney-General v Blake*[2]. Here the Crown was held entitled to recover the gains made by a former British spy who had defected to the Soviet Union in the 1960s and later published his very profitable memoirs in breach of the lifelong duty of confidentiality which he owed as an employee of the Crown. The House of Lords emphasised that the remedy was exceptional and allowed here only because none of the usual remedies would be an adequate response to the situation. Further, the claimant needed to have a legitimate interest in preventing the other party's profit-making activities. Otherwise little guidance was given for future cases, and *Teacher v Calder* was not mentioned. In some subsequent decisions the English courts have denied recovery of this kind[3]. The few successful claims have generally involved deliberate breaches of contract aimed squarely at either making a gain or saving expenditure[4]. Another important example which actually pre-dates *Blake* is a case which involved the defendant developer breaching a restrictive covenant by building more than the permitted number of houses on a piece of land. The damages were assessed on the basis of what the developer would have had to pay to get the covenant relaxed, with the major factor in determining that sum being the profit that the developer made and the sum awarded being about 5% thereof[5]. From a Scottish point of view[6] the attraction of the new remedy is its support for performance of the contract according to its terms: the taking away of gains made from breach gives parties an incentive to adhere to their contracts. But this may raise the possibility of a conceptual link between the remedy and specific implement: is it available only where the court might otherwise have ordered implement? On the other hand, if the remedy is limited to exceptional cases, it will in effect become a matter of judicial discretion rather than genuinely rule-based law, with all the consequential uncertainty for contracting parties; and if it is essentially a remedy against cynical or intentional breach aimed at making the gain in question, there will have to be difficult inquiries into the motivations lying behind people's conduct. There are other difficulties such as the application to awards of this kind of limitations found in the law of compensatory damages (and discussed further below), such as causation, remoteness, contributory negligence and (perhaps) mitigation.

1 (1899) 1 F (HL) 39.
2 [2001] 1 AC 268, discussed by *McKendrick*, ch 20.6 and *Burrows* pp 395–407. See also Edelman *Gains-Based Damages* (2002); Rowan *Remedies for Breach of Contract* (2012) ch 3F.
3 See eg *AB Corporation v CD Company, The Sine Nomine* [2002] 1 Lloyds Rep 805; *World Wide Fund for Nature (formerly World Wildlife Fund) v World Wrestling Federation Entertainment Inc* [2002] FSR 32, affd [2002] FSR 33 (CA).
4 See *Esso Petroleum Co Ltd v Niad* [2001] All ER (D) 324 (Nov); *Experience Hendrix LLC v PPX Enterprises Inc* [2003] EMLR 25 (CA). Note also the Israeli case of *Adras Building Material Ltd v Harlow and Jones GmbH* (1988) 42(1) PD 221 (SC); see also for a full translation [1995] 3 Restitution LR 235 (seller of goods who re-sold to third party before delivery to first buyer held liable to latter for gain from re-sale).
5 *Wrotham Park Estate Co Ltd v Parkside Homes Ltd* [1974] 1 WLR 798. In *WWF World Wide Fund for Nature (formerly World Wildlife Fund) v World Wrestling Federation Entertainment Inc (No 2)* [2008] 1 WLR 445 the CA controversially suggested that the recovery in *Wrotham Park* was 'compensatory' rather than

'gains-based'. This approach is however apparently confirmed in the Privy Council decision, *Pell Frischmann Engineering Ltd v Bow Valley Iran Ltd* [2011] 1 WLR 2370, where the defendants' gain from its breach of a confidentiality agreement was between $1 and $1.8 million, but the damages awarded were $2.5 million and explicitly stated to be compensatory in nature. This was reaffirmed in *Force India Formula One Team Ltd v 1 Malaysia Racing Team SDN BHD* [2012] EWHC 616 (Ch), paras 375–387.

6 For Scottish perspectives on the subject, see Thomson 'Restitutionary and performance damages' 2001 SLT (News) 71; Black 'A new experience in contract damages? Reflections on Experience *Hendrix v PPX Enterprises*' 2005 JR 31; and *Hogg* paras 4.123–4.131. Note also Campbell 'The treatment of *Teacher v Calder* in *AG v Blake*' (2002) 65 MLR 256.

6.18 It has been said that, in contrast to English law, Scots law resists the formulation of too precise rules on damages for breach of contract[1]. Nevertheless in both practice and academic writing English authorities are drawn upon with some freedom. This is particularly true with regard to a number of rules which operate to limit the amount of compensation which the aggrieved party can claim: remoteness, mitigation and, in some cases, contributory negligence. However, equivalents to these rules can also be found in the Civilian and other mixed legal systems[2]. An important consideration in the development of the law, past and future, is the relationship with the parallel rules of causation, mitigation, remoteness and contributory negligence in the law of delict[3]; are the rules the same or different, and if so, why?

1 *Duke of Portland v Wood's Trs* 1926 SC 640 at 651; *Hutchison v Davidson* 1945 SC 395.

2 Treitel *Remedies for Breach of Contract: a comparative survey* (1988) ch VI; Eiselen 'Specific performance and special damages' in *MacQueen & Zimmermann* pp 270–279; Rowan *Remedies for Breach of Contract* (2012) ch 3B, E. See also DCFR III.-3, sect 7; PICC, ch 7, sect 4.

3 For which, see Thomson *Delictual Liability* (4th edn, 2009) pp 139–147, 156–159, 301–307.

Loss

6.19 The amount of loss is in general to be determined by a comparison between the position in which the aggrieved party would have been had the contract been performed properly and its actual position as a result of the breach[1]. As a general principle loss is assessed as at the date of the breach but in exceptional circumstances account can be taken of events which occurred after that date, for example if the declaration of war after the date of the breach would have frustrated the contract or entitled the contract breaker lawfully to terminate the contract[2]. Damages can be said to be a monetary substitute for performance of the contract and to protect what is sometimes known as the 'performance' or 'expectation' interest of the aggrieved party[3]. Some illustrations help to make the idea clear.

(1) In a sale of goods, the seller fails to deliver on the due date. By statute, the buyer's loss is prima facie the difference between the contract price and the market price prevailing on the delivery date. Assuming that the contract price is lower than the market price, the buyer's loss is thus either (a) the extra cost of buying replacement goods if they were purchased for the buyer's use, or (b) if the buyer's purpose was to re-sell, the profit to be made on an immediate re-sale of the goods that ought to have been delivered. Obviously the buyer does not have to pay the price to the seller or, if it has already been paid, can recover it[4].

(2) In a sale of goods the seller delivers defective machinery which the buyer is going to use to manufacture other goods which he then re-sells at a profit. This time the price is paid, and the buyer repairs rather than rejects the machinery. The buyer's damages are the extra cost to him of repairing the machinery[5].

(3) The situation is as in (2), but the buyer uses the machine at a less productive level rather than engage in expensive repairs or rejection. The buyer's damages are the difference between the profits he has made and the greater profits which he would have made had the machinery not been defective[6].

(4) In a building contract the works are completed defectively or not in accordance with the contract description. There are two possible routes by which the employer can be put in the same position as he would have been had the contract been performed. First, the damages can be assessed on the basis of the cost of repairing the defect or bringing the building into conformity with the contract. Second, the value of the building received can be compared with the presumably higher value of what ought to have been received, and the employer awarded the difference[7].

1 *Houldsworth v Brand's Trs* (1877) 4 R 369 at 374 and 375; *Govan Rope and Sail Co Ltd v Weir & Co* (1897) 24 R 368 at 370–371.
2 *Golden Strait Corporation v Nippon Yusen Kubishka Kaisha* [2007] 2 AC 353 (by a 3–2 majority). See also *Radford v De Froberville* [1977] 1 WLR 1262; *Dodd Properties (Kent) Ltd v Canterbury City Council* [1980] 1 WLR 433 and *Douglas Shelf Seven Ltd v Co-operative Wholesale Soc Ltd* [2007] CSOH 53, para 603 (Lord Reed).

Damages for late payment?

i.e, not interest,

3 The terminology of 'expectation' was developed in a famous American article: Fuller and Perdue 'The reliance interest in contract damages' (1936) 46 Yale LJ 52 and 373 (two parts). See further Friedmann 'The performance interest in contract damages' (1995) 111 LQR 628; Macgregor 'The expectation, reliance and restitution interests in contract damages' 1996 JR 227; and Stewart 'The theory of the Scots law of contract' 1996 JR 403.

4 *Anderson v Croall* (1903) 6 F 153; *Marshall & Co v Nicoll & Son* 1919 SC (HL) 129.

5 *Gibson v Farie* 1918 1 SLT 404; *Waddington v Buchan Poultry Products* 1963 SLT 168.

6 *Gillespie v Howden* (1885) 12 R 800; *Duff & Co v Iron and Steel Fencing and Buildings Co* (1891) 19 R 199; *Govan Rope and Sail Co v Weir & Co* (1897) 24 R 368.

7 *Ramsay v Brand* (1898) 25 R 1212; *Prudential Assurance Co Ltd v James Grant & Co (West) Ltd* 1982 SLT 423; *Black v Gibson* 1992 SLT 1076.

6.20 In all of these situations the aggrieved party is being put in the same position as if the contract had been performed, at least in so far as money can do so. Two important ideas seem to underlie the various outcomes: loss is either the *difference in value* between the contractual and the actual performance or the *cost of curing* the breach. This shorthand is certainly a very useful way of approaching many typical situations of breach[1]. But it is not enough on its own to provide an immediate answer in all cases.

1 *McBryde* para 22.93; 3 *Stair Memorial Encyclopaedia* para 109, and 15 *Stair Memorial Encyclopaedia* para 911; Burrows *Remedies for Torts and Breach of Contract* (3rd edn, 2004) at 209–224.

6.21 First, both approaches may be relevant. At the very least, in practice both are averred in the pleadings as possible alternatives or as a means of cross-checking one result with another[1]. In some cases the approaches may appear to be combined. Thus for example, if a supplier delivers a defective building or defective machinery to be used by the recipient to create an income, then the recipient may be entitled to damages for both the cost of putting the defects right and the profit not earned during the period while repairs were carried out[2]. But there are dangers of overcompensation or double recovery in such cases. If the difference in value approach is applied correctly, the value of the contractual performance includes expected gross receipts to be earned by the asset less the cost of earning those receipts; that figure should then be compared with the value of the actual performance, which will take the cost of repairs into account. If, following such a calculation of difference in value, the cost of cure is again added in, then the pursuer is recovering twice in respect of the same loss. Express recovery of repair costs and lost profits as separate items should therefore only occur if profits are calculated net, that is, as gross receipts minus the cost of earning them. In general, the aggrieved party may choose which approach to follow and naturally will take the course which offers the higher recovery. However, in *Ruxley Electronics & Construction v Forsyth*[3], a swimming pool costing £17,800 was not as deep as specified in the contract and would have cost £21,500 to repair. It did not appear that the customer, F, would effect the repairs, since he was happy to use the shallower pool. In these circumstances, the House of Lords refused to grant cost of cure damages because the claim was unreasonable. Further, since the non-conformity with specification did not affect the resale value of the property, the difference in value damages were nil. The case presents difficulties inasmuch as it seems to give the green light to builders to save money by cutting corners in contracts. On the other hand, if cost of cure damages had been awarded, F would have had a perfectly good swimming pool for nothing plus some money in respect of a loss which would not in fact have been incurred. The case may demonstrate the limits of the compensatory approach to damages. A more attractive solution, not available in Scots law as a consequence of *Teacher v Calder*, might have been to award F a sum equal to the builder's savings in not carrying out the contract properly[4]. The problem does not often arise in commercial construction contracts because they usually contain an express right for the employer to have defects corrected at the builder's expense for a period after the apparent completion of the works, plus a retention of an appropriate percentage of the contract price until the end of that period. As it was, the House of Lords upheld a modest award of £2,500 to F for 'loss of amenity'[5].

1 *Duke of Portland v Wood's Tr* 1926 SC 640 at 651.
2 *Fleming v Airdrie Iron Co*(1882) 9 R 473.
3 [1996] AC 344.
4 See above, para 6.17, and discussion there of English concept of restitutionary damages.
5 See further below, para 6.29. In so far as the cost of cure would have made F better off, this could have been avoided by letting his contractual expectation act as a cap on the damages, ie only the increase in value, if any, of the pool after cure: see 3 *Stair Memorial Encyclopaedia* para 109.

6.22   Another difficulty may lie in calculating the value of the contractual expectation. The contractual obligation which is the subject of the claim may have given the contract-breaker an option as to how to perform. Damages for breach in such cases are usually calculated on the basis of the performance least onerous to the contract-breaker. But in *Paula Lee Ltd v Robert Zehil& Co Ltd*[1], the defendants refused to take any goods under a contract which obliged them to make a selection from a range of goods supplied by the plaintiffs. It was held that, in order to reflect commercial reality, damages would be assessed on the basis of a reasonable performance by the defendant and not on the assumption that it would have taken nothing but the cheapest of the plaintiff's goods.

1 [1983] 2 All ER 390. See also *Douglas Shelf Seven Ltd v Co-operative Wholesale Society Ltd* [2007] CSOH 53, paras 590–593 (Lord Reed).

6.23 Another situation is where the obligation breached is expressed in open-ended language such as a duty to take reasonable care. The approach to be taken is best illustrated through the surveyor cases in which a client who has purchased a property with defects which were not noted in the surveyor's pre-purchase report as a result of his negligence, claims damages for breach by the surveyor. In this situation, difference in value is not to be assessed with reference to the values of the property with and without the defects. Instead, the question should be, what would the position have been if the surveyor had reported the defects by acting with the care required? This leads to the conclusion that the purchaser would either have paid less or not bought at all. Thus the damages should be the figure produced by comparing the price which the client paid for the property with the actual value of the property at the time of purchase or by looking at the cost of repairing the defects[1]. Similarly, where a surveyor negligently overvalues a property for a lender who takes security over it, the lender can recover only the difference between the supposed and the actual value, not the difference between the amount lent and the amount actually realised when the security is enforced[2].

1 *Perry v Sidney Phillips & Son* [1982] 1 WLR 1297; *Watts v Morrow* [1991] 1 WLR 1421.
2 *South Australia Asset Management Corp v York Montague Ltd* [1997] AC 191. See for another example the Scottish case *Upton Park Homes Ltd v MacDonalds, Solicitors* [2009] CSOH 159. However, if the misstatement was fraudulent, the client can recover all the losses arising from the transaction but must, of course, sue in delict: *Smith New Court Securities Ltd v Scrimgeour Vickers (Asset Management) Ltd* [1997] AC 254. The *SAAMCo* case is criticised in depth by Burrows, pp 109–122.

6.24 In some cases, the problem is that the breach of contract denies the aggrieved party, not a certain benefit, but the chance of a benefit. The classic English case concerned the claim of a girl who through breach of contract was denied the opportunity to take part in and win what was effectively a beauty contest with a first prize of £5 a week for three years. Her damages were based, not on the value of the prize, but on the value of the chance to win the prize[1]. There has been at least one Scottish case in which an agent recovered damages for the loss of a chance to earn commission[2]. Despite doubts expressed in delictual cases on the subject, there seems no reason in principle against such recovery taking account of matters such as the number of contingencies upon which the chance depends and the likelihood of success[3].

1 *Chaplin v Hicks* [1911] 2 KB 786.
2 *Michael Robins etc Consultants v Skilling* 1976 SLT (Notes) 18.
3 *McBryde* paras 22.78–22.79; *Hogg,* paras 3.88–3.93.

6.25   However, in some cases the value of the contract-breaker's expectation is simply too speculative or uncertain to admit of valuation by the court. Examples of such situations include the salvage value of a shipwreck which did not exist and the profits to be earned by a film which was never made[1]. In such cases, the English and other Common Law courts have allowed plaintiffs to switch to an alternative way of assessing the loss caused by the breach, protecting what is sometimes known as the 'reliance interest', a form of what we have called the *status quo* interest[2]. The effect of this is that the aggrieved party recovers expenditure wasted as a result of the breach. In other words, there is an element of restoration to the position as though the contract had never been. Thus in the shipwreck case the would-be salvor recovered the costs of the abortive salvage expedition, while in the film case the wasted production costs were recovered. Indeed, in the film case the Court of Appeal allowed recovery of expenditure made even before the contract in question had been concluded, on the basis that the loss was a foreseeable result of the breach; but the result seems doubtful, given that such pre-contractual expenditure must have been at the risk of the plaintiff when made (ie it might have been a waste of money anyway), and there seems no reason why the position should be changed by the subsequent contract unless, perhaps, the expenditure was induced by pre-contractual representations or conduct of the other contracting party.

1 *McRae v Commonwealth Disposals Commission* (1951) 84 CLR 377 (ship); *Anglia TV v Reed* [1972] 1 QB 60 (film).
2 *Burrows* ch 5. For 'reliance' see Fuller and Perdue (1936) 46 Yale LJ 32, and for *status quo* see above, para 1.31 ff.

6.26   To let the aggrieved party return to the position as if he had incurred no expenditure upon the contract may allow him to escape from a bad bargain and to do better than he would have done if the contract had been fully performed. That might be said, for example, of the shipwreck case. The English courts have sought to avoid this result by finding that reliance protection is limited by the amount of the expectation interest. Thus in *C & P Haulage v Middleton*[1], a party occupying the ground of another under licence carried out work on the premises at his own expense and for the purposes of the business he conducted there. But the licence was wrongfully terminated early. Since the licensee could not have recouped his expenditure in the remaining period of the licence, recovery of that expense as reliance damages was denied. It is, however, for the contract-breaker to show that the expenses would not have been recouped on full performance[2].

1 [1983] 1 WLR 1461.
2 See *CCC (London) Films Ltd v Imperial Quadrant Films* [1985] QB 16; *Commonwealth of Australia v Amann Aviation Pty Ltd* (1991) 66 ALJR 123.

6.27 These issues have not been much discussed in Scottish cases but there are examples of reliance-based recovery being allowed[1]. In *Fielding v Newell*[2], for example, a seller of heritage defaulted and the buyer's claim to the following expenditure was held relevant, namely legal and survey fees, travel and accommodation expenses, and telephone charges. Moreover, the expenses were incurred before the conclusion of the contract of sale.

1 See, eg, *Daejan Developments v Armia Ltd* 1981 SC 48, and see further *Macgregor* 1996 JR 227 at 237–241; cf *Stewart* 1996 JR 403 at 409–411, Scot Law Com Discussion Paper no 109 (1999), paras 8.29–8.35, and *McBryde* paras 22.85, 22.96–22.97.
2 1987 SLT 530.

6.28 This discussion of loss has concentrated upon pecuniary or economic loss, which is, indeed, the characteristic loss arising upon breach of contract. But other types of loss are conceivable and relevant. In the context of commercial contracts, there may be recovery of at least small damages for the 'trouble and inconvenience' arising from the breach; the more serious the inconvenience, the bigger the amount[1]. This can be applied to non-commercial contracts as well[2]. But trouble and inconvenience are to be distinguished from injury to feelings or mental distress (*solatium*) and from loss of business reputation which, at least under the present law, are only recoverable in certain circumstances. So far as *solatium* is concerned, the general rule as laid down in *Addis v Gramophone Co Ltd*[3] is still against recovery. But if the dominant purpose of a contract is to provide pleasure or enjoyment (for example to take wedding photographs or videos[4], or to provide a holiday[5]), or to alleviate mental distress (for example a solicitor's undertaking to obtain a remedy to prevent a client's molestation by a third party[6]), and if by breach it fails to do so, then damages may be recovered for that loss. Surveyors who provided clients with a negligent report on a house which subsequently required major repair works have also been held liable for the 'anxiety, worry and distress' of the clients during the repairs[7]. In *Farley v Skinner*[8], the House of Lords awarded damages of £10,000 for distress and inconvenience caused by aircraft noise over the claimant's house which lay under the main flight path to a major airport. The defendant surveyor had reported, following the claimant's specific request when considering whether to buy the house, that such noise was unlikely to be a major problem. The court recognized that this was not the dominant purpose of the contract but held that nonetheless both parties regarded it as an important matter[9]. *Addis* itself concerned an employee's loss of reputation following wrongful dismissal: this was held not to be compensatable. This has been affirmed in more recent cases, together with the further proposition that there is no recovery for any psychological damage caused by the harsh and humiliating manner of a wrongful dismissal[10]. But a major inroad on the application of *Addis* in employment cases was achieved in *Malik v Bank of Commerce and Credit International*[11], where the bank which had been closed by regulators as the result of its involvement in drug-trafficking and illegal money-laundering operations, was found liable to a former employee who, despite his own personal honesty and integrity, had been unable to gain new employment in the financial sector as a result of his previous associations. The employer was guilty of breach of the implied duty of 'mutual trust and confidence' in employment contracts; the employee's 'stigma' damages compensated him for the loss of his reputation flowing from his connection with the bank.

---

1 *Webster v Cramond Iron Co* (1875) 2 R 752 at 754.
2 *Mack v Glasgow City Council* 2006 SC 543; *Smith v Park* 1980 SLT (Sh Ct) 62; *Gunn v NCB* 1982 SLT 526.
3 [1909] AC 488.
4 *Diesen v Samson* 1971 SLT (Sh Ct) 49.
5 *Jarvis v Swan Tours* [1973] 1 QB 233; *Colston v Marshall* 1993 SCLR 43; *O'Carroll v Ryanair* 2009 SCLR 125; *Milner v Carnival plc (t/a Cunard)* [2010] 3 All ER 701 (CA).
6 *Heywood v Wellers* [1976] 1 QB 446.
7 *Perry v Sidney Phillips & Son* [1982] 1 WLR 1297; *Watts v Morrow* [1991] 1 WLR 1421.

8 [2002] 2 AC 732.
9 For another case where an important but not dominant purpose of the contract was freedom from distress see *Hamilton Jones v David & Snape* (a firm) [2004] 1 All ER 657.
10 *Bliss v SE Thames RHA* [1987] ICR 700; *Johnson v Gore Wood & Co* [2002] 2 AC 1; *Johnson v Unisys Ltd* [2003] 1 AC 518. However, if the employee suffers a psychiatric injury as a result of the employer's wrongful behaviour before dismissal, damages are recoverable; *Eastwood v Magnox Electric plc; McCabe v Cornwall CC* [2005] 1 AC 503.
11 [1998] AC 20.

6.29 There is no doubt, however, that where the case is one in which breach causes *physical* personal injury then *solatium* is recoverable as it would be in delict[1]. With the expansion of the kinds of injury recognised by the law of delict since 1909 (for example, psychiatric damage or 'nervous shock'[2]), the restrictive general approach of *Addis* calls for serious reconsideration. In *Ruxley Electronics v Forsyth*[3],the House of Lords has given some indication that it might be open to a more expansive approach. Here, as we have already seen, F was given £2,500 for 'loss of amenity' in not being able to dive into his too-shallow swimming pool and at least one judge saw the result as a justified inroad upon the *Addis* principle. Perhaps the contract can be seen as one to provide pleasure or the damages might be regarded as representing 'trouble and inconvenience'. In the light of all these exceptions to the *Addis* principle, the Scottish Law Commission has recommended that damages should generally be recoverable for non-financial loss[4].

1 *McBryde*, para 22.104.
2 See Thomson, *Delictual Liability* para 16–12.
3 [1996] AC 344. Reference is made in this case to the important article by Harris, Ogus and Phillips 'Contract remedies and the consumer surplus' (1979) 95 LQR 581.
4 Scot Law Com no 174 (1999), Pt 3. Under DCFR III:3:701(3) loss includes non-economic loss and extends to pain an suffering and impairment of the quality of life. See also Palmer 'Contracts of intellectual gratification: a Louisiana-Scotland creation' in Palmer and Reid (eds) *Mixed Jurisdictions Compared Private Law in Louisiana and Scotland* (2009) pp 208–243; Rowan *Remedies for Breach of Contract* (2012) ch 3C.

6.30 If no loss at all can be established, then in principle no damages at all are recoverable. The dictum of Lord President Inglis that 'damages – at the lowest nominal damages' are always recoverable for a breach of contract[1], has been disapproved by a modern court on the basis that some loss must first be shown[2]. Assuming that by 'nominal damages' Lord President Inglis meant something different from the 'trouble and inconvenience' damages to which he referred in the same passage, two points may be made: (1) that there appear to be no reported cases of nominal damages in Scots law; and (2) that in England 'the term "nominal damages" does not mean small damages'[3].

1 *Webster v Cramond Iron Co* (1875) 2 R 752 at 754.
2 *Wilkie v Brown* 2003 SC 573 at 579C, per Lord Justice-Clerk Gill. See also *Aarons & Co v Fraser* 1934 SC 125 at 143 per Lord Murray; *McBryde*, paras 22.98–22.100.
3 *The Mediana* [1900] AC 113 at 116 per Halsbury LC. See for English cases of nominal damages in the absence of loss *British Westinghouse Electric & Mfring Co Ltd v Underground Electric Rys Co of London Ltd* [1912] AC 673.

Causation

6.31   The loss must be caused by the breach of contract. The test of whether a breach caused a loss is to ask whether 'but for' the breach the loss would have occurred. But it is not necessary that the breach be the sole cause. Rather, it must make a material contribution to the loss. Thus where the breach is the first step in a chain of events leading up to the loss, each connected with the other, there may still be liability. In the *Monarch Steamship* case[1], a ship's unseaworthiness at the outset of its voyage from Manchuria to Sweden was a breach of contract. As a result, the ship was delayed at sea and during the delay the Second World War broke out. The British authorities requisitioned the ship for war purposes and ordered it to Glasgow from whence its cargo was trans-shipped to Sweden at extra cost to its owners. This extra cost was held to have been caused by the unseaworthiness; each step in the chain of events led back to the breach on the 'but for' test[2].

1 *A/B Karlshamns Oljefabriker v Monarch Steamship Co Ltd* 1949 SC (HL) 1.
2 On the difficulties of establishing causation, see further *John Doyle Construction Ltd v Laing Management (Scotland) Ltd* 2004 SC 713; *Musselburgh and Fisherrow Co-op Soc v Mowlem* [2006] CSOH 39.

6.32   The difficult problem concerns the case where, in addition to the breach of contract, the aggrieved party may also be said to have contributed to the loss. There are clear possibilities of overlap with other relevant principles such as that of mitigation (aggrieved party will not recover loss which could have been avoided by reasonable action[1]) and contributory negligence (aggrieved party's damages will be reduced to the extent that the loss arises from its own fault), in so far as that is relevant in contract cases[2]. There are cases in which the aggrieved party has been held to have caused its own loss altogether: for example, through incompetent[3] or negligent[4] failure to deal with the breach when it became or should have become apparent. The initial breach in these cases did not cause the aggrieved party to act or fail to act in the way it did.

1 See further below, para 6.40 ff.
2 See further below, para 6.43 ff.
3 *Wilson v Carmichael & Sons* (1894) 21 R 732.
4 *Lambert v Lewis* [1982] AC 225.

Remoteness

6.33 The principle that loss arising from a breach of contract is only recoverable as damages if not too remote was well established in Scots law by the eighteenth century and has Civilian roots stretching back to the sixteenth century[1]. Nevertheless, all modern discussions of the subject in Scotland take the English case of *Hadley v Baxendale*[2] as their starting point. In *Hadley*, Alderson B formulated the principle of remoteness in a test commonly divided into two 'limbs' or 'legs': loss is recoverable if it either arises in the usual course of things or was in the reasonable contemplation of the parties as the probable result of the breach. This is taken to mean that there are usual losses and losses arising from special circumstances, the existence of which the parties must be aware before there can be recovery. In modern times, the English courts have tended to collapse the two parts of *Hadley* into a single test of reasonable contemplation or foreseeability, but this is not necessarily the approach of the Scottish courts.

1 It thus is found in DCFR III.-3:703 and PICC art 7.4.4.
2 (1854) 9 Exch 341.

6.34 The development of the law in this area has been bedevilled by consideration of its relationship to the rules of remoteness of damages in the law of delict, which also uses the language of loss arising 'directly and naturally' or which is reasonably foreseeable[1]. The present position seems to be that the remoteness test in contract is generally more restrictive than that in delict. This is sometimes expressed by saying that the test in contract involves 'reasonable contemplation' rather than the 'reasonable foreseeability' of delict. Many things are foreseeable but not likely or usual events; such losses might be recoverable in delict but not in contract. The reason for this distinction is that contracts are generally planned relationships in which the parties can apportion risk by agreement – for example, the price at which goods and services are supplied may reflect the risk that the supplier will be found liable for the customer's losses if the supply is late or defective or the liability may be excluded or limited by a suitable clause – while delict typically involves parties who are strangers to each other and cannot plan the consequences of an accidental collision between them[2]. But this is an uneasy basis for the distinction; many delicts occur between parties who are already in another legal relationship such as that of employer and employee. Lord Denning MR once suggested that there is in fact no difference between the tests in contract and delict; rather in each there is a distinction according to whether the loss suffered is economic (in which case the test is the restrictive reasonable contemplation) or involves physical damage to person or property (in which case the more expansive test of reasonable foreseeability is appropriate)[3]. This suggestion has however found no support amongst other judges in either England or Scotland.

1 See Thomson *Delictual Liability* paras 16.1–16.4.
2 See *The Heron II* [1969] 1 AC 350, especially Lord Reid.
3 *Parsons v Uttley Ingham & Co Ltd* [1978] QB 791.

6.35 It is clear that the *Hadley* test for contract was originally designed to limit the aggrieved party's recovery. Thus in *Hadley* itself, a mill-owner did not get the profits his mill would have earned had a carrier delivered a mill-shaft within the contractually stipulated period[1]. But the language of Alderson B is extremely open-textured and in modern times his famous dictum has been used in the English appellate courts to expand contractual liability considerably. In *Victoria Laundry (Windsor) Ltd v Newman Industries Ltd*[2], the purchaser of laundry machines delivered late was held able to recover the ordinary business profits which he would have made had delivery been on time, although not the especially high profits which would have been made from Government contracts of which the supplier was unaware. In *The Heron II*[3] a carrier who delivered a cargo of sugar late to a market was held liable for the profits which the owner would have made had the goods been delivered on time. Again, in *Parsons (Livestock) Ltd v UttleyIngham& Co*[4] the supplier of a defective pig-hopper was held liable for the resultant death of a valuable herd of pigs even though the actual loss was greater than could have been foreseen; it was enough that physical injury to the pigs was foreseeable to establish liability for the full (albeit unforeseeable) extent of the loss. This in turn raised doubts about

Victoria Laundry, where lost profits were held to be foreseeable and therefore the lost profit on the Government contracts, as merely an unforeseeably large loss of a foreseeable type, should have been recoverable. In *Brown v KMR Services Ltd*[5] the *Victoria Laundry* case was distinguished and *Parsons* applied to allow the recovery of losses made by Names at Lloyds against their agents, despite the unforeseeably high level of liability incurred by the Names through a series of major natural disasters between 1988 and 1990.

1 A similarly restrictive Scottish decision is *SS Den of Ogil Co Ltd v Caledonian Railway Co* (1902) 5 F 99.
2 [1949] 2 KB 528.
3 [1969] 1 AC 350.
4 [1978] 1 QB 791.
5 [1995] 4 All ER 598 (CA).

6.36 This trend of expanding liability was somewhat reversed by the decision of the House of Lords in a Scottish appeal, *Balfour Beatty v Scottish Power plc*[1]. In this case a concrete aqueduct was being built by BB to carry the Union Canal over the Edinburgh city bypass. The aqueduct was formed by a process of 'continuous pour' of concrete coming from nearby batching plants over many hours. A power failure halfway through this process, which constituted breach by SP, interrupted the pour and led, after some delay, to the demolition of the work done and later reconstruction at a loss of £250,000. The House of Lords held that this loss was too remote on the first leg of *Hadley v Baxendale*, ie the loss did not arise directly in the ordinary course of events. It would have required special knowledge to make SP liable. Although business people were to be taken to have knowledge of the ordinary course of each other's business, knowledge of specialist technical aspects such as construction techniques was not to be imputed to the parties.

1 1994 SC (HL) 20.

6.37 Although the case is carefully confined to its own particular circumstances, it does raise questions about some of the previous decisions. In *The Heron II* for example, what did the carrier know, and what should it have known, about the market in sugar? What does a supplier of pig-hoppers like the one in *Parsons* know about the risks of pig-farming? Was *Balfour Beatty* not, as the court below had thought, a case of an unforeseeably high loss of a foreseeable type? Conversely, *Balfour Beatty* also casts some doubt on Scottish cases in which recovery has been *denied* on the ground of remoteness. These cases have involved claims for 'finance charges' made necessary by a breach of contract. The courts have tended to find such losses too remote so that the borrowings and extended overdrafts of a party who has not been paid, or who has not received his building on the due date, or whose architect has negligently failed to control the expense of a building contract, are considered not to arise in the normal course of business – a view which seems to fly in the face of commercial reality. The few cases which go in the opposite direction may gain support from *Balfour Beatty* inasmuch as overdrafts and bank borrowings form part of the context of nearly all modern business activity and are not special losses falling only within the second leg of *Hadley v Baxendale*[1].

1 See further MacQueen 'Remoteness and breach of contract' 1996 JR 295.

6.38   In *Transfield Shipping Inc v Mercator Shipping Inc (The Achilleas)*[1], Lord Hoffmann set out with characteristic boldness a new understanding of the remoteness test in contract. He argued that remoteness is dependent on the parties' agreement (objectively determined in the light of the relevant background known to the parties), rather than an external rule of law imposed upon them unless they excluded it expressly. The question therefore is, from this objective perspective, what would the parties have reasonably considered as the extent of the liability being undertaken? This means that foreseeability of a loss as a not unlikely consequence of breach is neither necessary nor sufficient to make a loss recoverable. The significance of this approach can be seen from the facts of and the decision in *The Achilleas*. O chartered a ship (The A) to C1 with redelivery fixed for 2 May 2004. In April 2004 O chartered The A to C2 for 191 days at $39.5k per day, with C2 being entitled to cancel if the ship was not available by 8 May. C1 was delayed en voyage and became unable to redeliver by 2 or, indeed, 8 May. The ship hire market rate had meantime fallen, and O and C2 renegotiated their contract, extending the cancellation date to 11 May and changing the rate of hire to $31.5k per day. O subsequently claimed against C1 for the breach of contract constituted by the late redelivery of The A, seeking a loss of $8k per day for the whole of the C2 contract (191 days), ie nearly $1.4 million. C1 defended the claim on the basis that O could only recover the difference in value between the C1 contract and the market rate reflected in the original C2 contract for the actual over-run period of nine days, ie $158k. C1 was able to show that this was the market's general understanding of the loss payable. Anything more required special contemplation at the time C1 made its contract. The decision of the House of Lords was that O could not recover the loss it claimed. On Lord Hoffmann's approach this was because the parties had in effect not agreed to the liability claimed. Although other members of the House of Lords showed varying degrees of sympathy for Lord Hoffmann's idea, they felt able to reach the same decision on the more orthodox ground that O's full loss was the result of volatile market conditions beyond the reasonable contemplation of O and C1 at the time of their contract. It thus remains to be seen whether Lord Hoffmann's new approach will gain support as perhaps a more rational explanation of how the courts actually decide remoteness cases.

1 [2009] 1 AC 61. For further comment by Lord Hoffmann on this case, see his article '*The Achilleas*: custom and practice or foreseeability?' (2010) 14 Edin LR 47.

6.39 A Scottish case illustrating the fixing of a party with particular knowledge of special circumstances may be *Cosar Ltd v UPS Ltd*[1]. Here a delivery company failed to deliver tender documentation timeously with the result that the customer did not gain the contract in question. It was held that communications between the employees of the two parties about the nature of the package, plus labels referring to 'the tender opening session', could give the delivery company sufficient knowledge to make it liable for the loss of opportunity to tender and, more doubtfully, for the loss of the contract if the customer could show that the company's knowledge extended to the likelihood of the tender being successful.

1 1999 SLT 259.

Mitigation or minimisation

6.40 A loss which could have reasonably been avoided by the aggrieved party is not recoverable. The aim is to encourage the aggrieved party to take action rather than sit back and let the breach earn profits for him, while at the same time not letting unreasonable action increase the loss for which the contract-breaker is liable[1]. Thus, in general, a seller of goods refused by the buyer will be expected to take an opportunity to resell elsewhere, while the buyer confronted with non-delivery should seek replacement goods in the market. The principle will be important for the seller in a market where prices are falling and for the buyer in a rising market, as the table tries to show:

	Seller as aggrieved party (falling market)	Buyer as aggrieved party (rising market)
Contract price	£100	£100
Market price at breach	£90	£110
Market price at first chance to mitigate	£80	£120
Market price at second chance to mitigate	£70	£130
Actual loss	£30	£30
Recoverable loss	£20	£20

1 The principle is recognised in DCFR III.-3:705 and PICC art 7.4.8. See further Rowan *Remedies for Breach of Contract* (2012) ch 3E.

6.41 Sometimes the principle of mitigation is misleadingly described as involving a 'duty' upon the aggrieved party but there is no correlative right in the contract-breaker to have the loss reduced. The question is generally one of whether the behaviour in response to breach was reasonable or not with the contract-breaker having the onus of proving that an opportunity to mitigate was missed. The aggrieved party need not scour the market place to find a substitute performer while, equally, if the only reasonable substitute performer is much more costly, the contract-breaker will be liable for the full loss. The question has been most fully explored in cases where lack of resources or impecuniosity has prevented the aggrieved party from taking steps in mitigation of the loss flowing from the breach of contract. The clear trend in recent decisions in England and elsewhere is to take the un-minimised loss as recoverable in such circumstances[1]. As yet the Scottish courts have not addressed the problem directly, and have tended to see the issue of the aggrieved party's lack of resources as raising questions about remoteness rather than mitigation.

1 *Burrows* pp 144–147. See *Lagden v O'Connor* [2004] 1 AC 1067, over-ruling *The Liesbosch* [1933] AC 449.

6.42 Acute mitigation points arise particularly in the law on repudiation and anticipatory breach. In *White & Carter Councils v McGregor*[1], W refused to accept M's repudiation of the contract and performed his side of the bargain. He then brought an action for payment in defence to which M argued that in order to mitigate his loss W should have accepted the repudiation and brought the contract to an end. The House of Lords rejected this argument holding (1) that mitigation can only apply in an action for damages and not in one for payment of a liquid debt; and (2) that mitigation is only relevant after the contract is broken which does not occur until acceptance of the repudiation by the other party. If, however, a purpose underlying the mitigation principle is the prevention of waste, then there might well be sense in extending its scope to deal with situations like that in *White & Carter* as appears to be the case in the United States and, by means of other principles, Germany[2].

1 1962 SC (HL) 1; discussed above, para 5.34.
2 UCC, ss 2–610a, 2–723(1); *Treitel* pp 183–185 and 187–188. Note that Scot Law Com no 174 (1999) proposes reform of the rule in *White & Carter*: see above, para 5.34.

Contributory negligence

6.43 The Law Reform (Contributory Negligence) Act 1945 (LRCNA 1945) provides as follows:

'1. *Apportionment of liability in case of contributory negligence*
(1) Where any person suffers damage as the result partly of his own fault and partly of the fault of any other person or persons, a claim in respect of that damage shall not be defeated by reason of the fault of the person suffering the damage, but the damages recoverable in respect thereof shall be reduced to such extent as the court thinks just and equitable having regard to the claimant's share in the responsibility for the damage. …

4. *Interpretation*
'fault' means negligence, breach of statutory duty or other act or omission which gives rise to a liability in tort or would, apart from this Act, give rise to the defence of contributory negligence.

5. *Application to Scotland*
… the expression 'fault' means wrongful act, breach of statutory duty or negligent act or omission which gives rise to liability in damages, or would, apart from this Act, give rise to the defence of contributory negligence.'

The issue which awaits authoritative resolution in Scotland is whether these provisions, well known in the law of delict[1], also apply to claims of damages for breach of contract. The statute also applies in England: there it has been held at appellate level that contributory negligence can only be pleaded by the defendant in cases where the breach itself consists in negligence by the defendant. This can be characterised as either breach of an implied contractual term imposing an obligation to take care or as a failure to take care under a tortious (iedelictual) duty of care – that is to say, in cases where liability in contract and tort is concurrent. The defendant cannot plead contributory negligence where his breach is in relation to a term imposing a strict liability or where the law of tort could not have imposed liability in the same circumstances (for example, for breach of a contractual duty of care where tort liability is excluded). In a case of negligent breach of contract, the complainant will argue that his claim is purely contractual, while in order to reduce the damages by bringing in contributory negligence, the defendant will argue that liability arises in both contract and tort[2]. The basis for this approach is found in s 4 of the LRCNA 1945 (above) defining fault. Section 1 requires that two parties both be at fault, each contributing to the damage which one has suffered. The definition of fault in s 4 has two limbs. The first refers primarily to the fault of the defendant which leads to the loss suffered by the injured complainant and ends with the phrase 'gives rise to a liability in tort'. So the defendant's fault must give rise to a liability in tort (albeit, that the action is in fact brought for breach of contract). But it has never been necessary for contributory negligence to be conduct which, had it injured the defendant rather than the claimant himself, would have given the defendant an action. Hence the second leg of s 4 requires to be wider than the first and can only refer to the fault of the claimant.

1 See Thomson *Delictual Liability* paras 6.12–6.13.
2 See *Forsikringsaktieselkapet Vesta v Butcher (No 1)* [1989] AC 852; *Barclays Bank plc v Fairclough Building Ltd* [1995] QB 214.

6.44 In Scotland the issue has been considered in only two reported cases in the Outer House of the Court of Session. In *LancashireTextiles (Jersey) Ltd v Thomson Shepherd & Co Ltd*[1] a carpet supplier sued the manufacturer in respect of defective carpets which had previously been rejected by a customer of the supplier. The claim was for breach of the implied terms about quality in the SGA 1979 so the liability for breach was strict. The manufacturer pleaded that the supplier had been contributorily negligent in the way in which he had laid the carpet in the customer's premises. Lord Davidson held that before contributory negligence could be pleaded against a pursuer in a breach of contract case his claim had to be based on the defender's fault; since the claim here was not based on fault, the plea was irrelevant. In *Concrete Products (Kirkcaldy) Ltd v Anderson and Menzies*[2], two companies sued accountants for negligent breach of contract in auditing the companies' books. The negligence lay in the failure to check the books to detect frauds by the companies' employees. In their defences, the accountants pleaded inter alia that the companies had been contributorily negligent. The companies argued that a plea of contributory negligence was irrelevant in any case of breach of contract. Lord Dawson held that the averments were not clearly irrelevant where the breach of contract involved negligence and the contractual obligation broken was co-extensive with a delictual duty of care.

1 1986 SLT 41.
2 1996 SLT 587.

6.45 These cases appear to be in line with the English authorities. Yet a questioning note may be raised if the Scottish definition of fault in s 5 of the LRCNA 1945 is considered. Like the English s 4, s 5 has two limbs in its definition of fault, the second of them concerned with what will constitute fault on the part of the pursuer only (ie the part specifically referring to the defence of contributory negligence). The first limb, primarily concerned with the defender's fault giving rise to the claim of breach of contract, is different from the English first leg in that it contains no express reference to delict. Instead it talks about *'wrongful act'*, which is distinct from *'negligent act'*, and limits these only by saying that must give rise *'to a liability in damages'*. Now any breach of contract and not just those equally actionable as a delict, could be regarded as a wrongful act which gives rise to a liability in damages thus making contributory negligence universally applicable. *Cf Stewart's v Pare Ltd (2008)*

6.46 It must be admitted that, prior to the LRCNA 1945, *CJoH* contributory negligence as such was clearly no part of contract *49.* law and that it is unlikely that a change in the law was envisaged by the legislator at the time. Further, the function of contributory negligence may often be served by the other concepts used to limit damages claims for breach of contract such as causation, mitigation and remoteness. Thus in the *Lancashire Textiles* case it might have been argued that the specific loss which the carpet supplier was claiming was not caused by the defects in the carpets[1]. The Scottish and English Law Commissions recommended in 1988 and 1993 respectively that the plea of contributory negligence should only be available when the defender's breach involved negligence, whether in breach of a purely contractual duty of care or of a duty of care which could be either contractual or delictual[2]. While this would eliminate arcane arguments about whether a liability was purely contractual or also potentially delictual or tortious, there could still be arguments as to whether or not a breach involved negligence; while facts which would only reduce damages in a negligent breach case might conceivably give rise to a complete defence in one of non-negligent breach. The principled approach would be to allow contributory negligence as a general defence reducing the damages payable in all cases of breach of contract. In 1999, the Scottish Law Commission so recommended in a further report on the subject[3].

1 *Compare Lambert v Lewis* [1982] AC 225.
2 *Report on Civil Liability: Contribution* (Scot Law Com no 115) (1988); *Report on Contributory Negligence as a Defence in Contract Law* (Law Com no 219) (1993).
3 Scot Law Com no 174 (1999), Pt 4. See also DCFR III.-3:704 and PICC, art 7.4.7.

[handwritten: Interest on damages?]

Agreed damages[1]

6.47   Many of the difficulties which arise from the common law of damages can, of course, be avoided by appropriate contractual provision. Where the parties have stipulated a particular remedy for a particular breach, the contractually stipulated remedy is a substitute for and not a supplement to the remedies at common law[2]. Parties may wish to exclude or restrict the amount of damages recoverable and the law's response to such clauses is described elsewhere in this book[3]; here, we treat clauses in which the parties establish a regime under which damages are calculated and paid. Such clauses are known as *liquidated damages clauses*. Elsewhere, we have explained the meaning of 'liquid' and 'illiquid' in law: the former describes a sum of money which is fixed in amount and payable now, while the latter is any other sum. Prior to their assessment by a court, damages is the classic example of an illiquid sum. A liquidated damages clause is therefore a clause providing a mechanism whereby the damages payable may be calculated and made liquid in this technical sense.

1 *McBryde* paras 22.146–22.185; 15 *Stair Memorial Encyclopaedia* paras 782–801.
2 *Hutchison v Graham's Exec* 2006 SCLR 587.
3 See above, paras 3.20 ff, 3.75 ff and below, ch 7.

6.48   The freedom of parties to introduce such a clause into their contract is restricted by the law on penalties. The parties are not allowed to go beyond the compensatory function which the law assigns to damages and to seek to punish each other for breach of contract. Thus any clause seeking to provide for a penalty is unenforceable with the consequence that the parties are thrown back upon the common law to provide whatever remedy may be available. The classic test for the distinction between an enforceable liquidated damages clause and an unenforceable penalty was stated by Lord Dunedin who described the former as a 'genuine covenanted pre-estimate' of the damage flowing from breach, while the latter was 'a payment of money stipulated as *in terrorem* of the offending party'. A clause was to be tested for these qualities at the time the parties drew it up rather than in the light of circumstances as they had since emerged; so the damage actually suffered as a result of the breach, whether more or less or the same as the amount provided for, was irrelevant. Nor did it matter whether the parties called the clause one for liquidated damages or a penalty. A stipulated sum which was 'extravagant and unconscionable in amount in comparison with the greatest loss that could conceivably be proved to have followed from the breach' would be a penalty as would a payment greater in amount than the sum, non-payment of which constituted the breach. It would probably be a penalty if one sum was made payable for any of several different events of varying gravity. On the other hand, where the circumstances were such as to make a precise pre-estimate of loss virtually impossible, a clause agreed by the parties was most likely to be taken as one for liquidated damages[1].

1 *Dunlop Pneumatic Tyre Co Ltd v New Garage and Motor Co* [1915] AC 79 at 86–88.

6.49   Lord Dunedin's rules have been at the heart of the law on agreed damages ever since they were formulated. The commonest use of liquidated damages in modern practice is to deal with delay in performance: for example, in shipping or construction contracts[1]. The clause is then usually formulated along the lines of so much money per day; longer periods such as weeks and months create difficulties of enforcement in relation to the inclusion or not of fractions thereof. With an enforceable clause to hand, an aggrieved party need not be concerned with proof of his loss and he can simply deduct the sum involved from any payment which he may otherwise be due to make to the contract-breaker.

1 See for a recent example *Hill v Stewart Milne Group* [2011] CSIH 50.

6.50   Although the law is long established, it is not free from problems. First, one purpose of having such a clause, apart from the convenience factor mentioned in the previous paragraph, is indeed to provide the other party with an incentive to perform; but too much of an incentive runs the risk of becoming a stipulation *in terrorem*. Second, Lord Dunedin's test does not take sufficient account of the factor of equality of bargaining power: if such parties negotiate an agreed damages regime, why should the courts be empowered to intervene? Third, ignoring the actual loss means that a clause which is in fact grossly excessive may be recoverable while one which is in fact less than the actual loss may be struck down as penal. Fourth, and conversely in relation to the point just made, the controls do not reach far enough and are relatively easily evaded. They apply only to clauses dealing with breach of contract and involving payment of a sum of money by the contract-breaker. Thus when a contract contains a penalty clause which operates on the occurrence of an event other than breach, eg if a party exercises an option to terminate the contract, the clause is not subject to any scrutiny at all[1]. So the drafter of a contract wishing to provide contractual incentives to perform has only to design her clause appropriately and the clause will escape judicial scrutiny. Here are some examples of such clauses:

- *forfeiture clause*: provides that sums already paid under a contract (eg as deposits, booking fees, or instalments) will be lost if the contract is not performed[2]. The law of penalties only applies to sums to be paid *after* the breach;
- *accelerated payment clause*: provides that a party may terminate a contract early if he wishes without breaking it but that if he does so he becomes liable to make all or some of the other payments still due under the contract. Clauses of this kind are common in hire-purchase, conditional sale and leasing agreements;
- *'bonus'* arrangements: in a contract to be performed over a period of time, the clause provides for bonuses payable on 'early' completion;
- *'lane rental'* arrangements: these are often used in the construction of roads. The contractor pays a rental for each lane of the road occupied by him during the performance of the contract; so the quicker the work is done, the less the charges to be offset against the payments due to the contractor for the construction.

1 See *EFT Commercial Ltd v Security Change and another* 1992 SC 414. See also *Bell Bros (HP) Ltd v Aitken* 1939 SC 577 and note *City Inn Ltd v Shepherd Construction Ltd* 2002 SLT 781 affd 2003 SLT 885.
2 See, for example, *Zemhunt Holdings Ltd v Contract Securities plc* 1992 SC 58.

6.51 These developments in practice have led to recognition that the law on liquidated damages and penalties is out of date and in need of revision. This has even been accepted by the courts so far as possible: thus for example, it has been said that 'the power to strike down a penalty clause is a blatant interference with freedom of contract and is designed for the sole purpose of providing relief against oppression for the party having to pay the stipulated sum. It has no place where there is no oppression'[1]. Thus where the clause has been genuinely negotiated (as distinct from being a genuine pre-estimate of loss), the courts should not interfere.

1 *Philips Hong Kong Ltd v Attorney General of Hong Kong* (1993) 61 BLR 49 at 58, quoting *Elsey v J G Collins Insurance Agencies Ltd*(1978) 83 DLR (3d) 1 per Dickson J at 15. See also *EFT Commercial Ltd v Security Change and another* 1992 SC 414 per Lord Coulsfield at 427–428.

6.52 A more direct assault on the difficulties was proposed by the Scottish Law Commission in 1999, again starting from the premise of freedom of contract. Under its suggested scheme, only if an agreed damages clause is 'manifestly excessive' will it be unenforceable, thus allowing many more clauses than at present to be effective. However, the scope of control will reach more widely in another way: a clause may be penal, whatever its form, if its substance is that 'a penalty is incurred in the event of breach of, or early termination of, the contract or failure to do, or to do in a particular way, something provided for in the contract'. Thus the present limitation to clauses taking effect on breach and requiring the payment of sums of money will cease to have effect. Further, in determining whether a clause is penal, all relevant circumstances can be taken into account including those arising after the contract is entered; while the courts will be empowered to modify an excessive penalty in order to make it enforceable[1]. Although these proposals for reform followed the general drift of the DCFR and the Unidroit Principles[2], a Scottish Government consultation in 2010 showed divided views on the subject[3], and the Commission has the subject under review once more.

1 *Report on Penalty Clauses* (Scot Law Com no 171) (1999) (quotations from draft Bill appended to the report).
2 DCFR III.-3:708; PICC, art 7.4.13. See for further comparative analysis Rowan *Remedies for Breach of Contract* (2012) ch 5.
3 The Scottish Government analysis of the consultation is available at its website, http://www.scotland.gov.uk/Resource/Doc/254430/0110302.pdf.

Third party claims

6.53 A person with a *jus quaesitum tertio*[1] may raise an action for payment or performance of the benefit due to him under the contract. But some doubt exists about whether or not the third party can claim damages for breach of the obligation owed to him whether through non-performance, defective performance or delay. The better view is that a damages claim is competent and this is the direction which the law is apparently taking[2]. The claim might of course be excluded by provision in the contract and it is a moot point whether or not the controls of the Unfair Contract Terms Act 1977 apply[3].

1 For which see above, para 2.69 ff.
2 *Scott Lithgow Ltd v GEC Electrical Projects Ltd* 1989 SC 412; 15 *Stair Memorial Encyclopaedia* paras 837 and 838.
3 The Unfair Terms in Consumer Contracts Regulations 1999 do not apply in this situation.

6.54 Difficulties in relation to third parties have arisen in a number of cases concerned with buildings. For example, while a building is under construction or repair, the owner sells it to a third party to whom he also assigns the building or repair contract, ignoring the fact that it prohibits assignation without the builder/repairer's consent. The new owner discovers that the building/repair work is defective and sues the builder/repairer for damages covering the cost of curing the defective work. But the nullity of the assignation means that the new owner has no title to sue. The person who does have title to sue is the old owner who by virtue of the failed assignation remains a contracting party. But since he does not own the building, he has suffered no relevant loss and therefore cannot claim damages[1]. Thus we have the classic conundrum: the person with the right to sue has suffered no loss; the person who has suffered the loss has no rights. A similar example involves a group of companies, a member of which uses a building in law owned by another member of the group. The user contracts with a builder for work to be done on the building, which is then carried out defectively. The loss here is suffered by the owner but the contract is with the user[2]. In England, the House of Lords solved these problems by saying that the former owner and the user, respectively, could claim 'piggy-back' damages covering the loss of the third party owner. This approach, sometimes known as the 'transferred loss' or 'performance interest' approach, was followed in the Outer House in *McLaren Murdoch & Hamilton Ltd v Abercromby Motor*

Group Ltd[3]. Either the loss of the owner is by law transferred to the party with the contractual right; or the contracting party is entitled to the benefit of full performance of the contract, including damages protective of its performance or expectation interest, and it is not for the builder in breach to be concerned that the performance loss is actually suffered by a third party[4]. In *McLaren Murdoch* Lord Drummond Young preferred the first of these analyses. He rejected an argument that the loss arose as soon as the builder rendered its defective performance making it recoverable by the person who had the contract at that time regardless of the fact that the loss materialized later for another person; this could not be reconciled with the basic Scots law distinction between the wrong and the damage suffered as a result of the wrong[5].

1 *St Martins Property Corp Ltd v Sir Robert McAlpine & Sons Ltd* [1994] 1 AC 85;
2 *Alfred McAlpine Construction Ltd v Panatown Ltd* [2001] 1 AC 518.
3 2003 SCLR 323.
4 See the comparative studies by Unberath, *Transferred Loss* (2003) and Rowan *Remedies for Breach of Contract* (2012) ch 3D.
5 2003 SCLR 323, paras 41–42.

6.55 In the second of the English House of Lords cases referred to above, *Alfred McAlpine Construction Ltd v Panatown Ltd*[1], a further complication arose: the builder had granted the owner an independent right to sue by way of a duty of care deed. The owner seems to have preferred the 'piggy-back' claim because liability under the main contract was strict rather than negligence-based and therefore easier to establish. The House held by a majority of 3–2 that this independent right of the third party disabled the party with the right under the main building contract from recovering 'piggy-back' damages which only existed to ensure that loss actually suffered was recoverable by someone. This exclusion of 'piggy-back' damages where the third party has an independent legal claim in its own right may have significant effects in Scotland. In *Panatown*, Lord Clyde suggested that the building owner might also have a direct claim in at least some cases in Scots law as a third party beneficiary of the contract under the doctrine of *jus quaesitum tertio*[2]. This approach has been taken in one sheriff court decision enabling the third party to recover its loss directly and making 'piggy-back' damages unnecessary[3]. But as Lord Drummond Young pointed out in the *McLaren Murdoch* case, often the original building contract will not be one intended for the benefit of any third party thus eliminating any JQT claim[4]. Even if the third party loss is recoverable by way of a 'piggy-back' damages claim, there are enormous practical problems; notably whether the third party can compel the contracting party to hand over the 'piggy-back damages' awarded and, if so, whether it is a special claim to that money ahead of the latter's other creditors in the event of that party becoming insolvent before the money is actually transferred. Another problem arising from assignations in the context of building contracts is where A sells to B a building upon which work has been done under contract by C, and B subsequently discovers that the work was done defectively meaning that expensive repairs are required. A is the party with contractual rights against C but has suffered no loss. If A assigns his claim against C to B, can B claim his own loss or is he limited to the non-existent loss of A? The courts have so far allowed B to make a full damages claim for his own loss[5].

1 *Alfred McAlpine Construction Ltd v Panatown Ltd* [2001] 1 AC 518.
2 [2001] 1 AC 518 at 534–535.
3 *Clark Contracts Ltd v Burrell Co (Construction Management) Ltd* 2003 SLT (Sh Ct) 73.
4 2003 SCLR para 39. See also *Marquess of Aberdeen v Turcan Connell* [2008] CSOH 183.
5 *GUS Properties v Littlewoods* 1982 SC (HL) 157; *Darlington Borough Council v Wiltshier Northern Ltd* [1995] 1 WLR 68. For further discussion of the whole topic see MacQueen 'Assignation and breach of contract' (1997) 2 SLPQ 114; Thomson 'Restitutionary and performance damages' 2001 SLT (News) 71; Hawkes 'Emerging from a black hole' 2003 SLT (News) 285; *Hogg*, paras 3.174–3.202, 3.231–3.239.

CLAIMS BY THE CONTRACT-BREAKER

6.56 As already noted, one aspect of the principle of mutuality is that a party which has not performed or is not willing to perform its obligations cannot compel the other to perform. The Scottish courts have not shrunk from the logical conclusion that a party who has been in breach of contract cannot raise claims under the contract, at any rate those arising after the date of breach. This is so, it is said, even after the contract has otherwise been terminated[1]. Attractive though this may in many ways appear at first sight, it raises great practical difficulties. A supplies B with material which is admittedly not of the contractual quality but B is able to use it to manufacture other goods for resale and does so. Should A be denied payment?[2] C has sold land to D, the price payable in monthly instalments. D has discovered that C has failed to carry out certain works on the land despite a clause to that effect in the contract. But D is in financial difficulties which means that he has fallen behind in paying the instalments before discovering C's failure (ie he is not exercising the right of retention). Can D raise the question of C's breach? – and, indeed, can C sue D for the unpaid instalments?[3] E builds a house for F which is conform to contract in every way except that the specified mortar has not been used. Can F refuse to pay, even if the mortar is every bit or just as good as the one specified?[4]

1 The leading example is *Graham v United Turkey Red* 1922 SC 533, discussed above, para 5.47. See also *Forster v Ferguson & Forster* 2010 SLT 867, described above, para 5.16, and *Laurie v British Steel Corp* 1988 SLT 17.
2 *NV Devos Gebroeder v Sunderland Sportswear Ltd* 1990 SC 291.
3 *Hayes v Robinson* 1984 SLT 300.
4 *Steel v Young* 1907 SC 360.

6.57 To deny the contract-breaker any claim in the kind of cases described above may well be disproportionate where he has in fact rendered a performance substantially complying with the contractual requirements or which the recipient is able to use. There may also be absurdity, as in the C–D case above, if both parties are in breach: must a court refuse to hear a dispute of this kind? This would make a nonsense of the existence of procedures (*counter-claims*) which enable the parties to an action both to make claims against each other, to say nothing of the rules described earlier about set off and related matters[1].

1 See above, para 5.21 ff.

6.58 In fact the law does allow the contract-breaker to make claims against the aggrieved party in at least some circumstances, although the rules are probably in need of reconsideration and development. In construction contracts, a recognised possibility in respect of defective work which it would be impractical to have redone is a claim for the price subject to a deduction, usually based upon the cost of repair or difference in value[1]. This is distinct from setting off damages against the price inasmuch as it can be carried out by the employer without resort to court action. Other legal systems recognise this distinct price reduction mechanism[2], but Parliament in 1994 abolished a statutory version of it in the Sale of Goods Act[3] and it is not clear whether it now has any existence outside construction contracts and its recent reintroduction as a consumer remedy in supply of goods cases as a result of the Consumer Sales Directive.[4]

1 3 *Stair Memorial Encyclopaedia* paras 61, 72. The most recent example is *Bank of East Asia v Scottish Enterprise* 1997 SLT 1213, HL (above, para 5.15).

2 *Treitel* pp 107–111; CISG, art 50; DCFR III.-3:601. The rules derive from the Roman *actio quanti minoris*.
3 See SGA 1979, s 53(1)(a), disapplied in Scotland by the Sale and Supply of Goods Act 1994, Sch 2, para 7.
4 SGA 1979, s 48C, inserted by Sale and Supply of Goods to Consumers Regulations 2002 (SI 2002/3045). See above, paras 5.39, 6.16.

6.59 The mutuality principle denies the contract-breaker rights under the contract; but this has no effect upon his rights under other branches of the law. A contract-breaking party may still recover relevant property rights[1]. The courts have also indicated on numerous occasions that enrichment remedies may be available to a contract-breaker[2]. It seems that before the enrichment remedy may be used the aggrieved party must have terminated the contract for material breach; a non-material breach gives rise to a price reduction claim under the contract. The classic case is again that of the builder who fails to complete or completes defectively[3]; but a number of other situations are illustrated in the cases[4]. In *Thomson v Archibald*[5] for example, a builder abandoned the contract with the work only 45 per cent done. It cannot be pretended that the builder was in anything but material breach and it would be extraordinary if the contractual price was the starting point for any claim he might have. Equally, there can be no claim at all unless the employer uses the work done as the basis for completion by another builder because otherwise there can be no question of his being enriched. Given that the contract provides no answer if the employer does use the first builder's work as a basis for completion by another, it seems that resort must be had to the law of unjustified enrichment. Finally, this claim by the builder can, of course, be met by the employer's claim for damages for breach of contract.

1 *Forster v Ferguson & Forster* 2010 SLT 867 per Lord Clarke at para 20, citing *Gloag*, 261.
2 See generally for this and what follows MacQueen 'Unjustified enrichment and breach of contract' 1994 JR 137 at 149–166; *McBryde* paras 20.132–20.147; *Hogg*, paras 4.175–4.184.
3 Starting with *Ramsay v Brand* (1898) 25 R 1212.
4 Eg *Graham v United Turkey Red* 1922 SC 583; *PEC Barr Printers Ltd v Forth Print Ltd* 1980 SLT (Sh Ct) 118; *NV Devos Gebroeder v Sunderland Sportswear Ltd* 1990 SC 291; *Dollar Land (Cumbernauld) Ltd v CIN Properties Ltd* 1998 SC (HL) 90.
5 1990 GWD 26–1438.

6.60 The position which results may be complex. Suppose a building contract under which the price is £10,000. The builder abandons having done 45 per cent of the work; for simplicity's sake, suppose that work is worth £4,500. The employer completes through a second builder at a cost of £7,000. If he does not have to pay the first builder, the employer is in fact better off through the breach and can get no or only nominal damages from the first builder. If however the first builder has an enrichment claim, the picture begins to change. If he gets £4,500, then the building has cost the employer £1,500 more than the original contract price. He has a loss which he can set off against the builder's enrichment claim. Thus it is only if the builder's claim does not lead to the employer having to pay more than the contract price *in total* that it can be made good in full.

6.61 Other Civilian systems also allow the contract-breaker a claim, usually classified as contractual, if the innocent party 'accepts' the performance subject to cure of any outstanding defects at the contract-breaker's expense[1]. The key to this is that a contractual claim will tend to start, as in Scotland, with the contract price which incorporates an element of profit for the contract-breaker; a more appropriate starting point for recovery is surely the extent to which, if at all, the innocent party has been enriched by the performance actually rendered.

1 *Treitel* pp 289 and 308–310.

7. Illegal Contracts and Judicial Control of Unfair Contract Terms

ILLEGAL CONTRACTS

Introduction

7.1 A contract is defective if it is regarded by the law as illegal[1]. Unlike apparent contracts which are null or annullable because of defects in the parties' consent, contracts which are illegal (*pacta illicita*) exist and cannot be set aside by an action of reduction. Instead, an illegal contract is *unenforceable* by the parties. This means that where a party has refused to perform, the court will not order specific implement to compel performance. Nor will the court allow a claim of damages for the breach of a term of an illegal contract. Where there has been partial performance of an illegal contract, a party can pursue a claim based on unjustified enrichment: but where both parties are equally to blame for entering into the contract (*in pari delicto*) the court will allow the losses to lie where they have fallen. Since illegal contracts should not be enforced, the courts have been reluctant to open the way for parties to pursue claims based on unjustified enrichment. For if such remedies were generally allowed, this could undermine the sanction which is imposed for entering an illegal contract, viz that specific implement cannot be ordered and that a party's expectation interest cannot be recovered in an action for damages for breach of contract. Because the illegal contract is not null, ownership of property can be transferred consequent upon such a contract. The law of property operates in spite of the illegality inherent in the contract always provided that the parties concerned do not have to rely directly on the contract. The current law has been criticised as too draconian. This has produced two responses. First, to curtail a contract being classified as illegal in the first place; and second, if a contract is illegal, to attempt to mitigate the potentially drastic consequences of illegality. As a result, this area of the law is complex and unsatisfactory: a suitable case for law reform[2]?

1 See generally *McBryde*, ch 19; 15 *Stair Memorial Encyclopaedia* paras 763–769.
2 The English Law Commission has decided, however, that statutory reform is not possible in relation to contract law, and that development should be left to the courts: see Report on the Illegality Defence (Law Com no 320, 2010). For comparative law on the subject see DCFR II.-7:301-304 and MacQueen and Cockrell 'Illegal contracts' in *Zimmermann, Visser & Reid* (2004).

When is a contract illegal?

7.2   The first question to be considered is when a contract will be regarded as illegal. There are various circumstances where illegality can arise.

When the parties intend to perform a contract in an unlawful way

7.3   A contract is illegal if, at the time it is formed, both parties intend to perform it in an unlawful way either by committing a crime or a delict. For example, A and B enter a contract of partnership. At the inception of the contract, they intend to sell goods which they know have been stolen. The contract is illegal and unenforceable by both parties because they intended to commit a crime (reset) in the course of its performance. Similarly, if at the time the contract is formed, A and B agree to entice customers of C to break their contracts with C, the contract of partnership is illegal and unenforceable by both parties because they intended to commit a delict (inducing breach of contract) in the course of its performance. It should be emphasised that the contract is illegal because of the parties' *intention* to commit a crime or delict at the time the contract is formed. It is this *intention* which renders the contract illegal. In *Malik v Ali*[1], Ali (A) had financed the purchase of a house title to which was put in Malik's (M's) name. This was done to help M obtain a visa for her Pakistani fiancée so that he could enter the country. A lived in the house. It was accepted that if the money was not repaid, M would transfer the ownership of the house to A and, indeed, a disposition had been drawn up but not delivered to A. M claimed the money had been repaid and therefore she was entitled to possession of the house. She also argued that even if the money had not been repaid, A could not enforce the agreement that if this were to happen A should have the ownership of the house conveyed to him. The agreement was part of a fraudulent scheme to get the fiancé into the country and was a *pactum illicitum* and therefore unenforceable. It did not matter that the scheme had not in fact been carried out: it was the parties' *intentions* to evade the immigration laws which rendered the contract illegal. The Inner House allowed these averments to go to proof.

1 2004 SLT 1280.

7.4 A contract is also illegal if, at the time it is formed, one of the parties intends to perform it in an unlawful way either by committing a crime or a delict. But since the other party does not have such an intention, he is not regarded as culpable. We say that the parties are not *in pari delicto*, ie not of the same culpability. Therefore the effect of the illegality is that the party who at its inception intended to perform the contract in an illegal way, cannot enforce it; but the innocent party who is not *in pari delicto* can. For example, A hires B to do some repairs. At the time the contract is formed, B intends to use stolen wood for the job. The contract is illegal as B intends to commit a crime (reset) in the course of its performance. B cannot enforce the contract. But as A is not *in pari delicto*, he can sue B for breach[1].

1 See, eg, *Jamieson v Watt's Trs* 1950 SC 265.

Illegal contracts regardless of the parties' knowledge or intention

7.5 As we have seen, a contract is rendered illegal if at the time the contract is formed the parties *intend* to perform it in an unlawful way. But certain kinds of contracts are illegal regardless of whether the parties intend to perform it in an unlawful manner or, indeed, know it is illegal. This can be the result of common law developments or by virtue of statutory prohibitions.

(1) Common law

(a) Contracts which are per se criminal

7.6 When it is a criminal offence to make a particular contract, the contract is illegal and unenforceable. So for example, a contract of hire of an assassin is illegal because it is a criminal offence to hire a 'contract killer'[1]. It is a criminal offence to sell pornography and consequently the contract of sale of pornography is illegal and unenforceable. But it is not a criminal offence to sell a knife: a contract for the sale of a knife which the purchaser intends to use to kill his victim is not illegal and unenforceable unless the seller knows the buyer's reason for purchasing the knife.

1 Thus under Scots law, Rigoletto could not sue Sparafucile 'the assassin' for breach of contract in failing to murder the Duke of Mantua and killing Gilda instead.

(b) Contracts which are contrary to public policy

7.7   Over the centuries, certain contracts have been recognised by the courts as being illegal and unenforceable because they are considered to be contrary to public policy. As public policy changes, this will be reflected in the kinds of contracts which will be regarded as illegal so that certain contracts currently regarded as illegal may lose that status and vice versa. Contracts currently treated as illegal on public policy grounds include contracts which (i) interfere with the course of justice (for example, to bribe a witness)[1], (ii) deceive public authorities; (iii) oust the jurisdiction of the courts (iv) attempt to purchase honours; (v) involve trading with the enemy and (vi) involve doing an illegal act in a friendly foreign country[2].

1 Lawyers' contingency fee arrangements with clients may fall foul of public policy considerations as illegal *pacta de quota litis*: but cf *Quantum Claims Compensation Specialists Ltd v Powell* 1998 SC 316.
2 Contracts in restraint of trade should also be included here: see below paras 7.30–7.47.

7.8   The courts also formerly refused to enforce gaming contracts, regarding them as *sponsiones ludicrae*. These covered all forms of bets or wagers including football pools and lotteries. But given the social acceptance – let alone fiscal value – of these forms of gambling, it became doubtful whether the courts should continue with the blanket prohibition on the enforcement of gaming contracts. Reassessment by the judiciary of the policies which led to the categorisation of gaming contracts as *sponsiones ludicrae* in the eighteenth century did not however occur[1] although it was authoritatively settled that a contract to share winnings from gambling was not a *sponsio ludicra* and could be legally enforced[2]. Fortunately section 335 of the Gambling Act 2005 abolished the doctrine of *sponsiones ludicrae* when it came into force on 1 September 2007.

1 *Ferguson v Littlewoods Pools Ltd* 1997 SLT 309 was due to be reviewed by a Court
   of Five Judges in December 1997 but the case was settled after the pursuers ran
   out of resources: nor was the opportunity taken by the Inner House in *Robertson
   v Anderson* 2003 SLT 235.
2 *Robertson v Anderson* 2003 SLT 235.

7.9 Contracts which promote sexual immorality are illegal and unenforceable[1]. A contract to hire the services of a prostitute cannot be enforced by the prostitute or his customer. Similarly, a cheque to pay for such services cannot be sued upon if it is dishonoured. At one time, it would appear that an agreement to pay a lover's 'expenses' would be considered as contrary to public policy and consequently illegal. But given the number of couples who choose to cohabit rather than marry or register a civil partnership, such a prohibition is difficult to justify. Opposite sex and same sex cohabitants should be able to regulate the financial aspects of their relationship by contract without their agreement being undermined on the grounds of immorality. Since the nineteenth century, a contract providing aliment for a *former* mistress has been upheld[2] presumably because it no longer *promotes* immorality. Given the changes that have taken place since then in relation to sexual mores, we take the view that a contract to aliment a *current* sexual partner should no longer be treated as contrary to public morality. It should be noted that when property disputes have arisen between cohabitants, the fact of their non-marital status has not been used to argue that the law of property and unjustified enrichment should not be applied to their circumstances[3]. It is thought that such an approach applies a fortiori when the parties have attempted by agreement to anticipate any difficulties over the regulation of their property and financial affairs[4].

1 For an orgiastic case,see *Hamilton v Main* (1823) 2 S 356 (NE 313).
2 *Webster v Webster's Trs* (1886) 18 R 90.
3 See, eg, *Shilliday v Smith* 1998 SC 725; *Satchwell v Morrison* 2006 SLT (Sh Ct) 117.
   The Family Law (Scotland) Act 2006, ss 26 and 27 provide specific rules which
   are applicable to property owned by cohabitants.
4 This conclusion seems reinforced by the Family Law (Scotland) Act 2006,
   s 28 which provides a system of financial provision where cohabitation ends
   otherwise than by death.

(2) Statute

7.10 A statute may expressly declare a certain type of contract or a term in a particular type of contract to be illegal and unenforceable. Unfortunately the terminology used is not consistent. Sometimes a contract is simply declared 'void'[1]; in other cases, it is declared 'unlawful'[2]. The crucial point is that a contract illegal by virtue of express statutory enactment is unenforceable as *a contract* in exactly the same way as contracts which are illegal at common law.

1 See, eg, *Cuthbertson v Lowes* (1870) 8 M 1073.
2 See, eg, *Jamieson v Watt's Trs* 1950 SC 265.

7.11   There is little difficulty when a statute expressly prohibits a particular kind of contract. But sometimes the purpose of a statute can only be furthered if it is implicit in its provisions that certain contracts are prohibited. For example, a statute provides that it is a criminal offence to supply goods without an invoice being given to the purchaser. In order to give effect to the purpose of the legislation, viz the protection of purchasers, it has been held that as a matter of construction of the statute, any sale without an invoice is illegal and consequently the underlying contract is unenforceable[1].

1 *Anderson v Daniel* [1924] 1 KB 138.

7.12   On the other hand, because of the potentially drastic consequences of illegality, the courts have refused to accept that a contract is impliedly illegal simply[1] because its performance has involved a breach of statutory provisions[2]. For example, it is a statutory offence to drive a car at more than 70 mph on a motorway. A hires B to drive A to the airport. A notices that B breaks the speed limit during the journey. The fact that there has been a breach of the road traffic legislation does not impliedly render the contract of hire illegal. If B *intended* to breach the speed limit at the time he made the contract, the contract is illegal because B intended to perform it in an unlawful way. If B did not have that intention, the contract is valid and B can sue A for his hire charge even though B broke the law when he drove above the speed limit. Unlike the example of the sale without the receipt, the contract of hire of a taxi is too removed from the purpose of the detailed provisions of the road traffic legislation to be affected by illegality unless the parties (or one of them) intended to perform it in an unlawful way when the contract was formed. So if A agreed that B should drive him to the airport over the speed limit so that A could catch a particular plane, the contract would be illegal and unenforceable because the parties *intended* to commit a criminal offence at the time the contract was made.

1 Ie regardless of the intentions of the parties.
2 *St John Shipping Corp v Joseph Rank Ltd* [1957] 1 QB 267. Cf the approach taken by Lord Wheatley and Lord Johnston in *Dowling & Rutter v Abacus Frozen Foods Ltd* 2002 SLT 491 criticised in Thomson 'Illegal contracts in Scots law' 2002 SLT (News) 153 .

7.13 In *Archbold's (Freightage) Ltd v Spanglett*[1], for example, it was a statutory offence for goods owned by a third party to be carried on a lorry driven by a person who did not have an A licence. The defendant employed a driver without an A licence to transport the plaintiff's whisky. The goods were damaged in transit. The plaintiff sued for breach of contract. The defendant argued that the contract was impliedly illegal by virtue of the statutory provisions. The court held that the purpose of the statute was to prevent goods being carried by drivers who were not suitably qualified. This probably rendered impliedly illegal contracts of hire of a vehicle driven by an unlicensed driver. However, it was going a step too far to extend the illegality to contracts of carriage by land when the owner of the goods merely used the facilities provided by the carrier. In other words, contracts of carriage of goods by land, made between the owner of the goods and the carrier, were outwith the ambit of the mischief of the statute which was intended to regulate the relationship between the carrier and the drivers of the vehicles. The contract of carriage was therefore not impliedly illegal albeit that an offence had been committed by the carrier in performance of the contract.

1 [1961] 1 QB 374. In *Dowling & Rutter v Abacus Frozen Foods Ltd* 2002 SLT 491 the court elided the difficulty of determining whether as a matter of construction of the immigration legislation contracts of employment of unauthorised immigrants and contracts for the supply of the labour of such persons were impliedly illegal regardless of the parties' knowledge of the status of the workers.

7.14 What would have happened if the plaintiff had not paid the freight (ie the hire charge)? Prima facie, the carrier could have sued because the contract of carriage was not impliedly illegal. What is sauce for the goose is sauce for the gander. But if at the time the contract was formed the defendant had intended to use an unlicensed driver, then, as far as the defendant is concerned, the contract was illegal as he had at its inception intended to perform it in an unlawful way. Therefore he could not sue for the freight as the contract was illegal because he had intended to commit a criminal offence when performing the contract[1]. When a contract can be performed in one of two ways viz legally or illegally, it is not an illegal contract unless one or both of the parties intend to perform it in the illegal way[2].

1 For discussion, see above, para 7.3 ff.
2 *Archbolds (Freightage) Ltd v Spanglett* [1961] QB 374 per Lord Devlin at 391; *Robert Purvis Plant Hire Ltd v Brewster* [2009] CSOH 28 per Lord Hodge at para 20.

Consequences of illegality

7.15   The court may take notice of the illegality of its own accord (*ex proprio motu*) but will not assume that it is wise for a party to plead the point if possible[1]. Where the courts are prepared to hold that a contract is illegal, two important consequences follow. First, the courts will refuse to implement the contract or allow an action for damages for breach of the contract: *ex turpi causa non oritur actio* (no action arises from an illegality). Second, where both parties are equally at fault (*in pari delicto*) the losses arising from partial performance of the contract will be allowed to lie where they have fallen: *ex turpi causa melior est conditio possidentis* (in an illegal situation, the position of the possessor is the better one).

1 *Trevalion & Co v Blanche & Co* 1919 SC 617; cf *Designers and Decorators (Scotland) Ltd v Ellis* 1957 SC (HL) 69.

7.16   Consider the following example:

A is concerned that her husband will lose his licence for a public house. B who is a member of the licensing committee approaches A and tells her that the licence will not be withdrawn if she pays £8,000 to B. A transfers £8,000 to B. The licence is, nevertheless, withdrawn. The contract is illegal as contrary to public policy – a bribe to an official. Both A and B knew the contract was illegal *ie* both are *in pari delicto*. Accordingly, A cannot sue B for breach of contract (first principle above). Moreover, A cannot recover the £8,000 from B as the loss lies where it falls (second principle above)[1].

1 *Barr v Crawford* 1983 SLT 481.

7.17   The courts are prepared to alleviate the harshness of these principles if one party is considered less culpable than the other, ie the parties are not *in pari delicto* in respect of the illegality. This will arise in the following situations:

- if a contract is illegal because at the time of its formation one party intended to perform it in an unlawful way, then the innocent party can sue on the contract and recover any losses;
- where a person has entered into an illegal contract as a result of the other party's fraud, the innocent party will be entitled to relief;
- if a party to an illegal contract repents timeously, he can recover any payments made before the contract is performed;
- where a contract is expressly or impliedly illegal because of statutory provisions designed to protect one of the parties then that party is entitled to relief. For example, where the purpose of a statutory requirement to provide an invoice to a purchaser is to protect the purchaser, he can sue the seller for breach of contract even although the contract is illegal; of course, since the protection is only for the purchaser, the seller cannot sue on the contract for the price[1].

1 *Archbold's (Freightage) Ltd v Spanglett* [1961] 1 QB 374.

7.18 Where the parties are both *in pari delicto*, prima facie the contract is unenforceable and the losses lie where they fall. This might seem to exclude a remedy based on unjustified enrichment on the ground that to allow such relief would undermine the sanction imposed for engaging in an illegal contract. However, there is Scots authority that, in exceptional circumstances at least, a claim based on unjustified enrichment may be allowed. In *Cuthbertson v Lowes*[1], the Weights and Measures Acts provided that contracts for the sale of produce by the traditional Scotch – as opposed to Imperial – acre were to be 'null and void'. In breach of the statutes, the pursuer sold potatoes to the defender by the Scotch acre. After the potatoes were delivered, the defender refused to pay the price arguing that the contract was null as a result of the statute. The court held that the purpose of the statute was to promote the policy of using Imperial measures consistently throughout the UK. It was not for the protection of either party. Therefore both parties were *in pari delicto* and accordingly neither could sue on the contract for implement or recover damages for breach. But the court went on to hold that there was no moral turpitude involved in selling potatoes by the Scotch as opposed to the Imperial acre. In such circumstances, the court was prepared to allow the pursuer to recover the market value of the potatoes in an action of recompense for otherwise the purchaser would have been unjustifiably enriched.

1 (1870) 8 M 1073.

7.19   The difficulty with this conclusion is that, while it redresses the enrichment between the parties, it removes the sanction which Parliament may have intended in order to compel parties to contract using Imperial measures. Given the inconsistency in statutory terminology discussed above, it is not really sufficient to defend the decision by arguing that the contract was merely to be 'null and void' as opposed to 'illegal'[1]. Yet in *Jamieson v Watt's Trs*[2], the Inner House supported this distinction. In *Jamieson*, wartime legislation provided that licences had to be obtained to engage in building works. A joiner obtained a licence to do £40 of work. In breach of the statutory regulations, Jamieson carried out £114 of work. The defender refused to pay the balance. The contract was illegal because Jamieson had, at the inception of the contract, intended to perform the contract in breach of the regulations. Accordingly, he could not sue on the contract. Relying on *Cuthbertson*, Jamieson sought recompense for all the work he had done. This was refused on the ground that unlike the seller of the potatoes in *Cuthbertson*, his conduct in engaging in unlicensed work was a serious offence. The court also relied on the technicality that the contract in *Cuthbertson* was declared 'null and void' rather than 'illegal'.

1 Cf *Gloag* p 550.
2 1950 SC 265.

7.20   It is thought that the two decisions can be reconciled without recourse to the technical distinction. Like all claims based on unjustified enrichment, recompense and restitution are ultimately equitable remedies[1]. When a contract is illegal and unenforceable, it is contended that these remedies should nevertheless be available to redress the gains and losses between the parties. Put another way, the person who has benefited from the performance is prima facie obliged under the law of unjustified enrichment to make restitution or pay recompense in respect of any benefits received even although the contract is illegal and unenforceable. But because of the equitable nature of these remedies it is open to him to argue that in the circumstances it would be inequitable for him to be compelled to do so. This would most often arise where the parties were *in pari delicto* ie where the claimant was as bad as the defender: in such a case, the losses should lie where they have fallen. The moral turpitude involved in the parties' conduct will be an important factor in determining whether in the circumstances the defender should have to make restitution or pay recompense. In *Jamieson*, the pursuer committed a serious offence and it would have been inequitable to compel the defender to pay recompense. In *Cuthbertson*, the seller's conduct involved no moral turpitude; the contract was statutorily illegal regardless of the parties' knowledge or intention. In these circumstances there was no equitable reason why the defender should not have been compelled to pay recompense for the potatoes which he had received and sold on. In other words, the defender in *Cuthbertson* had no equitable defence to the pursuer's claim for recompense[2].

To summarise. Where there has been performance of an illegal contract it is submitted that prima facie the recipient of any benefits is obliged under the law of unjustified enrichment to make restitution or pay recompense. However it is open to the recipient to argue that in the circumstances of the case it would be inequitable to compel him to do so. Where the parties are *in pari delicto*, this argument will almost always succeed given the policy reasons why the contract was illegal in the first place. Consequently, in such cases the losses will remain where they have fallen. But in deciding whether it would be inequitable to order the restitution or recompense that is prima facie due, the court must take all the circumstances into account and in particular the extent of each party's moral turpitude: in each case, the onus lies on the defender to show that in the circumstances it would be inequitable to compel him to do so[3].

1 Cf *Dowling & Rutter v Abacus Frozen Foods Ltd* 2002 SLT 491.
2 Similarly, in *Dowling & Rutter v Abacus Frozen Foods Ltd* 2002 SLT 491 the defender could not show that it would be inequitable why he should not pay for the work done by the supply workers when unknown to both parties they were illegal immigrants.
3 Thus the factors which the court in *Dowling & Rutter v Abacus Frozen Foods Ltd* 2002 SLT 491 used in order to decide whether the contract was illegal should have been used to determine whether on the assumption that the contract was statutorily illegal it was inequitable that the defender should pay recompense for the value of the services he had received: it is thought that it would not have been inequitable to compel him to do so. See further Evans-Jones and McKenzie 'Towards a profile of the *condictio ob turpem vel injustam causam* in Scots law' 1994 JR 60; Macgregor 'Illegal contracts and unjustified enrichment' (2000) 4 Edin LR 19.

Property issues

7.21 When a contract is illegal, it is unenforceable as a contract ie the court will not compel performance through specific implement nor award damages for breach of contract. But although a contract of sale is illegal, the law of property continues to operate and ownership will pass to the purchaser. In other words, while the contract is illegal, the transfer of the ownership of the property from the seller to the buyer need not be tainted by the illegality[1]. For example in *Cuthbertson v Lowes*, although the contract of sale of the potatoes was illegal, ownership of the potatoes nevertheless passed to the purchaser when they were delivered to him. Indeed, it is precisely because title has passed that the seller cannot recover the goods from the buyer and prima facie the loss lies where it has fallen. Accordingly, in such a situation the purchaser has a good title to pass to a third party.

1 Smith, *Property Problems in Sale* (1978), ch IV.

7.22 Since the Sale of Goods Act 1893, in a contract for the sale of specific goods title will usually pass when the contract is formed[1]. In other words, the purchaser will have title to the goods before actual delivery. What if the seller refuses to deliver? It is thought that the buyer will be unable to vindicate the goods against the seller as this would be the equivalent of specific implement of the illegal contract. If the seller sells the goods to a *third party*, there is no reason why the purchaser under the illegal contract could not vindicate the goods against that party. Conversely, if the purchaser under the illegal contract sells the goods to a *third party*, the *third party* can vindicate the goods against the original seller.

1 See now SGA 1979, ss 16, 17 and 18, r 1.

7.23 When the illegal contract is one of hire or lease, it is thought that the transferor of the property will be able to recover it when the period of hire or the term of the lease expires. It is less certain whether the transferor could recover the property before such periods have elapsed even if the other party was in breach of contract: for example, if a tenant failed to pay rent. This is because the transferor would have to rely on a breach of the illegal contract in order to recover the property[1].

1 On English law, see *Bowmakers Ltd v Barnet Instruments Ltd* [1945] 1 KB 65; *Belvoir Finance Co Ltd v Stapleton* [1971] 1 QB 210.

Conclusion

7.24 At the outset, it was stated that this is a difficult area of the law. The major problem is that the sanctions for entering into an illegal contract are drastic and may not be commensurate with the moral turpitude of the parties. This is particularly the case where the parties do not realise their contract is illegal because they have no knowledge of the statutory provisions which render it so. With the proliferation of legislation, this is an increasingly common situation. It is surely unfortunate that one party may obtain a 'windfall' because she discovers a contract is technically illegal after the other party has performed. However, it may be possible to moderate the starkness of this result by recourse to the law on unjustified enrichment.

JUDICIAL CONTROL OF UNFAIR CONTRACT TERMS

INTRODUCTION

7.25 Since the seventeenth century, the Scottish courts have shown great reluctance to interfere with a contract on the basis that it contains terms which are substantively unfair to one of the parties. Of course, when a party was induced to enter into a contract as a result of a misrepresentation, then it could be set aside[1]. But the fact that the value of the exchange was grossly unfair (*enorm lesion*) was not in itself sufficient to annul a contract[2]. The reason for this reluctance was the perceived need in a mercantilist economy for certainty in contractual relationships: 'For nothing is more prejudicial to trade, than to be easily involved in pleas; which diverts merchants from their trade, and frequently marrs their gain, and sometimes their credit'[3]. By the nineteenth century, the predominant doctrine of freedom of contract demanded that the courts uphold the harshest of bargains regardless of the inequality in bargaining power between the parties. As Lord President Inglis observed in *Tennent v Tennent's Trustees*[4]: 'We are all agreed that inadequacy of consideration, however great, is not of itself a sufficient reason for setting aside a transaction.' Sometimes the judicial response verges on the hysterical:

'It seems to me so utterly wrong, when people have entered into a defined bargain, that it should be set aside upon some more or less fanciful notion of equity or right, that I will not discuss it ... I think it particularly mischievous that any notion of that sort should be countenanced nowadays when there is such a disposition, and such foolish, stupid, disposition on the part of people to think they can make better arrangements for those who have made their own, and that it is right to set aside a particular and distinct bargain that has been entered into.'[5]

1 See above, para 4.57 ff. And, indeed, the contract may be set aside as a consequence of any of the doctrines discussed in chapter 4. In the older authorities, many of these doctrines were simply classified as fraud.
2 See for example, Stair *Institutions* I, 10, 14; Erskine *Institute* III, 3, 4; *Fairie v Inglis* (1669) Mor 14231.
3 Stair *Institutions* I, 9, 10.
4 (1868) 6 M 840 at 877 (affd (1870) 8 M (HL) 10).
5 *Auld v Glasgow Working Men's Provident Investment Building Society* (1887) 14 R (HL) 27 per Lord Bramwell at 31–32.

7.26 In the twentieth century, the general principle remains the same: parties must be free to exercise their economic power to negotiate agreements which are in their best interests even if there is a serious imbalance in the value of the exchange[1]. Harsh bargains continue to be upheld[2]. Nor will the courts modify contracts. As Lord President Hope has observed[3], 'it is the function of the court to enforce contracts according to the bargain which the parties have made for themselves. It is not for the court to interfere in order to modify a bargain which one of the parties later considers to be unfair'.

1 See further Thomson 'Good faith in contracting: a sceptical view' in Forte (ed) *Good Faith in Contract and Property* (1999).
2 See, eg, *Edinburgh Corporation v Gray* 1948 SC 538. But note the two remarkable 'moneylender' cases where the courts refused to enforce contracts on the ground that they were extortionate, namely *Young v Gordon* (1896) 23 R 419; *Gordon v Stephen* (1902) 9 SLT 397, discussed in *McBryde* para 17.21. These cases may still be relevant given that there are well publicised lenders prepared to make short term loans at exceedingly high rates of interest.
3 *EFT Commercial Ltd v Security Change Ltd and another* 1992 SC 414 at 424.

7.27 That said, there are situations where the Scottish courts have traditionally scrutinised contracts and particular terms of contracts. As we have seen, contracts which are regarded as illegal cannot be enforced[1]. The common law controls on the enforcement of penalty clauses have already been discussed[2]. Here we shall consider other examples of judicial control of contractual terms. We shall also analyse two statutory regimes under which the courts are empowered to strike down terms in contracts which fail to satisfy 'fairness' criteria.

1 See above, para 7.1 ff.
2 See above, para 6.47 ff.

IRRITANCIES

7.28 An irritancy is a contractual right of one party to terminate a contract in the event of some failure to perform by the other party. In practice, they are to be found in leases. Where there is an irritancy clause, the landlord can terminate the lease if the tenant breaks the contract. The effect of the irritancy is drastic in that the lease comes to an end and the landlord can obtain possession of the property. In consequence, at common law a landlord could not irritate a lease without first obtaining a declarator of irritancy. This gave the tenant the chance to purge the irritancy before declarator was granted ie the tenant could remedy the breach, for example by paying arrears of rent. By the nineteenth century, however, the courts had become less prepared to allow the tenant the opportunity to purge the irritancy while maintaining the right to refuse declarator if the landlord's use of the irritancy was oppressive or being abused[1]. In practice, the courts rarely, if ever, exercised their discretion to refuse declarator[2].

1 *Stewart v Watson* (1864) 2 M 1414; *Hannon v Henderson* (1879) 7 R 389. Where the irritancy was legal, ie implied by law into the contract, for example non-payment of feuduty, the courts were prepared to allow the irritancy to be purged: but when it had been expressly agreed by the parties, ie it was conventional, it could not be purged in the absence of oppression or abuse.

2 *Dorchester Studios v Stone* 1975 SC (HL) 56; see in particular the speech of Lord Fraser at 73.

7.29 The law on irritancies was reformed in 1985. When the tenant's breach is the failure to pay rent, a landlord cannot irritate the lease unless he gives the tenant notice that he intends to do so[1]. The minimum notice period is 14 days during which time the tenant can purge the breach by paying the arrears of rent[2]. But once the notice period has lapsed without payment, the court has no discretion to refuse declarator: this is so even if the consequences of allowing the landlord to exercise the irritancy are socially and economically unpalatable[3]. In relation to breaches other than payment of rent, a landlord cannot rely on an irritancy clause 'if in all the circumstances a fair and reasonable landlord would not seek so to rely'[4]. In applying this test, the courts have recognised that in determining what a fair and reasonable landlord would have done, account has to be taken of the advantages to the landlord as well as the disadvantages to the tenant if the lease was irritated[5]. As both parties will usually be businesses, this is a very difficult, if not impossible, task. Where, as will often be the case, a landlord receives considerable benefits from exercising the irritancy, for example the value of improvements made to the property by the tenant, the tenant will usually have no claim in unjustified enrichment: since the benefits have been gained by an *ex hypothesi* lawful exercise of a legal right, the enrichment cannot be considered unjustified[6]. The law is thought to be unsatisfactory and the Scottish Law Commission has recommended radical reform in cases where the tenant's breach is remediable[7].

1 Law Reform (Miscellaneous Provisions) (Scotland) Act 1985 (LRMPSA 1985), s 4 (1) and (2).
2 LRMPSA 1985, s 4(3).
3 *C I N Properties Ltd v Dollar Land (Cumbernauld) Ltd* 1992 SC (HL) 104.
4 LRMPSA 1985, s 5.
5 *Blythswood Investments (Scotland) Ltd v Clydesdale Electrical Stores Ltd (in receivership)* 1995 SLT 150; *Aubrey Investments Ltd v D S (Realisations) Ltd (in receivership)* 1999 SC 21; *Euro Properties Scotland Ltd v Alam and Mitchell* 2000 GWD 23-896.
6 *Dollar Land (Cumbernauld) Ltd v C I N Properties Ltd* 1998 SC (HL) 90. But an enrichment remedy may lie if the windfall is not the result of the operation of a contractual term: *Mactaggart & Mickel v Hunter & Hunter* [2010] CSOH 130 per Lord Hodge at paras 97 to 105.
7 *Report on Irritancy in Leases of Land* (Scot Law Com No 191, 2003).

COVENANTS IN RESTRAINT OF TRADE

7.30   We have already seen how a contract can be unenforceable because it is illegal[1]. A covenant in restraint of trade is a specific type of illegal agreement which is prima facie unenforceable. What is a covenant in restraint of trade? In a way every contract operates as a restraint of trade: when she enters into a voluntary obligation, a party gives up a portion of her existing freedom at least to the extent that she is bound to perform the obligation she has undertaken. But it is a fundamental principle of a capitalist society that persons should be free to invest their wealth and exploit their capital and talents in the market ie should be free to enter into as many exchanges as possible. Where a provision in a contract purports unduly to inhibit this freedom, it has to be justified before it can be enforced. It is well settled that in particular types of contract covenants in restraint of trade are prima facie illegal and unenforceable.[2]

1 See above, para 7.1 ff.
2 See for further historical analysis Sutherland, 'Contractual restrictive covenants' in *Reid & Zimmermann* (2000).

7.31   On the other hand, by the end of the nineteenth century it came to be recognised that covenants in restraint of trade were not always designed to inhibit competition per se but were used to protect legitimate interests of the covenantee. The covenantee is the person for whose benefit the covenant is made ie the person who wishes to restrict the other party's freedom to trade. The covenantor is the person whose freedom is restricted by the covenant. As a result of the decision of the House of Lords in the great case of *Nordenfelt v Maxim Nordenfelt*[1], what is known as the restraint of trade doctrine was introduced into the law. Under this doctrine, convenants in restraint of trade remain prima facie unenforceable but they can be justified and consequently enforced if the *covenantee* can show:

(1) that the covenant is necessary to protect a legitimate interest of the covenantee: it is not sufficient that the covenantee wishes to avoid competition per se from the convenantor;
(2) that the restraint in the covenant is reasonable as between the parties; and
(3) that the restraint is in the public interest[2].

The onus rests on the covenantee to satisfy these criteria. If he can do so, the covenant can be enforced usually by interim interdict against the covenantor to prevent her acting in breach of the covenant. If he cannot, the covenant is illegal and cannot be enforced so that interim interdict will be refused. The test is ultimately one of reasonableness: the spatial area of the restraint, the duration of the restraint and the nature of the restriction will all be taken into account to determine whether or not the covenant is reasonable between the parties and in the public interest.

1 [1894] AC 535.
2 There have been few, if any, cases where a covenant has been held to be reasonable as between the parties but held not to be in the public interest.

7.32 Unless the covenantee can invoke the restraint of trade doctrine, restrictive covenants are prima facie illegal and unenforceable when they are included in the following contracts:

Contracts for the sale of businesses and partnerships

7.33 If A buys B's business, the sale price will often reflect the goodwill which B has built up over the years. To protect the goodwill he has purchased, A should ensure that the contract contains a covenant restricting B's trade for a period. While this covenant is prima facie illegal and unenforceable, A, the covenantee, can invoke the restraint of trade doctrine and attempt to show that it is reasonable. Because the parties have similar bargaining power and A has paid B for the goodwill that A is trying to protect, it is relatively easy to satisfy the reasonableness criterion. In *Nordenfelt v Maxim Nordenfelt*[1] itself, a worldwide restraint for 25 years was held to be reasonable since the customers of the business were governments; there were few rival firms worldwide that manufactured armaments; and the purchaser had paid a huge sum for the business. Conversely, when a business operates at a local level, the spatial restraint must be similarly limited if the covenant is to be reasonable[2].

1 [1894] AC 535.
2 *Dumbarton Steamboat Co v Macfarlane* (1899) 1 F 993.

7.34 Partnership agreements will often contain restrictive covenants regulating the partners' business after the partnership has terminated. Again, these covenants are prima facie illegal and unenforceable unless the covenantee can show they are reasonable and can invoke the restraint of trade doctrine[1].

1 See, eg, *Anthony v Rennie* 1981 SLT (Notes) 11 (neither partner would work for a period of five years within a six-mile radius of their practice: held reasonable).

Contracts of employment

7.35 A contract of employment may contain a covenant restricting an employee's trade after the contract of employment has been terminated, ie after the employee has left the job. Prima facie such a covenant is illegal and unenforceable unless the employer (the covenantee) can invoke the restraint of trade doctrine[1]. It should be noted that, unlike the contracts in paragraphs 7.33 and 34, here the parties do not have equal bargaining power nor, generally, has the covenantor received a sum of money to agree to the covenant. In addition, the covenant must not prevent the former employee from earning a living. Accordingly it may be difficult for an employer to show that the restraint is reasonable.

1 *Morris v Saxelby* [1916] 1 AC 688. See generally Brodie, *The Contract of Employment* (2008) ch 13.

7.36 An employer cannot protect himself from competition per se from a former employee. But he has the right to protect his trade secrets (processes, future plans etc.) and trade connections (including customers) from being used by the covenantor (former employee)[1]. Any trade secrets and confidential information must be capable of being identified[2]. Confidentiality restrictions without a time limit will be difficult, though not impossible, to justify[3]. In theory at least, the restriction on the covenantor's employment must be the minimum necessary to protect the employer's legitimate interests. In *Commercial Plastics v Vincent*[4], the court held that a covenant was not reasonable because it prevented the covenantor from working for rival companies on any type of research and was not restricted to the kind of work he had been doing for the covenantee, namely research into the adhesive qualities of plastic. The covenant was unenforceable even although the court recognised that the employer had a legitimate interest that could have been protected by a suitably drafted clause.

1 *Fitch v Dewes* [1921] 2 AC 158.
2 *Faccenda Chicken Ltd v Fowler* [1987] Ch 117; *Malden Timber Ltd v Leitch* 1992 SLT 757.
3 *TSB Bank Plc v Connell* 1997 SLT 1254; *International Computers v Eccleson* 4 May 2000 unreported; *Exchange Communications Ltd v Masheder* 2009 SLT 1141.
4 [1965] 1 QB 623.

7.37   The covenant must be read in the context of the relationship between the particular parties. A covenant restricting a milk roundsman from selling or serving dairy produce for one year to persons who had been his customers during the six months before he left, was held to be reasonable even although on a literal interpretation it would have prevented him selling butter in a supermarket[1] to a former customer. The court refused to take the clause out of its context where it was clearly intended only to prevent the covenantor from working on a milk round for a rival company. In other words, the court was not prepared to construe the clause in a way the parties did not in fact contemplate in order to decide that the restraint was too wide. A similar approach can be discerned in *Littlewoods Organisation v Harris*[2] where the employee was a director of a mail order company. He had access to valuable confidential information. The covenant restricted him from working for any rival for one year. Read literally, the clause prevented him from working in any part of a rival company's business, in any place in the world. The Court of Appeal held that the clause should be read in context and was intended only to apply to rivals in the UK and in the mail order side of their businesses.

1 *Home Counties Dairies v Skilton* [1970] 1 All ER 1227.
2 [1978] 1 All ER 1026.

7.38 It is important to stress that the onus is on the covenantee (employer) to justify the covenant as reasonable. At times the Scottish courts have failed to appreciate how onerous this task should be and have upheld extremely harsh restraints[1]. Where a restrictive covenant is designed to apply even after the employee has been wrongfully dismissed, there is Scottish authority that the covenant is unreasonable[2]. Similarly, a covenant stating that the parties accept it as reasonable is probably itself unreasonable[3].

1 See, eg, *Bluebell Apparel Ltd v Dickinson* 1978 SC 16; *Rentokil v Kramer* 1986 SLT 114. In *Exchange Communications Ltd v Masheder* 2009 SLT 871 it was held that a confidentiality clause without a time limit, and a covenant preventing the employee 'doing business' with any competitor in 'Greater Glasgow' for a year after he had left employment, could be reasonable.
2 *Living Design Improvements Ltd v Davidson* [1994] IRLR 69; cf *Rock Refrigeration Ltd v Jones* [1997] 1 All ER 1. It is no longer the law that a wrongful dismissal (ie when an employee accepts the employer's material breach of contract) automatically frees the employee from the operation of the covenant. See above, para 5.48.
3 *Hinton & Higgs (UK) Ltd v Murphy* 1989 SC 353.

Cartels

7.39 Agreements where manufacturers and traders combined together to regulate the market in goods or commodities – and the price of such goods or commodities – used to be governed by the restraint of trade doctrine[1]. The legality of such agreements is now regulated by statute and forms part of competition law[2].

1 *Pharmaceutical Society of Great Britain v Dickson* [1968] 2 All ER 686.
2 See generally Rodger and McCulloch *Competition Law and Policy in the EC and UK.* (4th edn 2008).

Solus ties

7.40 We have been considering contracts where it has long been settled that covenants in restraint of trade are illegal and unenforceable unless shown to be reasonable by the covenantee. There are also contracts which contain covenants, the legality and enforceability of which have never been challenged. These are covenants in dispositions, leases and standard securities regulating the way in which land can be used (real burdens). So for example, when A buys a house there may well be covenants restricting the use of the property to domestic premises as opposed to an hotel or a brothel and preventing the owner from having pigs or boiling blood on the premises!

7.41 For many years, it was thought that such covenants were beyond challenge simply because they were contained in deeds relating to land. However, in the 1960s, oil companies began to acquire garages which they would lease to tenants. It was a term of the leases that the tenants would buy their petrol from the oil company for the duration of the lease. This is known as a *solus* tie. Alternatively, the oil companies would lend money to proprietors of garages to improve the property and take a heritable security (mortgage) over the garage. The *solus* tie would appear in the security deeds. When covenantors attempted to challenge such agreements as being in restraint of trade, they were met with the argument that they were invulnerable simply because they were covenants relating to the use of land.

7.42 In the leading case of *Esso Petroleum v Harpers Garage (Southport) Ltd*[1], the House of Lords rejected the argument that covenants in deeds relating to land could not be attacked. In this case, the covenantor had owned the garage before entering into dealings with Esso. By agreeing the loan and the mortgage which contained the *solus* tie, the proprietors were giving up the freedom they had previously enjoyed to run the garage as they saw fit. In other words, they were giving up an existing freedom on how to use their property when they signed the mortgage. Because they had restricted an existing freedom, the majority of the House of Lords held that the *solus* tie had to be justified under the restraint of trade doctrine. To avoid this result, oil companies then engaged in complex arrangements so that an existing freedom was not being impaired. For example: X owns garage; X leases to oil company; oil company sublets to Y Co whose major shareholder is X. The argument that the restraint of trade doctrine did not apply because Y Co had no pre-existing freedom to use the property *before* the sublease which contained the *solus* tie was rejected by the courts. Instead, lifting the corporate veil, the elaborate arrangements were treated as one transaction in which X had restricted his existing freedom to use the garage as he liked[2].

1 [1968] AC 269. The same issues have arisen in Scotland where the *solus* tie was also in a heritable security: *McIntyre v Cleveland Petroleum Co* 1967 SLT 95.
2 *Alec Lobb Ltd v Total Oil* [1985] 1 WLR 173 (tie upheld as reasonable although it was for 21 years. The oil company had come to the financial rescue of the original owners and had paid them £55,000 for the lease).

7.43 If A *never* had any previous proprietary interest in the land before he takes a lease from the oil company, it is difficult to see that he has restricted an existing freedom since his first proprietary interest, namely the lease, contains the *solus* tie. In other words, since A purchases an interest in land which is already subject to the *solus* tie, he cannot be restricting any existing freedom because he had no rights in the land before he entered the lease[1]. For this reason, there is much to be said for the speech of Lord Wilberforce in *Harpers Garage*. He argues as follows:

(i) there are some contracts in which it is settled that restrictive covenants are prima facie illegal and unenforceable; for example contracts of employment.

(ii) there are some contracts in which it is settled that restrictive covenants are prima facie lawful and enforceable, for example covenants in deeds relating to land.

But a covenant in (ii) does not enjoy indefinite exemption: 'If in any individual case one finds a deviation from accepted standards, some greater restriction of an individual's right to "trade", or some artificial use of an accepted legal technique, it is right that this [covenant] should be examined in the light of public policy.'[2]

1 Compare the position of X in the example above, para 7.42.
2 [1968] AC 269 at 335.

7.44 The onus rests on the covenantor to show that the covenant should move from (ii) to (i). Once this is accepted, as in the case of *solus* ties, they become illegal and unenforceable unless the covenantee can invoke the restraint of trade doctrine. As a result of the litigation, the *solus* tie now only lasts for around seven years – as opposed to the 21 in the *Esso* case. But the importance of Lord Wilberforce's reasoning is its demonstration that, like negligence, the categories of covenants which may have to be justified under the restraint of trade doctrine are never closed.

Sole services contracts

7.45 A final example where the restraint of trade doctrine has been used is what we have called sole services contracts. The leading case is *Schroeder v Macaulay*[1]. Here a songwriter entered into a contract with a publisher under which he was obliged to hand over all his compositions to the publishers who were not under any obligation to publish the material. The House of Lords invoked the restraint of trade doctrine to argue that the terms of the contract were unduly restrictive of the songwriter's freedom to trade: given that the publishers were not obliged to do anything, the exclusive services obligation could not be shown to be reasonable[2]. *Schroeder* has been followed in analogous cases in England[3].

1 [1974] 3 All ER 616.
2 The publishers had also abused their strong bargaining position.
3 See, eg, *Clifford Davis v WEA Records* [1975] 1 All ER 237. In *Proactive Sports Management Ltd v Rooney* [2010] EWHC 1807 an image rights representation agreement between a company providing management and agency services to a professional footballer and the company to which his image rights had been assigned was held unenforceable by the management company as being in unreasonable restraint of trade. While the company was therefore unable to recover arrears of commission under the contract, it was entitled to recover recompense for the services it had provided under principles of unjustified enrichment.

Blue pencil rule

7.46 If a covenant cannot be shown to be reasonable under the restraint of trade doctrine, it is illegal and unenforceable. The whole covenant falls. The courts will not rewrite the clause to make the restraint reasonable[1]. But where the covenant contains two or more restraints, the court can 'blue pencil' out an unreasonable restraint while upholding the reasonable restraints. Before the blue pencil rule applies, it must be clear that the restraints are severable: if they are so intertwined that they cannot be pulled apart, the rule cannot be used. Provided the restraints are severable, the blue pencil rule can even be applied in a contract of employment[2].

1 *Dumbarton Steamboat Co v Macfarlane* (1899) 1 F 993; *Commercial Plastics v Vincent* [1965] 1 QB 623.
2 *T Lucas & Co Ltd v Mitchell* [1972] 3 All ER 687.

Effect of illegality

7.47 If the covenant cannot be justified, it is illegal. Like other illegal contracts, it is unenforceable: it is not null. Accordingly a covenant may begin as reasonable and enforceable but become unreasonable and unenforceable as a result of a change in the parties' circumstances. If these change again, the covenant could revert back to being reasonable and consequently enforceable[1].

1 *Shell v Lostock Garages Ltd* [1977] 1 All ER 481.

EXEMPTION CLAUSES

Common law controls

7.48   An exemption clause is a term of a contract under which one of the parties restricts his liability to the other. There are basically two types of exemption clause:

(1) *An exclusion clause.* Here one of the parties excludes liability which would otherwise arise. This is done by excluding the obligation. For example, in a contract for the sale of goods, there are important terms which are implied by statute into the contract including the obligation that the goods will conform to description and are of satisfactory quality[1]. With an exclusion clause, the seller can expressly stipulate that he does not undertake these obligations. Consequently, if the goods are disconform to description or are not of satisfactory quality, there is no breach of contract as these obligations were excluded at the outset. In these circumstances, the purchaser has no remedy since there has been no breach[2]. Moreover, in a contract a party can exclude any potential delictual liability which could arise from careless performance of the contract. For example in a contract of carriage, the carrier can exclude his liability for damage to the goods in transit caused by his negligence. However, it is not possible to exclude liability for fraud[3].

(2) *A limitation clause.* Instead of excluding the obligation, in this case the clause is used to limit the aggrieved party's rights to seek compensation or reparation after a breach of contract or breach of a delictual duty to take care (negligence). The most common example is to limit the amount of damages that will be paid in respect of a breach of contract or negligence. Rather than excluding the obligations that the goods will conform to description and are of satisfactory quality, a seller can stipulate that the maximum damages he will pay in respect of a breach of these obligations is £1,000, or £100, or £1, or 1p. Similarly, the carrier could stipulate that the maximum compensation he will pay in respect of damage to goods caused by his negligence would be £1,000, or £100, or £1, or 1p. Limitation clauses can also restrict the aggrieved party's rights: for example, by insisting that compensation will not be paid unless notice of the breach is given within a strict time limit or by stipulating that the seller is entitled to deliver substitute goods rather than pay damages.

1 Sale of Goods Act 1979 (SGA 1979), ss 13–14. On terms implied in law, see above, para 3.27 ff.
2 But if the seller excluded all his obligations, the agreement would no longer be contractual.
3 *H & J M Bennett (Potatoes) Ltd v Secretary of State for Scotland* 1986 SLT 665, 1988 SLT 390.

7.49 While the effect of both types of clause is often similar, it is important to stress that the theoretical basis of each clause is different. In the case of an exclusion clause, there is no breach of contract as the obligation was never undertaken: in the case of a limitation clause, there is a breach but the remedy for breach, particularly the amount of damages, is restricted.

7.50 Exemption clauses can be crucial in allocating potential losses between the parties and enabling them to acquire appropriate insurance cover for the risk. When the parties are of equal bargaining power, an exemption clause can determine the extent of their liability – thus avoiding expensive arbitration or litigation – and enables the value of the goods and services to be accurately priced. So for example, if A agrees to take the risk of damage caused by B in the event of B's careless performance of a contract, A will negotiate a lower price for B's services than if B had agreed to take the risk[1]. Put another way, the parties bargain on the appropriate balance between them of the risk of losses arising from defective performance.

1 This is important in building contracts when the employer often agrees to take the risk of damage caused by the negligence of the main contractor and nominated sub-contractors: *British Telecommunications plc v James Thomson & Sons (Engineers) Ltd* 1999 SC (HL) 9.

7.51 Where the parties do not have equal bargaining power, exemption clauses can be abused. Parties who have quasi-monopolies in the supply of goods or services can impose terms upon their customers who are, in effect, compelled to contract on the suppliers' standard form contracts which almost inevitably will contain exemption clauses: the '*contrat d'adhesion*', or the 'take it or leave it' contract[1]. Often the supplier's exclusion or limitation of liability will bear little relationship to the losses suffered by the other party as a consequence of defective performance. Yet because of the primacy of the freedom of contract doctrine, the courts have limited powers to control exemption clauses – even if they wished to do so.

1 See further above, para 1.47.

7.52 For example, in the context of partnership, Stair suggested that if one party has all the loss and the other all the profit, the agreement may be unenforceable as a *societas leonine* (a leonine contract)[1]. Throughout the nineteenth and twentieth centuries, there are dicta that on this ground Scottish courts might be prepared to strike down exemption clauses which were grossly unfair: nevertheless the courts have consistently found that the clauses in issue were valid[2]. In *MacKay v Scottish Airways*[3], the Inner House upheld a clause excluding the defender's liability to pay compensation for the death or injury of a passenger during carriage by air. In the course of his judgment, Lord President Cooper said[4]:

'Indeed, the remarkable feature of these conditions is their amazing width, and the effort which has evidently been made to create a leonine bargain under which the aeroplane passenger takes all the risks and the company accepts no obligation, not even to carry the passenger or his baggage nor even to admit him to the aeroplane. It was not argued that the conditions were contrary to public policy, nor that they were so extreme as to deprive the contract of all meaning and effect as a contract of carriage, and I reserve my opinion upon these questions.'

1 Stair *Institutions* I, 16, 3. The expression 'leonine' comes from the fable of the lion who carried everything off: *Fabulae Aesopiae*, I.5.
2 *Roberts & Cooper Ltd v Christian Salvesen & Co* 1918 SC 794 per Lord Skerrington at 814; *Bell Brothers (HP) Ltd v Reynolds* 1945 SC 213 per Lord Moncrieff at 222. But cf *Andrew v Buchanan and Henderson & Dimmack* (1871) 9 M 554 per Lord Neaves at 570. The House of Lords reversed the Second Division and upheld the validity of the clause.
3 1948 SC 254.
4 1948 SC 254 at 263.

7.53 Rather than develop the law on the lines suggested by Lord Cooper, attempts were made to control abuse of exemption clauses in two ways. First, as we have seen[1], it was sometimes successfully argued that the clause had not been incorporated into the contract and therefore could not be enforced[2]. But this device would fail if sufficient notice of the clause was given or the customer had signed the contract[3]. Second, the extent of an exemption clause could be controlled by construing any ambiguity *contra proferentem*[4]. Again, this device is of little value when a clause is unambiguously drawn in the widest terms[5]. Moreover, the courts became increasingly unwilling to engage in strained construction of exemption clauses. In *Ailsa Craig Fishing Co v Malvern Fishing Co*[6], the House of Lords held that limitation clauses should not be given an artificially narrow construction but should be given their natural meaning. The *contra proferentem* rule should only apply to ambiguous exclusion clauses[7].

1 Discussed above, para 3.20 ff.

2 See, eg, *Stevenson v Henderson & Others* (1875) 2 R (HL) 71; *Taylor v Glasgow Corporation* 1952 SC 440; *McCutcheon v David MacBrayne Ltd* 1964 SC (HL) 28; *Interfoto Picture Library Ltd v Stiletto Visual Programmes Ltd* [1989] QB 433; *Montgomery Litho Ltd v Maxwell* 2000 SC 56.

3 See, eg, *Lyon & Co v Caledonian Rwy Co* 1909 SC 1185, *Hood v Anchor Line* 1918 SC (HL) 43: *L'Estrange v Graucob Ltd* [1934] 2 KB 344. But the customer is not bound by his signature if specific notice has not been given to him of any unusual or special condition which might be regarded as something more than the normal ancillary terms of such a contract: *Montgomery Litho Ltd v Maxwell* 2000 SC 56 following *Interfoto Picture Library Ltd v Stiletto Visual Programmes Ltd* [1989] QB 433.

4 Discussed above, para 3.48. See, eg, *Hamilton v Western Bank of Scotland* (1861) 23 D 1033; *W & S Pollock & Co v Macrae* 1922 SC (HL) 192; *North of Scotland Hydro Electricity Board v D & R Taylor* 1955 SLT 373; *Graham v Shore Porters Society* 1979 SLT 119.

5 *Alexander Stephen (Forth) Ltd v JJ Riley (UK) Ltd* 1976 SC 151.

6 1982 SC (HL) 14.

7 See also *George Mitchell (Chesterhall) Ltd v Finney Lock Seeds Ltd* [1983] 2 AC 803.

7.54 While these devices may still be of some importance, the legislature has intervened and has given the courts powers directly to control exemption clauses. It is to the Unfair Contract Terms Act 1977 that we now turn.

The Unfair Contracts Terms Act 1977

7.55 The Unfair Contracts Terms Act 1977 (UCTA 1977)[1] sets up a statutory regime for the control of exemption clauses. The structure of the Act is complex and care is required to understand its provisions. At the outset, it should be emphasised that as a general principle the Act is concerned with the situation where a business is attempting to exclude or limit its liability through the use of an exemption clause. 'Business' is widely defined and includes a profession and the activities of any government department or local or public authority as well as companies and partnerships[2]. In short, all businesses are covered: manufacturers, wholesalers, sole traders, retailers and providers of services. Most contracts are included: contracts for the sale and supply of goods[3], contracts of employment[4], contracts for the provision of services[5] and contracts allowing persons to enter on to land[6]. That said, the Act does not apply to contracts which create or transfer a real right in land, for example the sale of a flat or a house[7]. Other important exceptions are contracts of insurance and contracts which relate to the formation, constitution or dissolution of companies, partnerships or unincorporated associations[8]. The statute appears to apply to contracts *stricto sensu*. Where an exemption clause appears in a unilateral obligation the statutory controls do not apply as the source of the obligation is not a contract. Similarly, where A and B create a *jus quaesitum tertio* for the benefit of C, it is doubtful whether C can challenge any exemption clause to be found in the contract between A and B as C is technically not a party to the contract[9].

1 In this section reference is to UCTA 1977 unless stated otherwise. On UCTA 1977, see 15 *Stair Memorial Encyclopaedia* paras 722–737; *McBryde* paras 18–02–18–45; Cabrelli and Zahn 'Challenging unfair terms: some recent developments' 2010 JR 115.
2 s 25(1).
3 s 15(2)(a).
4 s 15(2)(b).
5 s 15(2)(c).
6 s 15(2)(d) and (e).
7 s 15(2)(d) and (e).
8 s 15(3)(a). There are also special provisions relating to charterparties and carriage of goods by sea: s 15(3)(b).
9 See MacQueen 'Third party rights in contract: English reform and Scottish concerns' (1997) 1 Edin LR 488; above para 2.73.

7.56 The Act applies not only to exemption clauses in contracts but also to exemption provisions in non-contractual notices. So for example, if A, a surveyor, has a contract with B in which he excludes liability for negligence, the Act applies: but the Act also applies if A allows the survey to be used by C with whom he has no contract but has attempted to exclude liability for negligence in a non-contractual notice to C[1]. The occupier of land can only exclude or limit his liability under the Occupiers' Liability (Scotland) Act 1960 by agreement[2], ie in a contract, and therefore the UCTA 1977 applies.

1 Law Reform (Miscellaneous Provisions)(Scotland) Act 1990, s 68; *Smith v Eric S Bush: Harris v Wyre Forest DC* [1990] 1 AC 831; *Bank of Scotland v Fuller Peiser* 2002 SLT 574 . But before the non–contractual notice falls within the Act it must be established that A owed a duty of care to C: if A did not owe a duty of care to C, there is nothing for the non-contractual notice to exclude: *Gulliford Try Infractructue Ltd v Mott MacDonald Ltd* [2008] EWHC 1570 (TCC).
2 Occupiers' Liability (Scotland) Act 1960, s 2(1). If the occupier attempts to restrict liability by a non-contractual notice, it will have no effect.

7.57 The Act applies to limitation clauses, ie clauses which exclude or restrict the liability of a party who is in breach[1]. It also applies to exclusion clauses, ie where the clause allows a party to render no performance of an obligation or render a performance substantially different from that which the other party reasonably expected from the contract[2]. The theoretical difference between these clauses has already been discussed[3]. This is reflected in the statutory definitions. There is no difficulty when an exclusion clause allows a party to render no performance. However, if the clause expressly provides that partial performance does not amount to breach, it could be argued that such performance could reasonably be expected by the aggrieved party, at least when he was aware of the terms of the contract. For example, if A enters a contract to buy cheese from B and there is a clause which allows B to deliver chalk instead, is the delivery of chalk a substantially different performance from that which A could reasonably expect? If it is not then the UCTA 1977 would not apply. In *Elliot v Sunshine Coast International Ltd*[4] a holiday company's booking form included a statement allowing the company to alter the form of transport, while its coach holiday brochure promised that coaches would have toilets. The pursuer's coach had no toilets. It was held that to provide a coach without a toilet was to render a performance substantially different from what was reasonably expected and this could not be covered by the clause allowing alterations of the form of transport[5]. In *The Zockoll Group Ltd v Mercury Communications Ltd*[6] Lord Bingham MR argued that what was reasonably expected cannot simply be a matter of relying on the proper construction of the contract for that would mean that there was no difference between the other party's expectation and what, by reference to a term, the business claimed to be entitled to render : the court had to ask what reasonable expectations would a party derive from all the circumstances of the case including the way in which the contract was presented to him. Where a clause restricted a contractor's liability to the losses for which that party was responsible – thus excluding joint and several liability for losses caused by other contractors – Lord Glennie held that that was not an exclusion clause for the purpose of the Act[7]. In short ,whether or not a clause is an exclusion clause is ultimately a matter of fact and degree. Limitation clauses have an extended definition and include clauses which make the liability or its enforcement subject to any restrictive or onerous condition[8]; exclude or restrict any right or remedy in respect of liability or subject a person to any prejudice in consequence of pursuing such right or remedy[9]; and exclude or restrict any rule of evidence or procedure[10]. The controls of the Act cannot be evaded by means of a secondary contract[11].

1 UCTA 1977, s 17(1)(a).
2 s 17(1)(b).
3 See above, para 7.48.
4 1989 GWD 28–1252.
5 See also *Macrae & Dick Ltd v Phillip* 1982 SLT (Sh Ct) 5 for an unsuccessful challenge to a car dealer's pre-emption clause in a contract for the sale of a Rolls Royce. The English courts have taken a broad view. See, eg, *Johnstone v Bloomsbury Health Authority* [1992] QB 333 (clause requiring doctor to work 88 hours a week was an exclusion clause as it prevented the operation of an implied term that an employer would not overwork an employee to the detriment of his health). The courts have been enjoined to look at the substance, ie, effect of the term, not its form: *Philips Products Ltd v Hyland* [1987] 2 All ER 620 per Slade LJ at 626. See also *G M Shepherd Ltd v North West Securities Ltd* 1991 SLT 499, where a clause was held not to be an exclusion clause since the court held that there was no implied term in the contract which the clause purported to exclude.
6 [1999] EMLR 385 at 395.
7 *Langstone Housing Association v Riverside Construction (Aberdeen) Ltd* 2009 SCLR 639.
8 s 25(3)(a).
9 s 25(3)(b). This includes clauses which stipulate that defective performance must be notified within set time limits: see for example *Sterling Hydraulics Ltd v Dichtomatik Ltd* [2007] 1 Lloyd's Rep 8 (patent defects to be intimated immediately and latent defects within one week of discovery); *J Murphy & Sons Ltd v Johnston Precast Ltd* [2008] EWHC 3024 (TCC) (no claim in respect of goods being of unsatisfactory quality unless claim notified within 28 days after delivery).
10 s 25(3)(c).
11 s 23. See, eg, *Chapman v Aberdeen Construction Group plc* 1993 SLT 1205. This does not affect the validity of any discharge or indemnity given by a person in consideration of the receipt by him of compensation in settlement of any claim he has: s 15(1).

The controls

7.58 Exemption clauses can exclude or limit delictual as well as contractual liability[1]. Section 16 of the UCTA 1977 is concerned with clauses which exclude or restrict liability for breach of duty. Breach of duty is breach of a contractual obligation to take reasonable care or exercise reasonable skill in performance of the contract, breach of the common law delictual duty to take reasonable care or exercise reasonable skill and breach of the duty of reasonable care imposed by s 2(1) of the Occupiers' Liability (Scotland) Act 1960[2]. It does not matter whether the breach occurs as a result of an intentional act or negligence, while liability can be direct or vicarious[3]. The clause can be a contract term or a provision in a non-contractual notice provided it would otherwise be effective[4].

1 *MacKay v Scottish Airways* 1948 SC 254 and see discussion above, para 7.52.
2 s 25(1) On delictual breach of duty see Thomson *Delictual Liability* (4th edn, 2009), ch 5; on occupiers' liability, see *ibid* paras 10.9–10.12.
3 s 25(2). On vicarious liability, see *Thomson* paras 12.5–12.17.
4 s 16(1A).

7.59 Section 16(1) provides that where an exemption clause excludes or restricts liability for breach of duty arising *in the course of any business* or from the occupation of *business* premises the term or provision is void if it purports to exclude or restrict liability in respect of death or personal injury[1]. Thus for example, the clauses restricting the defender's liability in *MacKay v Scottish Airways*[2] for causing the death of, or personal injury to, its passenger would now be void. Whether the breach of duty arose in the course of business or from the occupation of premises used for business purposes is a mixed question of fact and law[3]. Personal injury includes any disease and any impairment of a person's physical or mental condition[4]. When the clause excludes or restricts liability for breach of duty in respect of damage to property or economic loss, the clause has no effect unless the party relying on the clause can show it was fair and reasonable to incorporate the clause into the contract or non-contractual notice[5]. Thus s 16 provides an important control in respect of clauses exempting a business from delictual liability or liability for breach of contract which arises from a party's negligence[6].

1 s 16(1)(a).
2 1948 SC 254 and discussion above, para 7.52.
3 *Harrison v West of Scotland Kart Club* 2001 SC 367.
4 s 25.
5 ss 16(1)(b) and 24(4). On the reasonableness test, see below, para 7.63 ff. See for example *Robinson v PE Jones* [2011] 3 WLR 815.
6 In England, it has been held that the equivalent section (s 2) does not apply to indemnity clauses unless the party bound to provide indemnity was itself the victim of the other party's negligence: *Phillips Products Ltd v Hyland and Hampstead Plant Hire Co* [1987] 2 All ER 620.

7.60 But contractual liability can arise where there has been no breach of duty in the sense described above. This is because many contractual obligations are strict in that there is prima facie liability if a party fails properly to perform her obligations even though the failure is not due to her fault. Exemption clauses which exclude or limit contractual liability are controlled by s 17. Section 17 only applies to clauses in two types of contracts, namely consumer contracts and standard form contracts.

7.61   A *consumer contract* is defined as a contract in which

(a) one party deals in the course of business; and
(b) the other party does not deal in the course of business; and
(c) in contracts involving the transfer of ownership or possession of goods, the goods are of a type ordinarily supplied for private use or consumption.

For example if A, a retailer, in the course of business sells a kettle to B which B intends to use at home, ie B does not purchase the goods in the course of business, this is a consumer contract because a kettle is ordinarily supplied for private use or consumption. Conversely, if A sells machinery to B which B purchases for use in B's business, the contract is not a consumer contract since B deals in the course of his business and machinery is not ordinarily supplied for private use or consumption[1]. As a result of the definition of consumer contract, s 17 does not apply to contracts between private individuals. Again we can see that the primary purpose of the UCTA 1977 is to control *businesses* from excluding or limiting liability.

1 In construing the equivalent provision (s 12), the court in England has taken a wide view of a consumer contract. In *R & B Customs Brokers Ltd v United Dominions Trust Ltd* [1988] 1 All ER 847, a company purchasing a company car for one of its employees was held to be dealing as a consumer since such a contract was only incidental to its business: cf purchasing commodities needed for its manufacturing process. It is thought this concept of dealing in the course of business is too narrow. On the other hand, there is Scottish authority that contracts of employment will almost always be consumer contracts for these purposes: *Chapman v Aberdeen Construction Group Ltd plc* 1993 SLT 1205 per Lord Caplan at 1209. Cf. in England *Keen v Commerzbank AG* [2007] IRLR 132 (CA) but the statutory background there is different. See further Brodie 'The employment contract and unfair contracts legislation' (2007) 27 Legal Studies 95. In any dispute over the nature of the contract in Scotland, the onus lies on the party who is contending that the contract is not a consumer contract to establish this is the case: s 25(1).

7.62   A *standard form contract* is not defined in the Act. However, the protections of s 17(1) are for the benefit of the customer who is defined as a party to a contract on the other party's *written* standard terms of business[1]. Consequently the contract must be in writing or refer to written standard terms[2]. The proposer of the standard terms must deal in the course of business. Once again we can see the emphasis of the controls on business liability. But unlike a consumer contract, the customer can also deal in the course of business[3] with the result that a standard form contract can be between two businesses. In a standard form contract, the majority of the terms are pre-arranged and not subject to negotiation ie the terms offered are the same for all the party's transactions. Where, for example, the price of goods or services is altered for particular transactions, the contract will still be on standard terms if none of the other terms is altered. Where there have been several alterations it is a matter of degree whether the changes are sufficiently significant for the parties no longer to be contracting on one party's standard terms[4]. When a standard form remains unaltered after negotiations about it, the controls still apply[5]. A proof may be necessary to establish that the contract is a standard form[6].

1 s 17(2). The standard terms must be imposed by that party on the customer. If both agreed to contract on industry-wide standard terms the Act does not apply: *Langstane Housing Association Ltd v Riverside Construction (Aberdeen) Ltd* 2009 SCLR 639.

2 *McCrone v Boots Farm Sales Ltd* 1981 SC 68 per Lord Dunpark at 74.

3 If the customer does not deal in the course of business, it will usually be a consumer contract.

4 *Ferryways NV v Associated British Ports, The Humber Way* [2008] 2 All ER (Comm) 504; *Yuanda (UK) Ltd v WW Gear Construction Ltd* [2010] EWHC 720 (TCC).

5 *St Albans City and District Council v International Computers Ltd* [1996] 4 All ER 481 (CA).

6 *Border Harvesters Ltd v Edwards Engineering (Perth) Ltd* 1985 SLT 128.

7.63 Provided the contract is a consumer contract or a standard form contract, any exclusion or limitation clause has no effect if it was not fair and reasonable to incorporate the term into the contract[1]. The onus rests on the party wishing to rely on the clause to establish that it was fair and reasonable to incorporate the clause[2].

1 s 17(1).

2 s 24(4). The defender must provide averments to assist the court in reaching a decision; see, eg, *Continental Tyre & Rubber Co Ltd v Trunk Trailers Ltd* 1987 SLT 58; *Landcatch Ltd v Marine Harvest Ltd* 1985 SLT 478.

7.64 Special rules apply to contracts of sale of goods and hire purchase contracts. In *all* sales – including sales between private parties – and hire-purchase agreements, an exemption clause excluding the obligation of the seller or hirer to pass good title is void[1]. For example, in a pub A agrees to sell B a DVD recorder. A expressly stipulates that he is not liable to B if B does not have title to the goods as they might have been stolen. This exemption clause is void! In consumer sales/hire, any clause excluding or restricting the obligations that the goods conform to description or sample, or are of satisfactory quality or fitness for purpose, is void as against the consumer[2]. In any other case[3], such a clause is unenforceable unless it is shown to have been fair and reasonable to incorporate the clause[4].

1   s 20(1). The seller's obligation arises under SGA 1979, s 12; the hirer's under s 8 of the Supply of Goods (Implied Terms) Act 1973 (SGITA 1973). The obligation arises even if the goods are not sold or hired in the course of the seller's/hirer's business.

2   s 20(2): the obligations arise under SGA 1979, ss 13–15; SGITA 1973, ss 9–11.

3   Eg sales between two businesses, whether or not on standard forms. A private sale is included only in so far as conformity to description or sample is concerned as the other obligations only arise when the goods are sold in the course of business.

4   s 20(2). There are similar controls in respect of the contract of barter, contracts for the supply of works and materials and contracts of hire: s 21. These are restricted to business liability. See for example *St Albans City and District Council v International Computers Ltd* [1996] 4 All ER 481 (CA).

7.65   We can see that the controls operate at two levels. First, some exemption clauses are simply deemed void and therefore unenforceable. Second, other exemption clauses will be treated as unenforceable unless it can be shown by the party wishing to rely on the clause that its incorporation was fair and reasonable. The reasonableness test is set out in s 24. The reasonableness and fairness of the incorporation of the exemption clause is determined by having regard to the circumstances which were, or ought reasonably to have been, known to or in the contemplation of the parties *at the time the contract was made*[1]. Where the exemption clause is in a non-contractual notice, whether or not it is fair and reasonable to rely on the notice is determined in accordance with the circumstances when liability arose[2]. When applying the test in the context of ss 20 or 21, the court is expressly enjoined to consider the factors in Schedule 2 to the Act: but these can be considered in any case when the reasonableness test is applied[3]. When a limitation clause 'purports to restrict liability to a specified sum of money' the court has to have regard to (i) the resources of the party relying on the clause to meet the liability and (ii) how far it was open to that party to cover himself with insurance[4]. Once again, it is submitted that these factors – in particular the availability of insurance – can and, indeed, should be considered in any application of the reasonableness test and are therefore not restricted to limitation clauses. A clause is fair and reasonable if it has been approved by a competent authority which is not a party to the contract[5].

1   s 24(1). Therefore what happened during the performance of the contract is irrelevant unless as evidence of what the parties might have contemplated: *Phillips Products Ltd v Hyland* [1987] 2 All ER 620 per Slade LJ at 628.

2   s 24(2A).

3 *Singer Co (UK) Ltd v Tees and Hartlepool Port Authority* [1988] 2 Lloyd's Rep 164.
4 s 24 (3). See for example *St Albans City and District Council v International Computers Ltd* [1996] 4 All ER 481 (CA).
5 s 29 (2).

7.66   The factors in Schedule 2 are as follows:

(a) *The parties' relevant bargaining positions including the customer's opportunity to obtain his requirements from an alternative source.* The mere fact that the parties contracted on the basis that the terms were non-negotiable is not in itself evidence of inequality of bargaining power and that the terms are unfair and unreasonable[1].

(b) *Whether an inducement was offered to the customer to accept the exemption clause or in accepting it, she had an opportunity of entering a similar contract with other persons without having to accept a similar term.*

(c) *Whether the customer knew or ought reasonably to have known of the existence and extent of the term.* Unless the customer has signed the contract or reasonable steps have been taken to bring the term to her notice, the clause will not have been incorporated into the contract and therefore is unenforceable without resort having to be made to UCTA[2].

(d) *When the term excludes or restricts liability if the customer does not comply with some condition, whether it was reasonable at the time of the contract to expect that compliance with the condition would be practicable.* Thus in *Knight Machinery (Holdings) Ltd v Rennie[3]*, the court was called upon to adjudicate upon the fairness and reasonableness of a clause which provided that a buyer was deemed to have accepted defective goods unless he had given notice of the defect to the seller within seven days of receipt of the goods. Since teething problems were common with the machinery bought in this case, an Extra Division of the Court of Session held that it was not reasonable at the time of the contract to expect that it would be practicable for the buyer to give the requisite notice. The court rejected the seller's contention that the clause only demanded that the buyer should inform the seller that he was having problems with the machine. Before it could pass the reasonableness test, the least that could be expected of a term conceived wholly in the interests of its proposer, at the expense of the other party's rights, was that the term should be clear and unambiguous.

(e) *Whether the goods were specially made for the customer.*

1 *Denholm Fishselling Ltd v Anderson* 1991 SLT (Sh Ct) 24.

2 On incorporation, see above, para 3.20 ff.
3 1995 SLT 166. See also *J Murphy & Sons Ltd v Johnson Precast Ltd* [2008] EWHC 3024 (TCC).

7.67   Since the test is ultimately whether or not the incorporation was fair and reasonable in the light of the circumstances which were known or should have been known to the parties at the time of the contract was made[1], it has been judicially recognised that it is impossible to draw up an exhaustive list of factors[2]. Among the most important are whether the parties are of equal bargaining power, their resources, the extent of the potential liability, the complexity of the language of the clause, whether or not it is ambiguous and, last but not least, the insurance positions. In *Smith v Eric S Bush, Harris v Wyre Forest DC*[3] the House of Lords held that a surveyor's disclaimer was not fair and reasonable when he knew that the survey would be used by persons of limited means to buy domestic property. On the other hand, a similar disclaimer was upheld in *Bank of Scotland v Fuller Peiser*[4]. Here the defender's valuation report was being used by a bank in deciding whether or not to grant a loan for the purchase of business property. As the bank and the surveyor were of equal bargaining power and could equally bear the loss, the incorporation of the exemption clause in favour of the surveyor was fair and reasonable.

It is only when it is clear that one party is in a better position to insure against the risk, that insurance will be a crucial factor. In most contracts for the sale of goods and the supply of services the customer will usually be in the better position to take out insurance for interruption of his business, loss of profits and consequential loss[5].

Where both parties are businesses of similar bargaining power and sophistication, it is unlikely that the clause will be found to be unreasonable[6].

1 s 24(1).
2 *Smith v Eric S Bush, Harris v Wyre Forest D C* [1990] 1 AC 831 per Lord Griffiths at 858–859.
3 [1990] 1 AC 831.
4 2002 SLT 574.
5 *Regus (UK) Ltd v Epcot Solutions Ltd* [2008] EWCA Civ 361; *Kingsway Hall Hotel Ltd v Red Sky IT (Hounslow) Ltd* [2010] EWHC 965 (TCC).
6 See for example *Regus (UK) Ltd v Epcot Solutions Ltd* [2008] EWCA Civ 361; *Food Co UK LLP (t/a Muffin Break) v Henry Boots Developments Ltd* [2010] EWHC 358 (Ch D); *Dennard v Price Waterhouse Coopers LLP* [2010] EWHC 812 (ChD); *Raiffeisen Zentralbank Osterreich AG v Royal Bank of Scotland* [2010] EWHC 1392 (Comm) (QBD).

7.68 Consider the following example. A purchases a machine from B on B's standard terms. In the standard terms there is a limitation clause which provides that any damage caused to A's business premises as a result of a defect in the machine is limited to £10,000. As a result of a defect in the machine, there is a fire which causes £100,000 of damage. Assuming that the clause has been incorporated into the contract and that as a matter of construction it does cover the losses incurred by A, can the clause be struck down by UCTA 1977? This is not a consumer contract. But the clause is in a standard form contract and is therefore unenforceable unless B can show that its incorporation was fair and reasonable. The court will consider the following factors:

(1) The relative bargaining strengths of the parties. If B was in a much stronger position than A, this would point to the incorporation being unreasonable: if equally balanced, this factor could be neutral. If A could not obtain an alternative supply, this would suggest that the incorporation was unfair.

(2) Did A receive an inducement to accept the clause? If so, this would suggest that it was fair.

(3) Did A know about the clause, or ought he to have known about it? If so, this would suggest that its incorporation was reasonable.

(4) Was the machinery specially made for A? If so, again this would point to the incorporation being reasonable.

(5) Was the clause ambiguous? If so, its incorporation would appear unreasonable.

(6) The resources of the parties. Who can better afford to suffer the loss?

(7) The insurance position. Since A should be insured against fire howsoever caused, the incorporation of the clause might be reasonable; the price of the machinery will increase if B has unlimited liability for all consequential losses caused by his defective product.

On balance, it is submitted that the clause satisfies the reasonableness test[1].

1 See *Watford Electronics Ltd v Sanderson CFL Ltd* [2001] 1 All ER (Comm) 696; cf however *St Albans City and District Council v International Computers Ltd* [1996] 4 All ER 481 (CA).

7.69 It will be obvious that, while not simply a matter of judicial discretion, the decision about whether or not the reasonableness test is satisfied involves weighing up a large range of factors, leaving room 'for a legitimate difference of judicial opinion of what the answer should be'[1]. In these circumstances, the role of an appellate court is narrow and it should not interfere unless the judge at first instance 'proceeded upon some erroneous principle or was plainly and obviously wrong'[2].

1 *George Mitchell (Chesterhall) Ltd v Finney Lock Seeds Ltd* [1983] 2 AC 803 per Lord Bridge at 815–816.
2 *George Mitchell (Chesterhall) Ltd v Finney Lock Seeds Ltd* [1983] 2 AC 803 per Lord Bridge at 815–816.

7.70   Finally, in a consumer contract, any clause under which the consumer has to indemnify another person (whether a party to the contract or not) in respect of any liability incurred by him as a result of a breach of duty or breach of contract, cannot be enforced unless its incorporation is shown to be fair and reasonable[1].

1 s 18 (1).

The Unfair Terms in Consumer Contracts Regulations 1999[1]

7.71   The purpose of these regulations is to implement Council Directive (EC) 93/13 on unfair terms in consumer contracts[2]. They replace earlier regulations introduced in 1994 and came into force on 1 October 1999. The essence of the scheme is to subject terms in consumer contracts to a fairness test. A term will be unfair when 'contrary to the requirement of good faith it causes a significant imbalance in the parties' rights and obligations arising under the contract, to the detriment of the consumer'[3]. When a term is held to be unfair, it is not binding on the consumer but the contract continues to bind the parties provided it is capable of continuing in existence without the unfair term[4].

1 SI 1999/2083. References in this section are to these regulations unless otherwise stated. See generally 15 *Stair Memorial Encyclopaedia* paras 738–752; *McBryde* paras 18–39–18—50; Ervine 'The Unfair Contract Terms Regulations Mark II' 1999 SLT (News) 253; Cabrelli and Zahn 'Challenging unfair terms: some recent developments' 2010 JR 115.
2 (OJ L95 21.4.93 p 29). The Directive is modelled on the German Standard Contract Terms Act 1976; for an English translation see Markesinis, Lorenz and Dannemann *The German Law of Obligations* vol 1 (1997), 908–912. DCFR II.-9:401-410 follows the Directive, but extends its scope beyond the consumer contract.
3 reg 5 (1).
4 reg 8 (1) and (2).

7.72   The regulations only apply to contracts concluded between a consumer and a seller or supplier[1]. A consumer is a natural person who is acting for purposes which are outside his trade, business or profession[2]. The seller or supplier is any natural or legal person who is acting for purposes relating to his trade, business or profession, whether publicly owned or privately owned[3]. Thus the regulations do not apply where both parties are acting for purposes not relating to their business, for example a sale of a second hand car between private individuals. Moreover, unlike the UCTA 1977, the regulations do not apply when both parties are contracting for the purposes of their business even if they are contracting on one of the parties' standard terms.

1 reg 4 (1).
2 reg 3 (1). See *Prostar Management Ltd v Twaddle* 2003 SLT (Sh Ct) 11 (professional footballer not a consumer of his agent's services); Joined Cases C-541/99, C-542/99 *Cape SNC v Ideal Service Srl; Idealservice MN RE SAS v OMAI Srl* [2003] 1 CMLR 42 (company cannot be a consumer). In the case of a guarantee of a loan, both the loan and the guarantee must have been entered into in a non-commercial context: *Barclays Bank plcc v Kufner* [2008] EWHC 2319
3 reg 3 (1). See *Khatun v London Borough of Newham* [2005] QB 985 (regulations apply to public authority contracts).

7.73   The contract is between a consumer and seller or supplier. It will therefore include contracts for the sale of goods and contracts for the sale of land[1]. In respect of the latter, the regulations are wider than the UCTA 1977 which does not apply to contracts relating to sales of land[2]. But the definition of seller means that contracts for the sale of land between private individuals remain excluded. Contracts for a wide range of services are covered including financial services and insurance[3]. But contracts of employment are excluded[4].

1 See *Khatun v London Borough of Newham* [2005] QB 985; *Shaftsbury House (Developments) Ltd v Lee* [2010] EWHC 1484.
2 See above, para 7.55.
3 Contracts of insurance are excluded for the purposes of the UCTA 1977: see above, para 7.55.
4 Unlike the UCTA 1977: see above, para 7.55. See recital 10 to Council Directive (EC) 93/13.

7.74   The regulations do not apply to contractual terms which reflect statutory or regulatory provisions or the provisions or principles of international conventions to which Member States of the European Community are a party[1].

1 reg 4 (2).

7.75   The regulations only control terms which have not been individually negotiated. These are contracts which have been drafted in advance so that the consumer has not been able to influence the substance of the terms[1]. Where a specific term in a contract has been individually negotiated, for example the delivery date or price, the regulations apply to the rest of the contract if an overall assessment indicates that it is a pre-formulated standard contract[2]. The onus rests on a seller or supplier who claims that a term was individually negotiated to show that it was[3].

1 reg 5 (1) and (2). A further question is whether the term is still to be regarded as non-negotiated when the other party has tried to negotiate a change but has failed to do so. It is thought that it would still be regarded as non-negotiated if it has remained untouched by the negotiations. In *UK Housing Alliance (North West) Ltd v Francis* [2010] EWCA 117 it was held that terms were not individually negotiated merely because the consumer was given the opportunity to negotiate the terms and chose not to do so.
2 reg 5 (3).
3 reg 5 (4).

7.76   A seller or supplier must ensure that any written term of a contract is expressed in plain, intelligible language[1]. If there is doubt about the meaning of a written term, the interpretation which is most favourable to the consumer is to prevail[2]. Neither Directive nor regulations state a sanction for infringement of this provision.

1 reg 7 (1).
2 reg 7 (2).

7.77   A term is to be regarded as unfair if, contrary to the requirements of good faith, it causes a significant imbalance in the parties' rights and obligations arising under the contract, to the detriment of the consumer[1]. Unlike the UCTA 1977, where the onus of establishing the reasonableness test rests on the party relying on the exemption clause[2], the regulations are silent on this issue. It is submitted that the onus should lie on the seller/supplier. A court may however raise the question of its own motion[3]. The unfairness of the term is assessed by taking account of the following:

(i)   the nature of the goods and services;

(ii)   all the circumstances attending the conclusion of the contract; and

(iii)   all other terms of the contract or of another contract on which it is dependent[4].

1 reg 5 (1).
2 See above, para 7.63.
3 Case C-484/08 *Caja de Ahorros y Monte de Piedad de Madrid v Asociación de Usuarios de Servicios Bancarios (Ausbanc)*, [2010] 3 CMLR 43.
4 reg 6 (1).

7.78 Factors which can be taken into account include the relative strength of the parties' bargaining power, whether the consumer had an inducement to agree to the term, whether the goods were specially made for the consumer, the relative abilities of the parties to bear the loss and the extent to which the seller/supplier has dealt equitably with the consumer[1]. Because the court can consider the nature of the goods and services, the fairness of the term can be assessed by taking into account the main subject matter and a price/quality ratio. So for example, if the goods or services supplied represent excellent value for money, a term, such as an exemption clause, may be adjudicated fair: the opposite conclusion could be drawn if the goods or services supplied represented bad value for money.

1 The 1994 Regulations contained a list of factors to be taken into account: such a list has been omitted from the 1999 Regulations. The factors in the text are drawn from Council Directive (EC) 93/13.

7.79 *Provided the contract is in plain intelligible language*, the *core* terms of the contract are not directly susceptible to the fairness test. The core terms are the terms which define the subject matter of the contract and the adequacy of the price or remuneration as against the goods or services supplied in the exchange[1]. Put another way, the terms which constitute the gist of the contract – the subject matter and the price or remuneration – remain invulnerable to the fairness criteria. The value of the exchange is non-justiciable and to that extent freedom of contract prevails. And so for example, the regulations cannot be used to help a consumer when a seller has sold goods or land to her at an exorbitant price or has supplied her with services at an extortionate rate always provided that the terms of the contract are in plain, intelligible English.

1 reg 6 (2) (a) and (b).

7.80 Sometimes it may not be easy to determine whether or not a term is a core term and therefore excluded from the fairness test. In *DGFT v First National Bank*[1] the term in issue was a clause in a contract of loan giving the bank in the event of default by the borrower the right to demand payment of the outstanding balance and accrued interest and further interest at the contractual rate after judgment up to the date of actual payment. The House of Lords held that this term did not fall within either the definition of the main subject matter or the adequacy of the price which were concerned with the parties' rights and obligations *in the due performance of the contract*. While important, a term for the provision of interest on default was a subsidiary or incidental term and not a core term. It was therefore susceptible to the fairness test. While the term in *DGFT v First National Bank* was accordingly subject to review, the House of Lords held that in the circumstances the fairness test was satisfied[2]. On the other hand, in *OFT v Abbey National*[3] the Supreme Court held that bank charges for an unauthorised overdraft were part of the contract price and therefore unchallengeable. The charges were not a penalty levied on customers but part of the overall contract package. Lord Walker concluded[4]:

'I would declare that the bank charges levied of personal current account customers in respect of unauthorised overdrafts...constitute part of the price or remuneration for the banking services provided and, in so far as the terms giving rise to the charges are in plain intelligible language, no assessment under the Unfair Terms in Consumer Contracts Regulations 1999 of the fairness of those terms may relate to their adequacy as against the services supplied.'

It is not yet clear what the impact of the Supreme Court decision is on such earlier decisions as *OFT v Foxtons Ltd*[5], where it was held that terms of a letting agent's contract with landlords under which the agent became entitled to commission payments from a landlord when a tenant found by the agent extended its tenancy, even after the original landlord's sale of its interest to a third party, did not relate to the core bargain and so could be reviewed for fairness. The approach in the *Abbey National* case has been applied to a 'subject matter' case where the contracts in question were for gym memberships. It was held that a term imposing a minimum membership period was part of the main subject matter, which was the right to access the gym facilities for a specific period. But confusingly the judge held that the term could nonetheless be reviewed for fairness in relation to the *consequences* under the term for members who terminated their contracts early, which was *not* part of the main subject matter[6].

1 [2002] 1 AC 481.
2 Cf *Bankers Insurance Co Ltd v South* [2003] EWHC 380; *Bairstow Eves London Central Ltd v Smith* [2004] EWHC 263.

3 [2010] 1 AC 696.
4 [2010] 1 AC 696 at para 51.
5 [2009] EWHC 1681 (Ch).
6 *OFT v Ashbourne Management Services* [2011] EWHC 1237 (Ch).

7.81 It has been noted that the fairness test comprises two limbs, namely that (1) contrary to the requirement of good faith, the term causes (2) a significant imbalance in the parties' rights and obligations arising under the contract, to the detriment of the consumer[1]. In *DGFT v First National Bank plc*[2] the view was taken that (i) the requirement of significant imbalance was met if a term is so weighted in favour of the supplier as to tilt the parties' contractual rights and obligations significantly in his favour; and (ii) the requirement of good faith was simply one of fair and open dealing. Good faith involves both procedural and substantive unfairness. There does not have to be a breach by the seller/supplier of the procedural aspect of good faith before the courts' powers are triggered. A significant imbalance in the parties' rights and obligations to the detriment of the consumer may in itself constitute a breach of the substantive aspect of good faith. It has been correctly said by an English judge that 'the words "good faith" are not to be construed in the English law sense of absence of dishonesty but rather in the continental "civil law" sense'[3].

1 See above, para 7.77.
2 [2002] 1 AC 481.
3 Per Evans-Lombe J, in *DGFT v First National Bank plc* [2000] 1 All ER 240 at 250. Note also on good faith *Munkenbeck & Marshall v Harold* [2005] EWHC 336 (indemnity and interest clauses in architect's letter of appointment unfair as unusual (although in use industry-wide), onerous, to the consumer's detriment and not brought to the consumer's attention at time of appointment).

7.82 Apart from the core terms, the regulations apply to any term of the contract. In this they differ from the UCTA 1977 which is only concerned with exemption clauses. Unlike the UCTA 1977, the regulations do not cover provisions in non-contractual notices[1]. There can therefore be an overlap between the regulations and the UCTA 1977 in respect of exemption clauses in consumer contracts but the UCTA 1977 will have to be used where the contract is between two businesses or two private parties. On the other hand, the regulations can control the fairness of a wide range of terms not covered by the UCTA 1977. These would include the following:

(1) Penalty clauses. Where these are not a genuine pre-estimate of losses arising from breach of contract, they can be struck down at common law[2]. But the common law does not control

penalties which are triggered by events other than breach, for example lawful termination of the contract[3], or when one of the parties becomes insolvent[4]. These, as well as the traditional penalty clause on breach, are subject to the regulations. So for example, if charges are to be paid in the event of early repayment of a loan from a bank or building society, these can now be challenged[5].

(2) Clauses which permit the seller/supplier to retain a deposit made by the consumer in the event of the latter deciding not to perform the contract. It is well settled that a deposit can be retained if it was intended to be a pledge or guarantee of the consumer's performance even if it bears little relationship to the seller/supplier's actual loss[6]. Such clauses can be challenged under the regulations.

(3) Accelerated payments clauses when the payment does not reflect the seller/supplier's loss[7].

(4) Clauses allowing the seller/supplier to cancel without a corresponding right in the consumer to do so.

(5) Clauses allowing the seller/supplier unilaterally to vary the terms of the contract[8].

(6) Jurisdiction clauses[9].

In short, the list is endless[10]. But it has been held in England that the regulations do not apply to terms implied at common law[11].

1 See above, para 7.56.
2 See above para 6.47 ff.
3 *Bell Bros (HP) Ltd v Aitken* 1939 SC 577.
4 *EFT Commercial Ltd v Security Change Ltd* 1992 SC 414.
5 Unless the charges are held to be part of the overall contract package and therefore unchallengeable if in plain intelligible language: *OFT v Abbey National* [2010] 1 AC 696 discussed above at para 7.80.
6 *Zemhunt (Holdings) Ltd v Central Securities plc* 1992 SC 58.
7 As in *White & Carter (Councils) Ltd v McGregor* 1962 SC (HL) 1. However the regulations would not apply on the facts of this case as it was not a consumer contract. For discussion, see above, para 5.34.
8 *Peabody Trust Governors v Reeve* [2008] EWHC 1432 (Ch).
9 Case C240/98 *Oceano Grupo Editorial SA v Rocio Murciano Quintero* [2000] ECR I-4941; *Standard Bank London Ltd v Apostolakis (No 2)* [2001] Lloyds Rep Bank 240; *Picardi v Cuniberti* [2002] BLR 487; cf *Lovell Projects Ltd v Legg* [2003] BLR 452; *Westminster Building Co Ltd v Beckingham* [2004] BLR 265; *Heifer International Inc v Christiansen* [2007] EWHC 3015 (TCC); *Malcrist Builders Ltd v Buck* [2008] EWHC 2172 (TCC). Adjudication clauses in building contracts have been held fair: *Bryen & Langley Ltd v Boston* [2005] BLR 508; *Allen Wilson Shopfitters v Buckingham* [2005] EWHC 1165; *Domsalla v Dyason* [2007] EWHC 1174 (TCC).
10 In *UK Housing Alliance (North West) Ltd v Francis* [2010] EWCA 117, for example, Francis sold his house to UK Housing. Seventy per cent of the price was paid at the date of settlement and the balance would be paid if Francis

remained in the property under a tenancy agreement with UK Housing for at least ten years. The tenancy agreement was terminated when Francis failed to pay his rent. A clause giving UK Housing the right to retain the balance in these circumstances was subject to challenge but held not to be contrary to good faith and that retention of 30% did not amount to an imbalance let alone a significant one. An indicative and non-exhaustive list of terms that may be regarded as unfair is to be found in the 1999 Regulations, Sch 2.

11 *Bagbut v Eccle Riggs Country Park Ltd, The Times,* November 13 2006.

7.83 Because it will be rare for a consumer to be able to afford to litigate, the Office of Fair Trading has a duty to consider complaints that any contract term drawn up for general use is unfair[1]. The OFT can then seek an interdict from the court to prevent the continued use of the term[2]. The interdict applies to existing as well as future contracts[3]. If the OFT fails in a collective action, an individual can still challenge the term on the basis that it is unfair in the particular circumstances of his case: but where the OFT has been successful it cannot be argued that the term is nevertheless fair in the circumstances of an individual case[4]. Qualifying bodies specified in Schedule 1 to the Regulations[5] may also consider complaints but must notify the OFT before doing so[6]. The consent of the OFT is required before a qualifying body can seek interdict.

1 reg 10(1). See also the OFT website on unfair contract terms, http://www. oft.gov.uk/Consumer/Unfair+terms+in+contracts/default.htm. The OFT is expected to merge with the Competition Commission in 2014, the two bodies together to be known as the Competition and Markets Authority.
2 reg 12.
3 *OFT v Foxtons* [2009] EWCA Civ 288.
4 OFT *v Foxtons* [2009] EWCA Civ 288.
5 These include the Data Protection Registrar, the Directors General for the various utilities, the Rail Regulator and every weights and measures authority in Great Britain. The 1994 Regulations did not allow for challenges by bodies other than the Director General of Fair Trading, which led to potential litigation in the European Court of Justice at the behest of the Consumers Association, claiming failure to fulfil the 1993 Directive; but this was settled after the change of government in the UK in 1997 and was followed by the 1999 adjustments.
6 regs 10(1)(b), 11 and 12 (1) and (2).

7.84 The regulations provide a further example of a statutory regime which allows courts directly to control the fairness of contractual terms. It should be emphasised that this is a measure for the protection of consumers who do not have sufficient bargaining strength to negotiate terms which are in their interests. But even here, the value of the exchange itself is not subject to judicial scrutiny provided that the contract is in plain, intelligible language.

Conclusion

7.85   As a consequence of a ministerial reference, the Law Commission and Scottish Law Commission brought forward proposals for a new scheme for the judicial control of unfair contract terms in 2005[1]. In effect the new scheme brought the UCTA 1977 and the regulations together and attempted to remove any overlaps and anomalies. In addition, it extended the protection currently enjoyed by consumers to small businesses. Implementation of the Report was delayed because the Directive itself was under review as (originally) part of the Consumer Rights Directive project. The non-inclusion of unfair terms in the Consumer Rights Directive in 2011 freed the UK Government to go back to the Law Commissions' 2005 recommendations. The controversial *Abbey National* decision however means that some further work is necessary to update the Report, and the Government asked the Commissions to carry this out in the summer of 2012. The Government has already made it clear that consumer protection will not be extended to small businesses. The UCTA will however survive in its non-consumer protection elements[2].

1 See the *Report on Unfair Terms in Contracts* (Law Com No 292) (Scot Law Com No 199).
2 See Law Commission and Scottish Law Commission Issues Paper, *Unfair Terms in Consumer Contracts: A New Approach* (July 2012).

Index